EMBRACING CANADA

An account of the realization of a naturalized Canadian's retirement dream to take a solo canoe to Montreal and retrace Canada's historic fur trade canoe route paddle stroke by paddle stroke westward across the country.

Jan Soukup

Tellwell Talent
www.tellwell.ca

ISBN
978-1-77941-085-6 (Hardcover)
978-1-77941-084-9 (Paperback)
978-1-77941-086-3 (eBook)

Acknowledgments:

I would like to express gratitude to Dr. Alexandra Bartell for a wonderful job of editing the manuscript and Dr. Lavinia Ionescu for the last professional formatting touches.

Text: Jan Soukup

Photography: Jan Soukup, Tony Netik, Milena Rigan, occasional nice strangers using my camera, rainbowcountry.com..

Illustration: Jan Soukup

Maps: created by Jan Soukup based on Google Earth, Google Maps, BWCA.com, Toporama.

Cover: Jan Soukup. Front cover top photo: the planet view with the chart of the historic fur trade canoe route across Canada. Displayed are the coats of arms of the Northwest Company left and Hudsons Bay Company right. Front cover bottom photo: paying tribute to the magnificent spiritual power and beauty of the Canadian nature on the shore of Lake Huron near Thessalon.

Back cover top photo: the author savouring a bright morning on Lake Superior past crossing of Shesheeb Bay.

CONTENTS

To my children, who'll never stop thanking

their parents for having had the courage

to surmount all barriers and establish a

new home in this magnificent country

to become the country of their birth.

And

to my grandchildren, who will

navigate Canada to greatness

in the cosmic age.

PREFACE

Ca-na-da…That name surely possesses a catchy cadence. My ears first caught its sound when they were still very young and sharp. I realize only now that I must have been my grandfather's favourite grandchild, because only for me, he had his loud cheery greeting of "Ahoj Kanado!" (Ahoy Canada!) whenever we visited him from Prague in his home nestled halfway into an aromatic pine forest on the outskirts of a small central Bohemian village. I did not know its meaning then, but from the context, I sensed that it had to be something grand.

The second clue to its meaning came from grandpa's boots. As a high-level forest ranger (a top forestry advisor to the Prince von Thurn und Taxis) he wore and lovingly cared for a pair of special high boots made of splendid, prime, reddish-brown leather with deep sole treads that laced up to just below the knee. The official term for this highly coveted kind of boots was "Kanady" (Canadas). That was the first hint to me that this name had to do with forests, nature and the outdoors in general.

Later years of elementary school provided a discovery to me that Canada was a vast country covering the whole north of the North American continent a hemisphere away. It seemed obvious to me that this country had to have a lot of forests and rugged nature if Grandpa's boots were worn there.

The next wave of information about Canada came to me courtesy of hockey. As a young boy, I grew up in a country where hockey was a national sport. Canada, at the time, ruled on the world stage of this game as the best. My first insight into the character of Canadians was through the members of the Canadian national hockey team. The Communist regime in which I grew up, tried to diminish their appeal by picturing them as — (what at the time was a widely used political derogative) — Hooligans. "Look at their square brush cuts;

look at them chewing gum when talking; look at their self-confident boasting; look at their fighting on the ice; look at their coach wearing that provocative loud-colored woolen coat with the red, green, yellow and blue stripes!"

The propaganda had the opposite effect. I started admiring these tall, broad-shouldered, free-spirited men and with them, I started to like their country. As I matured into my teens, I was forming my life's philosophy. It was putting equal emphasis on the desire to obtain good education and knowledge, inseparably coupled with achieving great physical fitness through exercise and competing in sports. I was developing a great adoration for nature.

With broader knowledge, my admiration for Canada grew through multiple sources. I admired it in films; in the paintings of the Group of Seven; in the books of James Fennimore Cooper, James Oliver Curwood, Robert Michael Ballantyne and other literature. My favourite author of the late teens was Jack London whose stories from the Yukon and his novels hit a great resonance with my soul.

I learned who the "voyageurs" were. I also learned that those red, green, yellow and blue stripes on the Canadian coach's coat were the colors of the Hudson's Bay Company — one of the icons of Canada's identity. Basing my lifestyle on living in harmony with nature rather than on politics, I liked that Canada had been basically neutral and provided freedom for its mosaic of aboriginal and immigrant populations. After all, the nature symbol of the maple leaf in its flag expressed its appeal to me the best.

Although my mind harboured a lovely image of Canada by the time of my university years, and in spite of it being the subject of my dreams, I never imagined that I could ever end up living there. It was simply "a pie in the sky" for me. Yet destiny can be friendly to those who are prepared. Within the turmoil of the Soviet-directed Warsaw Pact invasion of my country in 1968 to quash the newly sprouting liberation movement, a window of opportunity opened for me to leave for Canada.

It was in the interest of Canada to place fresh immigrants from then Czechoslovakia in locations like Edmonton and Winnipeg where there were unfilled jobs. Practically all of my Czech and Slovak fellow-immigrants were giving the Canadian consulate a hard time by demanding to live in Toronto or Montreal. I must have shocked the officers at the Canadian consulate in Paris when I asked to be sent to Edmonton. They might have been concerned that I was a mental case. Yet I was excited.

Although I heard of Edmonton for the first time only about a month before I set my foot on its soil, my adventurous spirit got interested in it as soon as I could see on the map that it was located in the brown color of the Rocky Mountain foothills and smack in the middle of the Canadian Wild West. The photographs in the tourist brochures that I saw in the waiting room of the consulate confirmed it to me with images from Jasper, Banff and the Waterton National Parks of Alberta.

Oh, what a shock it was when, upon my arrival, I took a taxi from the Edmonton International Airport into the city. I had a feeling that I would "drown" in that prairie flatness. The North Saskatchewan River valley appeared to be the only topography in the vast surrounding area. With $6 in my pocket, I was not bringing any monetary wealth to my new homeland. Yet in the young head of a strapping 24-year-old, I was bringing a fresh new Master's degree in Nuclear Engineering. I was going to deserve my new country!

Jan Soukup

CHAPTER I

A solo canoe voyage following the historic fur trade
canoe route from Montreal to Lake Superior
(June 4th – July 29th, 2010)

Why, oh why? — Because, because!

Allow me first, to give you a little explanation. I am well aware
that many people regard me as a bit of a crazy masochist. Who
in his right mind, they think, would be looking today, at 66, for
opportunities to tackle the wilderness in the ways that people had
to employ in traveling through Canada in the 17th century? Who
would voluntarily immerse oneself in the situations that many had not
survived? In fact, they did not even use to live to 66 in those times. ...
Well then ... First of all, I adore nature. Secondly, as a worshiper of
physical fitness, I admire Canadian history as it is woven through
with the thread of intimate co-existence of man with wilderness
in his unforgiving physical struggle to survive. In variation to an
average reasonable guy, my retirement dream of the last several years
had been to take a canoe to Montreal and then push it with steady,
determined paddle strokes back west along the historic water route of
the Canadian voyageurs. Who were the voyageurs? Voyageurs used
to be the "laborers of the wilderness," an analogy to modern truckers,
if you like, who propelled large freight canoes made of birch bark
with paddles. These were loaded up to the gunwales with bundles of
fur pelts when travelling eastward to Montreal, or with goods to trade
for them (such as blankets, rifles, gun powder, knives, axes, tobacco,
steel traps, tea, sugar, etc.) when moving in the opposite direction.
They worked for an outfit called Northwest Company that marketed
furs and had its headquarters in Montreal. The voyageurs used to
be recruited mostly as garçons of smaller stature (so they would

1

not add too much dead weight to the canoe), but of a tough, strong nature from among the French-Canadian farm hands of rural Quebec. The hierarchy of the company consisted typically of Canadians of Scottish descent, but, thanks to the head start of Francophones in penetrating into the Canadian interior, the business language of the fur trade was the archaic Québécois French. That's why Canada has so many French geographic names even outside of Quebec. Each spring during the break-up of ice on the rivers, fleets of big canoes (called "Montreal Canoes" or canot du maître), each with a crew of typically twelve, set out on their way west from Montreal. These carried the load of trade goods. They reached Lake Superior by the early summer and here they met with brigades of smaller canoes called "canot du nord" that arrived using a network of rivers and lakes from the northwest interior of Canada, also referred to as "Pays d'en Haut." The latter brought loads of fur from the winter harvest. For the purpose of this meeting, the Northwest Company had a base, Fort William, at the northwest end of Lake Superior. Following a two-week boisterous whoop-up "company party," as well as more serious board meetings to exchange news and business strategies, the loads of goods were exchanged and the fleets returned with the new loads to where they came from.

"It is a hell of a long journey!" I told myself. "But what the heck, being retired I will have plenty of time. I can add to it bit-by-bit with each new summer season for as long as my body holds together." This was two years before the planned realization of my dream. Back then, it still sounded like a romantic fairy tale. The closer to the magic date, however, the more often reality slapped my face to wake me up from dreaming and start with preparations. My shoulders started to feel an ever heavier burden of worries and uncertainty. I knew that I would not be able to find a partner who could afford enough time off for the trip and possess the necessary canoeing experience along with the sufficient standard of equipment at the same time. The vision of traveling alone — solo, did not terrify me. I had had plenty of opportunities to test this during my solo paddling in the Yukon and the Northwest Territories. I proved to myself then that I do not lack the necessary self-discipline and prudent patience required to avoid that fateful kind of a mistake for which such situations leave no room. What prevented me from sleeping at night was the agonizing over how I would move against the current on the rivers Ottawa and Mattawa. How was I going to cross the vast expanses of open water in the Georgian Bay of Lake Huron? My temples were pulsing against the pillow with questions like: Where will I camp in the section of the Ottawa River between Montreal and Ottawa city where, according to the internet, the river banks are lined with wall-to-wall stretches of private lots? Since the river flushes the very cosmopolitan capital of Canada here, I am not going to ingest its water even after boiling! Where will I find drinking water along the way? How will I find a canoe that would be both stable and well-tracking in the waves of the vast lake stretches while also yielding good maneuverability in the white water of the French River which I was to travel downstream? How shall it have sufficient load capacity for a multimonth expedition and yet be light enough for the countless portages of the water route? In the middle of the nights, I was solving the dilemma in my head of how I would get myself, the boat and the outfit to Montreal. My stomach, wrung with worries, had suppressed my appetite to the point where I had lost weight even before the first dipping of the paddle. In the end, everything unraveled positively, but this character of the constant uncertainty about what each new day would bring to solve stuck to the whole journey. Yet overcoming unexpected challenges is the essence of all adventures. Hence, it ought to be welcomed by the adventurer.

On the way!

I finally set out on my way for real on the last Saturday of May, the 29th. It started behind the steering wheel of a compact Toyota Yaris that I rented one-way from Edmonton to Montreal. The outrageously high rental fee helped me morally justify my mischief of tying a 15-foot canoe on its roof. It was pouring in Edmonton and

I was leaving it in a kind of "out-of-body-experience" where I was observing myself from above the road, asking myself: "What in the Lord's name are you, Grandpa, pushing your way into?" By the time of my crossing of the border from Alberta into Saskatchewan, it got colder and the road had even collected some five centimetres of snow! The trip to Montreal, however, takes five days. In Ontario, I was already expertly "sailing" with my long canoe on the roof of a short vehicle through 30°C side-winds in a sweat-drenched shirt. Luck was on my side and I navigated flawlessly straight to the yacht club on the western edge of Montreal that I had previously found on Google Earth. I expected this place to provide the most ideal point for the launching of my canoe. With the kind help of a sympathetic club member, I stored the canoe and gear here until I returned the rented vehicle. I slept in a hotel and returned to the club by taxi. My gear was locked in the cabin of the trusting Samaritan's own sailboat. He gave me the number combination to the club's locked gate and even showed me the secret hiding spot where he kept his boat key so that I could collect my stuff in his absence the next day. Not too far from there, the church of Sainte Anne de Bellevue was standing where the voyageurs used to make their last prayer before starting on the long dangerous journey. In their time, this represented the westernmost outpost of civilization. I was silently praying too, because, right at the start, I had to cross the wide expanse of open water on Lac Des Deux Montagnes. I had no idea yet how my brand new canoe, in which I had never sat before, would behave. Constricted, therefore, in a wetsuit and life jacket, I was soon sweating. The first skirmish with a stiff headwind thoroughly drained my out-of-fitness endurance. I ran out of all energy by early afternoon. I dropped off onto an inclined rocky beach of the Mohawk reservation shore about a kilometre past the Quebec town of Oka. I guessed that a few members of the Mohawk Nation, who crisscrossed back and forth in front of my spot shouting and gesticulating from a motor boat, were not very happy with me trespassing on their territory. Yet I was so beat that I could not move whether I wanted to or not. Luckily, the water was so shallow near my shore that their boat could not approach me for us to even understand each other's words. Frustrated, they soon left me alone. Here I recuperated in an emergency camp till morning.

The continuing dreadful toil of the slow progress against the current, wind and rain of the next several days would quickly crystalize into a rock-firm determination in my head that I would give up my nonsensical plan. Perhaps this would have happened were it not for the fact that both banks of the river were densely occupied with mansions and private properties that obscured my view of any municipal infrastructure behind them. Besides that, I was too afraid to abandon my boat filled with precious equipment, if temporarily, unguarded. Thanks to these technicalities, I found no practical way of quitting before further continuation on my journey showed me that my mode of travel was, after all, indeed possible.

Thanks to the fact that I traveled solo, coupled with my minimalistic outfit, I maintained a very low profile — i.e., I did not need a large campsite — I would be fine with a tiny one-tree island somewhere in a back slough of the river. In this way, I often "shared my bed" with muskrats and bullfrogs but I always found homey comfort and well-deserved rest in my tiny tent. I felt inconspicuous and I would blend in undiscovered for one night even somewhere on private property. It has always been my credo to never leave a trace of my camping. Mostly in this initial stage of the journey, but to a degree everywhere on it, I often felt like a fugitive. Being alone, I did not really fear wild animals so much, but I would always seek safety from malicious human characters. I had expected that the riverside vicinity of bigger cities might harbor homeless weirdos. Small islands thus became my camp spots of preference. Later on, above the city of Ottawa, such places would appear in very scenic or even romantic forms. No matter what, my river transit through the capital of Canada trumped over all my imaginings of difficult challenges. Its vision loomed like a dark thunder cloud. The Ottawa River, as my experience would show, is to a reasonable degree "friendly" to both travel downstream as well as upstream. It's because it does not shed its altitude in one continuous slope but instead descends a staircase of one-time waterfalls. These are all today harnessed into generating electric energy in a series of hydro dams. Above the waterfalls, equally as above the hydro dams today, the river has to a great distance possessed the character of a lake. A number of rapids that had to be portaged around in the past are drowned today under the surface of the dam-raised lakes. Yet some still exist today. They then bring a shocking surprise to an uninformed explorer and provide a heavy-duty test to his cardiovascular fitness. Just as voyageurs carried around waterfalls, so today, the river adventurer needs to find a way around the dams. In some cases, as I will describe later, overcoming a dam may be incomparably more difficult than it used to be for a waterfall.

The city of Ottawa

The city of Ottawa has one such waterfall right in its center. The natives had a name for it that translated as "Boiling Cauldron," or kettle for its part-circular rim and geysers of water spray, visible and audible from a distance. In order to appease the mean spirits who held the power of determining the safety of passage through here, they poured into the tumbling waters offerings of tobacco. French Canadians adopted the name in their French translation as "Chaudière" — kettle/boiler. Although the waterfall has become a dam, one has to portage around it. In combination with the size of the city, this obstacle eliminates the possibility that the river traveler might pass through it in one day. Where was I to spend the night? Yet at this phase of the journey I had already learned to deal with challenges as they came and not worry too much ahead of time. I thus established my camp right on the lower edge of the city on an island called Lower Duck Island. It poured the next day right up till noon and I was not able to start out until after 1:00. The day had then gradually blossomed into beauty and I enjoyed the full warming sun half-naked — like an Indigenous brave, while straining muscles in paddling against a strong current for a change. In doing so, I provided welcome entertainment for the otherwise bored tourists aboard some sight-seeing dinner cruise boat.

The first European who had traveled exactly the same water route to Lake Huron that I followed, was Samuel de Champlain, the founder of the New France in 1615. In those times, Indigenous nation groups were very powerful in comparison to the handful of white immigrants. They also happened to be in the midst of nasty feuds among themselves. European settlers' lives in that situation depended on alliances with the right Indigenous party and they had to resort to a great deal of diplomacy. Hurons were one of the Native nations that were friendly to the young white minority of French origin on the continent. Their name probably came from the French colloquial (or perhaps even derogatory) word "huron" that combined the meanings of wild boar, bristly hair ruffian, brute bumpkin, gross lout, etc., used for them by the French Colonial soldiers. The reason was an explosive shock of hardened hair that stuck out from the top of a Huron's otherwise closely shaven skull like the impact of a meteor on the surface of the moon. "Des hurons arrivent!" reported the guards from the walls of the fort located on the high Saint Lawrence River bank in the location of today's Quebec City when they spotted their approaching canoes. The name stuck and spread quickly. It would eventually also identify a large interior lake, the east shore of which Hurons inhabited. French missionaries eventually referred to this land in their Latin as Huronia. De Champlain and his escort traveled in canoes propelled by the skilled paddle strokes of the Natives. The Indigenous People had already used the route for, perhaps, millennia. His guide was a young Frenchman, Étienne Brûlé, whom de Champlain had dispatched to live with the Hurons and thus acquire the knowledge of their language and culture existing in 1610. As an 18-year-old, Étienne had easily assimilated and been thoroughly naturalized by the Hurons. Brûlé described the route to de Champlain in Montreal. Now he was contracted to lead him along it under the threat of hanging if he had lied. Having arrived to where the center of the city of Ottawa is today, de Champlain's attention was first attracted as was mine that day, by two white, smoothly continuous curtains of water that were falling from the left. In his diary he noted that the Indians led him to "walk behind the waterfalls completely dry." Naturally, the French then named them "Rideau" — curtain in French. The name endures to the present and again, it has spread to other nearby entities like Rideau River, Rideau Canal, Rideau Hall, etc.

Shortly after having passed under the rocky cliff with the buildings of the Canadian Parliament on its top, I finally reached the foot of the portage around the dam. Unlike the voyageurs who portaged along the Quebec side on a trail that is now obliterated, I had chosen the south — Ontario river bank — that has a paved recreation walkway called Ottawa River Parkway. Due to the busy traffic of pedestrians, cyclists, roller skaters and other fitness-bent citizens, I was placing my piles of repeatedly carried outfit about a hundred metres apart in order to be able to see them. Especially when I carried my canoe on shoulders around the dam and was crossing a major street artery, I again aroused attention and served as entertainment in a kind of acted-out rerun of the history. By the time I finished nudging my equipment, including the canoe, all the way to above the safety perimeter of the dam, it was already past 8:00. There was a null prospect of finding a camp spot somewhere upstream. It was very likely that darkness would descend before I would even be able to finish loading the canoe. What now? I was facing a fine if the park's security found me sleeping overnight in the park. I was out of options. Desperate, I was determined to neatly fold my weary skeleton onto a park bench and started preparing some words that could possibly wring pity from the park authorities. Tobacco to sprinkle about the bench, I had not. But as the dusk thickened, the traffic thinned. I spied a nice hidden dip with mowed grass under low branches of a tree right next to the Museum of War. I then gradually transferred everything there. When it got really dark after 9:00, I pitched the tent and unrolled my sleeping bag in it. Voilà! I had a comfortable bed if only for a short sleep. When dawn started around 4:00, I was already loading the canoe on a rocky riverbank. I had known about big rapids called Deschânes higher upstream in Ottawa but I was surprised to find that the river in the city above Chaudière had an almost continuous series of other smaller rapids. For the first time here, I learned to walk the fully loaded canoe up the strong current. In some places the water barely reached to my knees but there were also spots where I was in almost up to my neck. Experience taught me to turn the canoe stern forward. The reason was that after my disembarking, the stern was lighter than the bow and thus floated higher in the water. This stabilized the alignment of the canoe with the current in a natural way. Otherwise, the deeper-immersed end had a constant tendency to turn aft. I knew that the voyageurs carried around Deschânes rapids on the Quebec side of the river. Miraculously, though, I succeeded, if with heroic effort, in muscling the loaded canoe up the Ontario side by walking and dragging it directly up the staircase of the whitewater-washed boulders and plates. The rapids appeared to be a little milder there. Above them, finally, I paddled into flat (if strongly wavy from a mighty tailwind for a change) water of the natural lake, Lac Deschânes. The Sunday sun merrily baked my denuded back. I found myself paddling in the midst of a regatta of numerous sports yachts that had erected their balloon-like colorful spinnakers in a race down the wind. The lake is roughly two paddling days long and the river here is up to several kilometres wide.

Tackling the Chats

To return to the subject of hurdling the dams, the one that has particularly burnt itself into my memory is the one that came on the second day after passing through Ottawa. It is the dam called Chats Falls. It is one-and-a-half mile wide — just as the former very scenic waterfall Chute Des Chats that it obliterated. The name was given to it by de Champlain because when they arrived at it back in the early

1600s and had to haul their birch bark canoes up some steep rocky cliffs, the rocks scratched their bottoms like the claws of cats — chats in French. I knew exactly where the voyageurs portaged but the first thing I saw when I traced the path with my eyes was a big, red warning sign forbidding entry. Above it on top of the cliff, I could still see a low dam wall. No sign anywhere that would hint where to portage! For a long time, I crisscrossed along the bottom of the dam in my canoe, fruitlessly searching for any clue to circumventing it. Finally, I happened onto a noisy group of swimming and splashing children from some summer camp with their leader. Fortunately, this person had heard about the portage and indicated to me where it started. That place was just on the opposite-to-where-I-found-myself end of the dam (south) in a cove called Fitzroy Harbor. There was supposed to be the mouth of a small creek against which one had to ascend above the dam. By the time I finally found it, it was early evening. The creek had hardly any water. I was lucky that it was still barely capable of floating the canoe without me in it. I was leading the boat around and over sharp rocks. The real climb started with a short portage after which I assumed I would be above the dam at any moment. The portage was, however, followed by a series of high beaver dams with short, driftwood-congested ponds that morphed into a steep rocky staircase of the creek. I was often dragging the canoe over the creek bottom while removing and re-organizing rocks in it to avoid excessive scratching of the canoe. (Apparently, the dreaded Chats ruled here too). Dusk had slowly settled onto the dense hostile forest but I kept hurrying, convinced that I had to be almost at the finish. Early on, still in the vicinity of Fitzroy Harbor, I could occasionally see above me, high above the deeply incised creek bed, lit picture windows of the last, thinly scattered residences of the privacy-loving local families that were likely just seated around a dinner table. Not even in their dreams might they have had an idea of what strange kind of salmon was fighting its way below them up their indistinct stream through the semidarkness. After some time, the slope of the creek abated and I could thus paddle through a maze of dark sloughs. Yet these would again, from time to time, transform into a rocky staircase. When it suddenly turned pitch dark and I, completely wet, was being mercilessly eaten by mosquitoes, I had to quickly unload the canoe onto a spruce thicket-covered shore, pitch the tent with lightning speed in complete darkness, unfurl my bedroll in it, strip the wet clothes and jump in in one continuous motion with the closing of the tent zipper. The night under the dense, dark spruce trees was very intimidating.

It is interesting to see what a striking contrast there is between one's arrival into an entirely unfamiliar place in the back country under the darkness of a gloomy night, and awakening to a fresh, sun-gilded morning in the same spot filled with the happy chirping of birds. Everything looks different. Uncertainty, fear and pessimism miraculously transform into renewed energy, optimism and decisiveness. Before the expedition, I had agonized about how I would travel with a thick stack of detailed topographical maps that would cover my whole route. In the end, I accepted the advice of my technologically more advanced offspring and procured an iPhone. This smart phone has a built-in GPS and provides Google Maps in combination with a satellite view. One can thus see the terrain quite realistically and zoom into its finest detail. Moreover, the iPhone enabled me to contact my wife even when she was visiting her family in the Czech Republic. To recharge my phone and the AA batteries for my camera, I purchased online a very handy solar charger that folded down to wallet size. During the trip, I never ended up with discharged batteries. The only paper maps that I carried with me were a road map of Ontario and a map of the French River area.

When I finally had a chance to check my position on the iPhone in the morning, the puzzle of my dam-dodging route started to take shape. The detour followed a very small river with a rather pretentious and hardly original name of "Mississippi" that converged with the Ottawa River under the Chats Falls. Now, however, the raised surface of the dam's lake also touched its course above the dam by its enlarged bay. It was obvious that this was the point for which the detour aimed. Realizing that the creek had to gain an elevation rise equivalent to the height of the dam, which was about seventeen metres over the detour's course, the steepness of the climb made sense. The iPhone quenched my pride from the achievement of the previous day when it revealed to me that my existing location was barely about a third of the total detour length in. A quick morning survey indicated that I had to start with a quarter-kilometre portage. This was followed by paddling through a tangled rats-nest of lily pads and reed-congested marshes. Like the proverbial mouse in a maze, except for the technological edge of having the iPhone satellite view from above, I was able to connect through them the only right and very obscure course to a small side dam. Yet this last obstacle posed no serious threat as I tackled it in a final short portage. For the first time for a change, when I passed the first cottages on shore in the afternoon, the sight of motor boats moored at them brought joy to my heart. This was because the boats told me that from here on, there was an unobstructed connection with the lake above the dam. Finally I could enjoy a lunch break in the boat while I stripped my sweaty shells and exposed my body, protected by an application of sunscreen to the strong afternoon sun. Paddling on the smooth surface of the lake's flat water, until it reflected the red glow of the setting sun, tasted like paradise following the two-day bush and swamp slog.

The Allumettes Rapids

The character of the Ottawa River gradually changed. The higher I moved up its current above Ottawa, the more it approached (at least to some degree) what it might have looked like during the era of the voyageurs. OK, OK, wait ... I admit that there were cottages on its shores and even a couple of bigger cities like Pembroke and Petawawa. The latter has a large military base that seethed with aircraft traffic that provided security to the (unbeknownst to me at the time) G8 and G20 summits. But it started to abound with very romantic little islands, luscious forest growth and deserted little beaches of fine sand. From the North and East, the craggy, rugged edge of the Canadian Shield approached and it would then form the north bank of my route all the way to Lake Huron. In the area where the river splits around a pair of huge islands — Isle du Grand Calumet and Isle aux Allumettes around which the river flows in a six-paddling-day-long figure-of-eight, I luckily selected the right channels. I thus evaded a water-slalom paradise that I would have had to tackle against the current. My selected route necessitated portaging around one more hydro dam and the muscling of the canoe against two more rapids. These were the Bryson dam, where I had to survey my own, more than a kilometre long, portage and then the Lower and the Upper Allumettes rapids that the voyageurs used to portage around. But my choice made the difference between feasible and impossible passages up the river.

I arrived at the Allumettes unprepared for any surprises. I had read about them in historical literature but I never expected that they would still exist in modern times, unflooded by some dam. The Lower Allumettes posed no serious obstacle to my method of leading a loaded canoe. The Upper ones, however, prepared for me an ultimate test of maturity. They came inconspicuously in the first stages of dusk. The sky became overcast and sporadic droplets of rain started dappling the surface of the water. Seeing no suitable campsite, I continued paddling with the hope that something would pan out beyond the highway bridge that I could see up ahead. It was high time because the start of Pembroke was supposed to come some two kilometres beyond the bridge. Some distance before the bridge, I could see that the surface of the water up ahead was rippling. When I reached that, I was unable to gain any progress by paddling from the canoe, mostly due to the fact that the shallow water did not allow for any efficient paddle strokes. I quickly jumped out of the canoe and started leading it towards the bridge. By that time, a fully-fledged rain started falling. I sunk several times up to my neck into some deeper pools closer to the bridge in the next few moments. As I arrived under the bridge, I could suddenly see that ahead of me, I had about half a kilometre slope of strong rapids. My intention was to continue against the rapids only till I could see a suitable spot for camping. The bank was steep though, rocky and overgrown with dense wet bush. I could see a fairly large island in the middle of the river in front of me. I muscled the loaded canoe towards it in the hope that I would set up my camp on it. The island, however, had a shore of smooth rocky cliffs — unfit to support even emergency camping. Now I was already situated in the middle of the rapids. It felt more acceptable to me then to overcome the rapids completely and thus avoid the necessity of returning back into them the next morning. The sharp, chaotic rocks of the river bottom in the first part of the rapids suddenly transformed into smooth, algae-covered, super-slippery limestone plates. I moved over them with maximum caution on widely spread legs while desperately embracing the stern of the canoe that was pointing forward under my armpit. I was searching for spots that would provide enough friction for my water sneakers without constantly falling flat. I kept rising repeatedly with the support from the boat while I was also trying to prevent myself and the canoe from being dragged back down by the current. Now it was also pouring, getting dark, and my teeth were rattling under a wilted, wet sun hat. I was asking myself, as if I were watching myself on TV in a denial of reality, what in the hell persuaded me to end up in the situation that I was finding myself in. "Why do I need this? What's in it for me? Why am I not spending a relaxing summer with my wife in our beautiful log house on Lake Kootenay?" Racking my brain did not bring up anybody else to blame for this but myself. Finally, I conquered my advance all the way to the top edge of the rapids. Yet alas! The feeling of victory was yanked out of my grasp. The quieter water above the rapids was deep. Its depth prevented my jumping up into the canoe to paddle before I would be sucked back into the rapids. To be swept with the canoe backwards or broadside into the rapids would have meant a terminal disaster. The water between the bank and me was also deep and very fast. Some 15 minutes had passed in my agonizing about what to do. My legs were desperately feeling the bottom for some bigger rock from which to jump into the canoe. In the end, my fear brought a surge of adrenalin.

While swearing obscenely for courage, I jumped up into the canoe from a significant depth and still practically flat on my back on its spray cover, I started desperately paddling like a madman. My feet at that moment were frantically trying to find the opening in the spray cover so that I could plant my legs into the tight jumble of the load underneath it and sit up. I was battling in one spot for some time but the keen awareness that losing in this fight could bring a tragic end, helped me mobilize every last bit of strength. Slowly, inch by inch, I managed to overcome the mean sucking force of the rapids and win my progress upstream into quieter water — out of the reach of their power. It was still pouring. Now and then, a thunderclap ruptured the hiss of the rain drops on the water surface. The next milestone to survival was the erection of the tent, unrolling in it the sleeping bag and cocooning myself in it as quickly as possible. The left — Ontario bank showed the first, sparingly scattered acreage homes on the periphery of Pembroke. The right — Quebec bank — had a fringe of a sandy beach lined with cottages behind it. I aimed my paddling towards it. I dragged my canoe onto the beach, quickly unloaded it and unpacked the tent. Still in heavy rain, I erected it directly on the sand in front of one of the cottages. I did not care if somebody might raise any objections. This was, potentially, a matter of life and death. I pushed aside the sleeping bag on the mat in the tent, dried myself first with a towel and, keeping my legs that were covered with sand like ready-to-fry breaded chicken stuck out, I also wiped them with it. Then I finally zippered myself into my winter sleeping bag to arrest the rattling of my teeth. I fell asleep without supper.

The morning pretended innocence in its splendor. The bright yellow of the wet sand underfoot pleasantly harmonized with the complementary blue of the sky overhead. In the distance, diagonally across a several-kilometre width of the natural Lac Des Allumettes, a misty silhouette of the city of Pembroke stretched out. From time to time, came waves of the distance-muffled rumble of its industrial activity. Somewhere in the distance over there, the Trans-Canada Highway touched it. The highway was not visible, but betraying it was an occasional rapid-fire series of the retarder brakes on a semi-trailer truck. It is interesting to note that today's Trans-Canada Highway in its road form is more or less parallel with its historic water-based counterpart. Also interesting is that in spite of the varying combination of lakes and rivers traveled upstream and downstream, the water route stretches in almost a straight line from East to West. The smooth lake surface was spreading to the left — downstream only for about half a kilometre where it was breaking into a whitewater slope over the threshold of the rapids. Upstream, the lake was winding in a five-kilometre width up to where the eye could not see. My, Quebec shore had a sand beach lined with weekend cottages. Behind them, as far as one could see, a pine forest was stretching. As it turned out, nobody was in the cottages. It was a work day. Another discovery for me only now, was finding on my iPhone that the rapids of yesterday were the famous Upper Allumettes. I had had no idea of that when I was battling my way through them. I had also failed to notice that the river had a parallel, smaller channel with rapids on the Pembroke side that was separated from my main channel by big Cotnam Island. The voyageurs portaged along there when moving upstream, whereas they sometimes ran the river through the main rapids when they moved downstream, but on the other (north) side of the island where I aborted my camping plan last night. While wet items were drying quickly, spread on bushes and on the branches of a fallen tree, I sated my deprived stomach with a quick hot breakfast. The loading of the canoe and lacing of the spray cover was by then a fast routine. Soon afterwards, I was already pushing the point of a "V"-shaped wake, dotted with paddle stroke whirlpools on the smooth water surface in a beeline to the first point in the misty distance around which the river-lake bent its shape. I was digging the paddle in with a renewed zest for life.

Rapides-des-Joachims

With lesser population density in the upper reaches of the river, the character of the people living alongside it seemed to have changed. One no longer saw the super-powerful jet boats that lower down used to rocket like ballistic missiles with a deafening roar, skimming over the water towards an indeterminate target as if the owner's house there were on fire. Typically, in the next moment, they would be rocketing at a different angle back, where, apparently, the owner's second house was on fire only to "bounce" into a third direction, etc. In their wake, they would leave a thick contrail smelling of burnt gas. With my purposeful, hard-labor-earned progress, aimed at reaching a very definite destination in as muscle-saving a short line as possible, I defined that mode of "recreation" as the "mad buzzing of a housefly in a milk can." Here I only met motor boats with fishermen and even one canoe and one kayak propelled by paddles. Where have the times gone when canoes and paddles were the typical props completing the nostalgic Canadian river sceneries as depicted in archival black and white photographs?

The last dam to overcome on the Ottawa was one that was divided in two by a relatively large island in the middle. The island accommodated a nostalgic Indigenous People settlement with the interesting plural name of "Rapides-des-Joachims." A portage route that was over two kilometres long bisected the island through the village. The one-time portage trail of the voyageurs cut through a small lake on the island so that the weight of the load could at least, for a moment, be carried by water. With the aim to make it of minimum distance, though, the trail ran over steep slopes and now it was already overgrown with bush. The cove where it started was choked with deadfall. I was prepared to portage along a gravel road. I left my camp on a sandy point about half a kilometre downstream from the island before 7:00 in the morning. This was because I expected that the portage would take a long time. My final destination of the day was still over twenty kilometres above the dam. The Natives' village was still sleeping when I unloaded the canoe at its pier. The low early morning sun, reflected by the mirror surface of the water, provided blinding illumination for my work. I organized everything here into portage bundles and started the multiple carries. Two piles of my load had already been spread along the road when I was toting the empty canoe upside down on my shoulders on the last carry. At that moment, a pickup truck backed up into the road from a house, straight against me, making me worry that I would be run over. From the cab an old Native gentleman descended on wobbly bow legs dressed in tight jeans and a white, sleeveless undershirt. He must have been shaving when he noticed my activity on the road through his bathroom window. He turned his head with a prickly, black brush cut to me as he stepped down from his truck and with a no-talking-back expression on his face, dominated by a cucumber-like pock-marked nose that supported thick, black-rimmed glasses, he commanded: "Throw it on!" And he grabbed the bow of my canoe at that moment. It all came so suddenly that I had but a split second to mull over whether this would mean that I was cheating in my "voyageur game." But there was no way to protest. We put the canoe into the pickup bed and we gradually picked up my remaining load from the road. Then he took me all the way to the put-in place above the dam. As he was helping me to unload my stuff from the pickup and was putting down my plastic bottles with drinking water, he would not resist to advise: "My friend, there is no need for you to carry this water with you! Look! You are sitting on it here everywhere!"

Norma Pettigrew

My goal of the day, once I was above the dam, was to reach a private commercial campsite located in a bay of the lake that, from here, was in the farthest misty distance directly opposite the mouth of the Des Moines River. I had turned into it from the highway to research the river during my drive to Montreal. The campsite was still empty then before the season but its owner, an elderly lady, Norma Pettigrew, lives there year-round. The camping fee in it is high because it caters to motorhomes with all the hook-ups. In the form of small talk I jokingly negotiated what kind of bargain discount I could hope for if I arrived there by canoe from Montreal and only had a small tent. In the next moment, though, an idea flashed through my head that I could leave here one of my two drybags containing food that my wife had carefully packaged for each day. It would save me the portaging of an overly heavy bag around the dams. "If I don't show up by the end of the summer, the bag is yours!" I offered. Norma willingly agreed with the plan and readily stored the bag in the corner of her office. It is interesting that at that time I was 99% sure that the bag would become Norma's. She might have seen things in a similar way. When I finally found the right campsite and appeared before Norma hairy, suntanned, with a prickly beard, it took her a while before she comprehended what was going on. Then she immediately disappeared into her office and returned with my blue bag. I sensed that she would not ask any money for her service but I was eager to support her business by staying the night in her campsite and pay for once a full camping fee. I needed a hot shower anyway. But Norma would not hear of any money. "Nobody who arrives to us by canoe all the way from Montreal needs to pay here!" she proclaimed. Then she personally escorted me to an honorable camping spot right on the high river bank with a splendid view. Along the way, she stopped at every camping party and proudly introduced me to them: "This man traveled to us on the river by canoe all the way from Montreal!" It was very touching. As I was parting the next morning, I took a picture of Norma in front of her office. I sent it to her eventually with a Christmas card.

The Mattawa

The lake, raised by the last hydro dam on the Ottawa, reached upstream up to its confluence with the river Mattawa in a town of the same name. The river's name, in fact, comes from the Algonquin word for "meeting of waterways." The Mattawa was to provide the next leg of the water route to carry my canoe. Although I did not have to fight any mentionable current on the lake behind the dam, Mother Nature found another way to assert its authority and instill in me the appropriate respect for her by dealing me an ungodly, fierce headwind for all the remaining days on the Ottawa River. The first day, I simply stayed wind-bound in my camp for another night, hoping that the wind would abate. When this did not happen, I fought with it every day, sometimes metre-by-metre. In doing so, I "licked" the lee-side bank of the river and looked for shelter behind all points, overhanging trees and islands. My last campsite on the Ottawa was situated on a beautiful island right downstream of the town of Mattawa. I arrived there on Canada Day, the First of July. This lucky coincidence thus furnished fireworks for my successful completion of the journey up the Ottawa. Like all towns in Canada, even the small ones, Mattawa did an excellent job of celebrating the national holiday with great pride.

Once in Mattawa, I separated, for the first time, from my canoe that I had hauled onto shore at the point that the two rivers formed where they met. It was hidden to sight from the nearest vicinity by a grassy overhang but it was visible from the town's business center on the other side of the river where I walked across a bridge. In order not to be taken for a homeless vagrant, I carefully spruced up my hair and hung a camera on my chest. Still, I got a startling scare when I saw my reflection in the display window of a supermarket. My beard reminded me of my uncle's Bouvier des Flandres dog. Mattawa, and later on North Bay, were the only places where I made any significant food shopping along my voyage. In both cases, I still had sufficient supplies for more than a week. During a handful of other opportunities on my journey, I typically bought only snacks like ice cream and chocolate. Interestingly, a very special treat for me during my voyage turned out to be ice-cold diet Pepsi Cola, which in my circumstances, always tasted like God's nectar.

For canoe traveling, the Mattawa is a gem of the voyageur route. The Mattawa, in comparison to the Ottawa, is a small river. It winds through very varied, picturesque landscapes, rich in granite rock formations of the Canadian Shield and in scenic craggy islands. They are all dressed in the green of the forest giants emanating an intoxicating scent of resin. Dominating here is the white pine (*pinus strobus*). These trees anchor their roots even in the smallest cracks of rocky cliffs and comb the blue of the sky above with their unruly, wind-coiffed crowns of fine, long needles. Like the charms on a necklace, the course of the river is adorned with waterfalls and small and big lakes of crystal, clear water. I found here the true Canadian "Indian romance" just as I had imagined it when reading the books of Cooper, Curwood and Ballantyne during my boyhood in Prague. Both, the voyageurs` and the First Nation People's histories spoke to me here around each turn of the river, on the feet-smoothed rocks of the portage trails, in the scream of a circling bald eagle and in the refreshing mist off the waterfalls. The strongest link with the prehistoric past came on one scenically beautiful little island where my tent, anchored only with rocks in its corners, stood on an elevated granite bench with breathtaking views of Lake Talon through a veil of pine needle greenery. I felt a strong conviction that the Indigenous water nomads had already slept on this very same spot perhaps thousands of years ago. They did not sleep under a nylon tent in a down sleeping bag like me; they might have been comfortable with an armful of fur on the same hard granite but they must have enjoyed the same pleasantly hospitable atmosphere of the place and a refreshing swim in the clear, agreeably warm water. It is highly probable that their fire pit was in the same spot where mine was. "Archaeologically" stacked layers of ancient ash in the existing rock circle seemed to be the proof of my theory. In my imagination, a chance did not exist that they would have passed up this gorgeous campsite without using it. Especially here on the Mattawa, I could not help but muse about how the water route that I was following was discovered because its critical links are very obscure and often counterintuitive. Take for example the connection from Lake Talon to Trout Lake, which is west of it: it does not start in the western reach of Talon but in a small water-weeds-camouflaged little bay in its north. It was obvious to me that the route could not be discovered by one brave explorer who had set out to travel into the Great Lakes. Rather, it must have originated from the local knowledge of individual Native groups who traditionally occupied territories along it. The canoe-based cultures of Ojibwa, Nipissing and Algonquin, who happen to be united today under the name of Anishinaabe, used canoe travel for hunting and fishing and the gathering of edible plants. Most of them were likely peaceful home-bodies who got to know their water system of lakes, creeks and rivers in great detail but only in a limited range around their home. As in every human group, there must have existed a few braves with "itchy soles on their moccasins" who liked to range farther afield to get to see new lands and know new peoples. As they probably came to new places with friendship and in peace, they learned of further travel connections from the local people. In this way, some nomads united the isolated local routes into one grand water highway of trade and cultural exchange. The flip side of the coin here was the fact that it also opened a corridor for warring raids that could sometimes result in the annihilation of whole tribes. That is why some tribes jealously guarded the passage through their territory and tried to cloak it in secret and danger, such as when de Champlain arrived in the village of the Algonquin chief Tessouat on the Isle aux Allumettes during his first, unsuccessful attempt to penetrate up the Ottawa River in 1613. At that time, Tessuat prevented de Champlain from progressing further. To silence de Champlain's guide, who claimed to have traveled up the Ottawa and to James Bay via Lake Abitibi, Tessuat accused him of lying and sorcery, sentencing him to hang. Only desperate diplomacy from de Champlain eventually saved his man. Tessouat's security concerns were not baseless. His tribe would eventually be practically wiped out by the marauding Iroquois.

La Vase Portage

Historically, the Mattawa prepared for the voyageurs 14 portages. Of these, three are eliminated today due to raised water by small dams, leaving 11. I, however, carried the canoe and gear in repeated trips along the paths only about five times. In the rest of the portage locations, I was able to overcome them with my specialty which was the muscling of the fully-loaded canoe up the rapids by walking with it straight through the rocks and water. It always renewed abrasions on my knees and bruises on my shins but it was incomparably faster than the repeated portage. The longest one, though, and the most loathed by the voyageurs comes at the end. This is the 12-kilometre bushwhack and slog across the watershed summit that connects the head of the Mattawa River in Trout Lake with the very large Lake Nipissing — the head of the French River. The route of the portage takes advantage of marshy ponds, little swamp creeks and a small river with a mud bottom and muddy banks that flows into Lake Nipissing at the south edge of today's big city of North Bay. The voyageurs named the river La Vase — French for the mud — or Muddy. The name spread to cover the whole hated portage. It starts in the southwest reach of Trout Lake called Dugas Bay where it first crosses today's Trans-Canada Highway. It is commemorated there by a cairn with a plaque. Other than that, however, the portage route is not marked anywhere. Since there is zero traffic on the portage, it has no visibly trodden path that one could follow. Were it not for the ability of my iPhone to show me where I was located relative to the chain of ponds, and had I not found a schematic map of the La Vase portage in historical literature before the trip, I would never have succeeded in connecting its wiggly course. I was thus pushing my way through the forest with a dense undergrowth of fern, bushes and fallen trees to the first of the beaver lakes. Here for the first time, I discovered that they were all overgrown with water lilies and reeds. This is because the ponds had originally been created by beavers who were exterminated during the height of the fur fever. As a result, the ponds became overgrown with vegetation and then dried out. Today the beavers are back and they build their dams in the same spots where they did during the old times. The jungle of water growth, however, has never disappeared. Pushing my canoe, I struggled through forests of dense two-metre-high cattail reeds. These grew from floating root mats on which I had to step but sunk up to my neck into the black, stinking gravy wherever I slipped in between. I poled through the thick cover of lily pads with the long kayak paddle that normally served as my spare paddle, while standing in the canoe. I pulled leeches off my bloodied shins as I dragged the heavy boat over the high beaver dams. My nylon windbreaker that protected me from the bloodthirsty mosquitoes in the heat of the day, reeked of the soaked-up cesspoolish swamp liquid and my sweat. Later, I was moving through an unfriendly periphery of the city — forced to portage over a dusty road from a quarry and over an industrial rail spur from a chemical plant. I paddled past a jumble of wire and old tires, under multi-level highway and railway overpasses. I dragged the canoe over shallow rocky rapids on the edge of residential backyards, through a sewer-like tunnel under the city's Main Street, etc. I went through moments of psychological crises and depths of hopelessness when I doubted that it would be at all possible to connect the portage in this modern time. At last, though, the La Vase River quieted down and significantly widened as it started nearing its mouth into Lake Nipissing. By then, evening was slowly creeping in. One moment, a large dark beaver was swimming right next to the canoe. He might have failed to realize that I was not a floating log until I quietly spoke to him: "What are you up to old buddy?" His quick answer was an immediate noisy slap of his tail on the water and a perpendicular dive. Around the next bend, a good-sized raccoon gazed at me from the bank with the seeming grin of a Cheshire cat. Dusk approached. I spotted a pair of deer at the edge of the woods who were observing me while nervously flicking their short, white tails. When at last I triumphantly floated into the lake after a 13-hour dreadful ordeal, the sun was just dipping into its shiny, surface horizon. Beaching the canoe was not the last act of the hard day, though. Ahead of me was yet another, if definitely the last, half-kilometre portage from the beach to the tenting area in the back of a commercial campsite near the mouth. The tent went up by memory in the total darkness. But I felt immeasurable happiness from my success. I convinced myself that I had in me that something that De Champlain, La Verendrye, David Thompson, Alex MacKenzie and other famous explorers must have had in their characters when they all had passed through here. I was so thoroughly exhausted that I could not even straighten my chest. But suddenly, time stopped. I no longer had to hurry anywhere, strain my muscles and worry if I would be able to find suitable camping to lay my head down. In the cubicle of the shower shack, I pulled a plastic chair for changing under the hot shower and I sat in it after midnight when the camp slept, perhaps for an hour. I was soothing the pain of my achy muscles in it and I again and again savored the elation from successfully reaching my ambitious goal. "I can sleep in till noon if I want to!" I told myself. "I'll take three days of rest here!" A vision of breakfast at Tim Horton's washed down with ice-cold diet Pepsi, however, woke me up early. I visited the center of the city several times using a city bus and I resupplied my food. The mentioning of my epic voyage, following the historic route of the voyageurs from Montreal to the west, always worked like a magic wand. People would melt in friendly admiration and they would do anything to help me. They would personally

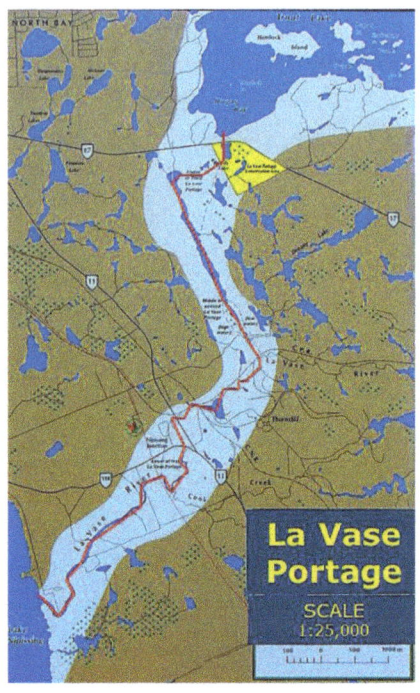

lead me to anything that I was looking for in a supermarket; in the campsite, I was given a substantial discount on the camping fee. A couple of times along the voyage I was invited by people to visit their house, join them for dinner, sleep in a clean bed, have breakfast and do my laundry that I always declined with thanks due to logistical reasons.

Lake Nipissing

Long before my arrival at Lake Nipissing, I heard warnings from people that this lake was known for its big waves. They predicted that I would likely not be able to meet this challenge in a canoe. This is because, they said, the lake is shallow. On that evening when I arrived, the surface of the lake was as smooth as a mirror. The next day, however, a storm came up in the afternoon that I slept through in my tent after a good beer. With the storm came change in the weather. Waves then rolled onto its beach shore day and night. I left the campsite on the third morning, still in the darkness, hoping that this early, the lake might still be quiet. I entered it again paddling out of the La Vase River since the river happened to be closer to my tent than the lake. But big breakers with foamy, white crests must have been rolling on the lake perhaps right through the whole night. The finding seemed crushing until I put my money on the theory that farther from shore, where the lake is deeper, the waves would not roll but rather just swell up and down. It turned out that I was right. As the dawn lit up the day, I was already paddling on waves like a skier on snow moguls. I must, however, state that I had a very happy observation. It would show up that I had chosen an excellent craft for this purpose. My Kevlar Evergreen Bob Special demonstrated incredible stability in the waves thanks to its wide beam. This, combined with its length of nearly 15 feet also yielded sufficient load capacity for a long expedition. It was a shorter tandem canoe with two seats but symmetrical. The stern became the bow for me and I sat backwards on the front seat that now became the rear seat. This brought me, as a solo paddler, closer to the center of the boat where I could more easily control it. At home before the trip, my wife and I had designed and sewn a light spray cover with a cockpit opening fitted with a skirt that could be sealed with Velcro closures up to the armpits. The cover attached to the canoe like the skin of a drum with lacing through a series of little loops that were sealed into both sides of the canoe. It protected the canoe from taking up water both in waves on a lake as well as in whitewater rapids, but it also shielded the load underneath it and the paddler from rain and wind. The spray cover had Velcro fasteners sewn on its top for holding a waterproof map case and a stretched-out, foldable solar charger. It also featured pockets and straps for holding the paddle and storing the spare paddle. The canoe had the hint of a keel that tracked well on flat water but it still allowed for sufficient maneuverability in rapids. The Kevlar material made the boat very light (20.5 kg) for carrying it on one's shoulders. A splendid woodwork of ash and cherry adorned it to complete perfection.

In the beginning, a wind from the right front accompanied by a gentle rain refreshed my face together with the whipped-up water mist. But with the progression of morning, it cleared up. The sun swung up the blue sky and the wind gradually weakened which was rather unusual. Step by step, this kept building up my courage to shorten the curve of my moving from A to B more and more. It was progressively approaching a straight line rather than the original scallops that were to carve out the southern bays of the lake. I thus often paddled kilometres from shore. When I beached the canoe for a lunch break, I could hardly discern the city of North Bay — my morning start — in the misty distance. In the view from my camp on the tip of an island looking east in the evening, North Bay was already hidden beyond the curvature of the lake horizon. I had spanned the vast, dangerous area of open lake in one day! This totally surpassed my expectations. I had reached the strategic start of a southwest panhandle of the lake in which location the French River — the continuation of the historic "water trans-Canada highway" — flows out of the lake to the west-southwest. Since the crossing of the divide on the La Vase Portage, I was now moving only "downhill" on the French, or "on a level" on the lakes Nipissing and Huron. The only "uphill climbing" waited for me just before the finish of the voyage in Sault Saint Marie when I would paddle upstream on the short Saint Marie River that flows from the higher elevation of Lake Superior into lower Lake Huron.

The French River

In this camp on the southwest end of Lake Nipissing, I had the last signal for my iPhone. From here on, west on the French River, I lost it. With this, I of course also lost the ability of the iPhone to show me Google maps. This could have been an utter tragedy since the river

French spreads in its flow through the Canadian Shield into its widely branching, innumerable, criss-crossing fissures and wrinkles in a chasm of channels and islands. Without a map, it would have been almost impossible for this first-time visiting canoeist to connect the way through. Fortunately, during one of my business trips in which I had crossed the French River in a rented vehicle on the way from the Toronto airport to a research lab in Sudbury, I turned off the highway to a small outfitter store on the river and bought an excellent local map. That became my reliable guide, although for a layman it was still difficult to decide which way to go on the upper French. This is because the river splits into two main systems. One of them is the main River French — used by the voyageurs with a long portage along (again) Chaudiére Rapids. The second one is the Little French which is the only possible one to travel through today. They both have dams on their courses — not for the production of energy but rather for regulating the water level in Lake Nipissing. In addition to the dam spillway, the Little French also has a parallel Free Flow Channel that allows for a passage down either by a portage alongside of it or by paddling through it. The latter, however, may only be feasible for a team of experienced slalom kayakers. A solo canoe paddler like myself, whose boat carries everything that he needs for his survival in the deserted wilderness, will obviously portage. No fishing boats venture into this area from above since they cannot pass through. Neither can they approach from downstream because it is isolated by rapids from below. I learned of the passage along the Little French only at the last moment when I was already churning my way towards the dam on the main French River. The fishermen in motor boats whom I had asked along the way did not know because, not being able to use it, they did not care to learn about it. They would not be able to pass down the river in motorboats here anyway. The correct information finally came from the young guide of a local outfitter whom the Lord sent my way in a boat with fishing clients at the last minute.

I then had to partially double back. After some improvisation in using a channel where I barely squeezed through with my canoe after getting lost, I victoriously emerged at the Free Flow Channel. I moved through this region totally alone. When I was below the Free Flow Channel, I flushed out a giant black bear. It was when I tried to provoke a response from a loon by imitating his hysterical laughing call. I was just paddling through a small lake in the advancing evening, looking for a camping spot. Naturally, the sighting of a bear then postponed my camping by another three kilometres. This part of the upper French River has a number of rapids, two of which, including the Free Flow Channel, were very difficult. I portaged around them. The voyageurs gave them names like: Five Finger Rapid, Little Pine and Big Pine Rapids, Little Paris and Big Paris Rapids, Rainy Rapids, Devil's Shute, etc. The Main and the Little French systems eventually merge again, increasing its width. The slope of the river lessens. It then has a few discrete drops, the biggest of which are the Recollet Falls. Several monks of the French Catholic order of the Recollets allegedly drowned here during the voyageur times when the canoes in which they were passengers on their way to become missionaries in Huronia, capsized.

The French River finally spills its waters into Georgian Bay of Lake Huron through a widely fanning delta. All its channels have a sudden drop that has to be tackled by passing watercraft. The voyageurs, as well as I, had chosen a channel that nowadays is called The Voyageur Channel. It has a relatively minor obstacle in the form of a small, rocky step called Petite Faucille, where the voyageurs had to portage. The channel also has sections, however, where the width of its granite course is so narrow that a large Montreal canoe could barely squeeze through. Over the centuries since the fur trade era, slow but steady erosion of the granite barriers that hold the water level behind them, caused the water level in the whole watershed to drop so that even my canoe, which has a maximum width of 93 cm, had a hard time easing through. In two places I had to lift and drag it over rocks. Modern maps do not even show the Voyageur Channel as continuous anymore. The voyageur route takes the maximum advantage of the relative wind shelter in the granite Shield by emerging into Georgian

Bay from the western-most channel. Here, however, I was suddenly assaulted by the overpowering force of the unbound wind that was driving its wrath against me across the enormous vastness of the great Canadian lake. It was a real interior freshwater sea as it was described by Brûlé to de Champlain.

When he arrived at the lake, de Champlain had fulfilled his ambition. He then continued south from the mouth of the French River through a connected chain of lakes and portages through Huronia until he reached Lake Ontario. From there he proceeded east into the outflowing Saint Lawrence River and back to Montreal. The neck of Étienne Brûlé was saved from the noose. In the end, however, he would not avoid a violent death anyway. He returned to his favorite lifestyle among the Natives. But his unrestrained sexual indiscretions not only offended the Catholic missionaries, whose work he thus undermined, but they even exceeded the liberal measure of tolerance by the pagan savages. They thus killed him before he lived to be forty. Thanks to his alleged betrayal of the French in providing guiding services to their British enemy, Brûlé offended even his onetime protector, de Champlain. This de facto Gouverneur de la Nouvelle-France would then not even bother to organize any punishing action against the Native culprits of his murder.

Georgian Bay of Lake Huron

In divergence with that of de Champlain's, my voyage now continued in the westerly direction. Although I got up very early and arrived at the lake by 11:00, there was no point in continuing further and fighting with the wind and waves. I thus put up my tent on a high, smooth granite bank among wind-sculpted pines. I resigned myself to suntanning, swimming in the refreshing, bluish clear water and cooking for the remainder of the day. I consumed four to six litres of unsweetened tea during each of my typical paddling days. In this way, I was adding a little flavor to the lake water that I sterilized by boiling. I filled with it one- and two-litre plastic bottles from Pepsi

Cola but only after partial cooling so the plastic bottles would not shrink. Because I only had one-litre and two-litre kettles, the brewing and cooling of the liquid normally took till the late evening. The tea would then become chilled by the overnight cold and stay cool in the bottom of the canoe. Since the two-litre kettle also served to cook supper, its taste to a small degree always found its way into the batch of tea brewed in it. No matter what, on a hot day on the water, the "tea" was always welcome, even if it sometimes tasted a bit like soup or an ashtray. My main courses consisted of naturally dehydrated foodstuffs obtainable in ordinary food stores, not of expensive freeze-dried meals from specialized outdoor shops. I went through repeating cycles of meals based on rice, pasta, potatoes and legumes. Most of the time, the contents of the Ziploc baggies only required boiling in water from a lake or river. Apart from legumes (like beans, lentils, peas), these represented mainly carbohydrates. I thus enriched the meals with beef jerky. I also cooked soups from bag mixes. When I had time in the camp in the morning, I would cook hot oatmeal or cream of wheat porridge for breakfast. The latter especially gained volume by boiling from almost nothing which I remembered well from a childhood fairy tale about a magic mug that overflowed with this concoction to the point where villagers returning home from the fields had to eat their way through it. One time I would make it from white wheat semolina, another time I would make it from yellow corn farina to lessen the chance of growing sick of it. With it I had hot coffee or mocha. In the later part of my journey when I resorted to launching the canoe before daybreak, I would usually have breakfast after two hours of paddling in the canoe. I would typically empty a paper packet or two of instant Quaker oatmeal straight into my mouth and chase it down with my "tea." The snack breaks on board would mostly feature protein bars, nuts and dried fruit. For lunch, I would often have crackers with cheese or a mini can of little frankfurters. Other times it would be jerky. I was able to pack six weeks-worth of food into two vinyl drybags. At the start, though, these were as heavy as if filled with sand. Although I carried a collapsible survival fishing rod with me, there was never enough spare time in my overly busy day to catch and clean fish. Traveling alone, I was also keenly aware of the risk of attracting a bear into my camp with fish scents.

The first day of my arrival at Lake Huron, whipped up by the wind into wild waves, gave me a big worry. How am I to continue? Then I realized that it was time to reach for the wisdom of the voyageurs and like them, get going in the mornings before daybreak. That is because at that time the lake surface was usually calm. I applied this masochistic idea the very next morning. In total darkness, I first changed into my mosquito-proof nylon pants and windbreaker before I left the tent. Still in there I also packed my sleeping bag, the mat and all my clothing. Then I took the tent down and packed it. Still in the darkness, I loaded the canoe. There would be no cooking this morning because the kitchen had been packed the previous night. Neither did I deploy the spray cover right away. Had I tried, I would have been eaten alive by the mosquitoes because the time around dawn and dusk were their ritualistic "witching hours." I planned to have a cold breakfast later on under the sun in the boat. I pushed off into darkness, dotted with fluorescence in the water, paddling in a west-southwesterly direction — a straight line among rocky islets that I had surveyed and predetermined the previous evening. Now I could see the scanning beacon of a lighthouse in that direction so I navigated toward it. I assumed that it had to be situated on a prominent shoreline point that I had to go around and which the voyageurs named Point Grondine. The name means Cape of Groaning or Growling because of the noise that the surf almost always makes at this location. At daybreak, I realised that the lighthouse was in reality situated on a very distant rocky island called Gull Island and I was by now finding myself quite a ways from Point Grondine on the open water. Under a very fine, gentle morning rain, I made an immediate correction to my paddling course — now towards the northwest. The waves had already started but I had proven to myself that, thanks to my canoe, I could successfully travel on. I was now moving through an interesting environment where smooth round granite ridges emerged in large numbers from the water. They were all oriented in the same way and of just the right size to look like the backs of a petrified pod of migrating whales. I landed on one of them after my sight registered very faint strobe flashes on a very distant, hardly discernible antenna tower. I tried my iPhone and indeed, I had a signal. Having completely forgotten that Milena's Edmonton time was two hours behind mine, not to speak of the fact that I had no sense that it was a Saturday, I then woke her up with a phone call at 6:00 in the morning. Not surprisingly she was not angry in the least. To hear my voice after five days of uncertainty with its assurance that I was still alive and well brought her a very soothing relief. Only here did I stretch my spray cover onto the canoe. By the shape of the coastline, I guessed that the antenna tower must have stood near the place called Killarney. In this location, the water passage squeezes into a narrow channel between an island and a peninsula, concentrating in it all boat traffic that follows the so-called North Channel (a buoy-delineated, safely deep route, loosely paralleling the north shore of the lake). I still had at least a day of paddling to it, though. Later in the afternoon I spoke with Milena again. She called in order to alert me to a weather advisory that had allegedly been issued for the entire area of Sudbury and Georgian Bay. It predicted a possibility of severe thunderstorms and even tornadoes. At the time, I had already been eyeing a darkening sky in the west with suspicion. Since I would never wish to be caught in an electric lightning storm on the water, I immediately aimed the bow of the canoe to the nearest island with a promising campsite on a granite shore bench. The downpour just started as I was finishing the erection of the tent. I then secured all the gear and drybags under an overturned canoe on the solid rock shore, and quickly crawled into the sleeping bag. I now braced myself for the development of a "devils' wedding" outside. But the rain stopped after about an hour and the weather warning missed its fruition. On a nice evening with a red sunset, I then stood on a jutting rock on the western point of the island and looking west, I watched the light of a very distant lighthouse. It must have indicated the entry into the Killarney narrows.

Killarney, Little Current, North Channel

I navigated straight to it the next morning, again in the darkness. I reached my target before 10:00 in a beeline across kilometres and kilometres of open water. My island where I camped the previous night was by this time invisible in the vapors of the distance. While on a shore leave in Killarney, I overindulged in junk food chased down with ice-cold Pepsi. I also bought two still warm, fresh loaves of bread for the way, but most importantly, I purchased a set of detailed nautical charts covering most of the North Channel. This is because the wireless telephone service in this area is very sporadic and I could not rely on my iPhone's navigation for this tricky island-channels topography. I then wreaked quite a havoc navigating around the luxury yachts and multi-story mega-motorboats of millionaire water tourists through the narrows as I boldly paddled my canoe west, proudly stripped to shorts like an Aboriginal savage. My ghostly appearance in the midst of the busy boat traffic must have served as a strong reminder that a canoe propelled by a paddle was the only true, traditional way of honouring the historic waterways of this magnificent country called Canada. On that day, I managed to battle my way through an afternoon headwind to make great progress thanks to a partial shelter from a long peninsula called Badgeley Point. I ended up on its very western tip. The camping here was awful. The shoreline granite was shattered into a sharp-edged jumble of rocks. Moreover, they were constantly battered by the surf. I had a very hard time unloading the canoe while standing next to it in the water and holding it from getting smashed on the rocks. Then I had to set my tent up beyond the band of rocky shore in the dense eastern cedar thicket. First I had to clear the spot using a machete and pushing away the gnarled thorny-like limbs to form a fence against imagined nasty beasts that must have lurked in the spooky forest darkness. The voyageurs had to cross a large spread of open water from here to the island of La Cloche (Bell). Continuing then through a narrow channel along its east side, they reached the north shore of Lake Huron that they would then follow. An out-of-place, glacier-delivered, dark-colored boulder allegedly existed in the vicinity of this route that when struck with a rock gave off a sound like a bell. Today not only the island is named after it (La Cloche) but so is the nearby mountain range, a provincial park and a number of other geographic localities. The narrow channel is no longer navigable having been interrupted by the causeway of a road that now connects the mainland with the islands. All boat traffic thus streams into another narrow passage between the islands of La Cloche and Manitoulin. This important spot again supports a small community called Little Current. A small boat does indeed feel a slight movement of the water flowing through here. The port of the village does again see a significant concentration of boats and ships. At the time of my arrival, even a cruise ship was anchored there. By its flags and the home port name "Valletta" emblazoned on its stern, it appeared to have come all the way from Malta. When I first saw it in the southeast on the sparkling lake horizon of early morning, it looked like a floating castle. I left my laced-up canoe at the edge of the port with peace of mind and set out to explore the village. My experience had taught me by now that in this neighborhood, no Canadian would touch my unattended boat. I enjoyed a nice relaxed dinner with two draft beers in a local corner restaurant. I topped it with a large bowl of ice cream. In the beginning, I could tell that the young waitress was wavering a little, unsure if she was allowed to serve a second beer to a homeless hobo. Only the ensuing small talk changed her distrust into admiration. On the way back to the canoe I, of course, picked up a couple of two-litre bottles of diet Pepsi. For a canoe, today's new route brings even larger crossings of open water than what the voyageurs had to overcome. The routine of starting out before daybreak, around 4:00 a.m., had thus by now become a daily affair in my movement along the North Channel. I would then span distances of up to around 40, even 50 kilometres during the extended days before I would start looking for a campsite around 4:00 in the afternoon. In this part of the journey, I enjoyed several very romantic campsites atop high granite islands with plumes of wind-combed pines and scenic views of the lake. In the evenings I would be gazing awestruck at picturesque groups of late sun-tinted small and larger islands. The landscape scenery was complemented by an ever-changing display of dramatic skies concluding with blood-red sunsets. I would frequently recognize the type of settings here that had been immortalized in the paintings of the famous Group of Seven. The nights were just as spectacular. It seemed that the mostly clear, very dark sky was so heavy with billions of stars that they would start snowing down at any time. One could almost touch the Milky Way. I was blessed with a full and later waning moon during the time of my voyage through the North Channel that provided adequate illumination for my early paddling starts. After a while, I arrived in that part of the North Channel that left the island archipelagos. I moved along the north shore. It was equally rocky and rugged as the islands, but when looking south, one would see nothing but an uninterrupted sheet of the water surface. Only later on, hovering above the southern horizon, a thin misty line would start appearing. It was the isle of Manitoulin, the largest freshwater island in the world that approaches the north shore towards the west. With a few exceptions, I was anchoring the corners of the tent with rocks everywhere I camped. Ever since I started traveling along the edge of the Canadian Shield that is on the Mattawa River, the tent mostly stood on hard level granite. In the beginning, I would carefully select only places for the tent where the granite was smooth and level. Later, misery would teach me to accept even surfaces that were a bit cracked, a tad sloping or somewhat bulging so long as I could arrange my weary frame flat on them. My experience had shown that a night on a bed of hard granite can provide the best rest for a back tired from the hard work of the day's paddling. Instead of pegs driven into the ground, I inserted about a foot long piece of a stout stick into each corner loop of the tent — perpendicular to the axis of the corner. I then pulled out the corner with the stick to stretch the tent taut and weighted it down with a rock or two. Thanks in part to its aerodynamic shape, my super-light MSR Hubba-Hubba tent for two never moved. It served me faithfully, especially in a wild storm with strong winds, pelting rain and lightning that slammed all around me like artillery bombardment. At that time, a fight with a strong afternoon headwind, a shoreline densely lined with cottages and the black wall of an approaching storm in the west forced me into emergency camping on the sharp granite "razor back" of an elongated narrow island. The top of the razor back ridge had only one spot where there was a bit of near-horizontal surface for the tent. Although severely exposed to the elements, the tent did not fail.

The Paradise Camp, the agony of exhaustion and the triumph of reaching Lake Superior

The exception in this final phase of the journey was a "paradise" campsite featuring a sweet horseshoe of a private little beach of fine white sand. Protecting it from behind was a parallel grouping of white pines. At the time, I was just paddling about a kilometre off shore to avoid just-under-the-surface-jutting rock snags, when the strengthening headwind made further fighting nonsensical. It was just before 11:00. My quick survey of the shoreline for a longer rest stop then aroused my suspicion that I was seeing a small beach. It seemed hard to believe. But when I came nearer and my suspicion proved true, I decided to camp here early and enjoy the beautiful day by swimming and resting. There was no sign of civilization as far as I could see. This allowed me to save the dryness of my swimsuit and swim and dry naked like in a real paradise. I had only a weak signal here for my iPhone yet it allowed me to describe the beauty of the wonderful place to Milena and to even send her a five-minute-old picture of it. As I was nearing the northwest corner of Lake Huron in my journey and its finish in Sault Ste. Marie, the fatigue of my hard daily toil exerted a stronger and stronger effect on my body. However romantic the voyage was, I could not wait to come to its end, drop the paddle as if it were made of red-hot steel and never touch it again. My experience brought a finding that might be of interest to performance athletes. This is that my body suffered from a lack of protein in my diet. My two bags of food, one of which I had left temporarily at Norma's campsite on the upper Ottawa, did not have equally distributed contents. The one at Norma's held, besides a bulk food reserve, the main significant supply of protein bars. I have mentioned that I had lost weight even before the voyage but my body still had reserves that were able to nourish my muscles without visible losses. I was losing mostly fat. When I picked up my food bag from Norma, I suddenly had no shortage of protein. In fact, I indulged on at least half a dozen protein snacks in one sitting on that very evening. The peak of my muscle development must have occurred somewhere on the Mattawa. In my subjective (relative) assessment, I was then representing a "lean and mean muscle machine." I bought a new supply of protein bars during my three-day stop in North Bay. But with their more frequent use when they had also served as a cold breakfast during my early starts on Lake Huron their supply had soon been depleted. Only carbohydrates remained. During the long seven-, eight-, or even up to nine-hour uninterrupted paddling stints, these were hardly sufficient to replace my spent energy. I continued to lose fat, but interestingly, without proteins, even my muscle mass started getting absorbed.

On the last day before Sault Ste. Marie, I paddled from 4:00 in the morning till 4:00 in the afternoon. The paddling against the current of the Saint Marie River seemed endless. The water streamed past the sides of the canoe with its usual speed but when I measured my forward progress relative to the river bank, it often seemed that I was stuck in one spot. In spite of this, I covered a distance that I had originally planned for two days. I did have a reason to hurry. Milena had already booked and bought for me a Greyhound bus ticket to Edmonton. It was to depart from Sault Ste. Marie in three days. Still ahead of me, was also the task of arranging the transportation of the canoe and gear by rail or truck to Edmonton. Milena found a motel for me on the internet that was situated right on the river bank. I found it successfully. Alas, it had no vacancy. The other motels and hotels were also fully booked, even the expensive ones. This was due to an unfortunate coincidence that the city was hosting an annual week-long reunion festival for Canadians of Finnish descent, the Finn

Days. Only with great difficulty was I able to find accommodation far from the river but the motel on the riverbank very generously agreed to store my boat and equipment till the shipping truck arrived to pick it up. When I finally saw myself in a hotel room mirror, the sore image of a human ruin reminded me of an unfortunate inmate of a concentration camp or perhaps a castaway, because of my beard and long hair. To further strengthen the reason for my self-pity, during the last 10 days, I also suffered from two broken toes. The bus trip from Sault Ste. Marie to Edmonton took almost three days. Even this represented a certain Canadiana experience in its passage through historical places, crossing the Canadian prairies and in the composition of the passengers. Represented here were the true average citizens, ranging from the Indigenous People, soldiers, farmers, seniors, to cowboys and young people migrating for work. To me the atmosphere of the bus ride was not too remote from that of a stagecoach. The combination of the car, bus and canoe travel back and forth over a major part of Canada brought me closer to her, amplifying my gratefulness for her acceptance of me. Should you ask me to characterize my experience from the cross-Canada voyage in one sentence, only two words keep creeping onto my tongue: "Embracing Canada."

CHAPTER II

From Sault Sainte Marie along the east and northeast coasts of Lake Superior to Marathon (August 5 – 29, 2011)

Well, greetings! Here I am, again afflicted with the "call of the wild" fever. It is nice to sit with you and chat again for a while.

When I finally gently nudged the bow of the canoe with my last paddle stroke into the sand of a short beach strip that belonged to Motel Algoma in Sault Sainte Marie on the 29th of July, 2010, I staggered onto dry land like a castaway. I dropped the paddle as if it were made of red-hot steel and was definitely determined never to touch it again. It was after an exceptionally hard day. My continuous 12-hour paddling from an emergency sleepover in a thicket next to a rocky point where I had to capitulate in my battle with ferocious headwinds the previous afternoon started while it was still dark at 4:00 in the morning. My plan was to conquer as many miles as possible of the distance that remained between me and the end of my torture from exhaustion before a new wind awakened. I paddled through darkness along the Canada-U.S. border and navigated only by occasional lights from thinly scattered dwellings on American Sugar Island. Twice I hit the bottom of the canoe on some shallow reefs but I entered Lake George otherwise unscathed. I was then traversing its vast spread in an almost straight line through its middle while dawn slowly diffused its pale light into the morning fog. Interestingly, the fog served as a friendly assurance to me that, at least as long as it persisted, there would be no wind. Lake George is very shallow and thus even in a canoe with its minimal draft I was forced to follow a shipping channel for boats. It was delineated with buoys that guided me like the gates of a giant slalom. The channel, in fact, represents the extension of the Sainte Marie's riverbed as it winds down the length of the lake through its center. I tried a direct line as a shortcut at one point but the bottom of my canoe immediately bogged down in a heavy rug of up-to-the-surface-growing aquatic weeds. Only with difficulty was I able to return back between the buoys. Had I met here with wind, the shallowness of the lake would have made for especially bad rolling waves. To my surprise, I eventually reached the north end of the long lake where the Sainte Marie River flows in, between 9:00 and 10:00 in the morning. This gave rise to a hope that, having half of the total distance behind me, I would reach Sault Sainte Marie not only on the same day but perhaps even quite early. Nature then made sure that I rediscovered my humility. The fog dissipated, a hot day started and the river, against which I earlier paddled relatively easily, soon came up with a strong current. I felt it especially around the mouth of the Garden River. I was slicing the water with the bow of my canoe like a racer, yet measured by the progress along the banks of the river, I occasionally wrestled the current in one spot. When nature detected that I was winning over her sabotage after all, she quite maliciously added a strong headwind. Following my juicy swearing at her with the rhythm of my paddle strokes, I now hysterically laughed and "congratulated" her for having done an "excellent job" — "just this had been missing." As it turned out, something more was missing that wouldn't let me wait for too long: A searing sun started burning in the clear sky from which salty sweat commenced streaming down my face. From under my hat, the flow split around my nose and settled into cracks in my parched lips that ushered it into my sandpapery mouth. A suburb of the metropolis of Sault Sainte Marie started populating the north bank of the river relatively soon. But the paddling along dwellings to reach the center of the city seemed to be endless. A can of diet Pepsi from a vending machine next to the office of the motel thus materialized as the attainment of an absolute Nirvana on this earth. At $40, Motel Algoma had an unusually low rate per night. Alas, due to that it was fully booked with long-term tenants. Its lady manager sympathized with my pitiful appearance and willingly spent about an hour on the phone trying to find me a substitute accommodation. As

I previously mentioned in my account of the voyage from Montreal to Lake Superior, thanks to an unfortunate annual reunion of Canadians of Finnish descent in Sault Sainte Marie that week, all motels, even expensive hotels along the water and elsewhere were full. In the end, I found a small hotel owned by a young East Indian couple who were willing to offer me a room to lay my head down and to store my gear. It was located about three kilometres away from the river. I had already accepted the unpleasant prospect of carrying everything to it in several trips as the last portage. But at that moment, a generous offer came from the Algoma lady manager for me to leave all in their motel except for my personal necessities and the backpack for the return to Edmonton by bus. This also solved my logistical dilemma by providing me with a mandatory physical address — a condition required by the truck of any road shipping company for picking up my gear. Indeed, during the next day, I had to find a suitable shipping outfit to secure the delivery of my canoe and equipment to Edmonton because the next day I had a bus ticket to depart from the center of the city for Edmonton with Greyhound Bus Lines. That had been arranged for me online by Milena. Multiple trips on foot between the motel and the hotel, together with the trips for food did not matter much to me, in spite of the fact that I had suffered from two broken toes on my right foot for the last ten days. The pain would always quickly subside as the injury broke in during the walk, protected by my sturdy hiking boots. I was now doing everything slowly and wisely. I thoroughly relished the happiness of reaching my goal and from the knowledge that the main self-torture was behind me for good. No wave could overturn my canoe from now on! The next day after my arrival in Sault Sainte Marie was Friday. I began calling several trucking companies from my hotel room and selected one. Instructed by the company dispatcher on how to wrap the shipped goods, I then located a building supply store in order to buy a roll of duct tape and a roll of foam underlay for laminate flooring. After I had brought all of this to Motel Algoma — all on foot — I tied all the paddling gear into the canoe and, with the help of a friendly motel tenant, wrapped her into the purchased material. My reward to my helper, Warren, was my leftover stock of nonperishable food. I then spent the rest of the day on the motel property sipping tea with the manager, Warren and a few of their come-and-go friends to wait for the truck from the shipping company. Their dispatcher had promised that they would pick up my shipment by 5:00. Yet when no vehicle turned up by 4:50 p.m., I roused the office of the central dispatch with my iPhone. It was just before they closed for the weekend. Apparently, due to a malfunctioning fax machine, the local branch had missed the order from the dispatch and nobody cared about my situation. After my angry complaints, the company finally intercepted the driver of their local branch — already on his way home for the weekend — and they remobilized him for the emergency mission. Only after the truck finally departed with the cargo of my canoe was I able to truly relax. I visited a restaurant that they recommended to me at the motel and here I savored an excellent steak dinner with good draft beer. My Greyhound bus was not leaving the next day until shortly before midnight. I checked out of the hotel on the morning of my departure and secured my monstrous waterproof backpack in a locker at the downtown bus depot. I was therefore free to walk through all the historical relics of the fur trade in town. It cost me a swollen foot for the three days of sitting on the bus but it was worth it.

With trepidations, yet hooked enough to go on

Well, my rock solid resolution to never touch a paddle again softened up somewhat by the next summer. The transformation in my desire progressed especially rapidly during July when we visited the old motherland. My wife and I went there to secure my mother in a reputable senior establishment with good care and to visit my wife's family. The step back with a view from overseas gave my solo voyage by paddle through the Canadian wilderness a new perspective. Suddenly I could not wait to return back to Edmonton, load the canoe onto the roof of Milena's economical Mitsubishi Lancer and hurry back to Sault Sainte Marie to resume my voyageur journey. Back in

Edmonton, I managed to squeeze the logistics of the preparations into just a few days and I headed east with the canoe on the car's roof. As usual, the closer I neared the place of launching the canoe into the water, the more escalated my worries about whether I was competent enough to tackle the challenges of lonely water travel. The views of the lake from the elevated stretches of the highway as it was winding along the top shore of the Superior filled the pit of my stomach with fear. I was looking at the enormous vastness of open water, the long stretches between islands and the long imaginary lines crossing the deep bays of the lake — the surface steel-dark from the chop of big waves. I was keenly aware that the biggest danger of Lake Superior lurked in its icy water. Its average yearly temperature was around 4 degrees Celsius. Although I used to compete in swimming and swimming a few kilometres is no problem for me, I knew that on the Superior it was different. If I overturned the canoe in the typical distance that I traveled from shore which is about a kilometre — to avoid the reach of chaotic surf-reflected waves — and made it to the shore, the body chilling would be so severe that I would likely require immediate hospital care. Especially without matches and fire, this kind of incident would inevitably end tragically. Most likely, though, total muscle paralysis from the cold would occur followed by death from hypothermia before I could reach the shore. I always carried a heavy neoprene suit, but paddling in it for a long time is so exhausting and so torturous in hot weather that this alternative is totally impractical. Transporting the suit in the canoe thus becomes only a psychological preparedness — a kind of sacrificial offering to the gods. What is important in the end is the overriding rule that one must proceed under all circumstances in such a way that he never tips. An easing of the stress only arrives when one is finally sitting in the loaded canoe and pushes it along the surface of the water with steady paddle strokes in the direction of the day's target. At last one feels that he is in control of his destiny. He must, however, be constantly keenly aware of the weather and wind developments so that he can responsibly judge when the degree of risk reaches a level where it is necessary to quickly terminate the cruise. Before every decision to cross a large bay or span a multikilometre gap in a chain of islands, not unlike in a high stakes game of poker, one must know how to read the signs in the sky in order to predict the risk of being caught in stormy weather before reaching the safety of a distant shore.

After I slept in a motel near the start of my new voyage and succeeded in securing the safekeeping of my vehicle — this even for free by the motel's sympathetic owner — the weather was friendly to me. The sun was burning and I had to protect my still tender skin with a thick layer of sunscreen. The lake's surface was remarkably quiet, hence my only initial obstacle turned out to be my physical shape. I had not yet gotten accustomed to sitting in the canoe and to the strenuous paddling routine. By August 8, I had already paddled along the tropical-looking sand beaches of Pancake Bay where the green crowns of pines substituted for palm trees. After a while, the beaches were succeeded by a ragged craggy shoreline. When around 3:00 in the afternoon, which was the time when I typically had enough of paddling during the first few days, I spotted a deep cove in the rock outcroppings in front of me, I headed for it. It seemed to be inviting, namely because from a distance it appeared to have a narrow gray beach. Only when I approached to gently push the bow of the canoe onto its water-washed edge, did I discover that the beach consisted of coarse pebbles from a small potato to football-sized and larger round rocks. At first glance, I was shocked to see how high up a relatively steep slope of the "beach" waves must have driven the moving rocks under different circumstances. Its upper edge must have been situated perhaps even ten metres above the normal level of the lake surface. The day was really hot, hence my first action after the takeout was to strip naked and dip multiple times into the icy water of the lake. Then I erected the tent on a pebble ledge about a metre-and-a-half above the level of the water. While cooking my supper towards the evening, I noticed that veil-like rags of clouds were quickly spreading over the sky from the west. It was an omen of a change in the weather. Before it got dark, the lake got churned up by wind. Huge waves arrived. The surf drove the round rocks into a steep ramp off the beach ledge and these rattled noisily back with each retreat of a wave. The noise disturbed my sleep. It escalated further after a while, especially when I started sensing that the surf was eroding the small gravel bench on which my tent stood and ate its way closer and closer to it. When surf spray started sprinkling onto my tent, I was forced into action. At 1:00 in the morning, I frantically moved the tent and its contents higher up on the rocky beach, luckily in the light of a full moon. The tent now stood on a slight slope and on coarser rocks, but hopefully, it was safely out of the reach of the waves. The battering surf had not abated by dawn. On the contrary, the waves had grown and roared against the outcroppings that confined my rock beach with five-metre explosions of spray. For me, this was a horrifying lesson about what energy can be possessed by this lake when whipped by a strong wind over an enormous distance. I was definitely wind-bound. I was a prisoner of the wind in my camp, waiting for the elements to come to their senses. These types of situations then arrived many times and more often — eventually even for more than one day. In fact, they say that "the window" of good weather for paddling on Lake Superior usually lasts from mid-July to mid-August. My late start of the voyage in the summer of 2011 made it spill beyond this favorable period. Spending my "bondage by the wind" in a camp has always been depressing for me. One wastes time without any progress in the traveled distance, consumes needed supplies and succumbs to melancholy from loneliness. This gets particularly amplified when the day crests its zenith and the late afternoon and evening set in. This first tangible experience with the lethal power of Lake Superior put me again into a state of doubt about the possible success of my travel on the lake.

At the wakeup time on the second morning in the camp, there were still waves but only of such scale that I could muster the courage to load and launch the canoe. I had to navigate precisely through the rocky channel of the narrow bay before I emerged onto the open water. Yet there, luckily, the waves exercised a regular rhythm. It wasn't until I had passed the mouth of the Montreal River, which was sending out evil invisible eddies far out from its bay, that my morale received a strong boost of optimism. From a great distance in front of me, I detected flashes of sun reflections on the wet paddles of a canoe that was approaching in the opposite direction. I steered my boat to meet it and say hello. It turned out that the crew of the aluminum Grumman canoe included two young women from Michigan who were circling the whole lake clockwise. They were only a few days from reaching the finish of their journey. Although, unlike me, they enjoyed road support with material and logistical aid, their success meant the injection of strong encouragement to me. They revealed that the Pukaskwa National Park was under temporary closure at the time due to an incident with a black bear. Allegedly, the animal had attacked a female tourist from Michigan and she ended up badly mauled. I still had at least a week of paddling ahead of me to reach this area so I hoped that the situation in the park would return to normal by then. The information only strengthened my discipline in conscientiously following my experience-proven rules of safety against bears. Around 3:00, I arrived at a granite island that happened to have in its center a sheltered lagoon of quiet water. It yielded an ideal port and a gorgeous campsite on a granite plateau rounded by glaciers above it. The hot afternoon air all around was permeated with an aroma of sun-heated resin from scattered white pines that valiantly faced the elements here and tenaciously held onto the creases and cracks of the granite formations with their stringy root networks. The crystal clear water of an emerald hue in the lagoon lured me to swim and even to go diving in it with goggles.

Agawa Devil — the canoeist's menace

When I sailed out of the serene water of the wind-sheltered lagoon that allowed me the luxury of a convenient loading and lacing of the spray cover onto the canoe, I hit large waves. I worried at first but the wind was blowing into my back for a change, hence I embraced the opportunity and tried to surf cautiously down the waves. Unsurprisingly, I moved fast along the rocky cliffs of the area known as Agawa Bay that abounds with ancient Aboriginal history. I was headed for a place where the ancient Ojibway culture, based on their canoe travels, left famous pictographs. These were painted on coastal rock faces with red pigment. When I finally located the rock wall on the shore on which the renowned "Agawa Devil," also known as "Mishipeshu" in the original Ojibwa language, was painted, the waves heaved my boat perhaps up to a metre up and down. In the Ojibway mythology, this feared monster — reminding one of a feline predator with spines along its back and with devil-like horns — is responsible for swallowing canoes by the waters of the Superior. Accordingly, it needs to be appeased and respected. The following is the explanation, in Wikipedia:

The most important underwater being for the OJIBWA is **Mishipeshu***, which means "the Great Lynx." This fantastic dragon-like animal resembles a feline with horns, symbols of his power. It has palmed paws that enable him to swim fast, and his back and tail are covered with scales. Mishipeshu lives in the depths of big lakes. Although he has a feline shape and is an amphibian, he is always described as a reptile. He is feared by all Ojibwa because he is the cause of waves, rapids and whirlpools, and he even breaks the ice in winter, thus claiming numerous victims. In the area of Churchill River, there used to be a game called "Mishipeshu" that symbolized this being's drowning power. A child, randomly selected, held the role of the aquatic monster; he had to catch his friends and throw them into the water.*

The legend of Mishipeshu is in line with general American Native mythology. Through my layman's research, I have found the following information on the internet:

Native American tribes of the Eastern Woodlands and the Plains viewed the cosmos as divided into three "realms": The Above Realm, the Earth Realm, and the Beneath Realm. The Great Spirit and the Thunderbirds inhabit the Above Realm, the Earth Realm is the world in which living humans, plants, and animals live, and the Beneath Realm is a watery abyss beneath the earth, inhabited by the Great Serpents. The ruler of the Beneath Realm is __the "Great Horned Serpent" or "Underwater Panther",__ a being associated with floods and danger, but also magic and medicine. A perpetual war exists between the Thunderbirds of the Above Realm and the Great Serpents of the Beneath Realm. This conflict is routinely acted out in the Earth Realm as the Thunderbirds hurl great bolts of lightning down upon the serpents whenever they use springs, rivers and lakes as points of access into the Earth Realm.

(From the article "The Spearhead Mound interpretation" at https://www.ancient-origins.net/ancient-places-americas/ spearhead-mound-0010681).

I extracted my camera and, risking getting it wet or getting the canoe smashed against the cliff by the waves, I teased the evil deity by attempting to snap a few pictures of the painting. Back then I thought that my efforts would be useless due to the jerking of the camera by the wave motions, but surprisingly, thanks to its technologically advanced stabilization, the snapshots turned up quite successful back home.

Soon after I rounded a point, wind hit me from the left side. By that time, it had strengthened to the level where I decided to wait it out in the lee of a small island. Although my constant observation while having a small lunch had not registered any change in the power of the wind, after about an hour, I impatiently set out to continue the voyage. This happened to be the period when I gradually got used to paddling in ever greater waves. In the next few weeks, when I had already decided to end the journey as soon as possible in Marathon, this would culminate in a really risky, stressful battle with the elements. In big waves, a canoe needs an especially strong forward drive from the paddle to maintain its directional aspect to the wave movements and to resist their attempt to toss the craft randomly downwind and thus overturn it. One thus cannot afford to stop the incessant, vehement paddling even for a few seconds. This state may have to last for many hours if no wind-sheltered spot avails itself for a rest. I constantly studied the shore looking for a suitable campsite. I entered and skirted around bays but no suitable spot had materialized until I reached the mouth of the Sand River. And that turned out to be worth the wait. The surroundings there were very scenic. As the name of the river hinted, it abounded with fine, yellow sand that was forming bars around its entry into the lake. Extensive sandy beaches stretched all around. Beyond the beach lining the shore, a bank of sand dunes rose parallel with it and backing it in turn was a forest predominantly of pines.

The macabre east shore

During the following few days, I moved around the next major curvature of the eastern coast that jutted into Lake Superior. Again, it was a very interesting area both from the nature point of view as well as of history. It was the vicinity of Cape Gargantua. Light gray and beige color shades of the granite crags mixed here with dark red to black formations of wild, bizarre shapes consisting of volcanic lava and ash. A number of these gigantic, natural sculptures had names that originated from the voyageur era. Interestingly, or perhaps unsurprisingly, they all derive from the word "devil." Some examples are "Devil's Warehouse" and "Devil's Chair." The Sharp edged rocks do not offer any campsites except for a couple of spots on the coastline where there are small coves with black, for a change, sand. I found my refuge for the night in one of these directly opposite the otherworldly-looking Devil's Chair Island that jutted out of the bluish-emerald waters of Lake Superior like Satan's stab at sculptural art. The black color of the rocks and the sand lent the surroundings of my camp a frightful, hellish morbidity. This was especially intensified by the loneliness of a solo water traveler. From my view out of the tent, the sun set just behind the Devil's Chair. Two blood red beams of its light shone through two roundish holes in the black silhouette of the red-haloed rocky island — straight at me — very much like the bloody eyes of a fiery monster.

During the next two days, I was forced by the wind to land. Fortunately, the forced landing brought me to a beautiful sandy beach. I found a pretty campsite here on the sand among small rocky formations. The spot was sheltered by a canopy of far-reaching branches from the edge of perfumed, resin-wafting coniferous woods. After being wind-bound for the rest of the day, the next morning I shortcutted deep bays across their entry. I passed a shoreline of high, vertical walls of granite. These rose straight from the water, forming ferocious rocky palisades. My map marked shipwrecks and I learned that this menacing barrier of Superior's east coast that stands against the wrath of western storms had become the burial ground of several large lake ships. The first of them, the steamship Acadia that was flung by a gale against a jutting out Grindstone Point on November 6, 1896, was totally crushed. It was carrying a cargo of prairie wheat from Port Arthur down to Sault Ste. Marie. In December of 1906, the large steamship Golspie got wrecked here while shipping a load of lumber for the construction of the Canadian Pacific Railway. It was sailing from Fort William (Thunder Bay today) to Sault Ste. Marie when it got caught in a massive lake storm. A western gale drove it like a walnut shell against the 50 to 100 metres high rock cliffs. All that the brave captain could do to stave off certain doom was to steer its course ever so slightly toward Old Woman Bay. The bay had a sandy beach in its farthest reaches. I cut across this large bay in a straight line about two kilometres from shore. The ship was driven high onto the beach where it crashed but the crew survived. A problem arose, however, when the sailors were forced to fight their way through thickly overgrown, rocky terrain along the lake's shore to the nearest settlement that happened to be a Catholic mission at the mouth of the Michipicoten River. The Trans-Canada Highway obviously did not yet exist. The humid, freezing pre-Christmas weather resulted in serious frostbite of the crew's limbs, especially for those who were fresh immigrants in Canada and were not yet used to its winters. The fates of these poor souls, tragically, called for many amputations after their arrival at the mission. One sailor allegedly lost both hands and both legs, another died of pneumonia. I paddled about a kilometre from the cliffs of the shore. About two kilometres before the mouth of the Michipicoten River, which during the era of the fur trade used to serve as a link to Hudson's Bay, I found a very romantic campsite on a sandy beach at the mouth of a small creek. In the evening, I savored its quiet atmosphere, half sitting — half lying in the sand close to my cooking fire of drift wood. I warmed up in the radiant glow of the hot embers whose redness competed with that of the sunset as it silhouetted a small island spiked with black spruce trees. I reflected on my life's happiness and on the modest fortunes that destiny had strung along my life's journey until the sun finally went down. My thoughts could not part from the sad visualizations of the horrific journey that, in contrast, destiny dealt to the unfortunate Golspie castaways.

Making friends at the Dog

In the morning, just as the oblique, golden rays of the early morning sun topped the tips of the coniferous woods behind my now vacated camp, they caught me lacing the spray cover on the loaded canoe. As I stood bent over in the shallow water, pushing the canoe with my shins against the sand of the beach to arrest its bobbing up and down in the waves, an aristocratic-looking lady appeared with a little dog on a leash. The beach apparently served as a morning promenade, especially for those locals, who followed a daily routine of walking their dogs. The woman was curious about what I was doing. After I explained my solo retirement canoe voyage, she dreamily sighed, "How romantic it must be! … Have you taken enough good reading with you?" she asked. She obviously must have held a somewhat distorted view of the hardship that travel by canoe on Lake Superior may pose. I just took my seat in the canoe, pushed off and bade her goodbye. I headed for a large teepee that I could see from a distance of about a kilometre, standing near the mouth of the Michipicoten River. I knew that there used to be a large Indian village there. Yet as I got closer, it turned out that it was only a decoration belonging to a local canoe-kayak club. From the mouth of the river, I took a straight course to the west far from the shores of the bay. I paddled stripped to my waist — like a stereotypical Native brave — among fishing boats of the real Indigenous people from the large local Indian reservation. The men wore full survival suits from head to toe for safety against an unlucky tipping accident. The weather was favourably hot. I had already attained a splendid paddling shape and was thus gobbling kilometres with the ambitious aim of reaching a mouth of the Dog River that I had chosen on the map for tonight's campsite. I passed several nice campsites situated in cozy coves with sand beaches bracketed by craggy cliffs. At one of them, a young couple of kayakers were suntanning and sleeping in the nude, oblivious to my involuntary violation of their privacy by quietly passing by. Yet the Dog River was nowhere in sight! I was already running on the last drop of energy when I decided to stop and set up camp on a large steep beach in front of me. By making that decision, I was giving up my target for the day which was to reach the Dog River. But after my landing, it turned out that the beach was, in fact, a peninsula enclosing a lagoon around the mouth of the Dog. So I had fulfilled my goal after all! I pushed off back into the water and rounded the tip of the beach peninsula to enter the lagoon of the mouth. Here I unloaded the canoe in quiet water. At the entry into the lagoon, I noticed a faintly discernible, lichen-covered petroglyph on the left rocky pillar of a natural gate that opened into the lagoon. It was a symbol that the Indigenous People used to mark a camping site long ago. It was an equilateral triangle that was engraved into the rock. Its symmetrically rising legs crossed with extensions above the peak forming a simple symbol for a teepee. The mouth of the Dog River apparently had served as a favorite camping ground since prehistoric times. Just as I was ready to start erecting my tent, which was always my first task after unloading the canoe and pulling it out high onto the shore, a canoe emerged with two young men from the river's upstream bend. When they saw me, they beached their boat to give me a friendly hello. I assumed that we would be sharing the campsite but their plan was to paddle on a bit further. They had traveled the same route as I had and had also heard that at some distance upstream on the Dog, there was a scenic waterfall. They were just returning from there. The men assured me that their side trip had been worth the effort. I therefore decided to hike there right after setting up the camp. Before they parted, the men inquired, *"Would you, by any chance, have any marijuana?"* Having digested the disappointment of my negative reply without much surprise, they then paddled out onto the mirror of a serene evening lake surface. I set out for the waterfall. First, it was about a kilometre up the river in a canoe, then through the forest on foot. It turned out that the path was quite breakneck — overgrown, steep, slippery when traversing moss-slicked rock slopes where I desperately grasped for tree roots. Soon I ripped my nylon pants on a wood knot while climbing over a fallen tree. Only my hat protected my head from a deep gash when I crawled under another one. I realized that I was absolutely alone in a location where nobody would look for me in case something happened to me. The evening was encroaching and I was aware that there were bears. I also realized that in my hurry to go, I had forgotten the bear spray in camp. To prevent surprising a bear, I sang loudly and felt more and more tense from the foolishness of my idea. Just before the waterfall itself, I had to jump from rock to rock in the river. The last of the oblique sun rays were gilding the green foliage and a smooth sheet of water that was descending to a bubbly embrace with the dark green depth of a pool below the waterfall. The direct light was going to leave the setting any minute, casting it into deep shadows just as the scene finally opened in front of me. I quickly snapped a few pictures and off I went, hurrying back to the camp at a fast clip. I sang valiantly all the way back to the canoe. My supper that was cooked on a fire, surrounded by still warm sand, was finished and eaten in darkness.

What a surprise it was when I woke up to the roaring of surf against the beach. The gobbling of kilometres would not take place today! I then spent the whole day resting on warm sand in a wind-sheltered spot, dozing and cooking. I had to wait out the boredom of being wind-bound. The only exceptions to the ennui were provided by the refreshment of multiple swimming dips in the warmer water that was confined to the lagoon. Perhaps the lady with the doggie was right when she visualized that I had to have a lot of opportunity to read during my travels. Alas, I had brought no book with me. All I could read were the accounts of all the lake's tragic shipwrecks appearing on the back of one of my maps. Sounding in my head was the ballad "The Wreck of the *Edmund Fitzgerald*" by Gordon Lightfoot. He sings about the huge lake ship Edmund Fitzgerald that broke in two during a hurricane storm with 11-metre waves. It sank with a loss of the entire 29-member crew on the November 10, 1975. No bodies had ever been recovered. Often during my voyage, I would notice that where the coastline and islands were exposed to the prevailing winds, their granite banks were absolutely bare of any vegetation — not even a blade of grass — up to a height of some 10 metres above the level of the lake's surface. It served as a testimony to the potential degree of the lake's fury during periods of storms.

The next morning, I impatiently pushed off very early hoping to travel some distance before a wind arose. Yet the wind returned very soon and from the front to boot. At 9:00 a.m., I feverishly searched again for a wind-sheltered cove in which to land. I found it in the lee of a small rocky peninsula. Here yet again, I whiled away the ennui of the familiar, well-rehearsed role of a prisoner of the wind. Yet at least I had a changed scenery. The wind continued to blow the next day but on a somewhat lower level. So early in the morning, I pushed the canoe into the waves. Especially encouraging was the finding that the wind had changed its direction overnight and now blew almost from the back. I cut across a broad bay far from shore and just as I was rounding a point at its end, a canoe set off perpendicularly from shore. In it were my recent two friends. Its trajectory soon curved in an arc into a direction parallel with the coastline. Although I almost ran into them, they did not see me and since they paddled as a team of two, their distance ahead of me was increasing. To call at them was useless due to the all drowning noise of the wind and surf. I only caught up to them when they stopped to rest in the boat. We greeted each other, cracked a few jokes and I continued on. They caught me, in turn, when I stopped for a snack in the canoe. I determined our position using my GPS unit during the break. We were all pleased with the result that showed surprising progress in our paddled distance. After that, we would travel together. When a change of wind direction eventually forced us to land in the late afternoon, we shared a campsite and cooking fire. The site abounded again with a vast beach of fine sand. The spot was surrounded by wildly beautiful scenery of high forested islands. My skinny-dip in the crystal clear, emerald water was rather short, though, because the water around here was especially frigid. I found my new friends very interesting. They were both around 26, just like my son, Alex, and they very much reminded me of him. I thus felt that I knew them inside out. Beau (the same name as my grandson) and Darren had set out early in the spring from their small town just north of Toronto. With backpacks and a tent, they traveled north on foot along Bruce Peninsula. They circled Manitoulin Island and continued on to Sault Sainte Marie. Here they bought a very cheap, square-stern aluminum canoe from a newspaper ad. It might have been used for hunting, judging from the camouflage paint that was now peeling off in places. Instead of drybags they sealed their backpacks and other modest gear into black plastic garbage bags. Following the initial success of their traveling, they had a somewhat fairy-tale plan to continue along the voyageur water route all the way to Winnipeg. From there, they planned to cross the Prairie Provinces on horses that they again hoped to buy cheaply from ads. In their view, they were going to reach Calgary just before the onset of winter. They planned to continue on snowshoes from there for a while and then wait the winter out in some mountain cottage in the Rockies. The following spring, they intended to proceed on foot to Vancouver. To me, their prospect represented pure utopia, yet I would never dare discourage them from their dream. I was only half-jokingly refining their ideas about what kind of horses they should be looking for, etc. I liked their youthful resilience and optimism. I admired what they had achieved so far with their primitive outfit. I especially admired their courage to venture into the waves in their open walnut shell. They in turn admired my experience-optimized equipment and my guts to set out on this voyage alone at my age. I shared my evening meal with them and I gave them some of my food provisions. I also squeezed half of my toothpaste, which they had run out of, into their Ziploc baggie. In the morning I did not feel like waking them up — I knew my son. So as their snoring, subdued by the tent wall, carried over the beach, I struck my tent, quietly carried my possessions past them, loaded the canoe and set out ahead on my own. Alas, after

10:00, menacing waves arrived. The coastline that I was just passing was very ragged and it was not too difficult for me to find a sheltered cove to wait it out. I was just lying down on a sun-exposed rock shelf, drying out from a mishap where, while pulling the canoe out of the rocking reach of the waves, I slipped on slimy algae into the water up to my armpits. But around 11:00, I suddenly noticed that from some distance among the scary waves, the canoe of my two friends was approaching. It shocked me but at the same time it injected me with an instant dose of courage. I launched my boat and joined them just as they were passing my position. I saw them alternately emerging and disappearing among the giant waves in front of me. Eventually, however, they would gradually stretch the distance between us. After an hour, I lost sight of them beyond the horizon of waves and jutting points of the shoreline. We would not see each other again for the next four days. Thunderstorms with lightning, wind and driving rain kept us wind-bound in separate locations from each other for two full days of this period. We skirted the wildly beautiful, yet menacingly deserted, dreamy coastline of Pukaskwa National Park. I exercised an extra degree of prudence around here. Choosing a spot for a campsite, for example, I would consider even such factors as the possibility that my canoe, stored on shore next to a vertical rock formation, could get hit and damaged by a falling rock if it rested too closely. Regardless of the fact that the big rocks I could see at the base of a rock wall might have fallen only every hundred years, I could not take that chance. I knew that if I lost the use of the canoe due to this, or a similar incident, I would be doomed. Without a watercraft in these haunts, I would be finished. The national park was situated on the area of a right-angle projection of the shoreline into the lake that the Trans-Canada Highway bypassed through a wide arc removed deeply inland. Consequently, there was no cell phone coverage here. A passage through the interior of the park to the highway would be, for all practical purposes, impossible. The topography of the landscape abounded with vertical rock walls of crags and canyons whose impenetrability was reinforced with thickets of tough, thorny bushes and wind-contorted, mutually-interwoven fallen trees. I did not need any proof of the possibility that I could suffer a wildlife attack. That I already had in the aforementioned bear attack incident that had taken place here not even two weeks before. In variation to other visitors, who had not traveled alone, I could not rely on any aid from somebody else in the case of an accident to call for help. Like wild animals, I had to be constantly on the alert and prudently decisive.

After the two days of being wind-bound, I finally continued on my way. Apprehensive, I pushed off the loaded canoe into the morning fog. The first hint of dawn from a yet unrisen sun tinted its upper fringes with a mauve-pinkish glow. About eighty kilometres remained to the nearest settlement that happened to be the town of Marathon. It was situated in an "armpit" shape of the upper coastline of Lake Superior. I conscientiously avoided the waves wherever it was possible by keeping on the lee side of the coastal islands. From behind one of them, a group of kayakers emerged who were traveling in the opposite direction. We greeted each other and stopped for a brief chat exchanging our experiences. "Do you speak Czech?" one of the paddlers asked me curiously when he recognized a sticker of the Czech flag on the left side of my canoe stern. "Of course!" was my answer. "But I have already lived here for 43 years." The man was a Czech visitor in Canada. The world is small and following the tearing down of the Iron Curtain Czechs are found everywhere now, especially in adventure hot spots. The group had a weather radio and before we said goodbye, they warned me of a forecast for a big storm, suggesting that I choose a well-sheltered campsite for the night. I then continued paddling long into the evening while the going was still possible. The sun had already descended to kiss the shining surface of the lake when I finally located a beautiful small cove with a scenic beach. It harboured quiet water in the lee of a bar of small crags. I weighted down the tent corners with especially heavy rocks and retired to sleep immediately after finishing supper and cleaning up. As I was falling asleep, which was not difficult after the hard day, I had a feeling that I heard faint voices. I immediately banished this possibility from my mind in worrying that my solitude was playing tricks on my brain. In the morning, though, it turned out that the voices had been real. That was because Beau and Darren were camped nearby where I saw a plume of smoke rising from low forest growth. Apparently, with my long paddling stretch of yesterday, I had passed them somewhere and they then caught up to me after dark. The voices that I heard in my sleep were their muffled outbursts of joy when they discovered my camp.

Gambling with life in a tempest

That morning they started out before me for a change. I spotted them again when Beau was waving at me from the rocky top of a small granite island where they stopped in its lee to erect a makeshift sail. The truth is that I transported a stunning homemade sail, sewn from a sheet of transparent plastic and a Canadian flag. It only required the cutting of suitable sticks for a mast and a yard. But for one thing, it was packed deep in the innards of the canoe below a tightly laced-on spray cover. Secondly, I would not dare to jeopardize my precarious maintenance of the boat's stability with the paddle in giant waves by the extra need to control a sail on top of it. I thus left them and paddled on following an alignment of points and islands while striving to stay not too far from some shore if I tipped over. When I carefully turned my torso back to find out if my friends had already started out, I didn't see them anywhere. But in heart-stopping shock, I suddenly noticed them on my left, far out on the lake's horizon in the direction of its center on the open water. A black silhouette of a tent fly that Darren held on paddles was repeatedly emerging and disappearing among the waves in the distance on a brilliantly glistening horizon. Beau was steering at the stern. "Madmen!" I thought. But I must admit that they sailed really fast. As for myself, I prudently moved between the shore and a stretched string of islands that lined it. My pair of buccaneers were passing around it all, way outside the band of islands. The strength of the wind and the size of the waves kept increasing during the day. When I did not see my friends' canoe in front of me after I stopped for a quick snack in the lee of an island, I seriously worried that they might have ended up in the claws of the Agawa Devil somewhere. I then continued alone, and driven by the waves, I would always pray for reaching the safety of a lee of each new rocky point that emerged in front of me. When I finally reached the state of total mental and physical exhaustion, I entered a deep bay where I found refuge from the wind and waves to have a rest. I started looking for a suitable camping site there but it was only noon and after some time of recovery in the boat, I gave in to the temptation to resume my battle with the elements. I wanted to advance a bit closer to the finish. The absence of cell phone coverage filled me with worry that Milena, who had not heard from me for some eight days now, must be worrying about me. Under the circumstances of advanced August on the lake, which was past the usual window of tolerable weather for tackling it, I longed to reach the nearest settlement on the coast that happened to be Marathon as soon as possible and end my stressful, risky voyage. The main problem of continuing the paddling was the fact that in the next ten kilometres the shore consisted of vertical, granite cliffs where no possible sheltered refuge from the wind existed. After hesitating for a while, I entered the waves. Soon I was surfing on waves double the length of my canoe. The white crest of the wave that reached the canoe from behind would get cleaved by the stern lifting it, at which moment I would time my paddle stroke to take advantage of gliding down the water incline. As the wave passed under the hull, though, it would lift the bow and the stern would simultaneously sink up to the gunwales into the hissy, bubbling foamy water. As the waves were not arriving straight from the back but at a sharp angle from slightly left, their component force tried to push the stern to the right and so rotate the whole canoe broadside to the direction of their movement. For this periodic phase, I had to time a superhuman stroke along the left side to neutralize this rotation. The movement of the waves was not the only terror. Even more intimidating was the constant thundering rumble and howling of the wind. The wind was already stripping water from the foamy, white caps behind me and from time to time, it sprayed my bare back with an icy spur, prodding me like a swish of Mishipeshu's cat o' nine tails to still more frantic effort. Eventually, I at last spotted a rocky point in the distance jutting in from the cliffs. My sole aim and focus then became to endure the onslaught of the waves all the way to it and around into its lee. I finally succeeded in this goal with the fervent invoking of Manitou but only just by the skin of my teeth. Entering into the lee, I pulled out the canoe on a rock shore and studied the terrain for the possibility of emergency camping. That proved to be impossible, however, due to a chaotic jumble of rocks and drift logs everywhere. But the effort paid off because I found out that standing up on the very tip of the point, my iPhone had just enough signal that I could intermittently talk with Milena and soothe her worrying about the state of my being. But in reality, my situation was far from satisfactory. I could not camp where I was and when I tried to rearrange rocks under water to create a safer port for my canoe, I managed to smash the tip of my middle finger between them. Bleeding profusely, I returned to dueling with the waves. My goal was to reach shelter behind an island that seemed to lie right next to the shoreline another kilometre farther ahead. Having overcome sudden chaotic waves that seemed to hold the progress of my canoe as I was entering the channel between the island and the shore, I discovered to my surprise that this was not a gap between an island and the shore but the mouth of a river. My map would later identify it as the White River. Looking for a suitable spot to camp a little ways upstream, I found an official campsite that was situated on a Pukaskwa Park trail that passed along the shore through this part of it. It consisted of two tent spots, a latrine and a sheet metal cabinet for securing food from bears. The spot offered heavenly serenity from the furious tempest of the wind and surf. I unloaded the canoe without any delays, set up the tent and finally bandaged my bleeding finger. I would spend, yet again, a day of being wind-bound here as the raging surf outside the shelter of the river mouth bombed against the rocky cliffs for the whole next day till the earth would shake. Interestingly, in the morning of the second day, bear scat appeared on the adjacent empty tent spot that had not been there the previous evening — about three metres away. Nothing disturbed me from my sleep, though, and my food stores endured in the safety of the metal cabinet. My cell phone had no signal here. I spent part of the stay studying evidence of ancient rock circles that, according to the info on a nearby plaque, represented the wall remains of prehistoric huts erected and used by the first people on this continent. In their time, the level of the lake surface stood much higher than in modern times, placing these abodes much closer to the shore.

The crash landing

The second morning in the river camp, I loaded up and set out to continue my paddling voyage. I started very early but the lake still had waves if somewhat smaller than those of the previous days. The driving force behind my resolute effort was the desire to have those last 20 kilometres that remained to Marathon behind me. After the delays of being wind-bound, I was prepared to risk it. I cut straight across deep bays with multikilometre gaps between their starting and ending points. The cell phone signal reappeared on the open water and several times I updated my plans with Milena. The wind inconspicuously but persistently escalated its power during the day and at the same time, it shifted more and more to my left — westward. After a few hours, in the distance ahead of me, I could finally see a tall chimney painted red and white of a power plant in Marathon. I knew from the map that the town had a harbor in a secluded bay that required circumnavigation of a conical mountain forming a peninsula on the south side of its entrance. On my right, the low rocky coast gradually transformed into a long — at first marshy — beach that eventually morphed into sand with boulders and a jumble of driftwood logs. The shallow bottom shaped waves here into the kind with rolling crests. They were now coming from my left — westward side. I strived to move farther from the shoreline into deeper water in the hope of avoiding them. I streamed in ever more extended and more powerful paddle strokes in the shortest line north — straight to the conical mountain that I had to paddle around. As the wind strengthened, I practically raced to reach my target before the task would become impossible. A large white-capped wave that rolled over the nylon deck of my canoe almost overturned me. This was sobering. I started eyeing the beach on my right that was about a kilometre distant. The beach was by now almost starting to transform into the rocky neck of the mountain peninsula. The entrance into the harbor seemed within reach but I knew that this was an optical illusion. I probably still had at least another two kilometres to it. The waves from the left — with their rolling crests paralleling my boat — grew in size and power. When the fourth wave rolled over my canoe and only with a good dose of luck I managed to maintain its stability, I realized that I had to deploy emergency action. I turned the canoe 90 degrees to the right and quickly headed down the waves toward the beach. While my boat surfed with the waves, my eyes were frantically scanning the shore of the beach, trying to find a section where there might be only sand without the jumble of rocks and wood. That I indeed discovered in the last moment. I managed to aim the canoe in time toward the clear beach's three-metre width and then I prayed that nature would not channel all that excess energy that had concentrated on my surfing canoe into some unforeseen tragic unravelling. When I came barreling down with the canoe to within 10 metres of the shore, it rode on the crest of a wave perhaps a meter or more above the level of the surrounding surface. "Excellent!" I naively rejoiced. "The wave will throw me high up on the sand and retreat back." Alas, just before landing, the crest of the wave passed under the canoe that suddenly sunk at least a metre lower. Its nose buried itself into a band of coarse pebbles under the zone of sand and the next wave threw its stern over the bow. The gunwale of the canoe painfully twisted my knee and my bare shoulder (I again paddled half-naked like a true savage) buried itself into the pebbles of the beach. I had never seen a single human being along the whole multikilometre length of the beach. Yet precisely in the spot where I had to land my canoe, I noticed an old man wearing a straw hat who was standing with his back turned to me. He must have been searching for some interesting pet rocks. My screams of warning him literally fell on deaf ears. He had no idea that I had performed a somersault with the canoe immediately behind him. Only after a moment did he turn around and, looking at me with baffled slowness, informed me that my shoulder was bleeding. Everything could have ended much worse. I escaped with scratches, nothing got wet that shouldn't have and the boat survived the crash landing without any harm. While I unloaded the canoe and hung up wet clothing on the bare limbs of surrounding driftwood logs to dry, the old man lay down about three metres away in the warm sand, contentedly snoozing. As I slowly recovered from the shock of the crash landing, my next step was to go and explore the flat plateau above a steep escarpment under which stretched the beach of my wreck. I wanted to find some way of ending my voyage for this year. I needed to find a place where I could carry my boat and equipment for temporary safekeeping while I traveled to Sault Sainte Marie to return with my vehicle. Luck was on my side. Straight from the spot of my crash, a steep path lead up the escarpment. On its top, about 400 metres away past a small grove of trees, the nearest building at the edge of a residential subdivision was that of The Royal Canadian Legion. I peeked inside and encountered a quiet, grey-haired senior behind a bar counter. He was busy polishing glasses and the already shiny surface of the bar counter top with the care and focus of a true perfectionist. "Hello, sir, my name is Jan. How are you?" I described my situation to him with a plea if I could possibly leave my gear with them for 48 hours. Paul introduced himself with a French-Canadian accent and, with polite kindness, immediately showed me to the basement where I could deposit the canoe and, in turn, where I could put my bags on a small music band stage right next to a piano in a dancing hall. It was surprisingly easy!

During the course of the next hour, I portaged my outfit piece by piece, climbing up the steep path to the top of the escarpment and on to the Legion. The canoe was the last. In the next stage, I only kept a fanny pack with documents, money, and items of personal hygiene. With that, I also carried my camera and a small drybag that contained all my electronic gadgets. I then walked two kilometres into the center of the town where there was to be a motel. The motel was not cheap but I was happy that all my heavy toil of the day was finally over. Following the 20 kilometres of gambling with life while paddling in boisterous waves, the repeated portage up the cliff and the long march to the motel, I could hardly move. To remain standing upright in the warm shower posed a challenge. Yet not even in the bed could I find a position for a relaxed rest. I fell asleep at the TV right after I turned it on. I did not find strength to go and have something to eat until morning.

And then I only had to cross the street to A&W fast food outlet. An interesting notice caught my eye as I was leaving the motel through a side exit. On the door, which automatically shut and locked, a warning was posted for guests not to prop the door open when they stepped outside to have a smoke. It said that "a black bear had entered this way several times in the past!!!"

Who did I run into in A&W but my young fellow Argonauts, Beau and Darren. What a relief that they escaped the evil designs of the Agawa Devil! They were ahead of me at the time when the storm forced me into the mouth of the White River to camp there, bound by the wind. They had managed to travel a few kilometres farther before they were also forced to seek refuge in a deep narrow bay. It turned out that there was a public campsite there and the headquarters of the National Park of Pukaskwa connected with the outside world by a road. When they were unable to start paddling again the following morning due to the wind, Beau and Darren hitchhiked into town. Here they befriended a local family who was amused with their adventurous story. The people readily offered them beds and logistics support. The rumour spread and the boys gained instant star popularity in the entire town of Marathon when a local radio broadcast an interview with them. It turned out that, independently from me, they had also decided to end their paddling voyage in Marathon. Their plan now was to resume their walking mode of travel and continue to Thunder Bay marching with backpacks along the highway. The weather for canoeing on the lake had become too dangerous. At 1:00 p.m. my bus arrived on which I traveled to Sault Saint Marie so that I could return back with my vehicle. All went smoothly. I slept in the motel where I reunited with my car. My drive back to Marathon started the next morning before 6:00. I worried that the Legion might close for the weekend (it was Friday) but I arrived there to pick up my equipment at 3:00 p.m.. Heading toward the Trans-Canada Highway West with the canoe on the roof, I gave my final farewell to Beau and Darren with a wish of good luck. These adventure seekers marched along the shoulder of the highway with their modest livelihood on their backs. Hitchhiking certainly did not fit into the etiquette of their standards for chasing the setting sun. We exchanged our e-mail addresses but the e-mail, in which I sent them my photos of them from the voyage, has never been answered. I firmly hope that they safely escaped the Mishipeshu's claws and that they happily reached their target destination in Vancouver.

After three years, I found a blog of Beau and Darren on the internet. http://voyagecanada2011.blogspot.ca/2011/08/short-break-beautiful-lake-nice-day.html#more

It contained a selfie of the three of us while camping together on the sandy beach shore with a caption:

"Jan Soukup, Canoeing Superior Solo at age 67! ... WOW!!!"

CHAPTER III

From Marathon along the north and the northwest coasts of Lake Superior to Thunder Bay/Fort William (July 4 – 20, 2012)

Although I felt infinite relief when I finally carried up and stored my outfit and canoe out of reach of the angry, malicious Lake Superior in the Royal Canadian Legion, the tooth of time would gnaw again at my resolution. As I walked on stupefied legs over the asphalt of Marathon's main street in the direction of the motel at its distant center, my recent experiences convinced me that I ought to obey sober reason. It whispered into my ear that I was getting a little too old for all of this. It said that I could only thank God for escaping with my lucky hide from the hungry claws of the Agawa Devil.

Hadn't the ancient Native tales said that this legendary lake monster was responsible for pulling boats under the surface of the Superior and swallowing them without a trace? Oh what a feeling of safety to be standing back again on terra firma, however physically thrashed I was.

It hadn't taken long, though, and I already rued the fact that I had been unable to finish my Lake Superior journey. At first, this would gnaw at me in secret. But later, it would surface in front of my wife. Eventually, it would be clear even in our circle of family and friends. Around Christmas, I was already spinning plans on how to prepare for the continuation of the voyage. I contemplated how to return next summer to the place where my journey came to an undignified end the summer before. If I still wrestled inside with trepidations, this stemmed from my look at the map. Because the coastline of the Superior runs straight west from Marathon, but instead of a solid line for following it safely, it is ripped up into deep irregular bays. These would undoubtedly require stressful shortcutting of long distances far from the safe reach of shore. After about a third of the overall distance toward the end of my voyage in the metropolis of Thunder Bay, the shoreline would diverge toward the northwest into the deep, giant bay of Nipigon. The skirting of this would nonsensically prolong the journey. Instead, the lake's topography offers a water route of fluent continuation on an imaginary gentle arc that extends the curve of the beginning of the coastline from Marathon along a discontinuous chain of islands and peninsulas. The curvature of this arc gradually aims more and more southwest. The vision of the gaps to cross between the islands — some of them multikilometre long — under the excesses of the weather that I had had the honor to get to know during the voyage from Sault Sainte Marie to Marathon scared me. Besides that, I knew that on the islands, many tens of kilometres distant from the Trans-Canada Highway, there would be no cell phone signal. Should I lose my canoe through some unlucky mishap, I would become a castaway without any means of returning back to civilization by walking. I could clearly see that the line of hopping from one island in the chain to another would eventually bring me to the tip of a peninsula known in the Native mythology as The Sleeping Giant (Nanabijou in the Ojibwa language). This jutted from the north far out into the lake and from its point an enormous spread of open lake surface would separate me from the destination of my voyage in Thunder Bay. The shortest direct distance there was of around 22 kilometres. At the time, I did not even want to think about how I would tackle this challenge.

As I did not have any other plans for the summer of 2012 and was retired, I was free to select the most suitable date for the start of my water expedition. Milena had again organized an annual visit to her family in the Czech Republic for herself and I was able to give her a ride to the airport on Friday, June 29. Her flight went through London directly to Prague. I then departed from home on Sunday, July 1st — Canada Day. Around 6:00 a.m., I was heading east in Milena's economical Mitsubishi Lancer with my gear inside and the canoe on its roof. The vehicle ran faithfully, hence on Tuesday I was already cruising through Thunder Bay. From the heights of the highway, I gaped in astonishment at the intimidating spread of the lake surface surrounding the peninsula of the Sleeping Giant. The reported temperature there was 31 C — the local record for that particular date — and a clear blue sky. As I continued eastward, I could not believe the news from the car radio reporting that Marathon had thick fog with a temperature of 16 C. But after a few more tens of kilometres, from a new height of the highway, I was indeed looking for the first time at perhaps a 300-metre-high wall of gray fog that shrouded the whole coast around and including Marathon. The water of Lake Superior that is up to almost half a kilometre deep, represents an enormous thermal mass that, at the beginning of the summer, is very cold. Any air humidity that drifts from the hot mainland over its surface thus immediately condenses into fog.

I drove through the town in a thick, milky haze by the late afternoon. When I left the vehicle to purchase some last minute necessities, I had to don a fleecy. It felt rather chilly around here. I was pondering a dilemma in my head about what to do. It was nearing 7:00 in the evening. "Shall I spend the night in a motel?" Under the given circumstances, I did not feel like coming to the water. Nevertheless, I continued heading slowly towards the edge of the cliff above Pebble Beach — the site of my crash landing last year — and to the familiar building of the Royal Canadian Legion. I peeked inside and whom did I spot behind the bar counter, like the old Paul — my Samaritan of the last year. His skinny head with long, whitish-grey hair — slicked high up on its sides to cover a glistening pate and converging down in a graceful arc into an Elvis-like duck tail — stared at me with an expression of a question mark on its forehead. "Hi Paul, do you remember me? I am Jan, the guy who crash-landed here with a canoe last summer and you helped me store my stuff. Any chance that I could leave my car on your parking lot for three weeks? I am willing to pay a reasonable fee." I was not a hundred percent sure that Paul recognized me but after a brief moment of thinking, he gave me his permission, even without any payment for it. His only condition was that I park at the farthest edge of the parking lot where my car would not be in the way. Encouraged by my unexpected luck, I made a Spartan decision: I would immediately start sorting my load and carry it in repeated trips down the steep path to the rocky beach. There I would sleep in a tent and thus be ready to resume my water voyage bright and early tomorrow morning. On top of it, I would save the money that I would otherwise pay for the expensive motel. Before I delivered everything, starting with the canoe down to the beach, the fog started quickly dissipating. Around 8:00 when my tent was up, a gorgeous evening set in with a warm sunset flooding my camp in a red-golden glow.

Off into the blue yonder

I was awakened by the sound of waves sloshing against the pebbles of the beach. I extricated myself from the zipper of my sleeping bag with worries that it would be difficult to load and launch the canoe. But even before I poked my head out of the tent, I sensed that there had to be a splendid, sunny day outside. My instinct proved right. The azure hue of the sky competed with the aquamarine color of the lake water that was heaving in regular swells. On the distant lake horizon where both elements came together, they fused into one blinding brilliance. Before I even emerged, I commenced the morning work. The logistics of sailing out is always a bit more complicated on the first day of the expedition. Yet most of it already represented a well-established routine for me: First, to empty the nylon stuff sac from the sleeping bag that was filled with all my clothing serving as a pillow for the night and compress into it the sleeping bag. Then to come out of the tent and store the packed sleeping bag at the bottom of the waterproof backpack with a frame. I would top it inside with all the clothing except those pieces that I would need while paddling. Rolling up the sleeping mat followed and then I strapped the roll tight onto the top of the canoe seat to softly raise my seating position for paddling. Sadly, after decades of almost daily jogging, my knees refused to tolerate long periods of kneeling. Meanwhile, I removed the fly from the tent and spread it inside-out over a sun-exposed jumble of driftwood. Both were thus well ventilated and drying from the early morning condensation. This done, I stripped and washed myself in the icy water of the lake. After brushing my teeth, rubbing my wet hair semidry with a towel and combing it, I donned the prepared small pile of clothing and rubber sandals. I stored the toiletry kit in a drybag with shoulder straps that also contained the kitchen gear, medical kit, spare material like ropes, strings, rubber cords, duct tape, a small repair kit, hiking boots and similar "hardware." I then brought the canoe right up to the edge of the water — parallel with it but out of the reach of the surf. This was to allow me slip it into the water when loaded with a minimum of bottom rubbing. I draped the wet towel as a throw over my seat of the rolled up mat. From the tent, I brought a waterproof map case, a brim hat, Gore-Tex windbreaker, machete, a belt with items of safety — like bear spray, a hunting knife, a flare kit and bear bangers complete with a pen-like launcher, etc. I stacked them in a small pile near the canoe. The tent was packed next, the fly and a poly ground sheet stuffed on top of the tent in its stuff sack and then the package went into the top of the waterproof backpack. The sealed backpack went into the canoe first. I slid it with straps up under the middle two thwarts from the front so that its closure pointed straight against me in front of my seat in the canoe. Its fit under the thwarts was tight so even in case of an upset of the canoe it would not get dislodged. It was still secured similarly to all the other canoe luggage with a waist strap snapped over a thwart. The bow of the canoe held two heavy drybags containing food that were tightly rammed under its back seat. (As a solo paddler, I sat backwards on the front seat of the otherwise symmetrical craft in order to be situated closer to the boat's center). The purpose of placing the drybags there was to hold the bow of the canoe low which is important when paddling against a headwind. The space between the food bags and the waterproof backpack got filled with the drybag containing cooking gear and other "hardware." The top arch of the waterproof backpack's aluminum pipe frame just in front of me then served as a rack for snapping on a small drybag with electronics and photo accessories. It also held the belt with my safety weaponry. I then jammed the sheathed machete into the pack frame with the handle towards me. On top of the backpack within easy reach, I laid the life jacket, the Gore-Tex windbreaker and extra clothing in case of sudden cooling in the weather or rain. A waterproof fanny pack, containing food for lunch and the day's snacks, mosquito repellent, sun screen, etc. was then clipped under the seat on the left. Under the right side of the seat, I snapped on a camera in a waterproof bag. On the bottom of the canoe behind the seat, there was a larger drawstring nylon sack with three two-liter plastic Pepsi bottles of tea, a camera tripod and sometimes my hiking boots for a quick change when expecting a portage. The unrolling and lacing of the spray cover onto the canoe followed. Once in place, the waterproof map case and a solar battery charger were attached upon its top with Velcro fasteners. The paddles — one a kayak type as a spare — were then inserted into the appropriate spray cover pockets. After putting on my hat, sunglasses and fingerless paddling gloves, the moment of slipping the canoe into the waves finally arrived. It was heavy, hence the launch required multiple alternate liftings of the bow and stern with their shifting towards the water. Everything, including pushing off, had to be accomplished quickly to prevent the waves from pressing the boat into the shallows, splashing water into it and tipping it over. The operation worked surprisingly smoothly. I commenced paddling before I even slipped my feet into the cockpit, draining water and sand from my sandals. I quickly reached deeper water, distancing the craft from the effects of the surf.

Soon I accelerated the canoe into its full traveling speed. Together with its direction, I maintained the speed with rhythmic paddle strokes on the left side. I left the shore of the launch with a touch of uncertainty as always when heading into the unknown. The thoughts were tumbling in my head like: "Is this reasonable? Is this a test of strength and courage or is it just proof of irresponsible madness? How is it all supposed to end? Happy ending? Or, does destiny have a tragedy in store for me? Will I always find a suitable spot to lay my head down for the night? Will my boat last? My tent?"

But the farther I worked my way into the blue world of the tame, regular waves coming from the front left under the canopy of the azure, clear sky, the more I slipped into the self-confidence of my old proven routine. The day was truly one of the best to banish doubts and restore courage. At the first rest in the boat after an hour and a half of uninterrupted paddling, I stripped off my top and spread sunscreen onto my as-yet delicate skin. I resolved that for the first few days of the voyage, a 1:250,000 scale map would do. I resolved that I would orient myself only by comparing the followed contour of the shoreline with that in the map. That way, I reasoned, I would conserve the battery power in my iPhone and in my GPS unit. The conditions were good, hence I aimed in a straight line for the narrows between a large island and a point of the coastline that glistened far out on the horizon ahead. Somewhere there, I thought, I would be looking for a campsite. An old song of the voyageurs sounded in my head. Its rhythm and words in archaic Québecois French, which celebrated the longed for moment of meeting the paddler's sweetheart back there somewhere, synchronized perfectly with the rhythm of my paddle strokes. Leaning out to the left and pulling the paddle with my whole body along the gunwale of the boat from the farthest forward reach that my stretched trunk and arms allowed, up to the moment of a brief steering twist of its blade at the stern to maintain a straight path, I felt as if I was synchronizing my movements with a voyageur crew around me. In spite of not having held the paddle for almost a year, I didn't need any focussed effort to find my old efficient style in handling the canoe.

I reached the predetermined destination when I had enough of paddling for the first day of the expedition. It was just before 3:00. As if by design, the contoured shoreline of smooth granite was very jagged and allowed me to find the protected lee of a cove facing away from the wind. I pitched my tent on the crest of a low granite peninsula that provided a view of my protected harbour on one side and of the vast spread of the fresh water sea in the opposite direction. I picked a spot for my cooking fire near the water in the wind shelter of a small grove of bushy growth that yielded a good supply of dry firewood.

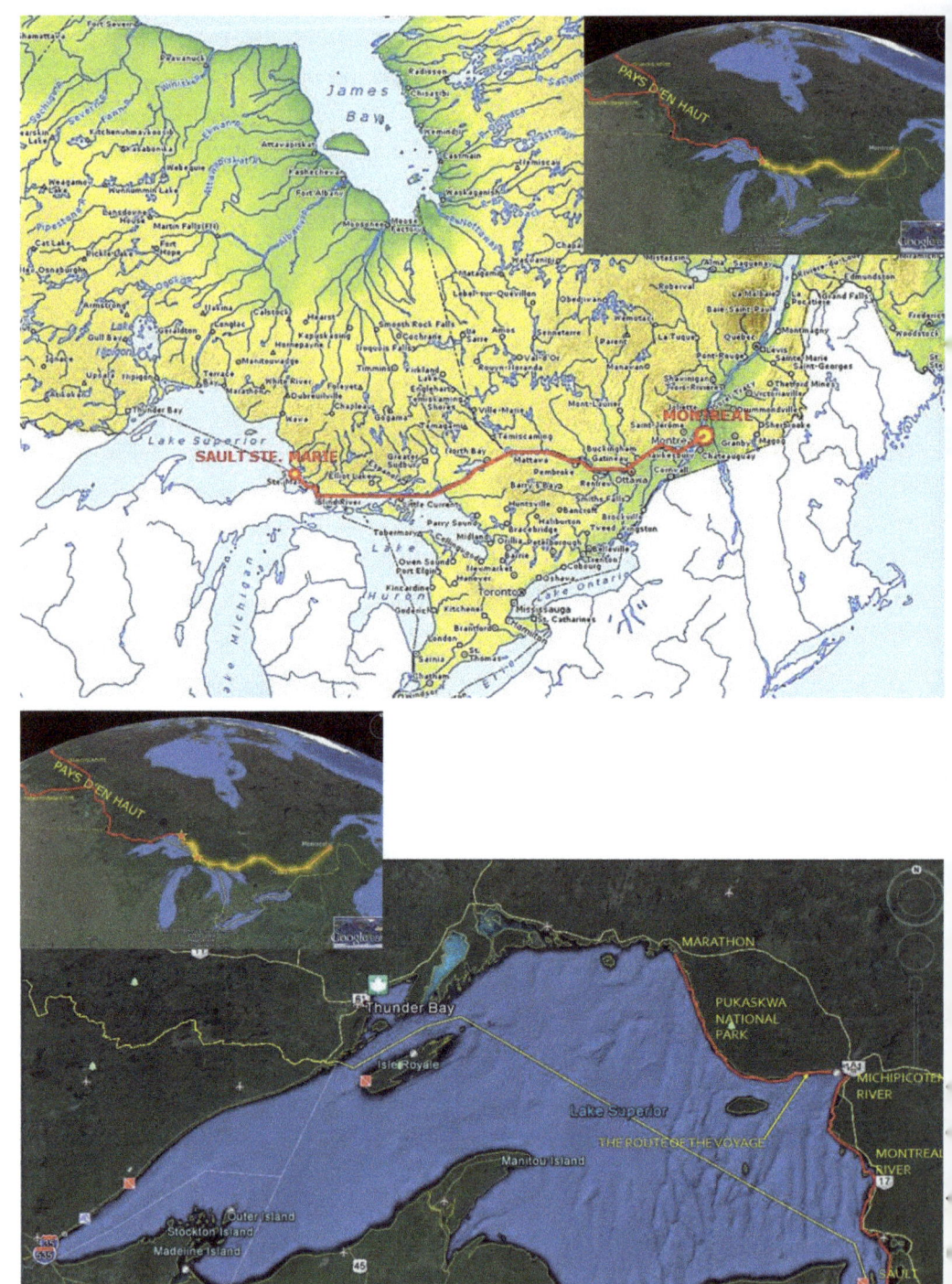

Travel map for Chapter III Part 1.

Travel map for Chapter III Part 2.

CHAPTER I.

Evening in the "Prehistoric Connection" Island camp. Lake Talon on the Mattawa Rive

Entry into "Voyageur Channel" on the French River.

My arrival into windy Georgian Bay of Lake Huron having descended the French River delta.

My arrival at Chenaux Dam in Portage-du-Fort on the Ottawa River.

Portaging through Portage-du-Fort.

Getting ready to start the portage around Chaudière Falls dam in the city of Ottawa.

Paresseaux Falls on the Mattawa River.

I found out that my fame preceded me when canoeists traveling in the opposite direct[ion]
had been informed about my approaching the portage around Paresseaux Falls and rea[dily]
offered to take my picture with mine as well as their cameras.

I finally reached Lake Nipissing just as the setting sun kissed its glassy surface following a 13-hour dreadful ordeal on the La Vase portage.

By the time I took my lunch break on traversing Lake Nipissing, the city of North Bay was already hidden beyond the Earth curvature horizon.

The hard granite had become my typical bed-rock when moving through the Shield country. Surprisingly, I, personally, discovered that sleeping on it provides the best overnight therapy for the back, over-worked from the day-long paddling.

Sandy beach camps which were rather rare provided contrast to sleeping on granite. Their great advantage was in the luxury of being able to enter the water in bare feet. The "Paradise Camp" before Thessalon Peninsula.

e historic Fur Trade Canoe Highway ovides a never ending obstacle urse for the poor water-wanderer: The first, Carillon dam, provides lock, the huge gate of which got ened for my tiny craft (fee by a ot= $17 total for me)
Falls within the city of Ottawa - Rideau The Upper Allumettes Rapids. Recollet Falls on the French River.
The weedy jungle on La Vase rtage. 6) The early morning fog is ing on Lake George.

My typical evening fatigue

Over the centuries since the height of the fur trade the natural water damming barriers have been eroding. The level of Lake Nipissing, for ex., is now maintained by an artificial dam. To avoid it, there is a branch outlet of the lake called Free Flow Channel that continues on as the Little French River. This, after a series of challenging rapids, eventually merges back into the French.

Top: The Free Flow Channel; Middle: My third carry around the Free Flow Channel; Bottom: My first carry around Five Finger Rapids. (All on the Little French River).

CHAPTER II.

My first wind-bound prison – a camp half a day past Pancake Bay – the first lesson in the intimidating power of the angry, frigid Superior.

The pictograph of the Agawa Devil – "Mishipeshu" in Ojibwa language on Agawa Rock in Agawa Bay of Lake Superior Provincial Park.
The scaled, horned panther-like monster of the Ojibwa canoe lore.

Devil's Chair Island in Agawa with its fiery eyes of a setting sun glowing through its two holes impersonated for me the horror of Mishipeshu's vile designs as I viewed it from my tent throughout my lonely evening.

The lower falls on the Dog River.

An island-with-a-lagune camp in Agawa Bay.

A camp near the Michipicoten River.

My "safe harbour" camp before a predicted storm when I was following the shoreline of Pukaskwa National Park.

My fellow
Argonauts,
Beau and
Darren,
whom I ran
into while
skirting the
shores of
Pukaskwa
National Park

A wind storm
on Lake
Superior.

CHAPTER III.

Soon after pushing-off, I found my well-entrenched routine of my paddle-travel. All prior doubts and stresses magically dissolved in the gorgeous morning.

In my start-up camp out of Marathon I woke up to a crisp beautiful morning on the spot of Pebble Beach where I crash-landed the year before.

A scenic campsite in the area of many smaller islands that I "won-by-a-nose" from the kayakers.

I luckily sighted, what I called "Sliver Island" in the last, desperate moment of the day following my crossing of the Shesheeb Bay. I first unloaded in its cove then pitched the tent.

My totally isolated, quiet cove camp that I had found on the north side of Edwards Island.

hat a shock to wake up into a wet fog morning for the crossing of the dangerous Black Bay.

he scene of a lucky unraveling to the serious survival situation that involved a crossing of
e Black Bay in an electric storm.

"Land on the horizon!!!" The distant view of the Pie Island. I was to aim for the low tip to the right of its mountains.

The "laker" ship that I narrowly avoided in the middle of the watery expanse.

Looking back at the "Sleeping Giant" the tip of whose peninsula is already hidden beyond the horizon of the vast watery universe that I had just successfully traversed. Phew!!!

Clockwise from top: Sunrise glow behind "Sleeping Giant" Peninsula on the morning of my 13km crossing from Pie Island to Thunder Bay. Fort William dock with Montreal canoes. The shop on the fort where birch bark canoes are still made. The south, riverside gate of the fort.

Soon the scene of a water traveler's camp with a tent and a pulled-out, overturned canoe on shore was completed with a thin ribbon of rising, aromatic smoke from a fire that was cooking supper.

The first night passed quietly without much excitement. I rested on a bed of hard, glacier-smoothed granite in the tent since perhaps 7:00 in the evening. I had to give my body and muscles the best possible chance to slowly acclimatize to the hard toil of the days ahead. On the other hand, I got up early. A strong wind blew from the left — the center of the fresh water sea — and slightly from the front. While I paddled in the lee of the big island everything was hunky-dory, but as soon as I reached the point of the coastline where the island ended, the wind struck my left cheek with full force. A big bay opened up ahead of me into which the whitecaps stampeded from the left. The other end of the bay could barely be seen in a hazy distance of some 17 kilometres. The coastline there appeared only as a darker, thin line hovering over the hazy, light water surface. There was no way that I would risk traversing it by paddling sideways to the waves. I therefore turned the bow right around the point instead and surfed down the waves into the depth of the bay. My movement was unsurprisingly fast. When I neared the deepest reach of the bay, I steered the boat to the left to take a shortcut sideways to the waves. I could afford the risk for I was no longer situated as if on an open sea. When I reached the opposite shore of the bay, I turned the canoe still more to the left to parallel its shoreline, about a kilometre away from it. At that point, I was already fighting the waves head-on, moving against the wind. My original dream had been to reach the other end of the bay for my campsite of that day. Yet, when I reached the lee of a small island about eight kilometres short of the planned target in a fierce paddling battle, I sweetly abandoned my resolution. I set up the camp right there, again on smoothed granite. Under the circumstances, I was quite happy with my day's accomplishment even as it was.

Disorientation

After setting up my tent and bed I cooked and ate dinner. Having accomplished that I still had the whole late afternoon and evening for studying of the terrain and the map. The shape of the bay more or less agreed with that which I identified in the map. Winding along the coastline in these parts is the Canadian Pacific railroad. In some places it is closer, elsewhere farther, so in certain places it is visible and occasionally at least audible when a train is passing by. But just that very railroad did not exactly mesh with my assumed position on the map. As it often happens, however, one is reluctant to admit one's own disorientation and instead, tends to blame the map. "I bet that it is obsolete and the course of the railroad must have changed since the map was printed," I foolishly assured myself. The unravelling of the mystery came the next day. After I rounded the point on the western end of the bay that I left behind yesterday and this morning, I followed the coastline in continuing embarrassment. The railroad continued to appear unpredictably where it wasn't supposed to be. Far ahead of me, I could see an infinitely long two-story freight train that was climbing serpentines of the railroad from the lake shore level into high hills. This was not on the map! Then a small railroad station took shape which also wasn't supposed to be there. That was when I started to accept that I was lost. I pulled out the GPS unit and determined my coordinates. I transferred the reading into the map and voilà! I was completely somewhere else than where I assumed I was. As it turned out, I happened to be almost three times as far from Marathon than I had expected. It seemed unbelievable. I confess that I again first suspected some malfunction of the GPS unit but even my iPhone confirmed its allegation. The coastline that I followed towards the climbing train led, in fact, into another, very deep, but narrower bay. I was moving north when I thought that I had been moving west. The shoreline that I saw on my left and had taken it for a large island was, in fact, the west shore of the bay. That's where I was supposed to move across the bay to continue along the route of my voyage. The wind-battered bay that I thought I was inscribing yesterday, I had actually crossed in a straightcut on the first day. The bay of yesterday was a farther one and much larger. All of a sudden, everything was falling into a picture and it meshed together like a jigsaw puzzle. It seemed incredible that with my sense of orientation, of which I am very proud and believe would never fail me, I could get so easily confused. It served as a valuable lesson to me that moving only by comparing the shape of the topography with a large-scale map (like 1:250,000), and especially during the first few days of the journey before one has had a chance to acquire a feeling for the map's scale, it is easy to lose orientation. With newly restored peace of mind, I now changed the course by 90° left toward the distant end of the bay. When a cozy little island with a wind-sheltered beach for easy landing availed itself half way to it, I anchored there for my campsite.

I again got up early and when the sun started rising, I had already paddled for almost an hour. The surface of the lake was as smooth as a mirror and the sun reflected on it with blinding brilliance. What was unusual for me was the high front of a dense, gray fog bank that was sliding over the lake surface from its interior directly towards me. I worried that I would get lost in it, but fortunately, I reached the far end of the bay before the fog engulfed me. After I changed my course to the west when I rounded the point, the fog and I were mutually separating. The ever strengthening sun was then sending its warming rays onto my bare back as it rose higher and higher above the eastern horizon. When I twisted my torso and neck 180 degrees backwards during a rest stop for breakfast, I could already see the fog in the distant east. Above me, an entirely clear, blue sky was spreading. Following the map and the shape of the coastline a lot more vigilantly now, the appearance of hints of closeness of the town of Terrace Bay where I had expected them, confirmed that I was oriented correctly. Just as I neared the mouth of the Aguasabon River, reflected sun flashes from wet paddles made me aware of a fast-approaching canoe. Discerning that its crew consisted of two women, my first reaction was to quickly pull on shorts over my underpants in which I had been sitting in my boat since morning. I suspect that the women also feverishly replaced appropriate pieces of textile over their suntanning bodies in the last moment before we met. They were ripe, forty-somethings, adventurous types sporting friendly smiles. They possessed very detailed maps. Having arrived from opposite directions, we were able to provide each other with valuable help by exchanging the descriptions of our previous travels. They had just been bunny hopping along the arc-like chain of islands which were part of my plan too, but in the opposite direction. They had not started from Thunder Bay, though, but rather from the tip of the Sleeping Giant Peninsula where they had been dropped off. In this way, they avoided the dangerous traversing of vast areas of open water. They raved about how beautiful the trip had been so far. The benefit to them from me was the revelation that I could download detailed maps into my iPhone. Using an app that works even outside of cell phone signal coverage, I can zoom into the finest detail and also see my exact position. My wallet-sized, fold-out solar battery charger became an instant hit — a source of their admiration. Each such encounter serves as encouragement with a valuable boost to self-confidence for the continuation of one's journey.

A strong headwind arose after noon and only in a heroic battle did I conquer my way to a small group of islands that the women recommended for good camping. My tent stood here on a beach of small pebbles in the shadow of a granite crag that was on the lee side of an island. It was my last campsite at the shoreline of the mainland before it diverged to the northwest toward the town of Schreiber. My route would then start hopping along the chain of islands to the west.

Following the experience of paddling in the previous years, I decided this time that I would have a regular weekly rest day every Sunday at my campsites. In this way, I hoped to give my body a chance to regenerate its strength and thus avoid states of total physical exhaustion. I considered it necessary in spite of my experience that, for a lonely traveler, dwelling another day in the same spot can be boring and even depressing.

Bunny-hopping the chain of islands

I pushed the loaded canoe off the pebbles of the beach at the crack of dawn on Monday morning to maximize the probability of a quiet lake surface. This was important because after about four-and-a-half kilometres of paddling along the mainland, I was to encounter the first open water gap of about seven kilometres needed to cross to the first island in the chain. My strategy would prove successful. The waves were small and my nervousness started to wane as I neared the forested point of the island. At first, I could barely see a faint, misty line merging at a great distance with the lake's horizon, until eventually I could see the individual spruce trees on land. After reaching its nearest point, I traced the southern coast of the island at a safe distance. The gap between this and the next island, named Wilson Island on the map, was a lot smaller. The day started with sunshine and blue skies, if eventually with the usual headwind. And so just as I reached Wilson Island and was paddling through the shelter of a river-like, narrow passage between it and a smaller island, I was thoroughly surprised by a blast of thunder. Only when I raised my eyes above the tall spruces could I see that from the north, an anvil of a huge cumulonimbus cloud was spreading — seemingly with the speed of a volcanic eruption. Another few thunders shook the air and lightning electrified the darkened atmosphere. I would never wish to get caught in an electric storm on the water. Accordingly, I franticaly returned to a small bay with a coarse beach for a quick landing. I jumped out of the canoe and pulled it quickly out of the water. I barely managed to close the drawstring of its spray cover apron when large rain drops started bombarding me. I just stood up erect under my hat in a Gore-Tex windbreaker, the zipper of which I drew up to my throat, in shorts and in rubber sandals. I was standing at the upper edge of the beach at a reasonable distance from the nearest spruce trees to be safe from getting hit by lightning. I had never seen a deluge like the one that ensued. The water surface of my bay turned into a "field of thistles" as dense, huge droplets of rain fell brutally on it and bounced upward drawing a two-foot column of water with a burst of a bubble on its top in lieu of a "flower." My shoulders underwent a vehement, chilling massage as if I were standing under a waterfall. Goosebumps popped up on my wet legs. The water of the bay literaly boiled both optically and acoustically. At one time, the lightning exploded with deafening noise directly above my head. The downpour stopped as suddenly as it started after about 20 minutes. When I assured myself that the center of the storm had sufficiently shifted and the danger of being hit by lightning no longer threatened, I relaunched the canoe and continued paddling through the passage. Due to the change in the weather, though, I decided to camp as soon as a suitable spot availed itself. I did not have to search long. As soon as I emerged from the narrow passage and reached the southern point of Wilson Island, I paddled by a deep, small notch in the crags that harbored a beach of round rocks. This was so secluded that I almost missed it. I immediately returned to it for a gorgeous campsite with a late warming sun. I even enjoyed an icy swim here. While cooking supper, I admired magnificent rainbow displays in the southeast that were following the departing storm above the lake.

The next day, I was faced with cutting across two gaps of about three kilometres each, separated by a small island between two large ones. The first of them was Wilson Island, the second one Simpson Island. The day started in a promising way, but around 10:00, a black cloud rolled in again from the north just when I was passing the little island between the water gaps. I landed at its suitable, rocky beach and prepared for the start of the menacing deluge, sitting on a drift log under a crag's overhang. I even had my lunch bag with me to make the break useful. Although the rain did start, its main strike missed my area of the island. It barely managed to make the surrounding rocks wet. As I was then approaching the nearest point of Simpson Island, I spied some fishing boats scattered in the distance around it. One of the motorboats floated between me and the coast of the island until I came to a distance where I could greet its crew. The two men had been distracted by their routine of fishing and had not noticed me until then. It seemed that I almost scared them and they could not understand where I had emerged from in my little nutshell. From their point of view, I must have seemingly arrived from the middle of the infinite lake. "And how did you survive that pelting rain storm that finished just a little while ago?" they wondered. It must have hit them much more fiercely than me. "And where are you traveling?" "From Montreal to Thunder Bay," was my answer. They thought I was pulling their leg.

Before noon, a headwind gradually arose and I fought an ever more vicious battle with it, right up to the time when I found a suitable campsite. It was a surf-eroded bowl in a basalt rock cliff from which a steep natural path led to its flat top. That's where I placed my tent. Surrounding the tent on the top of the rock cliff was a fresh green surface formed by low, creeping aromatic juniper. Backing it up, was a dense fir and spruce thicket. It was definitely not a suitable environment for making a fire, especially because the spot was exposed to the wind. That was now pushing waves in a noisy, thrashing, white surf against the rocks of the cliff. A small survey deeper into the interior with the kitchen bag and the food ration for today's supper in hands finally yielded a sheltered clearing paved with the round rock cobblestones of an ancient beach. It wasn't too far from here to the water for cooking. The surface level of Lake Superior had significantly dropped over the ages causing these prehistoric beaches of lichen-covered round rocks to lie higher and farther from the shoreline. Here I built my safe firepit from rocks and old driftwood logs. They also offered a seat while cooking and eating. The entire area was nicely level, surrounded by sheltering woods. It had gentle access to a small cove for a harbor. My imagination could visualize a grouping of birch bark wigwams or teepees of an old tribe of Ojibway People before the arrival of the white man with their birch bark canoes pulled on shore at the harbor. This vision mixed in my brain with the smell of smoke, rawhide and drying fish. Completing it was the occasional bark of a dog, the beat of a drum and womens' laughter. It seemed like an ideal spot for a smaller Indigenous People's village.

Acquiring great self-confidence

When I reached the large island of St. Ignace, which followed Simpson Island in the chain, I gradually found myself in a very pictoresque landscape. The main isles in the chain were lined with splashes of small, forested islands. The otherwise monotonous horizon of an infinite shiny water surface that merged in a featureless, indistinct line with the sky, was scenically broken into a contrast of dark, sharp silhouetes with the spiky contours of coniferous trees — so typical for Canada. A view into the distance, interrupted by scattered islands, thus gained dramatic depth. A red sunset can greatly emphasize this effect. More important, however, is the fact that one periodically travels through passages among scenic islands of varying sizes and shapes that yield protection from the wind and waves. In this way, one is often paddling in very close proximity to the shore and is thus able to admire the variety of rangy rock formations, trees, undergrowth vegetation, wild flowers and wild fauna. From time to time, a good size fish jumps out of the quiet water right in front of the canoe. The hot noon air in such places is infused with scents of resin perfume. Trails of fine natural litter like leaves, feathers, seed fuzz, little twigs, bark and cone scales left over from a squirrel's dinner float here by air and water currents, forming twisted spirals in the reedy coves of stillness. Paddling alone without the slightest sign of another human soul as far as the eye can see and the intuition can extrapolate beyond it, stripped only to shorts, shirtless under a sun-shielding brim hat, I felt more like a nature-raised savage than like a voyageur. I had neither a bow and arrow nor a rifle, but my paddle slipped into its pocket on the spray cover from time to time and my hand reached for the camera to free it from the waterproof bag under the seat and shoot some unforgettable sight. I felt strength now — both physical and mental. My muscles had already filled with what they needed for my daily achievement and my technique of paddle strokes had sharpened to optimum efficiency and endurance. My canoe was gliding on the water perfectly straight and its bow split the surface with a wave on each side like the prow of an ocean liner. My complexion had armed itself against the burning sun with a deep shade of bronze and toughened itself against wind and minor showers. While constantly moving, I did not need to don any top. A layer of sweat shined up my muscles, made the sun pleasantly warm and the breeze pleasantly cool. In spite of the knowledge that I was totally alone in a land that I had never passed through before, I now felt self-confidence that I was safe to rely on my physical shape, experience and decisivness. I had no signal here for my iPhone and my connection with the outside world could only be based on telepathy. The only living beings that knew about my presence were seagulls, the osprey and the eagle, maybe also a hidden moose, cariboo, bear or wolf. I knew what to do if the weather changed; how to pick my route to move through sheltered from the wind or within safe reach of the shore. I knew when I could afford to risk cutting straight across a multikilometre stretch of open water and thus entrust my heart into the palm of the Manitou. I knew that I would find a reliable campsite at the end of the day and that I would sate my hungry innards. It spread happiness over my shoulders. I would have smiled if I had had the assurance that it would make any sense in my lonely desolateness. I felt that I belonged here and that I was in harmony with nature — not altering the environment. I had found what I had been seeking — both in space and in time. The landscape surrounding Lake Superior is just as its fierce winters — harsh. It appears as if it were dreaming sad dreams, bearing its fate with clenched teeth. It adorns itself with a wild beauty of ripped-up, hard rock formation shapes and prickly-spiked, densely intertwined, knotty, knobby spruce and fir with wind-broken and sun-bleached bones of bare branches. On the wind-exposed headlands of its shoreline, the granite crags are totally bare, denuded of even a single blade of grass by the surf and storms, sometimes to a height of ten metres. Like a man who had suffered an unloving, stern childhood, Lake Superior is cruel, gravely short of tenderness and unforgiving. It only rewards those who are not afraid and who are willing to win its favors in an honest fight.

I enjoyed a broad variety of campsites here. Some days, I would sink anchor at a coastline point or in a sheltered cove. Another day, at an island. Sometimes what made the decision was a nice view, a pleasant beach, the scenic beauty of a rock formation. Another time, it would be the snug coziness of a shelter from the wind that would make any further paddling nonsensical. There were times when I would choose a spot for its luring access to a polar bear swim which I needed to cool myself from an especially hot afternoon sun. There were also occasions when, after rounding a point, the wind would strike my face with a force rivaling the thrust of a jet engine and only with the utmost exertion would I reach the lee of the nearest island, so small sometimes, that I could throw a rock over it. But in fact, even what I call "mainland," were actually islands, only disproportionally larger. The vegetation abounded with a broad scale of shades of green, from the darkest of spruce to the fresh green of desiduous bushes, to the particularly light green of peculiar small flowers that grew predominantly on black, volcanic ash. Not even the rocks were bland in color. They displayed shades of black to grey to blue, tan to richly red. Based on these hues, they than mixed infinite combinations of speckled patterns, mottled veins, etc. The lake water here was absolutely crystal clear. It changed in hue from emerald green to bluish. The richness of its shade grew with its depth. In all cases, though, it was ice cold. I often admired the beauty of diminutive, colorful blossoms of an alpine type in my campsites that one normally encounters in the harsh conditions of alpine altitudes. Once when I was packing my tent at daybreak, I discovered that a toad found protective comfort among the pebbles under tent's floor. Its color mimicry blended perfectly with the coloring of the rocks, making it hard for me to notice him.

I was just closing in on a very inviting site at one time that promised nice camping on a point with a beach of very fine pebbles. It was situated under low rock formations on shore that extended discontinuously out into the crystal clear, green water. When the prow of my canoe sledded gently up the edge of the beach following a successful slalom of dodging some rocky shallows, it stopped. From the other side of the point, one of two kayakers suddenly emerged. They were also looking for a campsite. I was prepared to generously share the place that I had reached first by a nose's length but the duo preferred privacy and hence, continued looking. I only had a chance for brief small talk with one paddler while his colleague was rounding the point in a wider arc. They were both from Thunder Bay and had traveled this route more than once before. As all the others that I had met on this route, they did not start out from Thunder Bay but had arranged to be dropped off at the tip of Sleeping Giant Peninsula from where they paddled. The kayaker wore neoprene from head to toe during the sweltering day, including a neoprene hood, black sunglasses and a life jacket. From my point of view, such a way of traveling would be unbearable torture for me. We discussed the possibilities of reaching the city by canoe. He confirmed my own speculations that the only option, besides transportation by a vehicle from the tip of the peninsula where they launched, if still with a great deal of risk, would be to split the direct line of 22 kilometres from the tip to Thunder Bay by a southward side trip to Pie Island from which to paddle directly to the mainland. As I had earlier deduced from the map, this alternative divided the distances over the open water into 10 and 13 kilometres. The vision of this prospect put butterflies in my stomach, yet from now on it represented the only tangible plan of how to reach the harbor of the metropolis. Should I succeed in accomplishing this feat, I dreamed of then paddling up the current of the Kaministiquia River all the way to Fort William where the canoes of the voyageurs once used to head. I saw in it a fitting coronation to the finish of my water voyage from Montreal.

The encounter with the kayakers renewed my comparisons of the pros and cons of using the two types of paddling craft for the purpose of the lonesome voyage along the giant lake water route by one's own muscle power. Before the start of my journey, more than one seasoned paddler recommended I use an ocean kayak. But even after my return, at my slide show from the trip, some listeners were asking why I had not used a kayak. I felt happy that I had chosen the canoe. It wasn't only for the fact that a canoe represented the traditional historical vessel of movement through the lake country of Canada — it had been used both by the Aboriginal People since time immemorial and by the Europeans from their first arrival throughout the era of the fur trade. In my view, a canoe also offered better advantages and comfort for my purpose than a kayak. For one, the load capacity of a canoe allows up to three times more cargo weight and volume. This is critically important in extended expeditions without the frequent possibility of resupplying. While a kayak is good for about a week or a fortnight-long trip, in a canoe I sometimes carried supplies for six weeks. Another of my observations had been that the kayak sits low in the water which is an advantage when there is a headwind. Yet I have noticed that the upper edge of its cockpit is perhaps only six to ten centimeters above the water level while in the canoe, I sit high — not below the level of the icy water. A canoe's gunwales on the sides are at least some 25 centimetres above water. The bow and stern of the canoe rise even higher. I am sitting upright in the canoe. I can change position by shifting to the left, right, lower, or higher. I can stretch my legs, or bend them, spread them apart to the full width of the boat or fold them crossed under the seat. I can kneel. I can turn around and reach for something in the back of the canoe or to extend my reach for something in the front. I can stand up in it and study the entry into a rapid up ahead or lie down flat on the deck of the spray cover behind the seat during a rest. During extended paddling this is extremely important. I felt more like a captain in his ship than as if tightly snugged up in a rigid floating shoe in the same position for long hours. My water journey had not consisted just of floating on lakes. My vessel had to have the ability to maneuver in river rapids. It also had to be carried on many portages. A Kevlar canoe is not only more suitable for zigzagging through rapids than an ocean kayak, but it is also significantly lighter and built for the ages-verified, classical way of carrying it upside down on one's shoulders behind the neck. My extensive portaging experience that included canoe travel in the Yukon and the Northwest Territories has convinced me that, in this fashion, I am able to pass with the canoe through everywhere, where I had been able to pass without it. Overturned on shore in a campsite, a canoe doubles as a reliable, protective cover for much of the gear from rain. Sometimes it can serve as a kitchen counter for the evening preparation of supper. Carrying an ocean kayak, on the other hand, is not a simple matter. Most of the time it requires a folding two-wheel cart for dragging it, but this is again feasible only on reasonable trails. I had heeded the advice to take a kayak paddle as a spare. Yet I tried to use it only once out of three seasons of paddling. This was when I had to fight my way against the rapids right in the center of Ottawa city. Still, this attempt did not last for even a minute. When I lost the battle with the regular paddle, I quickly switched it for the kayak type but found no difference. When the current started pulling me down, I was forced to jump out of the canoe and, submerged up to my chest, lead it against the waves. The only other occasion when I also used the kayak paddle was on the gruesome 12-hour La Vase Portage from Trout Lake on the Mattawa to Lake Nipissing. This being the only long object on hand at the time, I poled with it, standing in the canoe backward. I was moving backwards, pushing its stern through a blanket of lily pads, searching for a pathway through channel-like gaps — narrower than the canoe — left behind by beavers and muskrats in a thick rug of water-grass sod and rafts of reed roots. I philosophised then how much the landscape must have changed since the times when the voyageurs traveled through there. Only later would I learn that they, in fact, carried around this particular marsh. During this year's journey from Marathon to Thunder Bay, the kayak paddle served only as a holding boom for a small GoPro camera. That's because I stuck on the back side of its far end leaf the camera mount so that I could shoot the whole canoe from its front end in order to include me in action. When I needed to, I pulled the paddle from its pocket, mounted the camera on its far end and returned the paddle end with the camera back to the front. The Hollywood action could start. The movie clips have allowed me to enliven my PowerPoint slideshow presentations from the trip with inserts of animated action.

When there was no headwind that normally prevails during the movement from east to west — the direction I traveled — I used to make great distances. The landscape that I passed, paddle stroke by paddle stroke, had not changed since the time when it was passed by the voyageurs. I saw what they had seen. My map acquainted me with the names of prominent geographical forms that the voyageurs had seen. Some they named after animals of the wilderness of which they were reminded, others after the items of their outfit or after the names of members of the company brass after which the lakes and mountains were named. Otherwise, one encounters Otter Head Point, Hat Point, etc. These features separated sections of the voyage and served as milestones in measuring their travel progress. One day when I paddled among islands with large gaps in between, a distant view opened in which I could not overlook an almost identical pair of rounded green hills that were standing out from the broad plain of Black Bay Peninsula like a pair of woman's breasts. It is not hard to understand that that would be the very name that was attached to them by the hard-working, love-deprived voyageurs who must have longed for sorely missed embraces with their sweethearts. The name "The Paps" so endured into the modern maps.

After being forced by a ferocious headwind into spending a night in an encampment on a tiny island with a narrow sandy beach, I pushed off the next morning just as the blinding, reddish disc of the rising sun nudged its upper edge above the infinite horizon of the lake surface. The wind was not unfriendly; hence, I could afford straight-line shortcuts along the outside of a coastline-fringing group of islands. The situation also allowed me to perform daring straight traverses of deep bays and gaps between the main islands and the peninsulas of the stepping stone arc waterway. The wind arose from the left and a bit from the back only after I had rounded the rock tower of Roche Debout Point that was surrounded by treacherous shallows and jutting rock reefs just under the surface. Even with a canoe that had minimal draft, I had to be very vigilant here. The water was of a bluish hue and crystal clear. The refraction of light under the surface distorted the notion of depth and made navigation over the sharp, rocky reefs into a testing challenge. While the gradually rising wind already whistled by my ears, the broad maw of the deep Shesheeb

Bay opened up to the right of me. After a brief hesitation, I found the courage to paddle almost straight across it, frantically racing to have the most vulnerable position in its most-remote-from-shore middle behind me as early as possible. The shoreline that I approached had towering rock cliffs that dropped straight into the water without any possibility of landing. On my left, a large, high forest-covered island started looming. Although it provided some shelter from the wind after a while, it rendered itself unsuitable for camping on account of its steep treed shores. Finally, in a gap between the island and the main shore, a long narrow sliver of a small, rocky, but relatively low island came into my view. I was just at the end of my strength and thus, with a jubilant spirit I immediately headed for it. The landing at its wind-exposed shore of smooth rock was difficult. This was especially so because the wind kept trying to blow the canoe away. I was therefore forced to pull almost the whole loaded vessel onto the rock, even if just for the inspection of the island. That, however, quickly revealed that in about a third of the length of the island and on its other side, a small sheltered circular cove was situated with a gradual rocky shore. Behind it, on the crest of the island's spine, a flat spot for my tent was visible with a thick bedding of caribou lichen on granite amid aromatic, creeping juniper. I returned to the boat right away, slipped it from the smooth granite back into the water and rounded the end of the island into the espied harbor. The water here was shallow with a bottom of coarse sand yet sufficiently deep for the canoe. The first task after the bow touched the shore was to step out of the boat into the water, walk to its front, lift it and pull the canoe up halfway onto the shore. Then the unloading ensued. First the paddles went onto the shore together with all the other objects that detached from the spray cover. The untying and unlacing of the spray cover from the canoe with its spreading to dry on a flat rock followed. From this point on, I would not need to step into water anymore so I changed from my wet rubber sandals that were filled with sand and small rocks into much more comfortable socks and Gore-Tex hikers. These also provided protection while I was walking on sharp rocks and prickly vegetation. The drybags containing food were then unloaded from the bow and placed in the shade of the low branches around the foot of a young spruce. The yellow drybag with the kitchen and "hardware" moved to the vicinity of the spot that I picked for cooking. This phase in the disembarking of the boat allowed for its further withdrawal from the water onto the shore and this allowed me access to the large waterproof backpack in its middle. The latter was carried, together with the rolled up sleeping mat under my arm, to a spot I selected for the tent. The solar charger was unfolded on a rock surface that was the most perpendicularly exposed to the rays of the afternoon sun, its corners weighted with rocks so the wind would not flip it over. The bottles with the remaining drinking fluid and the waterproof fanny pack with day lunches and snacks in the canoe went to the shady vicinity of the food bags. When the canoe was empty, I lifted it onto my thighs by the gunwale in its middle and I carried it out of the water to a safe distance from the reach of the wind and waves. Here I overturned it bottom up. The map case, the photo and electronic equipment, as well as the machete and the items of bear safety now went to the tent spot. The tent was erected, its corners weighted and pulled out tight with rocks over short sticks passed through the tent corner loops. The mat was unrolled inside. The sleeping bag was pulled out of its stuff sack and unfurled on the mat in the tent to air out. The stuff sack was filled with clothing from the backpack to serve as a pillow. During extra hot days I could not resist refreshing myself with an icy bath and a brief swim in the lake. But in most cases, I would then crawl into the tent, over which, if it was hot, I would not place the fly yet. I would just remove my shoes and, protected by the tent netting from insects, would lie down on the sleeping bag to rest my overworked back. I then opened the map case and, lying down, studied the map with the use of the GPS to assure myself about where I was located, what distance I made today and what my route should be for tomorrow. Today I had conquered 28 kilometres. Sometimes I dozed off for an hour. I got up after the rest, stretched the fly over the tent and stored the safety kit in its back vestibule. I then moved to the harbor, namely to the place that I had chosen as a kitchen to start cooking supper. I usually located the fire pit close to water, typically in a rock fissure for a wind shelter and to limit the possibility of its spreading to combustible surroundings. I made use of a light, collapsible cooking grill as a platform for two stainless steel pots. I mostly burned small pieces of driftwood that I stacked under the grill beforehand around a core of tiny dry spruce twigs, birch bark, lichen, or dry grass to serve as a fire starter. I never needed to use paper and I almost always succeeded in igniting the fire with one match. If a breeze was blowing, I surrounded the fire and the grill with short chunks of logs, or rocks that allowed for air supply to reach the fire from below. The water in the pots boiled within a few minutes. I scooped it directly from the lake and boiled it for over five minutes to assure sterilization. Later even the surfaces of the surrounding pieces of logs burned and radiated heat. I then stoked the fire with thicker wood under the grill so that I didn't need to constantly be adding fuel. The great majority of my meals were based on naturally dehydrated pasta, rice, or potatoes purchased in common supermarkets that were packaged in light, foil baggies. These are mostly just boiled with added water. After the first boil, I reduced the fire and let the mix simmer while stirring it occasionally for another eight or so minutes. For this purpose, I folded away the surrounding logs and spread out the burning wood under the grill, letting it slowly burn up. I resurrected the fire after supper. After I washed the pots in hot water, I boiled water in multiple batches for four to six litres of tea. This served partially for drinking a cup after supper but mainly for the next day in the canoe. I cleaned all the cooking equipment after its use and stored it back in the yellow drybag designated for "hardware." When the fire fully died and cooled, I threw partially burnt wood pieces into the lake and swept all ashes into the water to erase all traces of my fireplace. I washed before going to bed and brushed my teeth. I then stored the toiletries into the "hardware" bag and stashed all the remaining gear like ropes, paddles, life vest, rolled up spray cover, sandals, gloves, water shoes, drybags, etc. under the overturned canoe in case of an overnight rain. Both the food bags as well as the bag containing items of personal hygiene were kept some 20 metres from the tent in order not to attract bears to it. Bears can be lured even by the scent of toothpaste. With dusk, the mosquito airforce usually scrambled to air duty but of my blood they would not imbibe. By then I would be comfortably lying down behind the mosquito netting in my tent and study the map again, the graph of the atmospheric pressure development on my watch, etc., in order to crystalize the details of the next day's plan. After that, I drifted into sleep, hypnotized by the scents of resin, the gentle lapping of the waves against granite and the nostalgic lullaby of a loon's haunting wail.

I left the sliver-like island just as the blinding disk of the rising sun swung above the horizon. The brightness of the morning was encouraging with the promise of a friendly day for a long journey. After a few kilometres, I passed another "sliver" of a rocky island and following that, I steered the canoe to the right into a narrow passage between the islands. I had chosen the optimal route on the previous evening while I lay in the tent exploring several imaginary routes through the islands with my eyes on the map. Soon I took off my t-shirt and assumed my favorite role as an Indigenous water nomad. The morning air among the islands was pleasantly fresh. In the shadows it even felt a bit too cool. I thus paddled through sunlit gaps among the islands where I felt the sun's pleasant, warming rays as they reflected from the water and the rocky outcroppings. This early, they formed sharp shadows. An occasional splash of icy water onto my bare skin from the paddle when it caught a little wave on the surface during its return forward only awakened my senses to a keener perception of the wild beauty. When a five-kilometre straight crossing of a bay opened up in front of me, I finally stopped at the last island. It was time to have the first rest and breakfast in the boat. That consisted of two paper sachets of instant oatmeal poured directly into my mouth and watered down with tea from a two-litre plastic bottle chilled over the last night. About 10:00, a slight wind arose from the left — east, but the day maintained its brightness. As it continued warming up, the wind was so far welcome. When a view opened up towards the southeast over an uninterrupted surface of a large bay, in the distance on my left, I spied a little steamboat-like craft of a fishing outfitter. It repeatedly stopped in previously-verified good spots to allow its clients to hook that sought-after trophy catch. The steamboat disappeared and re-emerged as I left the shelter of the islands. Even over the great distance, I could hear the boat's PA relaying the guide's information to the clients and when it called them to lunch. The wind strengthened around noon. It blew from my left — the direction from the infinite stretch of the giant lake's open water. My plan from yesterday to look for a campsite among the islands of a small archipelago, which was situated on the right side of the exit from the bay, soon fizzled when the setting on the low rocky islands did not prove friendly. Offering no good spot for putting down a tent made them unworthy of landing. The passing of a dark cloud with several rain showers just then, which I endured in the canoe, only deepened my reluctance to camp there. While stopping to eat my lunch in the boat during the light rain, I was even bothered by mosquitos here. In my present physical shape, I still felt fresh, hence a decision wasn't hard for me to continue on my way. From the map, I knew that no suitable islands would avail themselves for camping for some six kilometres. I thus continued gobbling further distance in long, smooth paddle strokes. The wind from the left grew inconspicuously yet tirelessly stronger, while the sky became a bit gloomy with long streaks of clouds. Once in a while, a drop of rain would fall. I was nearing the muzzle of Black Bay, the largest bay, whose depth seemed infinite on the map. It merged into the tip of Nipigon Bay on Lake Superior. The feature was basically just a corridor for the excesses of bad weather. When I was cutting across a fair sized bay a few days ago, about a kilometre from the coastline, I noticed a group of four ocean kayaks that "licked" the rock cliffs of the shore at close proximity to its edge. The kayakers did not see me but when I later stopped in a different bay to rest from a strong headwind and have a small snack in the canoe, a motorboat approached me. As it turned out, it served as a supporting escort to the kayakers. Three men of a ripe, fatherly age were interested to know if I had encountered the kayakers anywhere. Having affirmed that I had, I asked what kind of situation would unfold ahead of me from where they had arrived. According to them, there wasn't anything serious to expect ahead except for one thing that they wanted to seriously warn me about. It was the crossing of Black Bay. I was to pay special attention to avoid getting caught in it with bad weather. According to the map, a large island was situated in the mouth of Black Bay bearing the name Edward's Island. Under the given conditions, and in fact even if the weather were calm, I did not intend to risk circumventing it around its southern, to the fresh water sea-exposed side. It would potentially involve long, open-water crossings in strong side waves. Instead, I prudently opted for a somewhat longer trajectory of rounding Edward's Island on its inside — the northern side. I hoped that on its northern, lee-side coast, I would also find a suitable site for camping. Just before I reached the point of Black Bay's eastern edge, I passed through a narrow strait between the main shore and a sizeable island on which there was a fisherman's homestead with a port of several motorboats. I estimated that two families were living there because I saw two adult men and two adult women. They most likely were Indigenous People judging from the almost bluish-black raven color of their hair, which in my experience, is surprisingly distinctly visible from a great distance. Frolicking around them, was a group of children and teenagers. Apparently, they must have been preparing a Saturday afternoon barbeque. I cruised through the channel seemingly as if on a river. I raised my paddle several times to make sure that they would notice that I was greeting them. They briefly turned their looks to me and returned the salute by raising an arm but only in a lukewarm manner. I, however, felt their spying eyes on my back up to the moment when I disappeared from their sight as I rounded the point of the east edge of the bay and turned my course to the northwest. I had a suspicion that they might have exchanged perplexed questions like, "What kind of a nut is this?" We both found ourselves in an isolated water wasteland but they were at least connected with outside civilization by fast motorboats. Having rounded the starting point of Black Bay, I headed diagonally across its nearer and also narrower arm toward the northern point of Edward

Island. I was by now driven by a really strong wind, which, after changing my course, blew directly into my back. I felt a little ill at ease in the big waves and hence cut as quickly as possible across the width of the water gap in order to paddle at a safer distance from the shore of the island. When I finally reached and rounded its north point, I suddenly found myself in the quiet water of its leeward side. I could now afford to stop paddling and enjoy a little rest. While taking a few mighty swigs of cold tea and good bites of a protein bar, I studied with interest the northward expanse of Black Bay, uninterrupted up to the most northerly extents of Lake Superior shores, along which I knew the Trans-Canada Highway ran. I tried my iPhone, "Et voilà!" I had a faint signal. I did not catch Milena who was still at her home in the Czech Republic but I spoke with her mother who could relay the message to her from me that I was OK. I included the description of my present location. A search for a campsite was the next item on my agenda. In spite of the calm water and low flat shores, this goal did not prove very easy. The little islands here were covered with rugged sharp rocks while the main shore around them was marshy and covered with reeds. I seriously considered a site on a flat but uneven and prickly, blistered rock platform that was situated only a few centimetres above the lake surface level. But then I weighed the possibility of the tent being flooded by waves if the wind changed direction. I kept looking. I eventually turned into an unpromising, narrow strait lined with reeds. "Eureka!" I cruised into an inviting circular cove — almost closed, with shallow, flat and considerably warmer water. Its sandy bottom feathered into the horseshoe arc of a narrow sandy beach lined from behind with overhanging branches of dense cedar forest. What a reward for a long day of paddling! I had bagged 35 kilometres today! The beach did not look wide enough for erecting a tent at a safe distance from the water's edge at first. But eventually I did find a suitable spot. It only called for chopping out a sufficiently high room for the tent from the overhanging cedar branches with the machete. I slept here not even a metre-and-a-half from the water's edge but thanks to the cove's semiclosed isolation, the probability of larger waves that could flood the tent was sufficiently negligible.

I was totally cut off from the outside world here. Somebody would have had a hard time looking for me should I have met with a serious mishap. The cell phone signal in this location was again absent. Everything around was very still and eerily silent. The close proximity of the dense, dark forest immediately behind the tent gave me an uneasy feeling. All of that only sharpened my otherwise constantly wary senses of prudence and vigilance. Traveling through wilderness solo absolutely requires that. On the other hand, there was nice bathing and swimming here. The shallow, isolated water was somewhat more warmed up by the sun. The sandy bottom then yielded the luxury of entering the lake and swimming without rubber sandals. The next day after my disembarking here was a Sunday. I thus spent here my planned day of the rest. I completely washed myself, including my hair in the lake and rinsed out a richly foaming shampoo frolicking and swimming under water like an otter. I had time to cook both breakfast and dinner, I ventured for several small survey walks along the sandy beach. As always during these days of lonely rest, however, a nostalgic melancholy set in during the afternoon. I couldn't wait till the early morning when I would depart with the goal of crossing the main width of Black Bay.

The Black Bay

I woke up at dawn into a humid chill. Only reluctantly did I leave the cozy warmth of my sleeping bag. When I poked my nose out of the tent, I could see right away that the ideal day for overcoming the dangerous bay had not materialized. Everything was engulfed in dense, milky fog. Just when I had changed and packed away the sleeping bag the fog started precipitating drizzle. I quickly struck and packed the tent to minimize its getting wet as much as possible. I consoled myself with an old scouting rule of thumb that said a rain before 7:00 means the weather will clear up. Yet the fine rain did not stop when, after an hour, I pushed the canoe off and started paddling into the fog under a dark sky. I headed west for an imperceptible narrow strait that the map showed between the northern protrusion of Edward Island and another, long and narrow island directly north of it. Up to the very last moment, I could see no gap. I feared the possible need for an enormous detour if it turned out that the strait did not exist. Circumventing the long island would represent a multikilometre addition to the crossing distance. Thanks to an unrealistic, foolhardy faith, I slowly kept pushing the canoe in the direction of a grassy neck of land that seemed to be connecting both islands. The line of the tree cover on both sides tapered down to it and stopped leaving a grassy gap. I was practically sliding the canoe with a paddle over the rocks in flooded grass when it finally became clear that I would be able to pass through — yippee! — success! Ahead of me, a dark, vast spread of the wind-roughened water surface of Black Bay opened up. Under the gloomy overcast sky, it appeared really black. It kept raining. The wind, which was not screened here by Edward Island, blew from the left — the center of the Superior — and a bit from behind. The fog was driven away here by the wind but the shore on the other side of the bay was hard to see anyway. It was only a thin, fuzzy line on the horizon. I assessed the situation and it seemed to me that under the existing conditions, I could cautiously continue. I was still convinced that with the progressing morning, the weather would change for the better. From the map, I knew what course I had to follow to aim for a point on the far shore that represented the shortest distance. It could not be discerned by sight. The wind blew and a fine rain cooled my face while I vehemently paddled to cut as fast as possible through the stressful position in the middle of the bay from where it was the farthest to a shore. As I was leaving the more sheltered vicinity of Edward Island, the wind and the waves grew in strength and size. After some while, the point on the far shore started to appear discernible. Yet instead of the onset of feeling safer the exact opposite arose. When I was situated about a kilometre from the tip of the point, the wind suddenly exploded in a fit of fury and to top it off, a thunder clap rumbled. A storm cloud wall mysteriously spread in the direction opposite to the wind on the surface of the lake, thus directly against me. I really started paddling now toward the tip of the point as if my life was at stake. The direction of the wind, though, was sending rolling waves head-on against the point and the shoreline did not yield any leeward side. I steered to its left in hope that the shoreline of the point might reveal some hollow, but when it became fruitless, I just searched for a spot with a piece of smooth beach among the rocks where I could run up with the canoe onto shore. The spot availed itself at the last moment. It even revealed the mini-lee of a big boulder. I turned the canoe by its stern to the sand and pushed it up with the paddle while still sitting in it. I then quickly jumped out of the boat before the next wave could throw its front and I quickly pulled the whole canoe onto the sand. As I was pulling shut the draw string of the spray cover skirt and was propping it up into a peak with a stick to prevent the pooling of rain water, lightning flashed directly above my head and thunder followed it instantly. At the same time, as if the skies had ripped open, a deluge of a downpour descended. This drove me into the protective arms of the forest limbs. The forest lined the narrow beach and covered a rock wall that stretched along the whole shoreline of the point. Under my hat, in a chilling Gore-Tex rain jacket, shorts and bare feet in rubber sandals, I shook violently from cold. I wrapped myself into the wet cedar branches as if they were a robe and I wrung my brain for an idea of how to escape this precarious survival situation. The two-metre rock wall behind me with a thick growth on top of it eliminated any possibility of camping. A relaunching of the canoe in the hope of finding more suitable places somewhere farther on was, under the given circumstances, also beyond a realistic possibility. The beach was narrow and strewn with rocks. Clearly imprinted in its sand, I could see a well-trodden path of a wolf pack. It led along the beach length as far as I could see. The sole goal of my frantic attention to the beach, though, was scanning it for the remote chance of finding a wider, flatter spot that might accommodate the emergency erection of a tent. If faintly, this wish had finally started taking real shape. The beach was being whipped by wind and waves but after removing a fallen rotten tree, the tent might stand on it with about a metre's margin from their reach. I was finding myself in the middle of absolute nowhere and nobody, but I alone could save myself. The warmth of a dry sleeping bag now emerged as the only key to survival. When the worst of the rain temporarily abated, I raced to start the work. In a flash, I released the spray cover off the canoe on one end and pulled out the waterproof backpack containing the tent, sleeping bag and clothing. I managed to accomplish all the operations of the erecting of the tent and unfolding of the bedroll in it so quickly that the interior did not end up too wet. I still managed to access and collect a few protein bars from the canoe and, with them, I finally crawled into the heavenly, homey comfort of the tent. I dried my whole body with a towel and quickly slipped into my sleeping bag. The wind, waves and rain raged outside, but I now happily fell asleep in warmth and soft comfort. It wasn't even noon yet.

When I woke up in the late afternoon, everything was gilded by the rays of the lowering sun. The storm was gone but all was still wet. The evaporation of moisture chilled the air to such a degree that, to recover from my earlier hypothermia, I had to don woolly socks for my hiking boots, long thermal underwear, long pants, a fleecy and a woolen ski touque on my head. I walked on the moist sand along the beach, following the wolf tracks. They led me to the tip of the cape. An uninterrupted view north into the depth of Black Bay opened up in front of me. I tried my iPhone and, lo and behold, on the other side in Jilove by Decin in the Czech Republic, the voice of my beloved wife answered. "How is it going?"… "Now, that I hear your voice, everything is hunky-dory! I miss you here!" Everything instantly acquired the appearance of a stroll through a rose garden. I assured her that I had another dangerous milestone behind me and that I was approaching the final destination of my water voyage faster than expected.

But, of course, I did not tell Milena that the most dangerous challenge still awaited me. And not for too long. I was to arrive at my Rubicon the very next day. From here on, to the tip of Sleeping Giant Peninsula, I did not have to cut across any large water gap. My travel to it was now merely following the coastline of the peninsula itself. The morning after the early emergency camping on "the beach of the wolf pack" forced by the storm looked very promising. The sun rays had warmed since early morning and the lake's surface was undulating from a reasonable breeze. The wind was coming from the west but at the beginning it was screened by the east coast of the peninsula along which I paddled toward the south. It started right from the moment in the morning when I pushed the canoe off the beach sand into the waves. When the curvature of the coastline I followed guided me to its south point, my course aimed west from here and against the wind. Although the wind strengthened a bit during the morning, it was not strong enough to sap energy from my muscles and break my will to continue. I was moving slowly, methodically and resolutely along reddish hue-tinted rock cliffs that were covered on top with the greenery of aromatic, coniferous giants. I cut across one scallop of a small bay after another. It was not even noon before I finally approached the town and port of Silver Islet. Silver used to be mined here at one time and a road leads to it from the mainland in the north. This road had been used by all those water travelers who launched their boats here and whom I met during my paddling voyage in the opposite direction. At the same time, in the distance on the western horizon, a ridgeline appeared of the tip of the peninsula. It was not difficult at all to see in its silhouette an upward facing head of the sleeping giant with forehead, eyebrows, nose, mouth and chin. Even the long feathers of an Indian headdress that extended into the very point of land were easily apparent. *Nanabijou* — the Ojibwa name for the giant according to their legend — was turned into stone by Manitou as punishment for revealing the location of a fabulously rich lode of silver at today's town of Silver Islet to the white man. For a moment, I pondered the urge to stop in the port for a while and perhaps enjoy a diet Pepsi for which my parched throat yearned. But then self-discipline won. I instead continued in order not to get delayed. My plan was to arrive as close as possible to the point of the peninsula and find a camping spot there. I wanted to camp early and go to sleep early so I could get up optimally rested. I planned to push off at dawn the next morning in the hope that the lake surface would still be calm. It was needed for my enormous open water traverse to Pie Island. Its closest point, according to the map, was over 10 kilometres distant from the tip of the Sleeping Giant. The day after, the distance to overcome from the island to the mainland would exceed 13 kilometres. As I neared the cape, my emotional tension grew. It got softened only by a brief encounter with a guided group of ocean kayakers who were returning from a two-day trip along the coast of the Sleeping Giant back to Silver Islet. They set out after yesterday's storm and had only "licked" the shoreline of the peninsula. I revealed to them my intention so that at least somebody would know about my insane plan in case something happened to me and a search would occur. The guide had a radio and on my request he checked out what the weather forecast was to be for the next day. I do not remember that any special threat was to emerge. Following that, I kept dutifully shortening my distance to the point on the horizon. The headwind strength grew. I was looking forward to reaching the lee of the point's landmass and setting up a campsite on it. From up close, though, the shore would not prove friendly to camping. It was rough, consisting of big, angular rocks and raspy bushes. I was moseying around for a while and then I rounded the point. I was studying if it would be possible to disembark and camp in the vicinity of a now deserted small bird research station that was situated on the point. In front of me, a hazy outline of the metropolis of Thunder Bay hovered as a ghost at a great distance of over 22 kilometres.

The dice are thrown — crossing the Rubicon

For some mysterious reason the surface of the lake then started to calm down. It was just 1:00 in the afternoon. I was rocking slightly with my canoe on the glossy swells while taking bites of my lunch and studying the lake in the directions of Thunder Bay and Pie

Island. I moved a bit in the direction of Pie Island. I weighed a temptation similar to one who is considering jumping across a flood-swollen stream. The adrenalin then rushed into my face and I put on a racing pace towards the island. My sudden resolution was "now or never!" The island was taking shape at a great distance and I knew from the map that I had to be heading slightly to the right of the mountains in its outline to reach the closest little bay on it. I was hoping that it would possibly also yield good camping. The gamble proved successful. The water surface continued to calm down and I estimated that in my racing pace I might reach the coast of the island perhaps in as short a time as a little over an hour.

Out of the port of Thunder Bay, a giant freight ship emerged, perhaps over 200 metres long with cranes on both ends. It was a so called "laker" — the lake counterpart of an ocean-going cargo ship. At first it seemed that our trajectories would cross. Yet once they spotted me we avoided each other from a bilateral effort by a wide margin. The crew must have been shocked by the audacity of the canoeist in a paltry nutshell of a vessel whom they met in the middle of the freshwater sea far from the nearest shore. The sun was burning and I took a good gulp from my two-litre bottle of tea every once in a while but I would never slacken in my racing pace of paddling. I wasn't taking my momentary fortune with the calm water for granted. I knew that I had to forge iron while still hot. At last I started to perceive the bay of my destination. Not too long after that, I could even see individual trees on the shoreline. The bay displayed the arc of a pebbly beach and I aimed towards its right end, close to the point around which the course was to turn that I would take tomorrow in crossing to the mainland south of Thunder Bay. Oh what a feeling of temporary safety when I finally furrowed into the fine pebbles of the beach with the prow of my canoe! I disembarked into the water and turned back, looking in the direction of the Sleeping Giant's point. I could barely see it from here, only a mirage in the hazy distance. It was hard to believe that I had just surmounted all that vast watery universe. It had indeed taken me only a little over an hour. Then I stripped naked and threw myself into the waves in a thorough swim. A gentle breeze that now blew from the northeast skimmed water from the warmer top layer of the lake surface and pushed it against the beach. The result of this was an interesting effect of pleasantly warm water concentrating in the bay. It was apparent that in my sudden decision to traverse the water span to the island, I had taken advantage of the period when the wind temporarily abated and started to change its direction from western to northeastern. The tent sprouted on the fine pebbles quickly and the unfolded bedroll in it filled its purpose immediately when I laid my tired back down on it. I remained resting for an hour before I engaged in other camping chores. Everything around was absolutely serene — almost heavenly quiet. It seemed that not a living soul was sharing the island with me. Nobody was aware that I was camping here. I depended solely on my own ability for my return to civilization.

The second day on the island, I left the tent before dawn to take advantage of a calm lake surface. Yet I was surprised by splashing sounds of surf waves against the pebble beach. I was disillusioned but again, I assured myself that this early in the day, the situation meant nothing. It ought to soon quiet down, I thought, especially because there didn't seem to be any significant wind that would be pushing the waves. I quickly loaded the canoe and set out around the nearest northwest point of the island in the direction of the mainland coast. Soon the sun rose above the water level and hidden behind the black silhouette of the still sleeping Giant in the northeast it glorified it with a red-orange aura. The wind blew from it and so as I paddled west toward the main shore, the waves were coming from my right and slightly from the back. I again paddled as if in a race, especially since the wind and the waves grew in strength and size. But with my present level of experience I was successful in coordinating my paddle strokes with the rhythm of the waves so that they helped me with the forward propulsion. I advanced methodically. Slowly but surely I gradually resolved ever smaller details in the, at first, low and misty shoreline in the distance ahead of me. A feeling of relative safety finally arrived when I approached to within about a couple of kilometres of the mainland. I started steering my course to the northwest because Thunder Bay was located to the north along the shoreline from the place where the shortest line from the island led me. I focussed on finding and entering the southernmost of the three arms of the Kaministiquia River delta that my map was showing. But the wind kept growing and its direction was changing more and more to north which was against me. Besides that, the shoreline abounded here with many industrial structures including a power plant, warehouse docks of various businesses, etc., that masked and obscured the original, natural topography. Distracted by my battle with the headwind, I thus managed to miss not only the southern arm of the delta I had aimed for but even both of its farther arms. I fought my way north along commercial and recreational developments within the port region in vain, searching for the mouth of the river. When I eventually arrived at towering, concrete grain silos at the north end of the harbor, I realized that something was not right. I again invited help from my GPS unit and my iPhone. Again, I at first refused to believe what my electronic advisers revealed to me. It turned out that I had missed the mouth of the river by about five kilometres. Thunder Bay has a significantly extensive harbour. I had to turn back, but malicious Nature who had awakened to the realization of her missed opportunity to foil my long streaks to the mainland earlier, intended to make up for her hurt pride by changing the wind direction again, this time to a strong south-southeast one, or once more, straight against me. In this way, she hoped to sap the last drop of my energy. I paddled south right along the docks, fighting my way against the bucking waves and wind like a rodeo bull rider, metre by metre. I had been really lucky that I started from Pie Island very early because under the present conditions I would be forced to wait on the island, or else I would perish paddling to the mainland. When the mouth of a river finally appeared, which I took for the Kaministiquia's northernmost arm, I fought my way through shallows and against wind to the shelter of its channel. Here I stopped for a while to recover my strength and to phone Milena that all danger was behind me. I informed her that what remained to be done was merely to paddle 20 kilometres up the current of the river to Fort William. I announced that I would arrive there that evening and end my voyage. After that, I resignedly paddled up the river through the city with its commercial quarters, residential subdivisions and parks. After about two hours, the river was still not curving the way the map predicted and I again had a reason to suspect treason. My electronic advisers revealed that I had prematurely entered the mouth of a different river that led me into the centre of the city. This river was named the Neebing McIntyre Floodway, of which I had never heard. I swallowed the bitter pill and returned back down into the lake and the battle against the headwind and waves. When at last I gained the mouth of the northernmost arm of the Kaministiquia, it was already late afternoon. Besides that, I was totally drained of energy. Thus, although the surroundings looked very industrial, it was quite clear to me that I had to find a spot here somewhere for emergency camping. After several fruitless explorations, a spot indeed availed itself. It was a small piece of a wild meadow scented with sweet herb weeds, buzzing with honey-collecting insects. It was wedged between an industrial port and a thoroughfare that spanned the arm of the river on the high arch of a bridge. Crossing all around were pipelines and towers of high voltage lines but my camping routine was not significantly affected, provided that I ignored the constant industrial rumble and an over-abundance of various flashing strobes and other lights throughout the night that bestowed on the scene the atmosphere of science fiction.

Up the Kaministiquia River to Fort William

The river travel that started the next morning was hard work. As opposed to the movement on the flat water of the lake, I was paddling against the current. Yet here on a 50-metre wide river, wind did not play a big role. As the river constantly meandered, the problem expressed itself only over its short sections. The danger of big waves whipped up in size by the wind racing over enormous stretches of open water from sudden stormy changes in the weather no longer applied here. The day was really hot and I was sweating as I paddled along the industrial district first where the original, true Fort William used to be, and later by recreational cottages. At last, after some 20 kilometres, the final meander of the river appeared, beyond which, by the map, I expected Fort William. The river likely looked similar here as it might have during the times of the fur trade — a friendly flow, lined with dense greenery. The new section of the river bank on which the fort was expected to appear, rolled into view with every new paddle stroke. Finally, the green of the tree cover on the bank was pierced by a greyish/tan color of weathered wood structures. Above it, the colorful flags of Canada, the province of Ontario and that of the Northwest Company merrily flew in a stiff breeze, heralding the presence of Fort William. With a pounding heart and confident skill — honed by having paddled thousands of miles — I guided the canoe to the wooden pier of the fort's landing. Here I rubbed a gunwale with a 10-metre birch bark Montreal canoe. My toil was finally ending. I climbed onto the wooden platform of the pier, tied the canoe to it and pensively stood up looking around. I moved slowly. I did not need to strain my muscles any longer. At that moment, out of the fort's wooden gate, which was adorned with its own little tower, emerged a small electric truck driven by a park employee. It quickly passed along a palisade wall of fat, pointed, vertically-embedded posts. I waved at him to catch his attention and he immediately stopped. I needed to store my outfit somewhere until I returned for it with my vehicle from Marathon. I received a stern education that for the general public, landing with a private boat at the fort's pier was forbidden. Yet the hard, berating expression of the slender, blond man of Finnish origin, Henry Contio, quickly softened, when he heard my history of arriving at the fort. They had no facilities to offer the kind of services that I was asking for but he promised that he would check with his superior. We agreed that I would unload my canoe, organize my gear and Henry would return in an hour to load it up, provided he had been successful in persuading the person of authority. Henry indeed turned up within an hour with his bright green little truck and we transported everything, including the canoe, to a large warehouse behind the fort, which, by good coincidence, was in Henry's care. I promised that I would return to pick up my possessions tomorrow. What remained now was to find a way of getting myself to Marathon. I learned that the fort was serviced by a bus from the municipal public transport twice a day. The next bus was to arrive at 1:45 which still gave me enough time to buy an ice cold diet Pepsi in a park's vending machine. Ooh, what a heavenly nectar.

In spite of the serene peace in my soul and the slowly abating pain in my muscles, the adventure, as it later turned out, was far from over. The bus showed up at the stop exactly on time. I traveled with a minimum so as to avoid lugging a heavy pack. It was hot and I was wearing a light safari shirt with short sleeves and pants in the same style. I strapped a small fanny pack to my waist and carried a thin Gore-Tex windbreaker wrapped around one forearm. A camera and a small waterproof pouch with valuable electronics occupied my other hand. Why differently? I would only sit on buses and in Marathon, I would slip into my own vehicle right away. With just one transfer I reached the Greyhound bus depot in Thunder Bay and bought a ticket to Marathon. The next bus wasn't leaving until 9:00 p.m. I took a walk to a nearby shopping center that I recognized as the one that I had seen yesterday when I was paddling by it up the wrong river. Here I had a good meal and drink while waiting out the long afternoon. Watching the crowds of shoppers streaming by my table in the food court of the shopping center, I discovered a living connection to the historic past of the Great Lakes area in observing a significant percentage of Ojibwa characters and admiring the beauty of their women. A good while before 9:00, I patiently waited at the head of a queue of passengers to board the bus to secure a seat with a view in the first row. At the beginning, the bus ride still enjoyed enough daylight and this allowed me to get horrified again when eyeing the enormous stretches of open water around the Sleeping Giant Peninsula from the heights of the highway. The Giant was bathing now in the red reflections of the setting sun amid the mirroring waters. Soon, though, only the road lit by the bus headlights was visible.

Unreliable Paul

A majority of the passengers had already nodded off when I, as a lone passenger, disembarked at the bus stop in Marathon at 1:30 am. From the bus stop to the parking lot of the Royal Canadian Legion was a two-kilometre hike. The sleeping town was shrouded in a dark night chill coming from the icy lake and I thus walked as briskly as my legs would allow to warm up a bit at least in this way. The short sleeves of my shirt did not help and I thus couldn't wait for the moment when I would turn the corner of the Legion, unlock the car and start the engine. "I will crank up the heating to a maximum for the inside of the vehicle to warm up quickly!" I assured myself. "Only a few steps to the corner, peek, and I will see Milena's familiar silver Lancer." Yet, oops! I rounded the corner, saw the whole parking lot, and … no Lancer?! "Had somebody stolen it?" I was stumped. "What now? It is just after two a.m., everybody is sleeping. I can't even ask anybody." Then I noticed a faint light leaking out of the Legion. I grabbed the door handle and the door moved. I entered and saw two ladies wrapped up in counting of money that they had spread out over the table under a lamp. I will never forget the looks on their pale faces when they lifted their eyes and saw me. Blood just drained out from them. Only now did I realize what I looked like. Dirty, suntanned face, overgrown with a wild beard of whiskers, bloodshot swollen eyes, weather-beaten cowboy hat and a forearm pointing forward with a windbreaker wrapped around it. They were just about ready to raise their arms above their heads when I calmed them down with a soft voice in a friendly greeting. I quickly explained what I was looking for. "I had had a vehicle parked here and now it is gone. Would you know what has happened to it?" "Oh, aha, it had been here for some while," one of the women replied. "The club manager kept asking and searching to whom the vehicle with the Alberta license plate belonged. He had waited for a week and then had it towed away." It was obvious that dear Paul, who spent practically all his free time here, omitted to tell anybody about our agreement. When I mentioned his name, I learned that Paul was an "old senile coot." "And where might they have towed it to?" I asked. "Ooh, that, we don't know. One towing service is as far as Nipigon, 90 kilometres from here," they responded. Nobody could answer my question till morning when the key people would get up to leave for work. "What can I do? I have to wait the night out somewhere." It was already 2:30 a.m. and it made no sense to pay for an expensive motel for just a few hours. I learned that the only business in town that stayed open the whole night was Robin's Doughnuts. I dejectedly shuffled there, two kilometres back to the center of the community. Here I shivered from the cold until 4:00 in the morning. There was nobody in an overly air conditioned place besides a student employee filling the "graveyard shift" who would not dare changing the system's daytime setting and me who was desperately wrapping himself in a chilling Gore-Tex rain jacket and padded his ice cold iron chair seat and back rest with fliers and newspapers. I had learned that at 4:00, the motel's restaurant would open for breakfast. When I moved there full of hope, it was warm there. I ordered a breakfast to earn my right of a squatter in the corner of the cozy retreat. A motherly, congenial elderly lady, who was the sole person to open the early service, sympathised with my predicament. She informed me that the vehicle got most likely towed by the family business of a husband and wife who owned a car repair shop in the town. The local police allegedly had been using their services. Their daughter worked in the restaurant and was expected for a shift at 6:00 in the morning. The repair shop was situated in a back alley about two blocks from here. After breakfast, I set out into the darkness to have a look. I intended to verify if my vehicle might be there. I must admit that a mischievous thought flashed through my mind. Only I have the keys to the car. If I find it, what about quietly and simply eloping with it?

In the next few moments, however, I got educated about how grossly I had underestimated the vigilance of the local police force. The sheet metal Quonset of the garage was naturally locked up and surrounding it was a multitude of parked cars. I didn't see mine. It had to be in the locked garage. As I turned away disappointed from a garage window, out of the darkness, blue and red strobes started flashing against me. I was suddenly caught in the bright headlights of a police cruiser. A police officer emerged and with a flashlight shining straight into my eyes, blocked my way. His partner in the car probably rested his hand on the handle of a pistol in an unsnapped holster. He wanted to see my driver's license to identify me. They must have been sure that the unkempt homeless person hiding under a wide-brimmed hat and lurking in the dark shadows around a local business did not have benign intentions. I must have had the look of the proverbial "deer in the headlights." My voice stammered from being cold, from lack of sleep and also from my frantic effort to explain my way out of the embarrassing situation. Ahaah, slowly, but surely, the officer started grasping who I was. I represented a mystery to them. Allegedly, they found out that the mysterious vehicle parked for over a week at the Legion was registered to some poor female soul in Alberta (nobody else but Milena). Their detective investigations discovered that on its roof were imprints of the kind of foam blocks that are used for the transportation of canoes and kayaks. Somebody explained the unremoved vehicle with the theory that the poor woman, likely suicidal due to some unhappy love affair, launched a watercraft here and drowned. (A Mishipeshu notoriety in the local brains?) This was the last scandal that the manager of the Legion could afford. He called the police and by having them tow away the evidence, he rid himself of any responsibility and connection to the anticipated media circus.

Whether in a deep mess, or not, I at least had learned that my vehicle still existed and here in Marathon to boot rather than God knows where in Nipigon. What remained now was to wait till morning when the car repair shop opened. When I laid my sleepy head back on the table in the restaurant again, the daughter of the car shop owners was already there. I asked her if she knew what kind of a fine I would be slapped with. She replied that she had nothing to do with it but she knew that her parents were not cheap. She estimated the towing for some $75 and another $25 for every day of storage. I was devastated. Inside, I swore obscenely at the address of senile Paul. I learned what his phone number was and at 6:00 in the morning I called him at home. His wife answered and informed me that Paul was already at the Legion polishing the bar counter. My next phone call indeed caught him there. "Paul, you have to help me! You have to come to the repair shop at the opening time of nine and you have to testify that I had had a permit from you to park at the Legion!" "Yea, OK, I will be there!" Paul promised. At 9:00, I was waiting in front of the repair business for Paul to show up so that we would enter together. Yet he never showed up. On the other hand, the owners sure noticed me and they already knew who I was. It turned out that their daughter had already put in a good word for me. The husband, with a mischievous smile, sent me to pay in the office run by his wife. He tried to ease my evident trauma by saying that it would not be expensive. The wife smiled at me right from the door. "You know, you scared us all. We worried that somebody had drowned. But we are happy that everything ended up like this and, therefore, you don't have to pay anything. Take your vehicle for free. It is parked back over there." I could not believe that I had not seen it at night. It was right in front of my eyes. Nobody could understand how I could have made it all the way to Fort William in 15 days by paddling a canoe from Marathon. I thanked her very warmly and I assured her that she had restored my love and gratefulness to the citizens of the town. After that, without any further ado, I set out with my vehicle directly to Thunder Bay in spite of the fact that I had had practically no sleep for the whole night. The gesture from the owners of the repair shop seemed overly generous. Even the towing itself must have cost them at least an hour of labor with wear and tear on their machinery and the burning of fuel.

A similar generosity awaited me at Fort William. When I arrived there shortly after noon, with Henry's help, I started loading up my gear. I was just tying the canoe onto the roof of the Lancer when another electric cart arrived, the driver of which brought an important looking man. He introduced himself as the director of the historic park. Apparently, they had had a discussion about me. He congratulated me on the success of my solo voyaging from Montreal all the way to them and he informed me that I did not have to pay for the service of storing my possessions. The only condition attached was that I would buy a ticket and visit their restored fort. But this was exactly what I had planned to do anyway after I finished loading the car and parked it on the public parking lot. I even received a senior citizen discount on the admission.

My walk all throughout the fort and my stay of several hours left me with deep impressions. It was a hot, sunny afternoon, the air smelled of wood, hay, scents of a stable and of long-forgotten, old traditional agriculture. The authentically rebuilt structures omitted no details. This included all interior furnishing, dishes, tableware, utensils, bedding, tools and even personnel dressed in the style of the fur trade era and played by students in the form of a summer job. The place looked authentically lived in. When I struck up some friendly small talk with a young man dressed in a simple, balloon-sleeved shirt and old style woolen pants with a broad belt, he stuck to his role of a particular voyageur from some specific place in Quebec. He never strayed from it throughout our conversation. There was a main hall for the hierarchy of the company with tables set for a reception; there was a carpentry shop, black smith's shop and a shop where big birch bark canoes were being built in the present time. There were dormitories for the voyageurs as well as private residences for the full-fledged partners of the company with servants. There was a sick bay and a mortuary, even with a symbolic dead body of a just-deceased young voyageur covered with a sheet on a gurney. A handwritten note from a doctor tacked on a partially opened door assured that the malady of which the voyageur died was not contagious. An in-style dressed young lass came to sit on a rustic bench in the middle of the grassy plaza that smelled of hay and summer herbs. She then played a sweet Celtic melody on a primitive fiddle. With an occasional bark of a dog it still sounds in my heart and it will be forever associated with my memories of Fort William. After finishing my voluntary galley slavery and having overcome all the perilous situations that my voyage had laid out for me, I savored the fort's sweet atmosphere to the hilt in lazy reminiscing. Only after surviving such situations can one fully savor the infinite lightness and careless abandon of a normal life in the safety of civilization. At least for a few weeks before the old familiar stress returns.

After my return to Edmonton, I found a note taped to our mailbox. It asked me to contact a constable Harris of the RCMP. It turned out that the investigation of the case of the suspected drowning spilled over from Marathon all the way to Edmonton. Fellow employees of Milena were contacted at work to see if they knew where she was. Her momentary absence, thanks to her visit in the Czech Republic, did not help to diminish the suspicion. Even my neighbor across the street, Polak Andrzey, stopped me when I was mowing the lawn and informed me that the police had been asking about me. "What had really happened?" The closing of the case was fast. All were happy that no tragedy had taken place. Yet I still remain really awestruck to this day in discovering what concern the Canadian establishment maintains over my wellbeing. I bet that as a result, the Canadian unemployment figures must include more than one guardian angel. And all of this is the fault of that darned Paul!

CHAPTER IV

From Thunder Bay/Fort William along the northwest coast of Lake Superior to Grand Portage, USA, carrying all of the gear up the Grand Portage trail to the Pigeon River and following it upstream to Waterfowl Lake (June 4 – 22, 2013)

Historic Fort William with its log buildings and a palisade wall of winds, snows and rains of time-weathered grayish wood; rust-adorned iron of robust hardware; oiled leather of hinges, belts and harnesses; wicker work and basketry of willow twigs; handles, shanks and shafts of ash wood — stained with sweat and polished by callous hands; canvas of rough tarps, fine linen of bedsheets and embroidered tablecloths; stocks of oak kegs soaked with "high wine"; straw-stuffed mattresses; rolls of birch bark and thin cedar ribs for making canoes, a mixture of bear grease, spruce resin and charcoal powder to seal their watap-sewn seams; — the old classical materials — harmless to one's health, close to one's heart. All of this together with the scents of hay and horse manure under the blue sky of a hot summer day harmoniously converged into a sweet, nostalgic symphony of forgotten and newly rediscovered smells of childhood safety — the carelessness of my long ago youth. Set in nature's greenery on the bank of silently rushing, historic time-measuring cool waters of the Kaministiquia River, the realm of the fort was meant to be my final destination. It was to be the culmination of my ambition to repeat the old-fashioned way of travel along the water route of the fur trade canoes.

Not for long, however. I have always known that neither the bold ventures of the valiant French-Canadian explorers into the interior of this beautiful, wild, vast and varied country, nor the water arteries used to transport fur and trading goods ended at the northwest shores of Lake Superior. Fort William only represented the westernmost limit of the range of the large two-ton "Montreal Canoes" made of birch bark, each propelled by 10 to 12 paddling voyageurs. The latter used to be called "mangeurs du lard," or "pork eaters" in Northwest Company slang because their basic nutrition consisted of pork belly fat overcooked to mash in a kettle of beans or corn with wheat thickening. The most important purpose of this fort, however, was to serve as the company's forward base for the brigades of smaller, predominantly one-ton canoes of teams trading in the distant interior of the continent. These members of the Northwest Company did not return to Montreal for the winter. To the contrary, they overwintered in its far trade outposts. They were called "hommes du nord," "northern men," "hivernants," or "winterers." Their leaders were "wintering partners." As their water voyages were crossing or at least skirting the Canadian Prairies where huge herds of buffalo still roamed, the prairie Indigenous tribes supplied them with pemmican for their staple nutrition. This consisted of dried bison meat pounded to almost powder mixed with dried, wild berries like blueberries, Saskatoon berries or cranberries. The mixture was soaked with hot tallow poured over it into long narrow moose or deer hide stocking-like pouches. Once solidified, these were then typically portioned with an axe.

The boundary chain canoe highway

The territory to the north and the west from the end of Lake Superior is physically separated by a geographical step that rises steeply from the shores of the Superior to a higher elevated plateau. The height of land reaches its highest altitude some hundred kilometres west of the lake. From here further west, all the water flows into Hudson's Bay. The divide between the watersheds of Hudson's Bay and the Saint Lawrence River that flows into the Atlantic Ocean separates the rest of the country situated to the west and northwest of it. This land was called "pays d'en haut." The First Nation People, since time immemorial and the fur trade before some three to three-and-a-half centuries, connected a water route here through the thousands of lakes and rivers that pock mark a granite plateau. It winds westward to Lake of the Woods. Later on, this water route of trade and communication with the interior of the continent would define today's boundary between Canada and the United States. The river, which represents the easternmost link of the route, is called the Pigeon River. It still flows into Lake Superior but its final slope into the lake is too steep to be navigable. It descends in a series of cascades and waterfalls. The voyageurs and the First Nations People who showed it to them, thus bypassed this lower section of the Pigeon River by carrying their gear on a more than 14 kilometre-long, rough, climbing trail through the woods that is called "The Grand Portage." The Northwest Company built a big fort, called "Grand Portage" at its lower end on the shore of Lake Superior in a bay of the same name. At the upper end of the portage trail where it reached the bank of the Pigeon River, the company built another fort that they called "Fort Charlotte." When the boundary between the two countries had been established in this territory along the chain of lakes and rivers that connected the water highway to the west (and after decades of wrangling), it was officially charted in 1822 by a joint Canada – USA commission. For mysterious reasons, this charting omitted that the trade route detoured the bottom section of the Pigeon River over dry land. They defined this river as the boundary in its entire length to Lake Superior. The unambiguous determination of the boundary by a line as clear as a river would have made sense for the future. But during the era of the fur trade, the trail of Grand Portage, which lies to the south of the Pigeon River and had been critically important for trade traffic, ended up being fully in the territory of the United States. It might have been a technical omission as the spirit of establishing the boundary was for both countries to have access to the route. Yet the fierce economic and territorial competition that raged between the two countries at the time soon resulted in the U.S. bureaucratic abuse of this unfortunate advantage. The Americans demanded duty and other concessions from the Northwest Company for using their territory. As a result, this and other smaller Canadian companies were sufficiently disgusted after a while to find for themselves a new approach to the boundary water chain above and beyond the Pigeon. This went from Lake Superior on its Canadian side up the current of the river Kaministiquia and connected to the boundary chain on Lac La Croix. The Northwest Company abandoned its Grand Portage and Charlotte forts in 1808 and established a new base at Fort William. The new approach was longer and more complicated but it was situated fully on Canadian soil. This route nowadays, however, is interrupted with modern projects and it would be quite impractical if not outright impossible, to try connecting it again. Hence, for a nostalgic dreamer like myself, no other option remains today but the old classical bath in one's own sweat that is the Grand Portage. For a Canadian, this obviously requires crossing the border from Canada into the U.S. and associated with that, the necessary permits that require fees even today.

And now back to the topic. The successful achievement of my ambitious goal in paddle-pushing my Kevlar canoe (Evergreen Bob Special) of an unusual "mango" color along the rivers and lakes to the wooden pier of Fort William, tasted truly sweet for a while. My boat still proudly displayed the decals of the Canadian and the Czech flags on the cheeks of the stern and while being a bit banged up by now and fairly scratched on its bottom, it was also intimately familiar and loved like my faithful girlfriend. Yet, already in the Fort, a shadow of disappointment crept into the joy of my victory. "Does this spell the end to my professing of love to the spiky, wind-contorted pines waving at me from the rugged, granite crags above my passing canoe? What will replace the smell of resin in my nostrils that the heat of the summer day had evaporated? Will I only reminisce about the fragrant smoke from a cedar gum–saturated twig that shot little flames on a bed of still-glowing embers in a dying campfire? For whom will its gentle scent trail weave through the freshness of the cool night air? Will I ever again see so shockingly defined the Milky Way that stands out three-dimensionally in the black, infinite depth of a diamond-studded night sky? Will my summer-sun-heated bare skin never again be refreshed by a sprinkle from the icy little wave that my paddle caught on reaching forward for another stroke? Will my tired back never lay itself down to sleep on hard, flat granite that acts as the best of chiropractors for me? Who will worship the red sunset and express gratitude to it for the successful achievement of the day? These kinds of thoughts streamed through my mind with sad nostalgia like the summer clouds floating on the blue sky over lakes and forests.

It was a typical early evening at Christmas. I stood up the cross-country skis against the wall, stomped off the powder snow from my ski boots and entered from the sparkling frost of the wild lake country with towering snowy peaks and snow-burdened, coniferous giants above Lake Kootenay in British Columbia into the comforting warmth of our log home. The radiant heat waves from the red logs glowing behind the glass of the hot stove doors awakened the resin aroma in the Ponderosa pine walls and brought a moment when I ever more strongly started feeling that old familiar salmon instinct. You can call it "Call of the wild"; the itching of hands for the grip on a paddle; the yearn of boot soles for the rocks of the portage trail; of the shoulders for the straps of a heavy pack; of the face for the cooling droplets of a wind-driven drizzle; the longing of the ears for an echo of a wolf howl among the distant hills. It cannot be uniquely described, even if it all, I already well know. That was the time when I started to be overcome again with that old restlessness. When during the sunshiny days of spring at home in Edmonton, the "V"s of Canada geese started appearing on the blue sky and out of the heights the passing waves of migrating cranes sounded the ratcheting "gru-grus" in their push north, I had not an iota of strength left in me to resist. My plan of escape to the lake expanses and the rivers of the route of the voyageurs was again evolving at full tilt.

As I had found in my research of sources, I wasn't the only "weakling," who fell for the magic of life on the water — paddling a canoe and stumbling on foot under a heavy burden over rocks or through mud on the portage trail. Although their toil was much rougher than mine, even the voyageurs loved their life's deal. The following is a quote of what an unnamed voyageur in his 70s had said to a certain politician:

*I could carry, paddle, walk and sing with any man I ever saw.
I have been twenty-four years a canoe man, and forty-one years in
service; no portage was ever too long for me, fifty songs could I sing.
I have saved the lives of ten voyageurs, have had twelve wives and
six running dogs. I spent all of my money in pleasure. Were I young
again, I would spend my life the same way over. There is no life as
happy as a voyageur's life!*

The freedom of my logistical decisions for the details of the
expedition was somewhat limited this time because on July 27, my
youngest daughter, Olivia, was going to be married and I had to be
back for that. I anticipated that the movement along the boundary
route from Lake Superior toward Lake of the Woods, which called
for crossing into the U.S. by canoe on the lake and involved tackling
the Grand Portage, would be difficult. I therefore decided to start my
expedition early again. Shortly after dropping off my wife, Milena, at
the Edmonton International Airport in early June for her traditional
visit to family in the Czech Republic, I set out from Edmonton too.
Again I left in her economical Mitsubishi Lancer with a canoe on
its roof. This time I tried to conscientiously minimize the weight
of the travel outfit in view of the dreadful Grand Portage followed
by 40 more. Yet my stomach still wrung with worries when, after a
test packing of the equipment at home, I found that I would have to
move everything, which included the canoe on my shoulders, in three
carries for each portage. Especially my drybag containing food for
three weeks that was so stuffed that it was hardly possible to close it
by rolling and snapping its upper edge. It seemed to weigh a ton. In
fact, I had two, but I hoped to store one of them somewhere halfway
in Fort Frances for a later pickup. With two return trips between the
carries, the distance walked on each portage was to be the length of
the portage multiplied by five. It was a disquieting outlook. My future
son-in-law, Roland, who at one time worked in Fort Frances — a
town that grew out of the strategic fort of the Northwest Company on
the water route — had friends in town. He knew of my need to find
somebody who could temporarily store my second bag of food. Very

willingly, he arranged a meeting with the kind family of his friends who lived near the river in the town. They were willing to fulfill my need. They owned a second house in Thunder Bay where one of their sons went to university. When I eventually popped up in the record time of mere two days in Fort Frances, they even offered that their son could take me in my vehicle to the lake and subsequently store my car. It sounded ideal. No need for iffy arrangements with potentially unreliable unknown characters like poor old Paul in Marathon. They all warned me that the ice on Lake Superior went out only recently and that the lake would still be very cold.

A chilly Start

On the June 4, early in the morning, I picked up the student, Aaron, from their second home in Thunder Bay. We headed for the picnic site on the shore of Superior near the mouth of the southernmost arm of the Kaministiquia delta. After we untied the canoe from the roof of the Lancer and unloaded my expedition cargo on the lawn at the shore, Aaron left with my vehicle. I spent another hour in carefully sorting my outfit, loading the canoe and lacing on the spray cover. Sometime between 10:00 and 11:00, I at last pushed off, dressed in a hat that was pushed on up to my ears, long thermal underwear under nylon overpants, a fleecy and woolly socks that I wore in hiking boots. It felt really cold, especially so on the open water where there was stronger air circulation. The air was cool from the icy water of the lake and whenever a breeze stirred up, I shivered in the canoe. It forced me to paddle briskly to keep warmer. It was something that, after my last experience with the heat wave around Thunder Bay during the previous summer, I did not expect. When I left Edmonton this time, in spite of its notoriety for its late onsets of spring, everything there was already fully green. By contrast, around the Superior and on its islands, thanks to its enormous mass of icy water, spring was just awakening with buds barely open. Not for nothing, the lake is sometimes called "the liquid glacier," which it really had been until a relatively recent geological period. I was facing three days of paddling on the lake from the metropolis of Thunder Bay to Fort Grand Portage. On the third day, I was to cross the border from Canada into the USA on the water. It required the necessary permit for the back country border crossing. This I obtained in Fort Frances where there is an official border crossing. On the lake then, it was sufficient to merely call a given phone number from a cell phone while crossing the imaginary border line and give the serial number of the permit. Hard paddling was needed to keep the boat stable in the waves. I knew well that an upset of the canoe would leave no chance for survival. One paddles from one point of the shoreline to another up to five kilometres distant. In between there are the deep bays of a rocky shoreline. Often the wind would change its strength just when I was finding myself in the middle between the points and I then paddled with clenched teeth and a tight rear to reach the point of the shore or the lee of an island up ahead as soon as possible. In the evenings, I crawled into the sleeping bag in the tent somewhere on a deserted gravel bench of the shore or on an island before 6:00. This was due to my tiredness as well as to the cold that still ruled outside. Although one is constantly aware of the risk of overturning, the fact that he doesn't know of anybody who would have really perished, makes him somewhat lax and complacent. He then risks more than what might be reasonable. The weather during the voyage on the lake was not bad. Occasionally, it would sprinkle a little but it was mostly cloudy with sun-lit splotches between my boat and the lake horizon. When the sun showed up during the day, its direct rays were warming. But mostly, they also warmed up the land that caused the rising of warmer air above it. To replace it then, the colder air moved over the lake surface and this caused a breeze, sometimes even wind. The air predominantly streamed from the middle of the fresh water sea to shore, hence from my left. Besides the cold, with the wind also came waves and if that happened far from a point of the coastline, a stressful race was on. The only good side to such a situation was that it would warm me up a bit.

During all the cycles of my daily routine and the course of my lonely travels, I had plenty of time for musing. I tried to see the environment in which I found myself through the eyes of its original people, the Ojibway First Nation. It was not difficult because I saw practically no motorboats yet and the craggy shores revealed very scarce signs of human habitation. After repeated returns into the land of the Great Lakes, I gradually got to know more and more of the history of the Indigenous culture. My admiration for their life's philosophy — reflecting closeness to nature and their tight bond with it — never stopped growing. I have discovered that their orally relayed legends, which are a part of the Native folklore, strongly resonate with the emotional strings in my soul. I do not want to project my character as an overly emotional weakling which I am not. Yet I must admit that during the lonely moments on the water waves under the canopy of the vast open sky or under the stars at the dying embers of a little campfire, their recall in my mind was capable of pushing salty upwellings into my eyes. Two of them I must share with you.

Qu'Appelle

I do not remember when, after my arrival into Canada, I first overheard the name of the prairies-crossing river by the unusual name of Qu'Appelle. I know that this name is woven through Canadian history of the explorations westward and of the fur trade. When evening courses improved my knowledge of the French language, I recognized that the name meant "Who Calls?" What kind of a name is this for a river? I could not understand. During one of my long drives with a canoe on the roof of the car from Edmonton eastward to the Great Lakes about two years ago, I at last learned in Saskatchewan the origin of the odd name. It comes from the legend of the populous Indigenous prairie nation of the Cree. In their language it sounds like: "Kah-tep-was" (The River that calls).

The legend talks about a young brave who was returning in a hurry from a hunting mission in a canoe up the current of the river one day to arrive on time to his village on the prairie. Trembling with excitement, he was looking forward to his wedding with a beautiful girl that he loved with his full heart. As he vehemently paddled under the searing sun of a hot summer day through the valley of the river, somewhat recessed into the surrounding flat landscape, it seemed to him suddenly that he heard a girl's voice desperately calling his name. He stopped paddling, wiped the sweat off his forehead and pricked his ears. "Who is calling?" he shouted back. But only the echo of his voice came back from the slopes of the valley "Who calls...calls...alls". It disturbed him a little bit but then he reminded himself of the joy that awaited him at the end of his journey. He renewed his work with the paddle even more enthusiastically so that he would arrive home the next day.

Alas, heart-wrenching tragic news awaited him at home. He learned that his bride had fallen seriously ill in his absence and died the day before his return. With her last dying breath, she desperately called his name.

Even if only a legend, this story is based on an unusual phenomenon reported by a Metis trader, Daniel Harmon. According to him, the First Nations people of this region, whenever they heard (or thought that they heard) a voice, they answered: "Kâ-têpwêt?", "Who calls?" or "Qui appelle?" in Cree, English and French.

With this knowledge, this river can, from now on, never be a mere current of water that quietly flows past silvery waves of breeze-caressed willow foliage, the shaking leaves of trembling aspen and autumn-reddened foliage on wild prairie rose bushes. Hence forward, this river, at least for me, has a soul.

Another river got poetically personified in my imagination as a beautiful young woman with raven black hair. It was the river Kaministiquia. After the interior base of the Northwest Company transferred onto its bank in Fort William, the Kaministiquia would become an important artery of trade. The canoes of the northern teams used to return up its current from here to the boundary chain of rivers and lakes and then further beyond into the pays d'en haut. About the second day after leaving the fort, the canoes ran into the first major obstacle in the form of a high waterfall — Kakabeka Falls. Its circumventing demanded a challenging portage. The Trans-Canada Highway going east cuts across the Kaministiquia River about an hour before arriving in Thunder Bay. It winds not too far from the river and just about half a kilometre after it crosses its bridge, it has a small parking area on its right with a view of the falls. A stop here is well worth it. After another half a kilometre comes a small settlement — just two rows of low buildings on each side of the road, including a gas station, several fast food outlets, a motel, a church, and a fire hall — Kakabeka Falls. I have come to like a small cabin-like restaurant here where I have stopped a couple of times to order a grilled ham and cheese sandwich. On the placemat, laminated in plastic, I always read anew the following Ojibwa legend:

Maiden of the Mist (Kakabeka Falls)

Few visitors leave Thunder Bay without viewing the beautiful Kakabeka Falls. This remarkable work of nature is truly something to marvel at but the story of the heroism of a lovely Native Princess is still more enchanting than the rushing, swirling water and the crystal studded mist rising endlessly from the great gorge.

Chieftain White Bear, the peace-loving grand old leader of the Ojibway tribe was interested

rainbowcountry.com

145

only in the welfare of his people. One day Chief White Bear was greatly vexed to learn that large numbers of the fierce warlike Sioux were approaching his tribe's encampment at the mouth of the Kaministiquia River, bent upon the destruction of his tribe.

Being too old to go to battle himself and not knowing how to ward off the enemy, the old Chief was greatly distressed. Seeing her father's dilemma, Princess Green Mantle devised a plan. ...

Bidding her father farewell she hurriedly left the camp and paddled swiftly up the Kaministiquia River. Many times before she had gone for long canoe rides with her brother and she well knew of the Great White Falls. Leaving her canoe at the foot of the falls, she ran swiftly along the bank until she reached a point well above the waterfall.

She soon came within sight of the Sioux Camp. Boldly the young maiden walked into the camp of her bitterest enemies. At once they pounced upon her and captured her. Pretending to have lost her way, she led them to believe she was very frightened. Green Mantle was taken before the Sioux Chieftains and they decided to put her to death. Bargaining with them she followed through with her plan and told them that if they would spare her life she would lead them to her father's camp. The Sioux Chiefs were elated, thinking that they had indeed been blessed by the Gods.

The following morning the young Princess was placed in the lead canoe and the great band, in their war canoes followed, tied as Green Mantle suggested, one behind the other so that they would not get lost. However, she did not tell them about the falls and as they swiftly turned the bend of the river, they plunged headlong into the great gorge, killing all.

Princess Green Mantle of course lost her life also but all of her tribe were saved from the torturous hands of the most dreaded of all Native tribesmen.

The Great Manitou looked kindly upon the brave little Native maiden, and if one takes the trouble to walk down the viewing pods, the figure of Green Mantle can be observed in the mist, standing as a monument to the memory of the Princess who gave her life for her people.

The Grand Portage

On the third day of my paddle voyage on the Superior, I at last neared the long narrow spine of rocky land covered with forest trees — Pigeon Peninsula. Its point jutted far out into the lake from the mouth of its namesake river. The river defined the U.S. border and this continued an imaginary line out from Pigeon Bay further onto the lake. I stopped paddling some distance before the peninsula as this was already inside the territory of the United States. I was situated far out of the inside of the bay on open water on a straight line connecting the points of its edges. I extracted my passport and the Back Country Border-Crossing Permit from the waterproof map case and got my iPhone out of the small drybag with electronics. I spread everything cautiously between my knees in the wind shelter of the canoe spray cover and readied myself for a call from my cell phone. I knew that the official border crossing was situated on the road there somewhere in the farthest inner reach of the bay. When I was buying the permit, I was told that all that was required was to call the telephone number given on the permit and report the crossing of the border in addition to the permit's serial number. I visualized that I was talking to somebody who might be watching me with binoculars from the border customs building. Instead a woman's voice answered who didn't even know that the Grand Portage border crossing point existed. She talked about the town of Grand Marais that lies further into the States along the shore that I didn't know about at the time. Everything was unfolding very broadly and lengthily. As a thorough bureaucrat, the officer asked for a lot of information. For example, she wanted to know the serial number of the manufacture of my canoe that was contained on a brass tag riveted to the outside of the bow of the canoe under the gunwale. To read it for her, I would have had to take an icy swim to it. She would not let me give her the serial number of the permit, during which time the side wind and waves carried me hundreds of metres into the interior of the bay. Besides that, I was getting rapidly chilled from the long pause in my physical activity. Only after I warned her that my iPhone was about to run out of battery power with every passing minute, the officer finally accepted the permit number and we terminated the conversation. With the clear conscience of a disciplined citizen, I then continued across the border to the tip of the peninsula.

The name "Pigeon" of the boundary river and of the narrow peninsula is obviously derived from the by now extinct Passenger Pigeon, of whom huge — sky-obscuring — flocks welcomed the early European settlers to the New World. They became easy prey for the shooting weapons of the White Man and, similarly to the plains bison, the newcomers exterminated them all, both for food, and also merely for sport — as target practice. I passed the sandy point of the peninsula with its rugged rocks, paddling in close proximity to it. Just past it, I changed my course a bit more to the right — the southwest. I roughly paralleled the coast of the peninsula and later, I passed between it and a group of islands extended in the direction of my new heading. The previously port side wind thus became an almost rear one for a while. My original decision for the day was to arrive as near as possible to Grand Portage Bay and set up a campsite on some suitable island. In this way, I hoped to gain as much time as possible for the start of the Grand Portage trek the next day. The sky was overcast now save for an occasional cone of sun rays that pierced the grey canopy and gilded a brilliant patch on the chopped up lake surface. The wind kept steadily strengthening during the course of the day. If I wanted to stop paddling for a rest with a snack in the boat, I had to seek some labyrinth of a narrow bay sheltered from wind in the shape of the closest island. Otherwise, the wind would blow me far off the set course. Besides that, without paddling on the open water, the wind would also chill me to the bone. I was not finding any suitable camping on the islands that I had passed until I spotted the peninsula of Hat Point in the distance ahead of me. It is a peninsula of a circular domed shape that is connected to the mainland by a narrow isthmus. The spiky, domed forest cover indeed bestows on it the look of a fur hat with the connecting narrow bar representing a fur tail in the back. I was aware that this was to be the last protrusion of the coast past which, after its rounding, Grand Portage Bay was to open. The voyageurs would stop here before rounding it to wash themselves, shave and change into clean shirts. Only in their best, with red sashes around their waists and red caps or red bandanas on their heads, would they emerge into view from Fort Grand Portage paddling at full steam into the bay to the voices of heroic singing.

I was driven by a tailwind, surfing with growing and intimidating waves. But I still decided that I would reach the fort today. I couldn't wait for the moment when I would round the point and enter the shelter of the bay. The waves immediately past the tip of the peninsula formed tricky eddies but they did not fool me. Avoiding them with the finesse of a true pro, I, like the voyageurs, set the pace of a long distance racer. In the elegant style of long, mighty paddle strokes, I aimed diagonally across the bay to an inconspicuous gray spot on the distant shore where I sensed the ancient fort was located. I hoped that my performance would be admired by the Native people of the Chippewa tribe along whose village in the bay I paddled. It was already 4:00 in the afternoon. I left behind me a long, cold and stressful journey. I couldn't wait for the moment when, after mooring the canoe at the pier of the fort and erecting my tent on the grass next to it, I would crawl into my winter sleeping bag right at 5:00 to have a long rest for tomorrow's Grand Portage.

Yet as it often happens, my dream dissolved into sarcastic disenchantment. As it turned out, the newly rebuilt fort is a museum today — an attraction for tourists. As I found out, it is run by personnel consisting of seniors dressed in the period garb of the fur trade era. The men in velour knickers, white knee-high socks and buckle shoes, coats with tails and two rows of brass buttons, lacy collars and high hats of beaver felt on their heads; the women in full-length dresses buttoned with lacy frills up to their chins, wearing lacy bonnets. These people take their role deathly seriously. Intoxicated with their newly acquired importance, they abuse their pseudo powers here to the hilt. "What? To pitch a tent on the meadow where the voyageurs used to camp? You must be kidding! This is a museum! You have to go camping in a public campsite that is five miles by the road from here!" I was similarly verbally nuked when I mentioned my plan to use the Grand Portage trail for the same purpose that it originally served, i.e., to carry my outfit, including the canoe, up to the Pigeon River and continue along the fur trade route. "You must be joking! Have you lost your mind? And where is your permit? The trail is a National Monument. You cannot camp on it or make a fire!" I was supposed to go to process the permit somewhere at the office of the park headquarters, but in spite of my state of exhaustion and the late time of the day, I decided that I would rather start the portage right away. I will pack everything and disappear as high as possible along the trail into the forest, I thought. There I will camp in hiding. The disembarking of the canoe load, organizing it into three loads for the back and disappearing with two returns for two more loads, is not exactly a quick affair, though. Someone from the masquerading seniors must have ratted on me. Even before I started carrying my gear through the gate of the fort and up to the trail, two uniformed lady wardens representing the National Monument of The Grand Portage appeared. They had heard that I was getting ready to start up the trail and they came to process me by the rules. After my previous experience from the encounter with the senior citizens, I had expected that the wardens would lay before me a spike belt of bureaucratic obstacles and, in the best case, they would require fat fees. However, I found the warden lady who brought a writing clipboard with forms, intelligent and sports-oriented. She sympathized with me and knew that with a realistic cargo, which would require three carries with two returns in between, I could not accomplish the portage in one day. She knew that I would have to camp on the trail. She knew that the 14.5-kilometre length of the trail would thus multiply five times to a total of 72.5 kilometres. She did not express it explicitly because she was not allowed to but she indicated to me where it was suitable to camp. She also suggested where it was possible to filter drinking water from the crossed creeks and from a beaver pond. She hinted that the first evening I would have to carry everything at least two kilometres up the trail and above the Native village to avoid ending up in it for the night. At the upper end of the portage where there used to be a fort (Fort Charlotte) and where there is a campsite now of the same name, one is required to have a permit for camping. I thanked her but told her that I would pass because I would set up my campsite across the river on the Canadian side where camping was free, wherever it was suitable. I knew that now, at the beginning of June, there would be no one up there anyway, and I could easily put up my tent in the campsite. Yet once I was on my way, I discovered that the warden lady had issued me the camping permit anyway for free and attached its tag to my backpack with a wire twist tie.

It cannot be difficult to imagine how exhausted I was after almost 30 kilometres of paddling on the lake, reorganizing and repacking my load at the wooden pier of the fort and carrying all of it in three goes with two returns to over two kilometres above the shore. It was almost dark when I finally put up the tent about 50 metres away from the path in the forest, hidden from it by the large root plate of an uprooted, fallen spruce tree. I left my canoe on the trail some 500 metres farther so it would not betray my camping spot. Unfolding my achy skeleton in the sleeping bag on the uneven yet soft, bare soil exposed by the lifted roots of the fallen tree under the tent felt truly heavenly.

The next day, I started out early so that possible tourists would not catch me clearing my campsite. I always marched first with the load of my waterproof backpack with frame because its fit on my back was the best and it carried the most comfortably. Hence, with it I was able to perform a reconnaissance of the trail. The bright sun shone right from the early morning and I thus set out wearing shorts and hiking boots with Gore-Tex gaiters to protect my shins from the raspy undergrowth. I passed the canoe and continued about two kilometres farther along the path. Here I put down the backpack and turned back. Going back was easy and the return thus served as a rest for my shoulders and the muscles of my chest. The second burden for my back was much worse. It consisted of the light, aluminum structure of a hunting pack frame on the bottom shelf of which I strapped crosswise the super-heavy vinyl drybag with food. On top of that, I attached my second drybag with a kitchen set and similar type of outfit that I summarily called "the hardware." I had a well-rehearsed routine for lifting similar heavy loads into a standing position. I streamlined and tested it during our Canol Heritage Trail trekking in the Northwest Territories. I would stand the pack somewhere on a higher bump of ground, sitting on the ground below it with my back to it and passing my arms through its shoulder straps. Then I would roll sideways onto my knees and hands with the pack on my back, grasping desperately for whatever was around such as roots, bunches of grass, branches of bushes, etc. to help me accomplish this phase. Then I would straighten up on my knees and, pulling myself up with outstretched arms using some tree trunk or at least a vertical paddle, I would stand up. The straps of the heavy load would cut into my shoulders. I took some weight off them by jerking the pack up and simultaneously tightening the waist belt of the pack with lightning speed so that as much of the load as possible would end up resting on my pelvis. With every load on my back, I also carried fanny packs around my waist that were turned forward onto my stomach. In those I also carried a two-litre bottle of drinking fluid, for example, and a filter pump for its replenishing wherever there was access to water on the march. As a result, my waist was tightly constricted. In addition to the shoulder and waist-attached loads, I also carried objects in my hands like a small drybag with electronics, the camera, a plastic bag with more bottles of drinking water and one paddle each time that I used as a cane. On the second day, as I bent over to pick up stuff to be carried in my hands, the waist strapping cracked the lowest ribs on my front, right side. A day later, the same thing happened on my left side. I couldn't sleep on either side but I could otherwise continue. I did not consider this injury to be a show stopper. From then on, I prepositioned the items to be carried by hand onto some higher level platform like a log or a rock so that I would not have to bend down to pick them up. I performed the last carry with the canoe on my shoulders. If the going was satisfactory, I passed the previously dropped packs and continued for another kilometre or two farther. Hence I gradually moved all the outfit farther and farther along the trail that kept gently climbing through the mixed aromatic forest over rocks and through mud. I kept stumbling over exposed tree roots that stood up from the surface of the path that had been beaten deeper by ages of foot impacts. I often steeply descended to a primitive footbridge to cross a creek and then scrambled steeply up from its course that was deeply incised into the terrain. The more I climbed and got farther from the chilling influence of Lake Superior, the more the temperature rose. Soon sweat streamed down my face. The vegetation here thrived like in a jungle. With it came the true summer atmosphere. Alas, what now also thrived were the insects and hence, my hands passed objects from one to another every few moments so that my freed hand could swat a mosquito or a deer fly. From all this slavery I felt no hunger, just constant thirst. On the last day before leaving Thunder Bay, I bought myself a square loaf of soft, sliced bread and a package of cheese slices. Those I alternated with the slices of bread and forced myself to eat them like a simple sandwich. But I did not feel its taste at all. I just mechanically crushed and chewed the bites. It had the advantage that, in combination with some protein bar, I eliminated the need to make a fire in the evening to cook some supper. Towards the evening when I started precariously descending down to a larger creek, a more substantial wooden footbridge came into view with the sign "Poplar Creek." Bubbling up from my subconscious, a memory floated up that this name had been mentioned by the warden lady as a suitable place for camping and for filtering fresh water from the creek. I indeed found here a nice spot for the tent right next to the creek. I placed it carefully so that I would not crush the surrounding wild flowers. As I was undressing, I noticed tiny insects slowly crawling over my legs that reminded me of miniature crabs by their shape. After some seconds, I realized that I was dealing with ticks. They seemed a tad bigger than those that I remembered seeing in my childhood back in Czechoslovakia. I immediately and thoroughly inspected my whole body and carefully plucked off each tick that I found — it was easy — and destroyed it which was rather difficult. From the next day on, I wore long, nylon pants while walking. Even then, I picked some eight ticks off my legs every evening. Only much later would I learn that these were so called "Wood Ticks," unlike "Deer Ticks" that I had encountered in the past. Wood ticks are relatively harmless in regard to carrying Lyme disease, Boreliosis and other dangerous infections.

As I had expected, at the beginning of the season, the trail was empty. My movement along it was quite solitary. In several places, a big, healthy tree with a widely branched crown lay across the path that required me to thrash through thick bushes around it with my load. On the return trip for the canoe, I then broke branches from it to a degree where I would be able to pass through the tree with the canoe on my shoulders. In about three-fifths of the portage length, I came to a vast beaver pond. The trail led here onto an elevated walkway on stilts with a railing that sat on the whole length of a 250-metre beaver dam. However, when I came to the walkway, the platform was interrupted in its middle where the water of the pond spilled out over the dam. Apparently, the walkway section was swept out by the ice of the spring breakup. This necessitated precarious climbing over the railing and descending from the walkway height onto the beaver dam. Then I had to jump across the gap in the dam over the boisterous tongue of the water spill among jutting sticks of the beaver project and climb back over the railing onto the boardwalk. Especially with the canoe on my shoulders, all these operations turned into challenging acrobatics. The time to camp on the third evening on the portage caught me in a drizzling dusk in an eerie landscape where the trail was surrounded by a wet thicket with large, angular boulders. I was at about two-thirds of the total way. I pitched my tent directly on the trail and immediately crawled into it for a regenerating sleep. I needed liberation from my slave drudgery very badly. Falling asleep, I declared a silent oath that, if somebody tried to force me to repeat the Grand Portage, I would rather send a bullet through my brain.

My challenging experiences allowed me to intimately understand the philosophy of the operations of the Canadian fur trade and profoundly appreciate the bravery of the simple yet tough men who realized its success. The logo of the Hudson's Bay Company often returns to my mind, which, by the way, was founded in 1670 with the help of Prince Rupert, the son of the last Czech king, Fridrich of Falz. As a one-year-old infant, Rupert (Ruprecht) was almost forgotten at the Prague Castle in the confusion of his parents' escape following their defeat in the battle of White Mountain. He later earned his fame at the British court of King Charles II who was his cousin. The adult

Rupert was a very handsome and brave adventurer who accomplished many naval warfare successes for the British Crown. He was installed as the first governor of the Hudson's Bay Company. The enormous Canadian territory, consisting of the watershed formed by all the rivers emptying into Hudson's Bay, which this company was officially endowed with in its debut by the king for its operations, is known till today as The Rupert's Land. The coat of arms of the company contains a fox, two moose (sometimes two caribou instead) and four beavers. Underscoring it is a Latin slogan: **"Pro pelle cutem."** I personally translate this motto as: "A hide for a pelt." The Latin I know not and I only guess the translation, but I feel that I am interpreting it correctly. The motto obviously expresses the trade character of the company. But at the same time, I sense in it a degree of humor that was aimed at easing the stress from underlying danger and risks involved in its operations. For me, it expresses the awareness of the tenacious members of the company that they might have to be ready to sacrifice their "hide" (life) for the sake of successful trading in its commodity (the "pelt"). This, quite obviously, happened many times. The founding hierarchy and the investors of the company in faraway Britain in turn risked their financial "hides" (losing their investments) if the company failed. Today Hudson's Bay Company represents the oldest joint-stock company in North America that still prospers. Even if it ceded its vast territory to the Dominion of Canada at the end of the 19th century and fur is no longer its key commodity, it still owns a chain of department stores in Canada and the USA. The British Royal Family still owns a great deal of the company's stocks.

In spite of trudging on the trail through the wilderness quite alone, I felt safe. The toil of carrying the heavy load, which turned me into a beast of burden, ensured sufficient distraction of my thoughts from the dangers of an encounter with wild animals. Nowhere on the trail had I detected any sign of a bear in spite of my eyes constantly scanning the surface of the path in front of me for putting down my feet. My belt with safety items containing pepper spray was attached to my waterproof backpack and there it stayed even when I carried a different load. Only once was my attention fully sanctioned by a mysterious incident. I was walking upon rough-sawn, heavy boards that were laid down over the marshy terrain of a broadly spreading creek. The terrain was somewhat different from the most of the traversed forest. Everything here was freshly green from the luscious marsh grass with yellow buttercups up through a higher growth of thin alders and higher deciduous trees. The sun penetrated the greenery in a speckled mottling of bright green splotches. The weight of the canoe on my shoulders flexed the four-inch rough boards under my feet and I enjoyed springing on them with gusto on every sloshing step. Everything around was absolutely quiet except for the bubbling of the stream when all of a sudden a horrible crashing noise started in the area about 15-20 metres to my left. At first I suspected that I had startled a lying moose who might be frantically getting up. But the ruckus lasted perhaps for over half a minute and it seemed that the animal who caused it must have been heavier and more powerful than a moose. It thundered as if at least five trees had fallen with cracking and gotten crushed. I stopped on the board and turned only my look in the direction of the noise. Yet I was unable to see anything in the greenery. Surprised and embarrassed, I only mumbled below my breath: "Hello Sasquatch!" When all turned quiet again, I continued on in my voluntary slavery.

Fort Charlotte

A relative joy was brought to me by the moment when I attained the highest point of the trail. It was marked with a plaque on a small concrete milestone. From here, the path would slowly descend toward the Pigeon River. It seemed that I was almost at the finish of the portage but this was only a sad illusion. Two miles (3.2 km) were still remaining to "Fort Charlotte" and this, remember, I had to march out five times. Yet I delivered my waterproof backpack from here all the way to the yearned for campsite in one go. When, after a return trip, I also delivered the heavy freight pack, it felt almost as if I was home. The campsite consisted of two man-made clearings in the forest in the immediate vicinity of the river. This was just above its first cascade. It was empty. Each clearing had three wooden tent platforms and a couple of picnic tables. Each also had a concrete ring with a grate for a fire pit. Besides an outhouse latrine, the campsite also had a simple wooden pier for boats. It was a far cry from the onetime Fort Charlotte of which there remained not a trace. Yet at least in some aspect, it fulfilled a similar purpose. Right away, I set up the tent on one of the platforms and spread the bedroll in it immediately after that. All this because rain was looming. It gradually began shortly after I had finished. I was now still facing the last trip for the canoe that awaited me three kilometres back on the trail. Wearing my Gore-Tex rain jacket and Jackaroo hat, the rain did not affect me much. Marching under the umbrella of the inverted canoe it mattered even less. I delivered it into the campsite, stumbling over the wet roots with my last drop of energy. Yet I attained a hugely happy feeling from the successful reaching of my goal. A steady drumbeat of enduring rain was my lullaby for falling asleep. I was happy that I had managed to finish the portage before its path would become muddy and slick. "There is no way that any tourist would turn out here tomorrow under the present conditions," I assured myself. "I will sweetly sleep in tomorrow morning and I will give myself an extra day of rest here!"

Yet how flabbergasted I was when around 10:00 in the morning, still in the warm comfort of my sleeping bag while a persistent rain continued peppering the tent, I heard voices outside! I heard voices of children, the commands of an adult and the clanging of gear hanging off carried backpacks. "Unreal!" I exclaimed silently to myself. As it turned out, in spite of the bad weather, a troop of American Scouts had arrived at Fort Charlotte. There were about 20 of them, including the leader, accompanied by five fathers and even one mother as voluntary helpers. The sleepover in Fort Charlotte had simply been a part of the itinerary of their weeklong field trip that also included a trip into Canada with a visit to Fort William. They traveled in several vehicles that they had left about four miles back. This was at the point where an old (abandoned today and leading nowhere) road crosses the trail of the Grand Portage. From there, they came in the rain through the mud, carrying their huge and heavy tents; however, there wasn't enough room to erect all of them. Both clearings filled up even around the wooden platforms. The frustrated leader riled me up right from the beginning when he asked me suspiciously if I had a permit for camping at the Charlotte. Without batting an eye, I assured him of it and that was that. We were brought together again by the cooking fire when I taught the Scouts how to start it without using paper and how to maintain it while the firewood was wet. While we were cooking, I got to know the leader as a very friendly and intelligent man. He was a teacher who traveled a great deal and had even visited Prague. The story of my solo canoe travel along the voyageur route fascinated him. But he was not alone. The accompanying dads also sympathized with me. Especially admiring was a black man who was not an African American but had come originally from Ghana. He was a very pleasant, humble, constantly smiling gentleman who had the soft, kind voice of an African Bushman. In the evening, the Scouts had a bonfire in the other clearing but I was already gathering strength for tomorrow's canoe travel up the current of the Pigeon River in my tent. In the morning, the Scouts packed their wet tents early and, still in the morning fog, they sloshed away down the trail back to their vehicles.

The Pigeon River

I started the day by sorting and packing the load for my boat. One by one, each sealed piece of luggage went down to the pier at the river bank. Out of the fog, the day hatched into beauty. It promised bright sunshine with blue skies. Before I packed my tent last to give it a chance to dry, I stripped naked and dipped completely into the river. I had to wash away the sweat, blood and mud of the battle of the Grand Portage from my body and matted hair. Feeling like a brand new man, I then launched the canoe partially into the water and began to load it. I did not put on the spray cover yet because I had read that the voyageurs ran into the first portage shortly after leaving Fort Charlotte. Soon after, I pushed off seated in the canoe, very cautious not to get swept by the current into the fierce cascade of the river. That commenced immediately below the landing pier. The paddling up the current along the banks of spruce forest was easy at the beginning. But when I reached the first large bend of the river, I had to fight with a somewhat stronger flow. I managed to win over it by picking my way through the inside of the river's curve where I "licked" the rushes that grew close to the shore. They verified the calmer water. Here in the bend, I also, for the first time, noticed ice floe-like floating chunks of thick, creamy foam that were signaling the proximity of a waterfall upstream. I arrived under it in about half a kilometre past the river bend. I could not see the waterfall itself due to the high tree growth that covered it but I saw the water spilling from underneath the woods in two foamy streams down a steep, rocky staircase. Quite obviously, I also heard the main falls' rumbling, thundering noise. Since parts of the boundary water route are considered to be a popular playground by sports canoeists and kayakers from both sides of the border, I had expected that all the portages on the route would be reasonably marked. My first surprise came right at this first waterfall. With my eyes peeled, I vehemently paddled in the foaming current at the base of the waters that were descending from my right, searching to no avail for any sign of the portage. I dreaded the vision that I might be forced to find my own way around the waterfall when, on my last attempt, I fought my way through the strongest current to the far right side of the river immediately under the falls. Here I finally spotted a tiny point of the shore on which there seemed to be somewhat flattened grass. Indeed, when I approached it, I could see a steep muddy path disappearing from here into a fir forest. I pulled out the canoe and, betting all on the hope that I had found the portage trail, I unloaded everything and reset it into loads for my back. That done, I started out on a reconnaissance mission with the waterproof backpack. The path climbed rather steeply through dense spruce trees, many of which lay across it. After some half a kilometre, the path emerged onto a sort of primitive forest road that, at first, steeply climbed to the level of the river above the waterfall. But then it leveled horizontally and continued upstream through wet terrain along the river bank. At the next kilometre, it merged with a fairly reasonable gravel road that climbed up from the south and led at an angle to the river. It quite obviously served for the launching of motorboats or snowmobiles on a frozen river in the winter. This was at last the proof that I had found the right portage trail — at least in this case. On the way back for the next load, I stopped at the point above the waterfall from where I could see it. Yet the dense trees and steep, slick, rock drop-offs ensured that one could only see the upper part where the waters smoothly threw themselves over the lip into a narrow gorge between the rocks some 20 metres deep. I was glad that the portage prudently reconnected with the river far upstream. The vision of being swept by some unlucky blunder into the waterfall would not shape into a very esthetic picture. The river above the waterfall appeared to be calm for a significant distance. I picked my way upstream through the inside of its bends where there reedy grasses and bulrushes often grew. Here I almost regularly ran into families of swans. I never saw any young cygnets but the strange thing was that I always encountered a trio of the adults. They would always swim fast against the current ahead of me and only just as I caught up to their level and expected that my peaceful passing would calm them down, they took off with heavy wing flaps while frantically trumpeting. In a very shallow, slowly rising flight, they disappeared somewhere beyond the bend of the river upstream. It is conceivable that I kept flushing the same trio after each time they landed higher and higher up the river. The low banks of the river were covered with a thick jumble of willow and alder growth, beyond which spread a chaotic jumble of broken and inter-falling coniferous woods. I did not note any possibility of camping here, which, however, I did not need yet. As usual, when moving from the east to the west, I also had some headwind here. I was used to it by now. In the straight sections of the river open to the west where only the wind mattered, I applied my proven tricks of hiding from it, such as moving through reeds or under overhanging branches of bushes and trees that were growing down to the water, etc. Eventually, the current would grow stronger in places. I battled it heroically but situations arrived where I could not continue upstream by paddling. I never found any signs of portages even though I knew that the voyageurs carried on the Pigeon River several times. In the last moment, I would simply jump out of the canoe into the shallow water. Wearing my rubber sandals and the legs of my light nylon pants rolled up to my mid-thighs, I then led the loaded canoe against the current up the rapids. The water was not chilling and hence, I was reasonably able to continue.

A similar mode of advance used to be called "décharge" by the voyageurs. They would disembark from the canoe and lead it through the rapids loaded fully, partially, or empty, while others carried the removed load on a portage. Sometimes helpers also towed the canoe with ropes from the shore.

Several times, I spotted orange flagging tape tied to a branch near the river bank. It looked as if a trail was starting under the overhanging growth. Yet when I landed and went to examine the presumed trail, it would always turn out that the tape only marked a place where a trap for some fur-bearing animals had been placed. During winter, the frozen river apparently turns into a trap line for the Chippewa people from the local reserve who tend to it on snowmobiles. The travel along the border possessed one serious problem for navigation; the maps in my iPhone typically showed only one side of the boundary. The Canadian maps ended at the border and showed a blank area beyond it on the American side. The American ones displayed the opposite effect, i.e., emptiness on the Canadian side. Most of the boundary line winds through the middle of the lakes and, showing only half of the shape of the lake, confuses orientation. Due to the very long anticipated distance to travel, I wanted to rely on my topographic maps of a large scale of 1:250,000 that would be able to cover it. Unfortunately, it marked the boundary with a broad cross-hatched band that obscured the details of the topography along the very route of my advance. None of my maps showed the National Monument of the Grand Portage as a distinct band. So I easily became disoriented as to where I really started from on the Pigeon River. For a long time, I had expected that I would arrive at the next waterfall labeled on the map as "Partridge Falls" before which the river was crossed by some old road into Canada. Yet nothing of the sort materialized. Later on, though, some serious and truly challenging rapids came that I, at the time, suspected as a possible — grossly exaggerated representation of the waterfall. Here I was forced to fight a real life and death battle. The river narrowed down from 30 metres to some 10 and it steeply meandered. I led the canoe up the wild current that was tripping my legs. I kept falling on the rolling rocks of the river bottom, desperately clutching the stern of the boat. I was grasping for overhanging willow branches as if for the straws of salvation. I was picking my path of advancing through the insides of the bends where the current was weaker. Yet as the river meandered, I had to periodically cut across its middle, aiming for the inside of the next bend. The current in the outside of the bends was so ferocious that it was in no way possible to overcome. I realized very acutely that, should my canoe slip from my grip, I could never catch up to it in the current. It could be destroyed by wrapping itself around a rock and losing its contents. I was keenly aware that without the canoe I could not move through this area due to the dense growth along the shores. In combination with the merciless insects, I would undoubtedly be doomed. After an especially dangerous traversing of the center of the river when only with luck, all shaking, I reached the other side, I decided that I had to stop, calm down and conclusively determine where I really found myself. Standing in the fast current at the edge of the river, I took out the GPS unit and determined my coordinates. Those I then transferred into the 1:250,000 map and found to my shock that I was situated much higher up along the river than where I had assumed to be. "Definitely above Partridge Falls!" I concluded to myself. Suddenly, it seemed clear to me that if I somewhat stretched the day, I might be able to reach the first lake in the group that occupied the height of land of the Hudson's Bay watershed.

Having next overcome a series of the worst of the rapids, the river now calmed somewhat down again. I was now able to advance against it with long, regular paddle strokes. Also, the wind notably quieted down. It was already past 6:00 in the evening and dusk seemed to be setting in, mainly due to a now overcast sky. I sensed that I only had between one and two kilometres remaining to South Waterfowl Lake from which the river flowed out. The river, however, suddenly bent left and, following the next bend to the right, narrowed down to six metres. The compression of the river course brought rapids that were utterly impossible to tackle by leading the canoe through the water. On both sides of the river an impenetrable growth spread right down into the water. All I could do was jump quickly into the canoe that was already oriented by the bow downstream and cautiously navigate the whitewater back to the initial bend of the river. Previously, before the left bend of the river, I had noticed a tiny, grassy clearing on an elevated river bank, just large enough for my tent. I landed under it, unloaded the canoe and immediately erected the tent. Urging me strongly to do this, was the intrusive insect, which towards the evening, had its wildest ritual of blood imbibing. But I also could not wait to lay down my achy frame horizontally onto the sleeping bag. I maliciously spoiled the mosquito orgies by crawling into the standing tent, zippering up its no-see-um mesh door and slapping dead those bold intruders who had managed to sequester themselves in it with me. Following a supper of a mere protein bar, I was asleep before 8:00.

A chance portage to Waterfowl Lake

Last evening before retiring to sleep, I noticed a game trail behind the tent that led to the river. In its mud there were clearly imprinted tracks of moose and coyote. Curious, in the morning I explored it to see what other animal tracks I would find. I passed through its low marshy section with thick bushes where the trail was stomped into water-filled puddles fringed by slippery, gooey mud. Yet beyond the marsh, the trail rose to a higher level of dry coniferous forest. The path seemed to be more discernible here and moreover, it curved in the right direction toward Waterfowl Lake. A glimmer of hope quickened the pounding of my heart: "Is this a portage to the lake?" I almost trotted along the trail when at last I detected the first proofs that it had been used by humans. Laying across the path were many trunks of fallen trees but here and there a log appeared that had been removed from the way by now blackened old cuts of a chainsaw. With glee I returned to my camp. I immediately packed everything, had a quick breakfast and off I went, skiing through the mud of the marshy section of the trail with the burden of the waterproof backpack. Soon I marched through a dry forest of resin-smelling tall pines with occasional islands of thick, bright green undergrowth. I would often have to surmount big trees fallen across the trail or pass around them. The trunks of the conifers were easy to overcome by sitting on them and scissoring my legs over while rotating around. The branched-out deciduous trees had to be entirely circumvented, sometimes through thick undergrowth. When I anxiously anticipated that the trail would start descending to the lake, it suddenly veered to the right — not in the direction toward it. I had already walked about two kilometres. This caused spasms in my stomach as doubts crept into my mind. Was this really a trail to the lake? My pessimism grew when I suddenly noticed a trap for some small furbearing animal placed on a fallen trunk. "My God, is this just another trap line?" I had no other choice but to hold my cards and continue with a stone face in this game. I saw no other option. I stumbled along the trail for some three kilometres, watching for any possible signs to determine where the path was headed. I sensed that to my left the terrain had to be dropping off toward the lake. It seemed that I felt its moisture in the air. When I looked into the crowns of the forest trees, it seemed that they were thinning in that direction. Then all of a sudden, the path turned left and started dropping abruptly. Suddenly I stood at the edge of a ravine that dropped off to the lake. In front of me and across the ravine, an imposing granite formation loomed that looked like a castle with a tall tower. With joy, I descended a steep, rough, rocky path to the shore of a vast lake. At present, I did not pay attention to the fact that its surface was being whipped up by a strong westerly gale and the surf was spraying among the jumble of driftwood, rocks and wood chips pushed against the rocky shore of a small cove at the base of the ravine. Back on the trail in the woods, everything had been calm and sheltered from the wind. I did not waste much time at the lake. Ahead of me was another hard day of heavy carrying. I rested the waterproof backpack upon a small rock outcropping and immediately scrambled up the wall of the ravine. The return hike without a load was a refreshing walk. At last I could inhale the resin perfumes of the forest with full gulps of air. The woods were naturally mixed with areas where deciduous trees dominated, and others where towering lodge pole pines and fir trees prevailed. In the sunbathed spots of the trail, I ran into a fat, coiled garter snake several times who was soaking up the sun's warmth. It would always speedily slither off the path sensing the earth vibrations from my footsteps. On the rocks by the lake I even observed a garter snake in the act of trying to swallow a big, fat black slug. It seemed like an impossible feat because the slug tried desperately to spread its body, but suddenly the slug disappeared into the snake's head and the snake in turn vanished among the rocks. In one spot I marched through an alley within a thicker undergrowth towards a tall, thin pine forest when, beyond a turn, I caught a glimpse of the rear of some larger animal 15 metres in front of me who was disappearing in absolute silence among some deadfall into bushes. The being had jet black hair that attracted my attention for its apparent softness. It could have been a bear or a wolverine but they have coarser hair. I passed the spot of the disappearance within seconds but in spite of looking closely into it, I saw no sign of any living creature.

The trip with the loaded freight frame was by now already intimately familiar agony. Yet with the canoe I surmounted all the feared obstacles with relative ease. I delivered the boat all the way to the shore of the lake without a single stop. I estimated the total length of the portage at some three-and-a-half kilometres. Only now I realized how big the waves on the lake were. At the spot where I arrived, there was no possibility of camping. Some 400 metres from the shore where I stood with my possessions, I looked at a relatively large island on which I discerned a clear spot for a tent on its lee side that was turned towards me. The plan was obvious. I tossed the packs, as they were carried on the portage, into the canoe and, precariously stepping over the flotsam mess, I got into it. The paddling to the island was a Sisyphean struggle against the strong headwind and waves until I finally reached the lee of the island. On it I unloaded all and pitched the tent. Then I stripped and swam in the lake. It was about 2:00 in the afternoon and there was no rush to continue anywhere. The wind was bending strong birch trees and white poplars like stalks of grass. To fight it would have been a nonsensical, if not impossible, self-flogging. I decided to wait till the next morning.

By the next morning, the situation had not changed. The foliage in the crowns of the flexed trees wildly rustled as it was ripped by wind gusts. When I stood on the rocky outcrop of the windward side of the island, the wind howled around my ears, spraying my face with moisture whipped up from the crests of the white-capped waves. There would be no sense in launching the canoe. I cooked a hot breakfast as well as dinner on a fire in a sheltered spot. I filled all the bottles with filtered water from the lake and lounged in the sun on the leeward side of the island to rest my achy muscles. From time to time, I also sat on the windward rock outcrop and strained my eyes, focussing westward into the glistening narrows of the lake in the distance where my next travel would be headed and from where the wind now blew. As I studied the maps, I descended into an ever-deepening depression for which I had multiple reasons. Before the trip, I had relied on the assumption that it would not be difficult to find all the portages on the boundary water route that connected all the lakes in its chain. I had assumed that they would all be well signed. Yet my heretofore experience from traveling on it was a big disappointment. I was aware that a number of portages did not start at the ends of the lakes but often in out of the way side bays that would be hard to find without detailed information. There were also other portages that interconnected the network of thousands of lakes used by the First Nations people, fishermen and water tourists. In this labyrinth of the wilderness, where no human settlement exists far and wide, it would be extremely easy to get lost. Another concern of mine was the overall distance that remained for me to overcome before reaching the first community on the route, Fort Frances. It was covered not by one, but two maps of the 1:250,000 scale! My remaining food supply now covered only 19 days. Should I get lost or windbound several times, the trip duration could grow much longer. Another aspect was my injury. I had suffered fractured ribs on both sides of the bottom front in spite of trying to be maximally prudent as a lone wayfarer. If I perhaps fractured an ankle or became otherwise rendered immobile, my life's journey might terminate in the middle of nowhere. For almost 10 days, nobody had heard from me. There was no cell phone signal here nor did it exist along the whole way ahead of me. Without a satellite beacon, nobody would learn that I needed help in case of a serious mishap. Most likely, it would take weeks, if not months, before my carcass with pecked out eyeballs and gnawed-on ribs would be found by a search party. I reminded myself of the tragedies of adventurous enthusiasts about whom I had read. I sensed a similar kind of atmosphere in the air. In a self-critical look at my situation, I soberly came to the conclusion that I had reached the leading edge of irresponsibility. The whole difference between surviving and a tragic end rests in recognizing it. When I woke up the next morning on the island and the wind still blew with the same vigor, the decision was in for me. For this time, I had to terminate my journey!

The self-evacuation

The question now was how. I found myself in the middle of a vast wilderness without settlements or roads. The only way of self-evacuation that I could see was to backtrack to somewhere below Partridge Falls, where according to the map, I assumed that some kind of a small road crossed the river. There I would then try to arrange some transportation from the Canadian side. I was prepared to pay somebody a reasonable fee for the service. A weird thing, though, was the fact that I did not remember seeing such a crossing on the river during my travel upstream. I reasoned that I had somehow missed its signs thanks to some distraction. With sadness in my soul, I again repacked everything into carrying bundles and loaded the canoe. Then I cautiously navigated back into the cove under the ravine. As I emerged from the lee of the island, I caught large waves but I sailed downwind and hence I reached the landing spot quickly. Despite of all that wind, the sky was almost clear and I enjoyed a brilliant sun. While I repeatedly toted my burdens on the trail in the woods, there was not a breath of wind to be felt. The reverse portage took me a good half day. It was hot and I had to carry drinking water even on the return trips for the next load. When I had climbed up to the upper edge of the ravine with the last load of the canoe on my shoulders, I sadly turned to look back at the choppy lake. "One day, perhaps, I will be back and will continue. But I have to prepare better. The best would be with a partner!" When I delivered the boat to the river of the pigeons, it was only noon. I sat down on the spot where my tent had stood before and I had a quick lunch. During that time, I again studied the maps, both the paper one and the ones in my iPhone. At last I succeeded in finding a map in the iPhone that clearly showed the band of land that was designated as the Grand Portage trail. Suddenly it emerged with clarity that the Partridge Falls were, in fact, the waterfall around which I had portaged above the Fort Charlotte campsite. That "small road" that I intended to use as a way of escape from the route into Canada turned out to be the abandoned road that was used by the Scouts on their way to the campsite. But that one used to cross the river way down below the cascades — downstream from them. Furthermore, that road has been long discontinued and its bridge across the Pigeon River did not exist anymore. It was now quite obvious to me that I could not leave the wilderness by entering Canada. The only way of self-evacuation for me was to return all the way down the Grand Portage trail to its fort in the USA. After a while, I carefully loaded the canoe and stretched the spray cover on. That done, I cautiously pushed off into the current of the river. I proceeded prudently. In my mind, I constantly reminded myself how I would have to enter into the most difficult rapids and how to navigate through them. I realized that I did not have a whitewater canoe. With the canoe's keel, the maneuvering among the rocks would be harder. I knew that I would not leave all the dangers behind me until I showed up in front of the Grand Portage fort's gate. I knew that just one fateful lapse of judgement could end in tragedy. The script for the conclusion of my film, in which I played the leading role, depended strictly on my caution and the ability to control my destiny. It was not clear yet if I starred in a movie with a happy end or if the set was that of a tragedy drama. When I heard the rumble of the rapids up ahead, my knees were shaking and my hands were clutching the paddle with a white-knuckle grip. With my eyes, I burned out the line of my passing through the water-washed rocks ahead while I "read" the current to find sufficient depth for my canoe. But all was going well. I rubbed the bottom of the boat on a rock only once. At the time, when I passed through the most challenging rapid all tensed up, nature provided an added comical entertainment. The river was barely 10 or 12 metres wide. I slowly zigzagged along the right side of the roaring whitewater, when to the left of me in the water near its edge, a dark moose cow appeared standing with, apparently, a just-born calf. The calf with large eyes was of an unusually light shade of yellow, standing on widely-splayed, shaky long legs. They both gazed at me in shock, unable to move, as if paralyzed because, due to the overwhelming noise of the rapids, my sudden close appearance on the scene totally surprised them. The cow just shot off a thin diarrhea stream into the water from under her short tail. At that very moment — as if the scene were still lacking something and with the apparent aim of rejoining the duo — a buck deer jumped from the overgrown right bank into the river immediately in front of my canoe. He noticed me while already in mid-air. At the instant of landing in the river, he thus rebounded right back into the opposite direction and scrambled up into the thicket. I had been tempted to pass through the rapids with my GoPro camera on a headband but I did not want to anger the gods. So I banished the idea. Now, following my successful survival of all the whitewater, I sorely rued that I had not captured this unique action. Like several other most thrilling adventure moments in my past it will stay recorded only in my memory. Travel downstream on the swift river was obviously faster than in the opposite direction. It was around 5:00 when I arrived at the upper end of the portage around Partridge Falls. Yet I had had enough for the whole day. I quickly unpacked the tent and set it up right away so that, protected from the pesky insects by its bug netting, I could grant a horizontal rest to my fatigued back and achy muscles. My watch, which besides time also shows a graph of atmospheric pressure trend and the temperature, still indicated 29C in the evening. I fell asleep early and I slept for a long time.

In the morning, I started carrying around the waterfall in the early sunshine. Soon Partridge Falls was behind me. Before I reached the landing at the Charlotte campsite, though, I had yet another interaction with wild fauna. It was right below the falls when I paddled by the quiet water of a back eddy that was shaded by tall, dense fir trees on the river bank. Perhaps I approached too closely to the territory of a family of river otters when they started noisily frolicking around my canoe, snaking their shiny, water-polished, fur-dressed bodies out and into the water. Every once in a while, a snake-like head with wide bulging cheeks appeared above the surface with long whiskers at its sides and beady, black eyes sending flashes of anger at my intruding face. They emitted a ratchety, loud laugh that actually expressed their annoyance and had nothing to do with laughter. As, unfettered, I continued on my way, they must have thought that they had succeeded in chasing me away. Yet I only smiled, grateful for the performance. I jokingly chastised them with a quiet, "Shut up already!" At last, I cautiously touched down with the canoe at the collapsing wooden pier immediately upstream of the wild cascade. I reached the Fort Charlotte campsite around noon.

After erecting the tent on a wooden platform, I rested for some time while having lunch. I felt that it would be better to spend the night in the campsite rather than somewhere on the trail. Yet I wanted to take advantage of the rest of the day to make some progress in carrying the outfit down the trail for the next day. I could not leave the freight pack with food on the trail overnight without guarding it. But I realized that I could carry the canoe as far as possible along the path and leave it there without any worry. I could then return back into the campsite without a load for the night. That plan I immediately put into action. I jerked the canoe onto my shoulders and marched under it for some three hours on the trail, including the crossing of the beaver dam on the boardwalk. I continued on farther and farther. I only stopped within sight of the old road that crossed the Grand Portage roughly at its midpoint. The wooden walkway around the beaver pond was already repaired and the trees that had fallen across the path from my earlier travel up the trail had been removed with a chainsaw. The next morning, I left the camp with the heavy freight frame pack first in order to leave the tent and the sleeping bag drying and venting. I put it down on the trail only when I could read the signs in the sky of a change in the weather for possible rain. Then I hurried back to pack away the sleeping bag and the tent into the waterproof backpack to clear the campsite with this last load. It was already past 6:00 when I brought both packs to the canoe immediately before the crossing of the trail by the old road. It had been sprinkling for some while before that and when I pitched the tent on a somewhat dry spot of the trail where it was roofed over by a tunnel of dense spruce trees, it started raining in earnest. I was at the brink of my strength. My broken ribs were hurting and on top of it, an old athletic knee injury had awakened. No weapon happened to be on hand to realize my earlier resolution to send a bullet through my brains rather than to repeat the Grand Portage. But the nearest possible plan had hatched in my head. I had to find somebody with a pickup and hire him to transport my load down the old road. This obviously required that I somehow get down to the fort at the end of the trail.

At daybreak, I packed everything into the waterproof backpack that I would need for a possible multiday camping on the trail in case of a mishap with injury. It was practically all of my gear, including the sleeping bag and the tent that I normally carried in it, except for some unnecessary clothing that I added to the bag with "hardware" on the freight frame. On the other hand, I added a two-litre drinking bottle, the water filter in case of further need, all the photo equipment and all the electronics. I hid the canoe, the paddles and the freight pack so they could not be seen directly from the road. I donned the Gore-Tex windbreaker and Gore-Tex gaiters over long nylon pants. I stabilized my knee with a neoprene knee brace. Having put on my hat and hoisted the waterproof pack onto my shoulders, I started down the wet trail through the wet bush. I stepped carefully on rocks and over roots to protect my injured leg but I moved resolutely and quickly. When the sun pierced the crowns of the trees, Poplar Creek was already behind me. After some while, I heard sounds of human activity in the distance down below me. I emerged on the asphalt road just in front of the gate of the historic fort before 10:00. There I met an elderly, trustworthy-looking Native man. I asked him if he knew of somebody with a pickup truck who might be willing to fulfill my need. He thought for a moment and then sent me to the office of the park headquarters that was situated about a kilometre past the bend of the road. In a cabin-like office building of the complex with garages of the park's maintenance machine equipment, I found a uniformed Native female employee who called somewhere on the radio. A uniformed warden lady arrived shortly after with a park pickup. She was the same person whom I got to know before the start of my portage at the fort. When she heard of my plight, she urged me to heave my heavy backpack into the bed of the truck and without any delay we departed for the rest of my outfit. She wouldn't hear of any payment for the service. She knew the way well and soon we were bringing and loading into the truck my freight pack, the canoe, paddles and other pieces of equipment. She was stunned by the mountain of my gear and couldn't believe that I had transported all of it back and forth along the route that I had described. While riding with her in the cab of the truck, I investigated what options were available for traveling between Grand Portage and Thunder Bay. No means of public transport existed for this purpose. I speculated that I could reach Thunder Bay by taxicab, which would undoubtedly be very expensive, and then return for my outfit with my vehicle. But I immediately realized what kind of customs bureaucratic nightmare would be unleashed by my arrival in the U.S. with an empty vehicle, followed by an immediate return with a full load and a canoe on the roof, the serial number of which I had never declared. The only realistic solution that emerged in my mind was to return to Canada in exactly the same way as the one in which I had arrived in the USA but in the opposite direction. When the warden lady learned that I planned to travel from Grand Portage to Thunder Bay by canoe on the lake, she recoiled in horror. "You don't dare!" It is because she had grown up in this area and her father used to be a fisherman on the Superior. She still remembered the horror-filled nights that she endured with her mother during storms on the lake when they didn't know if her father would come home. She told me about a tragedy that occurred exactly the year before at that time of the year. They had exchanged goodbyes with a young American kayaker who was traveling around Lake Superior in a clockwise direction. He was headed from Grand Portage to Thunder Bay. They waved to each other with smiles and jokes as the kayaker pushed off. The kayaker promised that he would see them next year when he was planning to return. The kayaker then disappeared from their sight as he rounded Hat Point. As it later turned out, he passed by several points and when he rounded Pigeon Point he encountered big waves. These capsized his craft. The young man had a "Spot" device clipped to his life jacket that can send out an SOS signal with the GPS coordinates. He had activated this device by pressing the appropriate button to launch a rescue alarm. The Canadian Coast Guard search plane first discovered his overturned kayak in Pigeon Bay. The Coast Guard cutter reached the location in two hours. In the next ten minutes, they found the kayaker floating in his life jacket about one nautical mile from the point of the peninsula on the open water. His life, sadly, was already extinguished due to hypothermia. Not too long ago, I discovered the original announcement of this tragic incident in the press:

Kayaker apparently dies in Lake Superior near Grand Portage
Duluth News Tribune
Posted: 06/19/2012 12:01:00 AM CDT

The body of a man was found Sunday morning in Lake Superior near Grand Portage, Minn., by a Canadian Coast Guard aircraft and Cutter Cape Chaillon. The U.S. Coast Guard command center in Cleveland was notified of the alert of a personal locator beacon at 9:21 a.m. The emergency signals are activated if a button is pressed. The Coast Guard checked the beacon, found it was registered and made calls on the account, said Chief Petty Officer Kyle Niemi with the Ninth Coast Guard District in Cleveland. A kayak was found at 11:20 a.m. on the Canadian side of the lake, in Pigeon Bay. The man, whose identity has not been released, was found at 11:30 a.m. one nautical mile east of Pigeon Point. He was wearing a life jacket.

For me this was a sad and finally concrete reminder of the fact that paddling a small craft on Lake Superior can be a game with death and its threat has to be taken deadly seriously! The warden took me to the public campsite and helped me unload my cargo on the spot that I had selected for my tent. On parting, she suggested that from time to time they had a business trip to Thunder Bay to which they drove an empty pickup. Allegedly, they could take me. But she was not aware of any concrete date when they might take the next trip. I was very grateful to her for this kind gesture but I only took it as such — a gesture. That's because I could not afford to wait for weeks in the campsite in the hope that the employees of the National Monument might have a trip to T-Bay.

The public campsite had its own harbour for the mooring and launching of motorboats. Besides that, it also had hot showers. At night, a storm came with a downpour deluge that threatened to flatten my tent. It was still sprinkling in the morning and an unfavorable wind was blowing to threaten my possible departure by water. Hence, I hiked on foot down the road to visit the small local museum joined with an Information Centre for tourists. Of course, I also visited the Fort Grand Portage. Here I mainly admired the tables in the Great Hall that were set as they used to be for the great reception held on the occasion of the annual meeting of the partners of the Northwest Company. On the embroidered tablecloths the finest china dishes were laid out together with polished gold-inlaid silver cutlery. The menu listed the best delicacies not only from the hunts and harvests of the generously rich, local land, but also imported from the farthest trading corners of the once mighty British Empire. They were washed down with the finest "high wine" and liquors poured into splendid crystal. Only the highest quality tobacco was smoked. During my visit, I finally caught my dear wife on the phone in the Czech Republic. She was certainly happy that I was still alive. Before I ended our conversation, I obliged her with a sworn promise: "Darling, should I ever start talking about a desire to return back to the route of the voyageurs, please shoot me!"

The weather started clearing up during my return to the campsite. Out of the west, a blue sky commenced to spread. The wind turned into the right direction. I quickened my steps. In the campsite, I started packing right away. I carried the canoe and loading-ready cargo down to the harbor. Soon I laced the spray cover onto the loaded canoe. At 3:00, I pushed the canoe into the water so that it rested only by the tip of the stern on the concrete ramp. Then I cautiously crawled into its spray cover cockpit from the stern with my hands and knees on the gunwales to save my feet in rubber sandals from getting chillingly wet. It needed only a minimal push-off to fully float. An elderly gentleman who had watched me for some time leaned down from the concrete wall and asked where I was sailing. He could see that this did not look like a short outing. "Thunder Bay," I replied briefly. He nodded his white head seriously and with a worried expression stayed silent. I renewed my show when, with long, mighty paddle strokes, I elegantly stretched my wake diagonally across the Grand Portage Bay toward Hat Point. I wanted to travel as far as possible today. The day was already fairly advanced, but with the wind in my back I was moving fast. By the time the growing waves forced me to look for a suitable campsite, I had almost arrived at the tip of Pigeon Peninsula. Here I spent a nice evening at a small fire thinking of the unfortunate kayaker who had perished not too far from where I was. His fate was sobering to me. It constantly reminded me to be prudent. This I religiously heeded the whole way back on the lake when I had earlier thought that all its dangers were finally behind me. Now I was back here. Had destiny, perhaps, a different ending in mind? Yet with caution and the protection from my guardian angel whom, I admit, I do work hard, all converged to a happy ending. When I was rounding Pigeon Point at sunrise, the lake could not have behaved more peacefully. In the east, its surface glistened like a mirror. Over the morning vapours above it, the mirage of the large island — Isle Royal — hovered, as if a space ship of extra-terrestrial aliens were lowering itself for a touchdown to a massive invasion of Earth. I doubt that anybody would have noticed my measly "walnut shell" of a watercraft when I crossed the border with all my possessions in it back into Canada. I did not make a call anywhere this time. Still, no guided missile annihilated my ship. I, of course, did get to "enjoy" more episodes of upwelling adrenaline together with surging sprints in the blood flow of my cardiovascular system thanks to my stressful relationship with the wind and waves before I was finally able to phone Aaron to pick me up. He showed up faithfully with my (in fact Milena's) car at the lake's shore. After I let him off at his house in Thunder Bay, I headed home. I traveled via Fort Frances where I picked up my leftover second drybag of food. I returned to Edmonton in time to fulfill my important role of giving my daughter away to her groom at the altar. It was a splendid wedding. I even returned in time to pick up Milena at the Edmonton International Airport from her vacation in the Czech Republic.

Milena's faithfulness failed me in one aspect, yet in another, she reassured me of the kind of stone from which she is chiselled — how I can rely on her. After a while, I started to regret that I had not continued when I reached the Waterfowl Lake. Didn't I have the worst behind me there? I could have fished to supplement my nutrition! The fish are supposed to bite on every cast out there. I could have perhaps encountered a Sasquatch who allegedly thrives there in peace from humans. I started to talk about returning but Milena failed to shoot me. I had resolved, though, that I wouldn't want to continue alone again. When Milena saw that for two years it had been hard for me to find a partner, she came up with a shocking offer — this already for the fourth time in our adventurous life together! It was that she would go with me! Our new greeting: **"Pro pelle cutem!"**

CHAPTER V

From Waterfowl Lake along the Quetico - Boundary Waters Canoe Route to Fort Frances (August 30 – September 19, 2012)

"Oweeee!!!!" — A scream pierced the silent darkness of a late evening. Its gravity was legitimized by muscle tissue-muffled thuds of a human body collapsing onto the kitchen floor tiles. Sitting in front of a computer in the ground floor office, I had no idea that Milena was returning from the upstairs bedrooms to join me. Allegedly, she wanted to help me check which items on a predetermined list still remained to be added to the packed gear for our very challenging canoe expedition. We had planned it for over a year and were to depart in two days. It turned out that after an evening bath and the application of complexion creams, Milena descended in her nightgown and raised-heel slippers down the carpeted stairs — in darkness! Fate struck on the second to the last step. Her instep slipped sideways in her slipper and got violently twisted into a position in which it wasn't meant to function in any other way than to drop the rest of the body similar to a tree cut from below. The first was an instinctive reaction — a response to the sharp pain — with attempts to assess the level of injury. But soon cool reason followed as to what impact this unfortunate accident could have on our plans. Unwilling to accept the thought of cancelling our ambitious project, Milena bravely stood up and tested whether she could put weight on the affected leg. She hoped that this would turn out to be just a severe sprain — something that might, perhaps, postpone our expedition a bit but not cancel it. Yet the x-rays at the emergency room the next morning painted a different picture. It showed that Milena had fractured the navicular bone in her foot. This diagnosis eliminated any possibility of her tackling the 40 difficult portages that the route of our planned travel through the lake country wilderness involved. Don't they shoot race horses when they suffer this kind of injury? Milena's leg went into a cast and her spirit sank into deep depression. She feared that I had to be disappointed. Although I assured her that everything was OK, that this was simply fate — things happen for a reason and you can't do anything about it, my mood was low from the inability to resolve anything.

When I aborted my canoe voyage across Canada along the water route of the voyageurs at Waterfowl Lake in June, 2013, I determined then that to continue on, among other factors, without a partner was too dangerous. But during the whole next year when I had not found one, it was Milena again who voluntarily stepped by my side, offering to accompany me as a partner. I valued that gesture strongly but I worried that the present kind of undertaking could be somewhat over her head. Yet at the same time, I fully realized that I would have a hard time finding a better partner. I knew Milena well and knew that in critical situations she would be able to mobilize all the abilities that she had to her disposal, focusing them towards a positive outcome. I knew that she would never panic. Didn't we successfully complete a trek with a canoe over the mountains of the Continental Divide to the Nahanni River in the Northwest Territories in '97? Hadn't we descended the rivers Tsichu, Keele and Mackenzie in the Northwest Territories completely alone and trekked back to our vehicle in Yukon along the Canol Heritage Trail in '99? Following my initial doubts, it was quite clear to me that Milena didn't view her offer as some heroic sacrifice or an attempt to somehow prove her faith and love. It was obvious that she was genuinely looking forward to the adventure. The preparations thus started a year in advance. Sometime during November, I discovered a new tandem canoe for us in the Edmonton Mountain Equipment Coop store. It was hanging on the wall, smiling at me with its slender, shining yellow hips right from the moment when my eye roved over it. It was love at first sight. The canoe had the classical "Prospector" shape. It was also created to the same high quality as my thoroughly test-proven solo canoe. It was made from even lighter Kevlar and thus, although a whole 17 feet long, weighed even less — 20.5 kg. It was again adorned with splendid ash woodwork, including an artfully sculpted center yoke for its most comfortable carrying behind the neck on the shoulders. Its original price was no less than $3,300. This factor posed a high enough barrier for me to forget about it. But as I continued to visit the store during the winter, I noticed with surprise that after Christmas, the price started to drop. The store was to receive a new shipment of boats in the spring and it needed to make room for them. I entered into a kind of a poker game with the store by cautiously postponing the purchase. When at last the price dropped to $2,200, I was ready to close a deal. Only as a last-minute prank, I proposed a very improbable offer of $1,800. To my shocked surprise, the sales person accepted it. After its transportation home, a lot of work still remained around the new canoe. A new spray cover had to be designed and sewn for it — already our fifth. This meant we needed to source out waterproof Life Jacket Nylon for it and drill a row of small holes on each side of the canoe in order to pass nylon cord loops through them that we glued from the inside. They were to be used to lace the spray cover on. We managed to overcome all the related snags and pitfalls. We completed the task less than a week before the planned departure. And now, this!

Milena was given sick leave from her employer and I was racking my brains trying to come up with some idea of how we could use her time off together. It would have been nice if we could spend the Indian summer at our log house on Kootenay Lake in British Columbia. ... Alas, the conditions of her sick leave stipulated that Milena was not to leave Edmonton. Even if I wanted to, I could not leave her alone for a few days either, because as long as she had a leg cast she could not drive. Ergo, I had to constantly be on hand to drive her to checkups and for unforeseen incidentals. Only after the cast had been removed and the doctor suggested that Milena cautiously start walking on her leg and drive, I made a spur of the moment overnight decision. I would head east and continue on the voyageur route alone again. Everything had been ready for two weeks. What remained was to replace the tent and the canoe with the solo versions. Small repairs that my solo canoe required took me only one day. By now, it was the end of August. The time for realizing the trip was quickly passing away.

The challenge of returning to where I had left off

My flash decision filled me with fear. Am I not contemplating a return to where I considered my situation lethal two years ago? Moreover, I did not even know if I would succeed in getting my gear and myself to Waterfowl Lake, the location from where I turned around to go back at the time. While pouring over the terrain around Waterfowl Lake in Google Earth, I finally discovered a spot on its Canadian shore where, in the maximum zoom-in level, four-wheel drive trucks and all-terrain vehicles appeared parked in the shade of the trees together with motorboats and boat trailers. They hinted that a way had to exist to get to the lake from the Canadian side that would allow these kinds of vehicles access. Indeed — I was then able to trace a mud or gravel track on the screen that disappeared and reappeared from under the forest canopy that had peeled off of a small paved road. "There is my only hope!" I concluded. On it, I should be able to get reliably to the lake in my Jeep Wrangler with the canoe on its roof. But to leave the Jeep unattended in the middle of nowhere for maybe even a month? And how was I supposed to get back to it from Fort Frances after I finished my canoe voyage there? I was prepared to generously pay Aaron, my Good Samaritan who had provided me with transportation to Lake Superior and stored my vehicle in Thunder Bay two years ago. But he was now finishing his master's degree at the university and couldn't free himself for this service. In spite of keeping several "irons in the fire" — promises from friends to find something for me through their acquaintances in Fort Frances, nothing materialized in the end. Finally, I again turned to my electronic friend — the World Wide Web. I managed to find two taxi companies in Fort Frances that were willing to take me to Waterfowl Lake even though they had never heard of it and didn't, in fact, know what they were getting into. Yet the problem was that

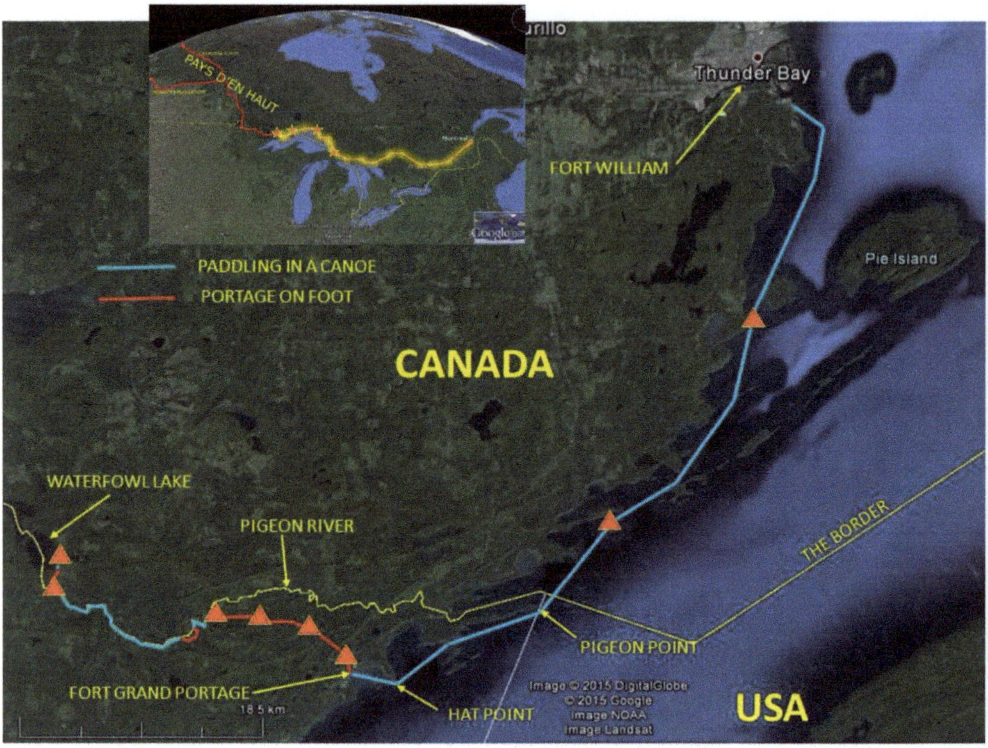
PAYS D'EN HAUT
Thunder Bay
FORT WILLIAM
PADDLING IN A CANOE
PORTAGE ON FOOT
Pie Island
CANADA
WATERFOWL LAKE
PIGEON RIVER
THE BORDER
PIGEON POINT
FORT GRAND PORTAGE
HAT POINT
USA
Image © 2015 DigitalGlobe
© 2015 Google
Image NOAA
Image Landsat

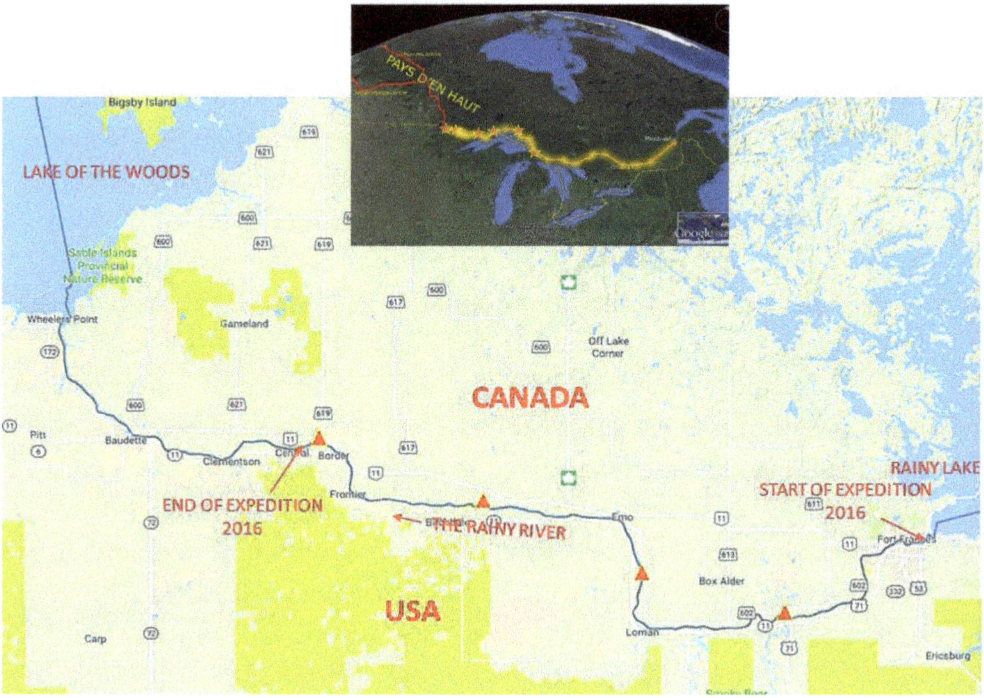
PAYS D'EN HAUT
LAKE OF THE WOODS
CANADA
END OF EXPEDITION
2016
THE RAINY RIVER
RAINY LAKE
START OF EXPEDITION
2016
USA

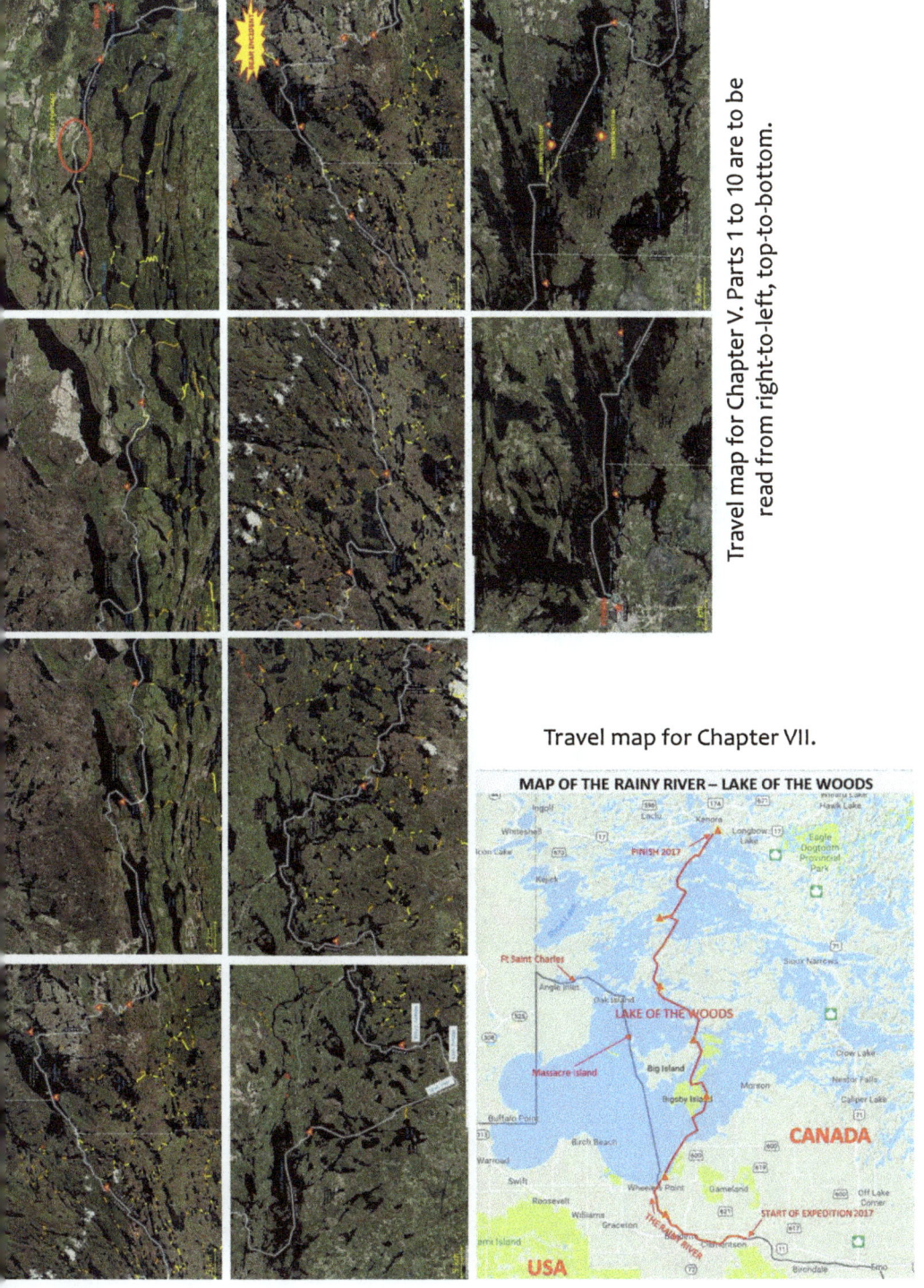

Travel map for Chapter V. Parts 1 to 10 are to be read from right-to-left, top-to-bottom.

Travel map for Chapter VII.

CHAPTER IV.

A chilly early evening on Lake Superior. Notice the barely budding trees on June 5th.

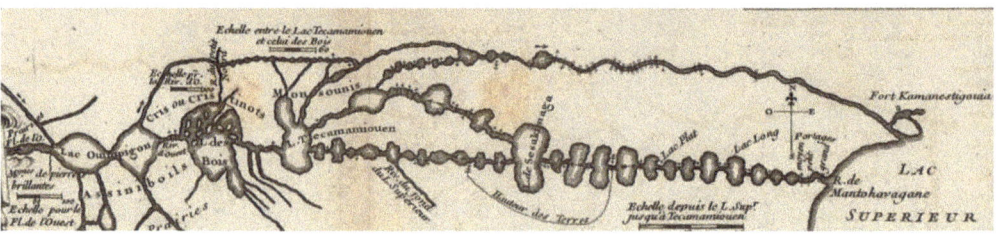

The map of the water route from Lake Superior west that Ochagach drew for La Vérendrye on a scroll of birch bark.

Top: A replica of Fort Grand Portage. Bottom: View of Grand Portage Bay with Hat Point Peninsula left and Mutton Island in the middle after my arrival to the fort's pier.

Left: Here I had an experience while carrying the canoe. It involved an act of thrashing of trees some 15m off the trail that lasted about half a minute. I attribute it to a Sasquatch intimidation behaviour.

A well-deserved rest on the portage trail.

Grand Portage Trail is skirting a vast beaver pond on some 250m long elevated boardwalk atop the beaver dam. Likely being one of its first users in early June, I had to overcome an ice-jam-caused gap in the structure by descending it, jumping over the pond outflow and climbing back on.

The only visible top of the Partridge Falls portaged on the navigable part of the Pigeon River.

The lower of the Pigeon Falls on the un-navigable, bottom part of the Pigeon River that has to be circumvented by the Grand Portage.

An evening meditation in the camp on Pigeon Peninsula only two kilometres away from the place of the fateful end of the American kayaker.

CHAPTER V.

Top: When I found the start of the portage from North Fowl Lake to Moose Lake in a jungle of wild rice, the unloading was tricky in deep mud. Bottom: A colourful scene of my last minute camp on the Canadian side of Mountain Lake.

My frequent companions on the Fur Trade Canoe Route from top: loon, otter, turtle.

The evening and morning light show scenes around my Pine Islands camp on Basswood Lake.

Ready to push-off into Rat Lake after a very short carry.

Ready to start the portage from South Lake to North Lake over the Height of Land. Notice the boundary marking cone.

A narrow curving channel connecting North Lake with Little Gunflint Lake that I shot in the canoe without hitting and thus saved myself the portage.

Lake Saganaga - the scene of my stand-off with a black bear that was dead-set on taking over my food laid out all over the flat rock behind the canoe where I was making its inventory. Later, it is hermetically sealed back in the drybag and hanging from a pine tree.

Lower Basswood Falls.

My arrival at Curtain Falls.

Curtain Falls.

An early morning scene and a Canadian float plane base on Lac La Croix.

My first camp on the east part of Rainy Lake.

My arrival at Fort Frances on the 19th September, 2015.

CHAPTER VI.

My first day out of Fort Frances on the brim-full Rainy River.

Poison Ivy is enjoying rampant growth along the banks of the Rainy River.

My rushed camp of probably "squatting" on a private property, unaware at the time of what Poison Ivy looked like. Notice the healthy bush of this plant behind the rail of the old fence. I went to take this picture in shorts and bare feet.

CHAPTER VII.

To make sure that one finds the right channel between many islands over vast stretches of open water one has to resort to tools for precise orientation.

Protected by Gore-tex, the canoe loaded, we are ready to set out into a blustery day on the Rainy River in our moving towards Lake of the Woods.

Preparations for an early morning launch from our camp on Lake of the Woods near the mouth of the Rainy River.

A view from the top of Sable Island sand bar in Fourmile Bay.

The narrows between Bigsby and Gooseneck Islands offered a cozy sandbar for a scenic camp.

The second day in our movement northward on Lake of the Woods we returned to the Canadian Shield. Picturesque little granite islands provided nice spots for a lunch, or snack stops with nice swimming refreshments.

A family of Canada geese is nearly mature for the winter migration.

Right: My SPOT device allowed me to send a predetermined list of addressees an e-mail message over satellite that "I am OK", "I need help", or, after flipping over a protective cover, an "SOS" messages. They came with an interactive map and a pin head of my position. The "SOS" message would activate an international rescue activity.

A scene of a lull period in a series of spectacular thunderstorms in our camp on a northwest granite point of Big Island.

Our accidental camp in a fiord of Kennedy Island where we believe that we had possible interaction with Sasquatches, likely attracted by the smell of Milena's freshly baked bannock. Bottom: departing it early next morning.

the price for the service was on the level of taxi fares. For several hundred kilometres, this was really high. The first company had a standard price of $500 for the trip from Fort Frances to Thunder Bay. My lake was situated another 150 kilometres further south on the border. Consequently, I should have expected a total sum of some $700. Besides that, I was to pay another $100 for the safekeeping of my Jeep at Fort Frances. When I mentioned to the second cab company, a competitor of the first one, that I had another option, its owner immediately offered to take me to my destination for a flat fee of $500. Without much hesitation I accepted the offer on the phone. We were to meet early the next morning at the parking lot of the Gold Star Taxi company. During the night in the motel, however, I hardly slept. The stress from the uncertainty of my success would not let me sleep nor eat. Through the whole night, I was thinking. The Gold Star was planning to use a regular Chrysler minivan with front-wheel drive. It had no roof rack and thus we would spend a lot of time untying my canoe from my Jeep and tying it in an improvised way onto the rooftop of the minivan. Besides that, I wasn't even sure if we would find the way to the lake at all.

In the morning, I turned up at the taxi company's parking lot, which was still in darkness, before 6:00. Its owner, Doug, was already there with a Dodge Caravan. We introduced ourselves to each other and shook hands. I revealed a bold plan that had emerged from my sleepless meditations: "Doug, look, this Jeep would have no problem making it to the lake. The canoe is already reliably affixed to its roof. The gear is inside, the tank is now full of gas. If we drive in it together to the lake and you then return with it to Fort Frances, I will pay you $200. If you park it at your house and guard it there until I reappear in town by canoe, I will pay you yet another $60. What do you say?" There was no problem. Doug immediately agreed. It was likely that he had been, in fact, worried about his vehicle. Without delay, we jumped into the Jeep and started out. I was driving and maintained a conversation for the long hours of traveling along the highway in the direction of Thunder Bay. Doug didn't do much talking. He was roughly my age, a slender cowboy type, apparently a heavy smoker.

In Kakabeka Falls, we turned south and followed secondary paved roads in the direction of the border. The settlements along the way gradually petered out until we finally drove through vast forests on pavement that seemed to be wide enough for only one vehicle. I turned off onto a gravel road at the right spot. After crossing a small river, I followed an arc of the road that curved in the right direction. These roads no longer showed on the map and the electronic navigator on the screen of my Jeep displayed only an arrow of my position that hovered in empty space. I knew that we should arrive at a fork in the road where we were to choose its left branch. A turn-off from it to the right should then appear after some distance. This was supposed to lead to the lake. The fork in the road soon appeared. Its left branch seemed to be well traveled. We followed it. After some while, a right turn-off appeared and, even though somewhat faint, we turned onto it. The new track turned very rough, going through rugged terrain. The Dodge Caravan would have barely coped with it. The turn-off, however, curved into the wrong direction after a while when it also started climbing steeply. In the end it petered out. We were forced to turn back. I tried to determine our position using an app on my iPhone, but, for an unknown reason, it failed. Every time I opened the app, the cell phone crashed. What now? I despaired. We had already lost over an hour in fruitless wanderings and the tank contained enough gas for only 100 kilometres. The nearest gas station happened to be 80 kilometres away. I was already dreading that we would have to return with me having wasted the transportation money for nothing and, in the end, I would reappear back in Edmonton in a few days humiliated. I had a nagging feeling that we had turned off too soon at the wrong fork. The arrow in the navigator seemed to be hovering too close to the asphalt road. Furthermore, I remembered that in the satellite view of Google Earth, the correct right turn-off to the lake had been situated past the ridge of a rocky escarpment that we now saw in front of us. I was freaking out. Fortunately, Doug remained admirably cool and let me make decisions without any comments. When we returned to the fork, I decided on a daring last ditch attempt. Instead of turning toward the asphalt road, I turned to the left and followed the right branch of the fork. God had listened. After a few hundred metres, he sent a local old-timer in a pickup traveling in the opposite direction. I immediately jumped out of my Jeep and flailing my arms wildly above my head, flagged him down. "Sir, I hope that you can help me. Do you know it around here? We are looking for a way to North Fowl Lake!" The man raked his hand through his massive gray beard and replied: "Well, you are on the right track. After about 300 metres, you will arrive at a fork. Take the left branch. You will round a long corner to the left and a turn-off will appear to the right. That one will bring you to the lake. "Praise the lord!" I immediately jumped back behind the wheel and after some while we were sloshing through axle-deep, liquid mud to an opening panorama of the lake shore. In spite of his stoic nature, not even Doug could hide his utter delight that, in the end, our efforts were not in vain. After we untied the canoe and unloaded the equipment from the Jeep, he wanted to help me get ready for sailing off. But I thanked him and sent him back. I knew that the logistics of my preparations would demand at least a couple of hours. While doing this, I like to think alone. Doug now had only 80 kilometres worth of gas left in the tank to the nearest pump that was 80 kilometres away. Yet it did not seem to have fazed him in the least as he was disappearing through the deep mud into the shadow of the forest.

Alone again in the wild

All of a sudden, I was alone again in the middle of the wilderness. Among the trees on both sides of the road's end, 4x4 pickups, Jeeps and boat trailers were silently snoozing. It seemed as if they were waiting like Sci-Fi robots to be activated for the final Armageddon — exactly as I had seen it at the maximum zoom-in level on Google Earth. But otherwise, nary a living creature stirred anywhere. I sorted out my gear and found that it included several pieces of clothing and other small items that were meant to stay in the Jeep. Now I would have to transport them in the canoe and on the portages all the way to Fort

Frances. I felt fear. My self-confidence was depressed to a minimum. I was hardly 50% convinced that I would successfully make it to Fort Frances. Yet once my Jeep was gone, I was committed. Bailing out anywhere along the route before Fort Frances was next to impossible. Was my risky adventuring perhaps finally embarking onto that tragedy scenario? Would my aging body be able to cope with the hardships of 40 portages and daily paddling marathons? Not even the hardy adventurers at the peak of their strengths — who represented the paddling troop of the first Europeans who in 1731 had the courage to penetrate up to these parts and explore the territory beyond Lake Superior — were willing to risk their lives. They mutinied against continuing on this way. It was the expedition of the Frenchman, Pierre Gaultier de Varennes, Sieur de La Vérendrye (1685 – 1749), who had resolved to find a way across the continent to the western sea and to the riches of the Orient. Discouraged by the dreadful toil of the Grand Portage and scared by the horror stories related to this journey, which were maliciously spread by the envious enemies of La Verendrye before he left Montreal, the group then split. A mere half of the bravest continued on up to the outflowing river, the Rainy (or Rivier La Plui for the voyageurs), from the lake of the same name. On a land point there, they built the westernmost base of the emerging young Canadian civilization, Fort St. Pierre, which became today's Fort Frances, the final destination of my present voyage. They had traveled through here during roughly the same month as I did now. The second half of the outfit, including La Verendrye himself, then returned to overwinter at the mouth of the Kaministiquia River (the location of the later Fort William and today's Thunder Bay).

There was a small wooden pier here where I finally loaded the canoe and stretched on its spray cover. Then at last, I pushed off into a narrow, clear channel through the band of reeds that lined the lake's shores. When we had arrived, the lake surface was as smooth as a mirror. Yet by now, a strong southern wind had risen and its side waves challenged my progress towards the portage out of the western extremity of the lake. Behind me to the left rear, I could see through narrows the island where I had camped two years ago and from which I returned back to Thunder Bay. Like Verendrye, I thus got to know the way to Waterfowl Lake from Thunder Bay by wayfaring upon Lake Superior to Fort Grand Portage in the USA, by carrying all the gear repeatedly up the Grand Portage trail to the Pigeon River and up the river to it, all in both directions, up and down. Now I was at last aiming for the far tip of the lake, covered in a thick growth of wild rice. After searching in the reeds for a while, I finally discovered the approach to the start of the portage. That led to the next lake on the boundary water route, Moose Lake. The access was extremely muddy. I poled the boat up the goo with the paddle like a sled as far as I could before I carefully disembarked, stepping on bent bunches of marsh grass. I then dragged the canoe upon the mud still higher before I could at last gain access to remove the spray cover and start unloading. The portage was rough in comparison to those that I had hitherto experienced. With three repeat loads and the return trips in between, I had to walk its length five times. Exhausted from a lack of sleep, the long hours of the last three days behind the wheel of the Jeep and a loss of appetite, I luckily and gratefully found a relatively nice campsite on the Canadian side of the Moose Lake shore near the end of the portage. I quickly erected the tent, unfurled the bedroll in it and at 5:00 in the evening, I curled up to sleep. My sleep was restless, yet thanks to its length — further extended by a morning rain — I felt relatively refreshed. I didn't eat supper or breakfast. I had no appetite for food. This condition would last for almost three days before I gradually rediscovered my lost instinct to eat. I packed all and loaded it into the canoe. The fly sheet of the tent was still wet and I placed it separately on the top so it could dry and not get other things wet. This time, I stretched the spray cover on the canoe because I was not quite sure that it wouldn't rain again during the day.

Moose Lake was higher up than Fowl Lake in altitude and it possessed a somewhat different character. There were less of the reeds, rushes and other signs of muddy marshes here that had appeared on the previous one. There, they likely attracted the aquatic fowl that

gave the lake its name — Waterfowl, or Fowl. The voyageurs had a
French name for it, Lac Aux Outardes, or Oies. It also used to be called
Goose Lake. As I learned later, so was the long portage to it from
Pigeon River, which back in the summer of 2013, I stumbled upon
and used merely by sheer luck — the "Goose Portage." Moose Lake
was surrounded by a hilly landscape that was covered with mostly
coniferous forest. I had crossed its length in a relatively relaxed pace
well before noon and reached a ruggedly rocky portage at its end.
It led to the next lake, another degree higher, Mountain Lake. The
rather long portage to it was broken into three by two small lakes that
had to be paddled across in the boat. I thus delivered the whole outfit
to the first lake. Here I reloaded the canoe without disassembling the
packs for the back, re-embarked it and paddled the kilometre plus of
the lake's length through reeds and lily pads to the start of the next
segment of the portage. All was repeated to the second little pond.
Having overcome a deeply muddy beginning of the third leg of the
portage beyond it, I finally reached the shore of long Mountain
Lake. I had, of course, traversed the length of each portage five
times. Hence, I did not start paddling on the lake until after 3:00. I
resolved to paddle as far as possible towards the end of the lake and
stop when I saw a possible camping spot on the Canadian side. On
the Canadian side, one is allowed to camp "wild" (back-country)
wherever it is suitable, while on the American side, camping is only
allowed in designated and marked campsites. The latter, however,
are equipped with cast-iron forestry fireplaces and leveled spots for
two to three tents. They are even equipped with a plastic, roofless
forestry commode as a toilet along a path deeper in the woods. It is
important to note that the historic water route of the fur trade, which
my expedition followed, wound constantly along the border between
Canada and the United States. In fact, it was the other way around.
The boundary between the two countries in this region was actually
defined by this route. It was officially established at the beginning of
the 19th century. When I was getting ready for this stretch in 2013 and
researched what kind of a permit I would have to acquire for crossing
the border from Canada into the USA on Lake Superior on the way

to Grand Portage, I had to have a so-called "Back Country Border Crossing Permit" from the American authorities. But to my surprise, I also had to get one from the Canadian ones. I had to pay fees for both. This time, I decided to ignore these requirements and have no permits. My rationale was the following: In the first place, I would not venture anywhere deep into the territory of the United States this time. I had launched from the Canadian side and I strived to keep to it during my travels. From the beginning, I therefore always looked for camping on the Canadian side. In any case, I prefer the free "wild" camping. I did anticipate that the border could be guarded and I had a logical explanation prepared for a possible border control inquiry. According to the Webster–Ashburton Treaty from 1842, the spirit of establishing the border on the fur trade route was to make travel along it readily accessible from both sides. And this not only exactly along the border line, but with access to all the elements facilitating travel on it. This means free access to portages for a Canadian, if they happen to be on the U.S. side, and vice versa for the American on the Canadian side, as well as to a distant American shore of a lake and vice versa if it is necessary to move along its shelter for safe travel due to wind and waves. I felt confident that I could successfully refer to it if I ended up in a legal situation. It remains an interesting fact that during the entire voyage from Fowl Lake to Fort Frances, I never met with any border patrol while I moved freely, sometimes as far as five kilometres into the U.S. territory. During all this time, I displayed decals of the Canadian and the Czech flags on the stern of my canoe. I must admit that this situation brought up another level of adventure for me. I constantly felt like a fugitive to some degree and I analyzed every motorboat that raced from a distance towards me as possibly being the border patrol. This certainly had a reinforcing influence on my credo — always followed anyway — never to leave any trace of my passing through the wilderness and to maintain a minimalistic profile.

Before I reached the end of Mountain Lake in the canoe, it was already past 5:00. The sun had considerably lowered itself toward the western horizon. I paddled directly against it. To top it off, its reflection on the waves was blinding me. In spite of the shading from my hat brim, my eyes could see nothing on the passing coastline but deep shadow. This strongly hindered my ability to find a campsite. Sites for backcountry camping are rare as it is because the shores of the lakes are mostly lined with shattered granite and dense forest growth right down to the water's edge. Hence, one usually has to look for a flat rock platform that juts out from the shore into the water. It seemed to me that I was passing a small black beach. But I rejected it as likely muddy. Only when my hope for a possible campsite on a point with a tall pine up ahead turned false, I turned around for a second look at the black beach. I now had the sun behind me and could see right away that what I had taken for a beach, was in fact, a granite slab gently sloping into the water. The unobstructed part of it was not very wide — I could hardly place a tent on it. But the weather was clear and calm. After a moment of walking from one of its ends to the other, I unloaded the canoe onto it. First, I pitched the tent as usual and prepared the bed in it. In the next phase, I attended to the kitchen. That is when I discovered that somebody had used the site before me since it already had a good fire pit built from stones. When the water was heating in the kettles to boil four liters of tea for tomorrow and for supper from a food packet, I jumped naked into the lake and had a swim to relax my arm muscles from paddling, my leg muscles from stumbling along the rocky portages and those of my back from toting the heavy loads. The water in these smaller lakes, after the exceptionally warm summer, was pleasantly warm. No threat of hypothermia in the case of a canoe upset was of any issue here this year. In the twilight of the evening, the place quickly turned into a cozy home. My stress from the uncertainty started to dissolve.

In the morning, I set out relatively early. I did not cook any breakfast. The kitchen outfit had been stashed in its nylon stuff sack and that, in turn, was packed in the "hardware" drybag since last night. My breakfast, consisting of a protein bar washed down with cold tea, got postponed until the time when, after a short paddle, I reached the portage at the end of the lake. Everything around there reeked of a fishy odour. It was apparent that a bald eagle had chosen a flat granite rock outcrop here as his countertop for gutting and pecking his catch. Remains of fish heads, fins and tails in varied stages of rot that lay scattered around testified as evidence. There was also a border marker here. It was in the form of a concrete pedestal with a shiny, metallic cone jutting vertically up from it. The boundary was further made visible here by a recently-cleared, wide cutline. This lay across a low ridge that separated Mountain Lake from long and narrow Watap Lake. The latter was the next link in the chain of the boundary route. The roughly kilometre-long portage trail at first wound through the cutline, then slipped into woods on the American side and then returned back into the border cutline near its end on the shore of the next lake. Near the shore, there was another border marker. Watap Lake snaked among densely forested shores like a motionless wider river. When Milena and I printed out a series of satellite maps covering the boundary route, I did not consider any need to print out further close-up details here. At the time, the topography of this section appeared simple to me. My negligence now cost me almost an hour of lost time when, after a while, I arrived at a false end of the lake and could not find the portage there. Only after I had fruitlessly explored every beaver chute into the water did I turn to analyze the shoreline somewhat back from whence I came. To my great surprise, I found that I had missed the continuation of the lake. It peeled off in an inconspicuous little bay that was shrouded by shadow against the noon sun. I had not seen it the first time. Now I paddled into it through a shallow narrows where the bottom of my canoe rubbed against a rock. The voyageurs likely had to lighten the load off their birch bark "canots du nord" (*"dé*charge*")* here to safely pass through. The new part of the lake bore a new name — Rove Lake. At the scale in which I had printed out the satellite view of lakes Watap and Rove, the map covered over their narrow width in many places by a relatively wide band displaying the border. Only with the benefit of the lesson provided to me by my previous lapse of attention, I noticed a second extension of the lake, again through an obscured narrows that finally brought me to its real end. This was the beginning of an over three-kilometre portage to Rose Lake. It was only 2:00 in the afternoon. Yet I knew that I would have to walk some 16 kilometres on this portage, of which nine-and-a-half would be with heavy loads. For that, I would need the greater part of a day. There was not enough time remaining now. I could not count on camping somewhere along an unfinished portage. I had to postpone it till the next morning. I therefore looked for some wild camping around the Canadian side at the end of Rove Lake. Several kilometres back, I had seen a pretty spot on a point with mature pines, but I would not want to lose time in the morning by repeating the paddling gain that I had already achieved. In the end, I thus chose a true emergency type of camping on the narrow strip of a spongy, moss and low bushes-covered shore between the water's edge and thick young spruce growth. I had to use my machete to chop out sufficient room in the low spruce branches for my tent. It wasn't cozy here, yet I took advantage of the still warm sunny afternoon for a rewarding swim in the lukewarm water of the lake. Soon after, I retired to an early rest in the tent upon a bed of deep moss. I planned to get up the next day with the crack of dawn.

The lake and my camp were shrouded in a low, heavy fog. But as the sharp rays of the rising sun started penetrating it, my loneliness was broken courtesy of a show from an otter. With a noisy splish-splashing he weaved through the lake surface and snaked with his flexible shiny body to the left and right. Every once in a while, he thrust his head and neck out of the water and sent me an angry look accompanied with rattley snorts. I had likely settled too close to his nest or perhaps I had simply just trespassed on his sovereign territory. What must have brought him satisfaction was the fact that I tossed my gear roughly into the boat and set out toward the portage. It had its beginning only a little over 100 metres away from my camp. Once there, I carefully sorted everything out and assembled it into loads for my back. The first one was my waterproof frame pack that contained the sleeping bag, all the clothing, the tent and a Bio-Lite stove. The stove was rather heavy — even heavier than my minimalistic tent — yet unlike other typical models, it didn't use liquid fuels. Instead, one could use pieces of wood, pine cones and other natural fuel in it. It generated its own thermal electricity that powered a fan. This blew the flame into the mightiness of a propane torch. The excess electrical energy was then made available through a USB outlet on the stove for charging camera batteries, cell phones, etc. It was meant to be my backup mode of charging in case there wasn't enough sun for my solar chargers. I must admit, though, that I hardly ever used this contraption. Next time, for the situations where there is a need to minimize weight, I would leave it at home. For a portage, I would add a waterproof map case to the pack, a small drybag with electronics and one two-liter bottle of tea. To the top of the frame, I would still strap a rolled up sleeping mat. The second load for the portage was assembled on the hunting pack frame. It was welded from light aluminum tubes. On its bottom shelf, I strapped a drybag with food horizontally. At the start of the expedition, the latter represented the heaviest object to be transported. Atop of it, I would then vertically strap on a second drybag with the "hardware." If the tent fly was still wet at the time of packing for the portage, it went into the top of this bag. The third load for the portage was the canoe. With it, I also carried a large lumbar fanny pack, which, in addition to a shoulder strap, had a waist strap. In it, I carried rubber sandals, fingerless leather paddling gloves and a second bottle of tea. I also slipped the lifejacket on my shoulders but would not zip it up.

I started the portage with the waterproof backpack. With it, I also carried a waterproof fanny pack that contained items for day needs and food for lunch and snacks. This I carried turned forward on my stomach. In my hands, I carried a camera and the spare (kayak) paddle as a walking cane. The path was very rough, bristling with large pointy rocks that jutted out in all angles. The rocky stretches alternated with muddy sections where one was forced to balance like a rope walker on the edge between the limbs of the trail-lining tree growth and deep liquid mud in the path. It wound and climbed through young deciduous woods as well as through tall conifers. The trail occasionally provided a hurdle in the form of a large log that lay across to stimulate a wakeup from the beast-of-burden-lethargy. The fresh morning sun made the greenery glow in the vivid yellow-red hues of autumn foliage, creating a merry carnival atmosphere. In about a third of the distance, the path had a junction with a turn-off to Daniel Lake in the States. From here, in the direction of Rose Lake, the trail had a long stretch of relatively smooth promenade-like walking up to a region of marshes where beaver mega-projects flooded a short spread of the passage, submerging it under water. This called for a great deal of acrobatics on slippery, fallen tree trunks, bent bushes and the skirting of the deluge through thick growth. Especially when passing through here with the canoe, there was no threat of boredom. Right here, in a tight wiggle of the path through tall marsh reeds, I almost collided with a trio of Americans who were travelling in the opposite direction with one canoe. While I still faced two more returns for the next loads ahead of me, they only had to walk once on each portage. It was an inverse proportion formula that one would readily deduce on the way; three paddlers in one canoe = one trip on the portages; two paddlers per canoe = two trips; a solo paddler = three trips on all portages. The last third of the trail continued straight to the lake under the canopy of a coniferous forest. But this was again over rough rocks scattered in chaos throughout the trail. At long last, the shore of Rose Lake revealed a welcoming scenic beach of coarse sand under tall, mature pines. The deep blue surface of the lake glittered in the prenoon sun with thousands of starlet reflections on fine rippling waves from a westerly breeze. Before I finally slaved my way up to it with the canoe on my shoulders, I had to circumvent the beaver flood zone while bending young two-and-a-half-metre birch trees under my crotch like a bulldozer. By then, the sun had long swung past its zenith and late afternoon set in. Sweat was pouring down my face and my weary skeleton screamed with pain. I saw not a living soul anywhere around. Hence without much hesitation, I stripped all and gleefully plopped myself into the welcoming arms of the crystal clear waters of the lake. For a while, I frolicked in it like a happy amphibian and weaved through its surface in dolphin-like leaps, not unlike my morning otter visitor. Once I had a satisfactory swim and relaxed my abused muscles a little bit, I dressed up again, loaded the canoe and pushed off into the lake. By then, it was already around 4:00 and evening was approaching. Like practically all the lakes on the boundary route, this narrow lake stretched from west to east and for me, a headwind prevailed. But now toward the evening it had somewhat abated. On this part of the canoe route where it rises through its highest altitude on the divide between the watersheds of the Saint Lawrence River and that which drains down into Hudson's Bay, I encountered a relatively populous traffic of canoes from the U.S. side. This was because Minnesota, as a lake country state, abounds with many bases of outfitters who rent out canoes and gear to water tourists together with detailed descriptions of multiday canoeing loops. There the clients are dispatched, sometimes even with paid guides. The loops encompass various lake chains of which many partly overlap the boundary canoe route. Interestingly, practically everyone that I met on this route, moved from west to east and so took advantage of the prevailing westerly winds. Only a masochist like myself resolves to face the winds and waves in travelling from east to west. Yet this is exactly the way in which Canada was discovered and this is how I wanted to discover it for myself.

After a while, I met a pair of canoes with American tourists who despaired that all the campsites on the American shoreline were already taken. They asked if it was possible to camp at the end of the lake from where I came. When I assured them of it, they in turn, expressed concern about where I was going to camp. I replied that I would be looking for a wild camp site on the Canadian side. This reaped me a smile of silent admiration with a "V" of two raised fingers as a sign of wishing me success. Not in the least, though, was I sure that I would really discover any campsite on the Canadian side. Not until past the half-length of the lake when I became uneasy from the lengthening of the evening shadows, did I suddenly notice what looked like very inconspicuous descending steps from the shore to the water with a seemingly worn and newly regrown grass cover. Rather skeptically I halted here, stood up in the canoe to look and "Voila!" — saw a beautiful little meadow shaded by a grove of young birch trees whose snow-white trunks encircled it. There were signs of its prior usage that included a rock fire pit. The whole area was overgrown with tall, wild oat-like grass and perhaps unused this year. In a flash my tent stood here, flames licked the bottoms of the kettles and I was enjoying another refreshing swim before the water would start boiling. It had once again become my home — an oasis of sources to regenerate my strength and boost my hope for the success of my continuing journey.

To the west of my camp, Rose Lake markedly narrowed down and wound shallow in between woody shores with a muddy bottom. Alex Mackenzie, the prominent explorer for the Northwest Company and the first man whose team reached the Pacific coast by canoe across the continent in 1793, notes in his journal that the shallow end part of Rose Lake had a strange effect on their canoes. It allegedly imposed drag on their canoes' movement, as if the shallow muddy bottom sucked on them. I do not know if I experienced something similar but the fact of the matter is that the next morning my water craft did not develop any racing speed here in spite of my vigorous paddling. This was partly due to the fact that every once in a while, I poked the paddle into the soft bottom and could not perform a proper stroke. Here I passed the iconic Canadian loons whose haunting wails or hysteric laugh periodically pierced the silence of the misty morning ambiance above the surface of the lake. Yet my interest was piqued mainly by a family of pure white, large trumpeter swans — two adults and an adolescent youngster — who aristocratically arched their slender long necks in minuet-like bows.

Before its end, the route left the lake in a short portage — perhaps only three or four canoe lengths long — over a small rocky ridge into short Rat Lake. Soon after I reached the next portage at the end of this lake, a party of young Americans in three rented canoes also arrived. While carrying on the portage trail, I mingled with them. During the ensuing small talk, I was pleasantly surprised that one of the young fellows recognized the Czech flag in the decal on the stern of my canoe. He must have been an educated university student. We instantly became friends. As to their canoeing experience and the optimum physical style in paddling, they were badly lacking and I was thus way ahead of them on the next lake right after leaving the end of the portage.

Height of Land — becoming a "Home du Nord"

The next lake was South Lake. This lake was long. It was the last one in the chain of the Boundary Route that still drained into the watershed of the Saint Lawrence. The portage out of it, sometimes called "The Height of Land Portage," into the next lake surmounted the ridge of the divide into the watershed of Hudson's Bay. Its start was situated on the north shore of South Lake, in roughly two-thirds of its length. The next lake — on the Hudson's Bay side — was North Lake. The crossing of the divide used to possess great significance. By crossing it, the "pays d'en haut" — the upper country — was officially reached and the new recruits of the Northwest Company underwent a ritual similar to the christening by Neptune on the occasions of crossing the equator at the sea. The newbies were patted with wet cedar boughs that officially installed them into becoming the "Hommes du Nord" (Men of the North) and, of course, it provided another reason for cracking open a keg of the "high wine." I arrived at the Height of Land Portage on a rather choppy surface of South Lake shortly after noon. On the portage, I met an interesting trio of Californians from San Diego — two young men and a very athletic young woman — who traveled in the opposite direction, and this on stand-up surfboards. At the time of our encounter, they had been facing a rare headwind in their direction of travel, while I, for a change, enjoyed a wind in my back. I could not believe that they also transported large rubber packs on their surfboards but they insisted that this had not been a problem. In my opinion, though, the standing position on the board represented the major unsuitability of this mode of travel for this lake wilderness with its high incidence of headwinds and waves.

By the time I pushed off from the portage into North Lake, it was already past 4:00. I first sought the possibility of camping on the Canadian coastline. But the narrow sandy beach, which only looked promising, turned up to have been abused in the past by untidy fishermen who left the bush behind it disgustingly littered with scattered garbage. To be fair, it might have been deposited as flotsam by the prevailing winds-driven surf. I therefore focussed my attention across the lake to its American side where in about the distance of a kilometre, I suspected signs of a campsite that was marked on the map. Nowhere on the lake could I see anybody. The lake landscape appeared to be dreamily deserted. As I neared the intended spot, a vividly green stripe on the small length of a bare beach under it worried me that I was looking at a green canoe pulled up on shore and that the site would hence be occupied. Yet on further approach, the stripe turned out to be a lusciously-green strip of tall grass. The campsite was free — waiting just for me. This was the first time that I used a campsite on the American side of the border. I enjoyed the comfort of a leveled spot for the tent here and the log seating configured into a square around a cast-iron grid fire pit. I also admired the plastic commode of a toilet deeper in the woods. Thanks to the lasting warm weather of Indian summer, I again enjoyed a nice swim in the small sheltered bay of the camp's landing. The only disadvantage of the site was its lack of firewood. Everything in the near vicinity had its dry wood supplies thoroughly picked over. In a serene moment, I was sitting on a log by the fire while savouring gulps of delicious Drambuie on my palate from a light flask to celebrate my crossing of the divide. At that moment, a family of Ruffed Grouse — a cock with four hens — gradually emerged from under the surrounding growth. Just like domestic chickens, they started peacefully pecking the ground right around me, making almost inaudible clucking murmurs. Then they slowly shifted off to have a drink from the lake. It is possible that some of the visitors of the site before me might have fed them here.

As I had reached the start of about a 50-metre portage by paddling to the end on the deserted lake the next morning, the water flowing out of it through a narrow winding channel reminded me that from North Lake on, I would be descending. My traveling along the boundary route chain would be downhill. I had not expected a portage, hence only with contempt, I went to survey its path. In the morning before the launch, a dramatic sky in the east seemingly threatened with heavy, rain-laden clouds. I therefore laced the spray cover on the canoe. Now I was reluctant to remove it again after such a short paddle for the sake of such a short portage. The inconvenience from this point of view on one hand outweighed the danger of a risky operation on the other. That is, I started to study the narrow channel of the outflow from the lake. The truth is that this was only about a metre-and-a-half wide and it snaked in three serpentines among large rocks. Yet… "Shall I try it?"… I planted myself firmly in the canoe and wrapped my hands around the paddle with a vise-like grip. Then I slowly moseyed towards the sucking maw of the lake outflow while constantly analysing the structure of the current in front of me. I was deciding what maneuver would be required where. The current set the speed. I just tilted the blade of the paddle in flash movements and stabbed it left and right as needed with lightning speed. In a few seconds, my canoe shot into the wide calm water of the lower lake. The hull had not even touched any of the rocks of the channel. Great pride from the significant saving of time and from eliminating the need to portage spread over my shoulders.

I now moved on a narrower water body — almost as on a wide river — between low shores lined with areas of reeds. A low ridge rose on the north side that was covered with a coniferous tree forest that consisted of many pines — both the majestic Eastern White Pine as well as the red pine. The left bank contained a low, green growth with thinly scattered bare masts of tall trees, burned by a forest fire. This was Little Gunflint Lake. After some distance, the lake narrowed further and paddling through thin reeds and water lilies, I slipped twice with the canoe down an overflow of beaver dams, the only spots where there was a discernible current. When it seemed that I had reached a dead end where the lake terminated, a narrow right-angle turn around a sharp point of red sand appeared. I ascribed it in an elegant move, tilting the canoe. I now emerged into a vast open surface on the large and long Gunflint Lake. On the right, a long beach of red sand stretched out. The setting appeared to be an ideal site for a camp but it wasn't even 10:00 in the morning yet. Towards the west, about an 11-kilometre length of the lake stretched out in front of me, the end of which faded out in the misty distance. The lake was over three kilometres wide. It had road access from both sides — the American and the Canadian. As a result, motor boats appeared here and even cottages. At first, I moved along its right – the Canadian side, aiming in a straight line to a place on the right hand shore near the end of the lake where an inconspicuous narrow channel was supposed to usher me into the lake of the route's continuation. This lake is called Magnetic Lake. As the day progressed, a steadily strengthening wind blew that gradually shifted from the southeast to the southwest. First, the wind sent its component of a headwind against my face. Second, it whipped waves that grew in size across the lake's width. At the north shore, there was already surf like at a sea. This forced me to traverse across the width of the lake to its left — the American shore and then paddle in its lee all the way to the lake's end. Only then, I had to cut across it again to the sought-after narrows of its outflow.

Magnetic Lake was surrounded with cottages, hence it did not offer any chance for camping. I hurried to paddle across it and enter its narrow outflow, the Pine River. Here I ran into a waterfall called Little Rock Falls. It was preceded by a short chute through a rock ledge that I shot through with a pounding heart and a white-knuckle grip on the paddle — again without the canoe's belly touching. I shortened the portage in this way but had to carry around the waterfall itself. It was already rather late and I was by then thoroughly exhausted from paddling against the wind on Gunflint Lake. I was pondering if I should set up an emergency camp somewhere before the portage but there was only rough and uneven rocky surface. In the end, I opted for a portage followed by looking for a wild camp somewhere beyond it. The carrying around the waterfall was really rough. It bordered on rock climbing as it traversed a steep side wall of the falls' canyon. A real challenge came when I was carrying the canoe as its length would not yield to the sharp wiggles between the rock wall and trees. In several spots, I had no choice but to hold the canoe on my shoulders with only one hand while I hung around tree trunks with the other. The continuing river Pine wound crookedly between granite rock banks, varying in its width from some 20 metres to 70. In its character, it was really a lake that filled a long fissure in the granite crust. There seemed to be no discernible current. Its shores were covered with low, young growth above which loomed the bare skeletons of sparse, tall trees burned by a vast forest fire in 2007. Several islands appeared in the river. One of them, picturesque with its silhouette of unburned mature pines on top of its granite platform — perhaps only a mere 10 metres in diameter — I finally approved for my campsite of the evening. According to the map, the island was situated on the Canadian side of the border. It was nice here. On one side, it was possible to dock with the canoe at a rock edge. Under the canopy of pine branches, a shallow rock saddle lined with a bedding of moss offered a cozy spot for my tent. Soon flames of a fire of pine cones and dry sticks blazed under the kettles. Meanwhile, once again, I slipped from the granite edge into deep water and had a swim at dusk.

The Pine River zigzagged through the granite crust, occasionally dropping by a waterfall or by a wildly cascading rock staircase. Twice I stuck out my neck to fate when I shot through the rock threshold of an initial chute. By doing that, I shortened the portage around the rest of the obstacle. Several times, the earth crack opened wider and the water filled to create smaller lakes. Only upon them, the wind mattered a bit. Otherwise, the incised narrowness of the river yielded reasonable wind shelter. I underwent four portages that day, which at the time, represented my utmost accomplishment for one day. The evening had caught up with me before yet another portage. Neither time nor energy in me remained for it. I found myself on one of the smaller lakes, this one called Granite Bay. I was forced to look for a wild camp on the Canadian side. A hilly terrain that surrounded the lake fell off steeply towards the water into a very uneven, marsh grass and bushes-covered shore line. The wistful, deserted landscape was littered with burned black trunks lying among the fresh greenery of new growth. Above it, blackened skeletons of still-standing trees jutted up. Like raised fingers, they threatened revenge for the crime that was committed on this corner of wild nature. Following a stint of breakneck climbing uphill and over the black chaos of deadfall, I erected the tent on the crest of a hill among sparse, broken-mast-like stumps. Then I quickly fulfilled the chore of cooking leaving all the rest of the outfit down on shore at the boat.

I left the spongy shore that consisted of an unkempt tangle of blackened, dead sticks and bleached branches that continued into the water under the azure sky of a sunny morning. The start of the next portage happened to be only some 200 metres from my landing spot. But first I wanted to have a look at the outflow from the lake that was only a little bit farther. As I neared it, I could hear the violent rumble of the water. I prudently floated closer to see the whole length of the channel. It seemed that I could paddle through the first part of the narrow passage in the boat, then stop, disembark and lead the canoe through the rest of the channel while walking in the water. For that, I needed to change from my socks and hiking boots into rubber sandals. Yet after stopping in mid channel and looking for the sandals in vain, I realized that I had left them on shore at my last campsite. They had been drying there since yesterday. The price of my attention slip was to drag the canoe back up the current, stepping carefully among the sharp-edged rocks on the bottom of the channel in bare feet. Then I would paddle back to pick up the sandals. But when I returned to the outflow again, now changed into the sandals, a sudden surge of bravery allowed me to shoot the whole length of the channel without stopping and disembarking the canoe. And this again, without touching a single rock with the bottom of the canoe. With boosted self-confidence, I then descended down several more drops of the river during the day. The name, according to the map, had now changed to the Granite River. One portage then brought me to Gneiss Lake followed by Devil's Elbow Lake. The route around the "Devil's Elbow" offered a shortcut by way of a portage over a narrow neck of land. For my case though, however long a loop of paddling on flat water while sitting in the canoe, is shorter both time-wise and hardship-wise than walking a portage five times. The river had narrowed again and led straight north now heading for two more drops. I portaged here around boisterous "Horse Tail Rapids." And then, "Saaaganaaaga!!!!" — my victory yell resounded with an echo of a happy "Yee-haw!!" from the people-less, wooded horizons as I finished carrying around Saganaga Falls and dipped the paddle again. I was finally entering vast Lake Saganaga. Its Ojibwe language name means "lake of many islands." From the map, I was aware of an American campsite on an island that was immediately past the inflow of the Granite River into the lake. Yet, as I approached it, a green canoe that was pulled up on shore, betrayed quickly that the site had already been taken. I had no choice but to continue along the route that now wound among the lake islands and look for wild camping on the Canadian side. It was high time. The lengthening shadows signaled the arrival of evening.

A bear stand-off on the Saganaga

Not before I had paddled about two additional kilometres around a large island with an unsuitable shoreline did I spot a site about half a kilometre across the water on the next shore that carried promising signs. It was a point with a flat rock platform under a thin grouping of tall pines. As I headed to it, my speculation proved true. There was a campsite here, likely infrequently used, if apparently by untidy fishermen. There was a rock firepit here with a square configuration of logs to comfortably sit around. Built near it, there was even some sort of a kitchen counter. Yet the counter was partially burned and tossed around were several soot-blackened grills from frying fish. Behind my tent, I later discovered a shallow pit where they disposed of spent frying oil. A thought flashed through my head that this campsite had to be known to a local bear. Yet I was happy that I had found a place to lay my head down just before darkness fell. In any case, I had never experienced any problem with bears during my entire canoe voyage from Montreal to here. After setting up the tent, I quickly readied myself to cook supper. In order to do that, I had to remove things from the drybag with food and make an inventory. This was needed because of food items that I knew had been put in but that I had not seen so far. I laid out the whole contents of the bag on a rock platform to have a good view of everything for a thorough examination. I gratefully found a baggie of dehydrated tropical fruit that I tore open right away and rewarded my neglected taste buds with a sizeable plug to chew. The dried fruit smelled heavenly. Similarly, a promise of otherworldly bliss was emanating from the chocolatey protein bars. Mixed with it were the aromas of spices, garlic and jerky. I could smell all those goodies from three metres away. I chose a package of Uncle Ben's rice meal with mushrooms, quickly unpacked the kitchen, collected firewood and started cooking. In the meantime, I ran from the canoe to the tent and back to place items in their proper places as I finished unloading the boat.

Somebody else must have smelled my goodies from up to five kilometres away. After some while, I could occasionally overhear a suspicious sound from behind a young spruce thicket that surrounded my campsite from behind. This sounded sometimes like a step, another time like something rubbing through the branches. Yet when I raised my head from work to listen, there was always silence. "I heard similar sounds around my campsite yesterday and still nothing came out of it," I comforted myself. I ate my supper with a healthy appetite and saved half of the mushroom risotto for tomorrow's cold lunch. When I returned to the canoe looking for an empty ziploc bag, the moment of revelation arrived. I sensed that somebody had just stepped out of the spruce thicket and, perhaps, even said something. I looked up in the direction of the sound and ... I froze. The evening was darkening and I was not wearing glasses but I could clearly see that in front of the thicket stood a big black bear looking daringly straight at me with its head lowered between shoulders. "This is just what I needed!" In my head, I feverishly started developing strategies. There was no way that I could back out of the place somehow. "It is going to be dark in a few minutes and I would never be able to find another campsite." The bear stood with his rear still just inside the

thicket, some 10 to 15 metres from me. "I will surely scare him away!" I declared hopefully. I started shouting at him as one would at a nosy stray dog while I swung my arms in shooing away motions. Yet the bear

advanced a step closer to me. I grabbed a paddle and started to amplify my yelling by slamming it against the trunk of the nearest pine tree. The bear advanced another step with a stiff, ruffled nape, his muzzle of a reddish tan aiming straight at me. Now he reinforced his threat with a rapid clicking of his teeth. "This expresses an aggressive challenge in them," I recalled from some Nat Geo TV program. Just yesterday, I had pondered about the usefulness of my belt with the attached items of protection against bears. "I have been carrying that bear spray, bear bangers and flares with me on various expeditions in the wilderness for some 20 plus years now. Never in my life have I had to use them. The next time, at least for trips where weight matters, I will leave them at home!" Now I quickly leaped to the belt that happened to still be at the canoe and extricated a bear banger from its belt pouch. I now tried to screw it onto a pen-shaped launcher. The bear banger had a fine thread in plastic though, and this was steadfastly cross-threading as I struggled in vain to attach it. "Finally!" The bear banger rested on the tip of the launcher. But now, in turn, the trigger wouldn't work! I repeatedly pulled the spring of the trigger down and let go but nothing happened. "Could the bear banger be too old — corroded?" After about the fourth attempt, the strike of the hammer finally hit home and fired off the banger. It made sort of bang but I had not known how it, in fact, worked. With the bang, a bright crimson flare also launched. It flew in a steep ballistic arc and, as I held the launcher with random aim, it fell into the spruce thicket about 20 metres away from me and about 30 degrees to the right of the bear. The landed flare immediately ignited the dry undergrowth. The threat of causing a forest fire rose greater fear in me than the bear. Without a second of hesitation, I sprinted to the fire and, barely in time, managed to stomp it out. Luckily, I wore my hiking boots and shorts. When I returned to my layout of food on the rock platform, the bear was yet another two steps closer to it, steadily clicking his teeth. I did not need an explanation. I knew exactly what was of issue to the animal. He had an irresistible desire for my laid-out food and was challenging me to a duel for it. Yet he was hoping that I would give up without a fight and run away. "Had he not spent a long enough time verifying that I was just alone?" Yet I had no choice. "I must stand my ground!" I extricated another bear banger and screwed it onto the launcher. This I now carefully aimed. Not directly at the animal because I did not want to cause him injury. I felt self-confident that this would work without violence. The banger exploded and the burning flare landed five metres to the right of the bear and a bit in front of him. Yet again, it ignited the surrounding parched growth. Terrified, I once more sprinted to the fire and feverishly stomped it out. I was happy that I succeeded. Only then my attention returned to the bear. But suddenly, there was none! He must have finally gotten scared — either by the flare or possibly by the fact that I daringly darted practically against him when I hurried to put out the fire. He must have come to the conclusion that I wouldn't be easily intimidated.

"The first battle has been victorious," I patted myself in self-praise. "But when it gets dark and everything is quiet, the bear will undoubtedly be back!" I feared. "Yet I have nowhere to go! What choice is there remaining for me but to wait the night out in the campsite?" I immediately collected and stowed away all the food items from the rock back into the vinyl drybag. I then hermetically sealed it by rolling its top and snapping the corners together. I detached the rope from the bow of the canoe and tied a rock to its end trying to throw it over a high branch on a leaning pine tree. I finally succeeded on about the tenth attempt. I attached the food bag to the carabiner at the end of the rope and tried to hoist it by pulling on the rope over the branch. It did not work. The friction of the rope on the branch was too high. Only after I lifted and pushed the bag up with my right arm as high as I could reach, standing on my tippy toes while simultaneously pulling down on the other end of the rope with my left arm, the bag ended up about two-and-a-half metres above the ground. Thanks to the tilt of the tree, it hung almost two metres from its trunk. Allowing that the result might not have been ideal, I did not think that I could do any better. "It will have to do, even if bears are known to perform surprisingly acrobatic feats sometimes." I then decided that I should eat the rest of my saved supper and I packed the kitchen into the drybag with "hardware." Having brushed my teeth and packed away the items of personal hygiene into it, I carried the bag away from the camp to the very tip of the rocky shoreline point some 20 metres away. Then I returned to the tent. I marked my territory around it by peeing on multiple spots of its perimeter — the language that the wilderness understood. I then lay down to sleep, my head sandwiched between bear pepper spray on one side and the machete and hunting knife on the other. For a long time, I would not sleep, but listened. I was waiting for when the cracking of the bear's footstep on a dry twig would betray his return. If I had fallen asleep several times during the night, it would not have added up to even a third of its length.

Yet the bear did not return. Or at least, if he had, I did not know about it. In any case, he had not succeeded in taking over my food supplies to gain an easy way of adding to his development of sufficient fat reserves to survive another winter. Nothing in my camp had been disturbed. This, thus far, had been the only camp since my leaving Montreal where I would have to hang my food supplies on a tree. Otherwise, the food bag had always rested near the shore under the overturned canoe. Besides this time, I had never experienced any bear problem during my entire voyage.

In spite of sleeping little, I got up shortly after 4:00. I had a long way ahead of me on a large lake where I was to move against the prevailing winds. I could not have afforded not to take advantage of the early hours with the calm before 10:00 — the time around which the wind would usually start rising. When I was taking down the tent it was still dark twilight, but by the time I loaded the canoe and finally took off from the bear encounter battlefield at 5:30, there was already daylight. Lake Saganaga with its multitude of islands confused my orientation. Even voyageurs frequently used the help of Native guides here to lead them through. The boundary line, which followed the historic route of the birch bark canoes and which one clearly saw on the map, quite obviously was not also painted on the water of the lake surface. I thought that I knew where my camp was located. Yet after the morning start when I arrived at a dead end of the channel that I had followed, I had to admit that I was lost. I returned to the campsite and tried a different water channel, still deeper into the Canadian side, but it dead-ended too. By then, I had already lost an hour. In the end, I returned all the way to the island with yesterday's occupied campsite on the American side and from there, I at last followed the channels that I assumed to be right. Still, I needed some kind of proof that I had recaptured the true sense of orientation. On my right, I was just passing an island with cottages, which, if I was correct, should have been on the Canadian side of the border. Some cottages along the way used to fly a flag. I now wished that I would see just that Canadian one somewhere to confirm my assumption. At last, around a corner, a flag emerged above the tree tops with the red maple leaf. I rejoiced. Spotting a Canadian flag in the middle of the border wilderness had always affected me as the touch of a friendly arm around my shoulders. I was surprised when, after completing the bend, it turned out that the flag flew over a building of the Canadian Border Inspection. A billboard on shore announced it and I guessed that it requested a CANPASS ... permit from Canadian citizens, who had crossed the border and were returning from the U.S. I moved immediately underneath it. Technically I did not cross the border from the U.S. but I turned my eyes away anyway to have a clear conscience that I had seen no announcement. Now I paddled at a fast clip in extended strokes to disappear as fast as possible from the view of the building beyond the nearest rocky point. Nobody stopped me, however. It was still only 7:00 in the morning and work in the office likely hadn't started yet. I escaped the law. Now as a fugitive, I weaved with the canoe among the islands towards the west-southwest along the edge of a large area of open water. This I followed for easier orientation. On the other hand, on the more open water, I now paddled almost directly against a rising headwind. Around 10:00, I finally arrived at the end of the islands. A vast bay opened up ahead of me, which in my direction of travel, I had to cut across. Its water surface was now menacingly black as it was chopped up in high waves from a strong southwest wind. There was no other choice but to take it on. The waves tossed the bow of the canoe and bucked it up like a rodeo ride on a wild bronco. I moved at a small angle to the right from the straight against the wind direction. The wind maintained a constant attempt to turn the bow of the canoe to the right, but at the mentioned aiming angle, only to the point where I managed to resist it with mighty paddle strokes along the right side of the boat with no need to correct the strokes by steering. When the bow wandered off to a bit of a larger angle, the canoe immediately turned broadside and it took a superhuman effort to return it back to its correct aim. I could not skip a single stroke. The battle lasted for 45 minutes while the headwind and the waves grew steadily in strength and size. I was forced to maintain a racing pace of paddling on the right side during the whole time. When my right arm was dying of exhaustion, I at last reached the lee of the opposite side of the bay in front of me. I then moved in its relative shelter, closely hugging the coastline to a point on its end marked on the map as "Rocky Point." This I was to round to continue on my way. As soon as I poked the nose of the canoe out past the rocky point, however, it became instantly obvious that to continue would be utter nonsense. Luckily, there was a marked campsite on the rocky point that happened to be situated on the American side. I landed at the lee side of its rocky shore and unloaded the canoe. It was only around noon but I put up the tent. I was "wind bound" – "*dégradé*" - in the language of the voyageurs. They used to make offerings of tobacco to "La Vieille" – the Old Lady of the Wind, so she would ease up on her blowing. Yet there was nothing in this situation to be sorry about. My body was exhausted to death anyway and my back and my arms screamed for a horizontal rest in the tent.

I used the lost time due to being wind-bound in an early sleep. The idea was to wake up early the next morning. I could not again allow a newly risen headwind to catch up to me on the remaining length of the lake. The sky was still dark — just a narrow band of orange glow spreading above the eastern horizon — when I pushed off the canoe and rounded the rocky point in the west-southwest direction. Lake Saganaga tapered down that way into a long spear. The narrow point of it eventually snaked through wiggly narrows into a chain of smaller lakes strung together by portages. This commenced with Cedar Swamp Lake and followed with Plume Lake, Ottertrack Lake, Knife Lake, Seed Lake, Carp Lake and Birch Lake. The fresh morning had just started awakening when I arrived at the portage leading from Plume Lake into Ottertrack Lake. Divine serenity hung over the small lake. Just a short while ago, I had escaped the wind as it started rising when I neared the end of the long tip of Lake Saganaga. The water surface before the portage was thickly dappled with green plates of water lily leaves and the ivory white crowns of their blossoms. All around, birds sang in the crowns of the surrounding birch trees. The end of the lake was shallow with deep black mud making its bottom. To make it possible to dock with the boat and disembark, there was a long board pier jutting from the shore into the lake. Something similar must have existed here during the era of the fur trade. When my carry with the waterproof backpack had swung past the crest of the lakes-separating ridge and I was descending to the shore of Ottertrack Lake, I ran into another lone wolf who had been traveling solo but in the opposite direction. He was stumbling on the rough rocky path in knee-high rubber boots under the weight of a hybrid between a canoe and a kayak. He was an American who had allegedly grown up in this Minnesota environment of hundreds of lakes. Although now living in Colorado, he still returned here for his vacations. Perhaps 10 years younger than me, he was also up in years. He complained that his lower back had ached from the extended kayak sitting. This allegedly to the point that he was actually looking forward to portages. His soft, friendly and politely aristocratic demeanor with the somewhat neglected physical shape of his tall figure betrayed somebody in a position of importance and influence in his professional career. Dean was quite obviously an adorer of nature and a lover of the lake wilderness with which he had grown up in his backyard. We struck up an instant friendship in the mutual admiration and understanding of each other. Traveling along only a part of the boundary route, he admired that I planned to complete the whole thing. He warned me with an expression of deep concern that big problems inevitably would await me in my planned attempt to paddle the length of the enormous Rainy Lake from east to west.

I now paddled on a very long, yet narrow Lake Ottertrack. Though I had been looking forward to not encountering the need to carry for a long time thanks to its length, I soon discovered that for me, the lake stretched almost directly against a now already strong headwind. I tried hiding behind the mild bends of the lake's course but the mostly cedar-forested shores acted as a guiding wind tunnel for the air current and aimed it against me, whether the lake angled one way or another. For most of the time, the progress along the surface of Ottertrack Lake was a strength-sapping, clenched-teeth battle fought with the paddle against nature's mockery. Only at its end, I temporarily breathed a sigh of relief in the momentary refuge of a wind shelter. But as soon as I summited the top of a short portage and descended down to the shore of the next lake, Knife Lake — again oriented straight against the wind — it was immediately obvious that I would not be able to continue until the wind abated. It was still only shortly after noon. I rested while eating lunch and pondered whether I should wait out the afternoon here. Yet there was no indication that the wind would have a tendency to stop, if at all, before evening. I knew from the map that just around the corner, some 50 metres from the end of the portage, an American campsite should be located. In the end, I loaded the canoe in difficult surf upon the shoreline of knife-sharp rocks that gave the lake its name. I then set out to rodeo-ride the reflected waves along a high, rocky cliff in the direction of the campsite. I succeeded in locating it after a while. But the landing in the persisting surf proved to be a hard job to accomplish. I managed to abut the canoe to the metre-high edge of a smooth granite outcrop. After several attempts, I successfully grasped a rock crevice and scrambled up from the boat atop the shore. I immediately reached back for the bow of the canoe and tried to pull it up fully loaded onto the rock platform. When the canoe's center of gravity rested on the rock edge, it still leaned towards the water and the spare kayak paddle suddenly slipped out of it into the lake. I sprang to rescue it and, holding lightly onto the stern of the canoe, I leaned out to the paddle as far as I could. At the very moment, when I touched the floating paddle, my imperceptible pressure onto the canoe tipped its balance and the whole works slipped back into the water, myself included. Luckily, the canoe neither tipped nor took on water. Now I swam fully dressed, hat on, up to my neck in the water around the canoe and the paddle. The lake was really deep here. In spite of the crystal clear water, the bottom could not be seen at all. I threw the paddle out as far as I could onto the shore. Then

I climbed again atop the slippery rock like a flooded-out mouse. This time, I brutally hauled the whole boat so far onto the shore that it could not slide back. The campsite atop the high craggy shore was nice and cozy. It was quite fortunate that it was baking in the afternoon sun making it really warm. Hence, I could blithely free myself from the wet cladding and spread my dripping clothing on the surrounding bushes and rocks to dry. The spot was simultaneously exposed to the strong southwest wind and the clothing thus dried quickly. Meanwhile, I put up the tent and started the fire for cooking. There was a pleasing setting here for serving out yet another wind-bondage sentence.

It was understandable that after my recent experiences with the headwind, I again arose right after the walls of the tent started to turn perceptibly pale. This was somewhat after 4:00. Still in the tent, I first changed from the long thermal underwear in which I slept into clothing for travel on the water. This consisted of a black silk t-shirt; a blue, thermal long-sleeved shirt with a zip-t collar; nylon swim trunks; black, silk long johns and long nylon pants with full-length zippers along the sides. With it I wore woolly hiking socks, and early in the morning a compact insulated windbreaker on top. Dumping the clothing from the sleeping bag's stuff sack, which when full, served as a pillow, followed. The sleeping bag was then compressed in to replace it. In hiking boots outside, I placed the packed sleeping bag into the bottom of the waterproof backpack and added all the dumped clothing into it. I then tightly rolled up the closed-cell mat. The latter I carried to the canoe which I turned upright and strapped the rolled mat to the top of its seat. Taking down the tent and packing it in the waterproof backpack was next — all actions so far practically in the darkness. The sealed waterproof backpack was now moved to the boat together with items like the machete, the belt with bear security items, the map case, the hat, the camera and the Gore-Tex windbreaker — all that had occupied the rear vestibule of the tent. By the time I floated the canoe and loaded it — no longer stretching the spray cover on it because after the very first morning it would never rain again during the day — daylight started dawning. Now I changed into rubber sandals, embarked the boat and pushed off into the long, dark shadows surrounding the smooth water surface. I got immersed in the silence of the awakening early morning. All was still sleeping except the echoes of the occasional knock of the paddle against the gunwale of the canoe reflected from the granite walls and dark forest giants that lined the shores. Low fog slowly folded over the water. In grimly dark coves, ghost-like tatters of vapors stood just above the surface. The cool temperature of the morning air condensed the evaporation from the relatively warm water of the lake. The tips of the tall fir trees and pines in the higher positions on the west escarpments commenced to turn gold from the sun rays that fought their way over the edge of the jet-black horizon in the east. The lake surface glistened with blinding glare in that direction. Of the eastern coastline and islands, only their black silhouettes, like theater props, interrupted the liquid shine. Sometimes, the long wail of a loon pierced the morning stillness and in my soul it sounded equally as if he called "Caaaanadaaaa!" My canoe glided smoothly upon the quiet mirror surface. I had a feeling that I would be trespassing against some ritual etiquette if I disturbed the temple-like silence with even a single splash of the paddle.

By the time I reached the end of the 17-kilometre long narrow Knife Lake, I was again wrestling with the headwind. In that situation, I actually welcomed the change of routine in the form of a series of portages on smaller lakes. Of these, there were no less than five. The wind was not the dominating issue here. At the end of one of the portages, I ran across a forgotten, brand new, splendid-looking U.S. Army canteen. It was of rectangular shape with round corners, made of light yet robust durable plastic. It was, of course, a khaki color. On the outside, it was protected by a tight-fitting shoulder bag-like canvas sheath in the shade of the "desert sand" with the large black letters of "U.S. Army." I was musing about how somebody would be grieving its loss when he or she discovered this prestigious and likely well deserved possession missing somewhere.

But at that moment, a canoe emerged from behind a point with two frantically paddling men. They were from a party of three canoes of middle-aged military-looking paddlers led by a man with an aura of authority. They addressed him as "colonel." The group had overtaken me on one of the past portages. With loud hollering they let me know that the canteen belonged to one of them. They had not hesitated to return for it from as far away as the next portage.

It wasn't until after 4:00 with the sun already headed for the horizon that I restarted my paddling into its blinding glare upon a now again larger Birch Lake. Here I looked for a campsite. I had hoped to find it toward the end of the lake. I wished to get as near as possible to vast Basswood Lake on which I was to travel tomorrow. Indeed, I did find a campsite on a low, level point of a forested island on the Canadian side. The spot was really nice and cozy. Also, the wild fauna came to greet me here in the form of a tame rabbit who hopped blithely right around me while I was cooking. I was now skirting the southern edge of the Canadian "Quetico Provincial Park." The map also marked Canadian campsites, the majority of which were utterly gorgeous.

Getting up just after 4:00, still in the dark, had by now become "de rigueur" for each new day of my water voyaging. The inhumane slavery of fighting with a headwind or risking an upset of the canoe in whipped-up huge waves by a side wind, had forced me to extend the productive part of the day before 10:00 — the time when the winds usually awakened — in this way. Early morning hours yielded the lion's share of the distance traveled every day. The voyageurs waited out the middle part of the day on land and after the winds died down towards the evening they resumed paddling until dark. They, however, already knew the places where they were to camp every evening. The collective work sharing in the camps made a quick process of completing all the necessary chores before sleeping. I had to find a campsite between 4:00 and 5:00. Still, it would take me until dark to complete all the required tasks and duties before laying my exhausted skeletal frame onto the sleeping bag in the tent. This was typically sometimes around 9:00 in the evening. The combination of 11-hour paddling marathons — interlaced with stumbling under heavy burdens on the portages, as well as the constant bending down to lift miscellaneous, often heavy objects — all from the ground level — in the evening camp, turned the moment of finally reaching a horizontal position in the tent into a true feeling of being liberated from slavery. The idea of evening paddling sounded absolutely unreal to me.

Basswood Lake

I reached the portage into Basswood Lake really early, still in darkness and in chilly fog. Just then, fast motorboats of outfitters from the USA were converging on it as they were bringing their clients — mostly for fishing. Their headlights beaming through the fog, some boats carried up to four upsidedown canoes on an overhead pipe rack. The outfitters stayed in contact with their canoe-paddling clients by radio. In this way, they could pick them up to "rescue" them from situations where they had requested it due to a headwind or bad weather. The waterfall into the lake had been replaced with a small concrete dam. On the Canadian side, there was a foot portage for canoeists, while the American side had a road for a truck that loaded motorboats with a winch and transported them between the lakes. The truck's headlights had been visible from quite a distance. The entrance beach of Basswood Lake was covered with tatters of dirty foam from surf that had whipped it since the wee hours. It did not serve as an encouraging sign. Gone were the cigar shapes of the lakes' outlines elongated from east to west that I had passed before the crossing of the divide. Large Lake Basswood spills into a torn up, complicated shape. The water route weaves through it in several giant zigzags. Depending on their direction, a strong, west-southwest wind thus asserts itself either as a strong side wind, or a merciless headwind. When moving northward, I had trouble stabilizing the canoe in large side waves. Moving westward, I was bronc-riding big waves straight against the wind. If I ignored the hard, as well as risky labor of fighting with the headwind, Basswood Lake and its surroundings were very scenic and romantic. The adjacent ridges were treed predominantly with tall pines that spilled their rich greenery over granite crags all the way to the water of the lake. From the lake surface up the gullies and ravines of inflowing creeks and streamlets, the yellow-gold of the birch, aspen and alder foliage that was starting to turn autumn colors dissolved into green. Here and there, a lonely maple screamed with a splash of fiery red. A few times, a "V" of migration-ready geese carried across the blue sky above a distant horizon, its point aiming south. The motorboats and the canoes of the outfitter clients dispatched onto the lake dissolved in time into its vastness. I paddled alone, forsaken in the deserted wilderness. Around 10:00, the sun started blazing in the clear sky. Sweating from the searing heat, as I did during most days up till now, I stripped shirtless and paddled like an Aboriginal water nomad. The wind cooled my sweaty muscles and brought the aroma of coniferous resin to my nostrils. Around 2:00, I rounded the sharp point of a wooded shore on the inside of a giant bend of the lake into its next segment that aimed westward — directly into the wind. I suddenly felt that any further battle with the wind was pointless. Seeing an empty campsite on a granite cliff on the American side, I traversed the width of the lake and landed there to inspect it. The site turned out to be nice but I was reluctant to unload the canoe yet. I felt sorry that I would be losing a significant part of the paddling day in an early stop. Reclining on a sun-warmed patch of grass high up on the crag, I enjoyed a nice view of the lake below and ahead of me. In the distance, I glimpsed a reflection of the sun on a wet paddle. Focussing on it a bit sharper, I discerned a trio of canoes engaged in a battle against the wind. They were seeking the advantage of coastline protrusions and little islands. This prodded me to an instant decision to continue a little farther. After a few kilometres of slow progress against the waves and the wind, I at last arrived into the vicinity of a group of islands topped with a growth of tall pines. One of them, according to the map, had a campsite on the Canadian side.

As I rounded the high granite edges of its shoreline, I could not see a campsite anywhere. It was not until I had touched at a high granite bank, scrambled up it and surveyed the island's crest that I saw a gorgeous site here on a high, grassy plateau among sparse, tall pines. A rock fire pit certified its official status as a campsite. From here, I could now see an access point along a slanting granite ramp from a small notch in the rock shore on the opposite side of the island. Right away I returned to the canoe and, after rounding the island, disembarked again in the newly discovered harbor. It was one of the "Pine Islands" on Basswood Lake that the voyageurs relished and which were particularly praised by the explorer of the Northwest Company, David Thompson. The evening sitting by the fire on the platform of the high island camp could not have had a more relaxing atmosphere. The scenery opened into a beautiful panoramic view of the lake with its multiple silhouettes of islands and shorelines — each spiky with the tips of coniferous trees. They were receding one behind another into the backdrop of long shadows, mirrored in the colorful reflections of the evening light on the water surface. Competing with the colors of the reflections were the reddish-pink hues across the blushing lace-work of clouds in the west. This was not to be the last feast for my eyes on Lake Basswood.

All of this would be upscaled by the performance of the awakening morning lights. It started from the very hint of dawn up to the diffusion of the rising low sun in a dense fog over the shiny lake surface. By then, I had already paddled for some while towards the portage around the outflow of the lake in the form of the scenic Basswood Falls. Ethereal outlines of islands and points of the shoreline kept emerging like ghosts, seemingly suspended in milky weightlessness in front of the canoe. One after another they film-faded into view at the last moment as I quietly paddled along the coastline. At first the fog had thickened. I moved through it practically by memory holding in it the map's shape of the shoreline. I oriented myself by the spot of brightest concentration of the diffused light up behind my head. This signaled the position of the morning sun. Only when the sun had moved higher above the horizon and its reinforced rays started to burn through the fog from a steeper angle, did it commence to thin and reveal the lines of the landscape surrounding the lake. It was still only around 6:00 when I passed by an American campsite with many small watercraft lined up on shore. I faded in from the fog like an apparition to a man who had just sleepily stumbled out of one of the tents. Clad in long underwear with a woolly toque on his head, he started to look around. It was apparent that he was spooked when he noticed the soundless phantom of a mist-shrouded figure in a hat — glorified with an aura of the sun glow penetrating through the fog — just passing by in a smoothly gliding canoe. The group was moving in the opposite direction and his colleagues were still sleeping. On my query, he confirmed that the start of the portage was to be found just beyond the nearest point.

The first, higher drop of Basswood Falls was followed by a series of smaller drops and rapids that curved in a long arc to the left between banks of granite outcrops overflowing with forest growth. The portage around this natural obstacle was significantly long. Its name is "Horse Portage." This may indicate that during the time of the busiest traffic along the water highway, horses might have been used here to help with the carrying. The Portage is over two kilometres long, but after two-thirds of its length from upstream, it has a short detour to the water. Those who travel upstream obviously undergo the whole length of the portage. But the more courageous of those who travel downstream can shorten the walking Calvary by some 700 metres if they launch the canoe at the detour and shoot the remaining length of the river's rapids. With shaking knees and a vise-like grip on the paddle, I did this. A person in my situation, who is forced to move through the length of each portage five times naturally profits from this kind of risky enterprise the most. All went well, though, and with a new injection of pride, I continued on the voyage. The Basswood River then led me to its magnificent end in Lower Basswood Falls. The portage trail here offers a nice vista over the roiling rush of the hurtling waters. I took time here to strap my camera onto the trunk of a young spruce tree and snapped a self-timed selfie. I hoped that it would enliven my future slide presentations. I even took a short video here of me carrying the canoe.

Crooked Lake, which followed and first appeared more like a river due to its narrow width, revealed another interesting curiosity. Not too far below Lower Basswood Falls, the vertical rock walls that were lining the narrow stretch displayed Native pictographs from the prehistoric past. Red paintings in vermilion exhibited wild animals like moose, pelicans and bipedal figures. For a long time, colorful feathered ends of arrow shafts jutted out of a horizontal crevice high up on a rock cliff overhang that were shot in by members of a marauding Sioux war party at one point. They were serving an intimidating message to their foes, proving the deadly prowess of the Sioux in the use of bows and arrows as weapons. By now, though, the bottom rock part of the crevice had fallen off and with it, also the relics of the arrows. I felt lucky. At least this kind of danger no longer looms over the intrepid canoe passer-by of today.

The Canadian side of the border here offers another splendid campsite on top of a sharp, high rocky point around which the lake breaks its shape in a tight switchback to enter into narrows toward the north. The grassy platform of the site with a thin growth of mature pine trees spreads on the flat crest of the point's ridge — a level of some 10 metres above the surface of the lake. A little meadow drenched by the late sun, to which I had climbed along an incline of granite from the canoe, had a surprise for me. As if prepared just for me, right in its middle, a large, single eagle feather rested. I accepted it as a reward from Mother Nature — who surely must have appreciated my resilient perseverance in passing the dreadful gauntlet of tests to which she had subjected me. To me, it was a coup for a special achievement by her "savage" worshiper. I truly treasured this as the symbol of my Boundary Waters adventure. I guarded it as an eye in the head while it traveled with me all the way home to Edmonton. Now it rests in our Kootenay log house.

Crooked Lake possesses a truly crooked, complicated shape. It zigzags in turns to the north and the west, aiming on average toward the northwest. From my eagle-feather campsite, I still had its main length ahead of me. A strong southwest wind blew after noon while I paddled on its last segment, leading me to the north-northwest. Admittedly, it did not act against me, but it tried its best to overturn my canoe with sinister side waves. I had bravely resisted its vile intentions for quite some while before I finally rounded the last point and reached the sheltered refuge with a bit of smooth water just before the rim of Curtain Falls. Another portage had its start here to bypass this obstacle. I chased the prow of the canoe up onto the coarse sand of a small notch in the granite right next to the edge of the waterfall and stepped out from the boat onto shore. Welcoming me here was a beautiful, scenic setting. The lake's water was throwing itself in a smooth sheet over the granite lip before it shattered into thundering white lace-work on a ripped-up, rugged rock incline, spreading like the bottom of a richly-ruffled crinoline. The whole scene was framed in the healthy forest greenery of pine limbs that were combing through moisture-filled air full of fresh scents on a sunny day with an azure sky. The fine long tufts of the white pine needles as well as the rough resiny tassels of the red pine needles saturated the ambient atmosphere of the warm autumn day with an intoxicating aroma of resin. When I stepped closer to Nature's wonder to revel in its beauty, a young man approached me. He was also traveling solo and had rested here before the portage, sipping tea from a metal cup clutched by both hands. "How are you? Nice seeing you again!" He claimed that we had met on some of the previous portages, which I did not remember, but we warmly shook hands. Brad had a very light, short canoe and also very light baggage for a shorter expedition. He was able to carry his canoe together with a backpack and consequently he went only once on each portage. His canoe was too narrow, however, and Brad thus suffered stability problems in side waves. I could tell from his wide open, shaking eyes that he had just experienced long moments of terror with the side wind on the last stretch of Crooked Lake before the falls. Below the end of the portage, it was still necessary to run a short series of mild rapids. I could see that Brad prudently hesitated for a long time, kneeling in his canoe, deciding how to pass through the first chute of the rapids. I hollered encouragement to him before I had to return for my next load. Alas, the rumble of the water drowned my acoustically-dispatched injection of bravery into nothing.

The sun of the ripe afternoon saw me wrestling with waves and a headwind in a battle for meter-after-meter in the south-westerly direction on Iron Lake. Following my passage through a rocky narrows into small Bottle Lake, the gaze of a late sun watched me start the portage toward a mighty big lake — Lac La Croix. The portage on the Canadian side had several stretches of deep liquid mud here, which together with rough, chaotic rock sections elsewhere, made the life of this lonesome exhausted voyageur dreadfully hard. The sun sat beyond the horizon by the time that I, at last, pushed off again and paddled into the lake and wind. A campsite on an American island, which I had hoped to use, alas, proved to be occupied. I could see from a distance that two canoes were drawn up onto shore. Yet fortunately, not too far from the main route around there, another island campsite was situated that was empty. Having found it already in half-darkness, I disembarked, erected the tent and supped on a couple of protein bars. There was no time left for cooking that evening.

Getting lost on Lac La Croix

A strip of orange glow had just started forming behind the black stage set of the eastern horizon when I slipped the loaded canoe from the granite slab into the dark water of Lac La Croix. I stepped into it with my right foot and pushed it off with the left. I seated myself on the soft rolled mat and started to paddle towards the north, pushed in part by the south-southwest wind. It had blown through the whole night and it ruffled the surface of the lake into black waves. The campsite with the two drawn canoes appeared dead as I passed it. All were still sleeping. Most likely, they were traveling toward the east and did not have to worry about starting the day early. Lac La Croix is really vast. One origin of its name comes from the fact that a long time ago, missionaries erected a giant wooden cross on one of its islands. But secondly, the lake also represented a crossroad of two fur trade water routes. It's because the later trade route of the Northwest as well as of other Canadian fur trade Companies, which was leaving Lake Superior up the current of the Kaministiquia River, joined the old boundary route from Grande Portage here. My way through the lake followed the line of the border. This wound through the enormous water area, strewn with islands, in a giant horseshoe with both its ends in the south. The highest point of its bend is in the north. While I traveled from the southeast end of the horseshoe to the north, I had another chance to admire more native pictographs on high granite walls dropping vertically into the lake. The waves tossed with the boat, though, and made it hard to photograph the graphics. Moreover, the sky had a gloomy overcast that created somber twilight and supressed all shadows. As a result, the coastlines of the shores and islands around the widespread lake surface merged into one black mass that made it impossible to recognize their shape. After infinite hours of paddling, I expected my arrival at the end portage out of the lake. Yet the geographical elements around would still not quite agree with those on the map. I suddenly ran into a fly-in base of float planes above which a Canadian flag was flying. I landed here to go and ask where I could find the portage. Right away, a chap in a baseball cap came forth to meet me, who as it turned out, was the pilot of a plane that I had seen landing over my canoe a short while back. He willingly escorted me along the floating pier to his plane, took a pilot's map from the door pocket of the aircraft and spread it on the deck. Radially diverging pencil lines on it converged into one point that was supposed to be the spot where we were finding ourselves. I couldn't believe my eyes. At first, I totally rejected the pilot's claim because I had been thoroughly disoriented. The base was situated in the center of the bend of the horseshoe on its very highest point. I therefore had a whole half-length of the horseshoe to the end of the lake still ahead of me. I had no idea where I had wandered off-course till I arrived at my present position. But knowing now where I was and where north was, all that remained to be done was to reprogram my brain. Then I set a hard racing pace, resolving to make up for the lost time and reach the end of Lake La Croix before dark. The headwind that I now faced in my southward movement, fortunately abated a bit with the advent of evening. I knew from the map that on a point of the left shore almost at the end of the lake, an American campsite should be situated. I only prayed that it was free.

The campsite was on a point that was more like a small island joined to the main shore by a short, narrow isthmus. The spot that I had taken for it from a distance as I approached it with my eyes glued onto the greyish rock slab looked empty. But it did not, in fact, turn up to be the campsite from up close. I despaired and readied myself for the need of emergency camping. Yet only after rounding the peninsula to its southern side where it formed a sheltered little cove with the main shore, the right signs emerged. Here was a harbor consisting of a granite platform. Higher up, in the back on a grassy clearing under tall trees, there was a fire pit with comfortable log seating around it, opening onto a scenic view of the bay. Not much daylight remained, but all the necessary chores were by now a well-entrenched routine. I stood up the tent in a blink of an eye and when the fire was already licking the kettle bottoms, I managed to jump into the now serene water of the bay and wash my hair with shampoo after two weeks. This took place in dim light. I then dried myself in the warm, radiant heat at the fire while I finished cooking supper, drank the tea and ate. *(Only much later, in fact at the time of this writing, did I discover from a view in Google Earth that what I took as the horseshoe shape for Lac La Croix from my detailed series of one-page, overlapping satellite-view printouts at the time of my voyage, had a much more extended shape from east to west. I might not have strayed off the route that I should have followed after all. It was just long — I paddled over 50 kilometres that day.)*

I launched the canoe at 5:00 the next morning. The lake was quiet but the light fog above its surface this early was freezing. I paddled in a light, insulated jacket with the zipper drawn up to my throat. Even the hat jammed up to my ears filled its function in holding my body heat. At the end of the lake where I had expected the portage, a small, rural, stucco house emerged from the misty twilight — likely several generations old with various additional structures similar to a small village settlement. There was mowed grass here and a pier with moored boats. I took it for private property and searched farther beyond it. But it was already the end of the lake with no sign of a portage trail. It was only 5:20 and I knew that I could not wake the owner of the property up to ask. Yet at that moment his voice thundered out from somewhere around the door of the house where I could not see anybody: "The portage is to the left of the pier!" What? Isn't this just a lawn of a private lot? I did not understand. Again the voice bellowed, this time separating individual words with short pauses to sound more comprehensible. "The-portage-is-on-the-left -of-the-landing-pier!" I detected a hint of ire in the undertone and hence I obediently turned my canoe around right away and headed to the indicated spot. Only now could I see rails over the lawn that led to the water for the transporting of motor boats. Only now did I notice a greyish figure in high rubber boots and a ball cap standing on the entrance porch of the house. From it must have come forth that angry voice from the heavens. As I would soon find out, it was Mr. Beatty and the whole settlement, in fact serviced the portaging of fishing motor boats between the two lakes. It made a living from the corresponding fees for the service. A sign burned into a wooden board on the front of a shed hung here: "Beatty's Portage." The Beatty family apparently had been on the scene here for several generations. My quintuple, non-motorized trek, counting two returns, through the morning dew across the property to the water of the next lake naturally was not subject to the list of fees for powerboats that was conspicuously posted here. I therefore quickly disappeared from the annoyed Mr. Beatty's eyes. Who knows, maybe he had had a bad dream or could not sleep.

Now I moved to the south against a southern wind. My route today was to travel a big square "U" and I couldn't wait to have its first leg, aiming south and against the wind, behind me. After that, I would move more or less toward the west-southwest where the wind should be coming from the left side. Some distance beyond the next portage on the Loon River, the route should even bend to the north and thus downwind. Up to the first corner of the "U" and for a great part beyond it, the route stretched through irregular-shaped Loon Lake. Before I rounded the corner, the wind had already changed to south-southwest and I consequently still had a bit of a headwind with strong side waves. But as soon as I entered into the narrow Loon River, which aimed more or less directly to the west, the wind was seldom channeled against me by the trough of the forested banks. Soon I arrived at the second portage, which, as it turned out, also had a set of rails over a small hill for transferring motor boats. It bore the name "Loon Portage." The trail for canoes had a small landing here in a cove full of reeds and mud. I located an extension of the path from the shore into the water in a strip paved with flat rocks. I poled the canoe along its side up the mud with the paddle all the way to a mowed lawn so I could step out of the boat with dry feet in hiking boots. It was right at that moment that a man with a canoe on his shoulders and a huge rubber pack on his back from the other side of the portage came to the stone strip. I greeted him and apologized, asking him to wait a second so that I could pull the whole canoe out of the water and make room for his launching. Yet he assured me that there was no problem. He said that he was OK, that he would pass by me. What a shock awaited me when, having pulled the full canoe onto the mowed lawn, I turned toward the water and saw the man standing up to his waist in the black muck. With a brimmed hat on his head and the pack on his back, his chest was at the level of the canoe's gunwales next to him. Horrified, I rushed to help him, but again he claimed that he was OK, that he did not need any help. Ergo, I delivered my first load to the other end of the portage. I thought that the man traveled alone like me but soon his wife appeared on the scene with another big rubber pack. They were both around 55, dressed by the latest outdoor fashion in perfect synthetic tops — him in blazing red, her in turquois — in brand new fast-drying cargo pants with many pockets, excellent mountaineering boots and glowingly new waterproof hats of the "Outdoor Research" brand. He, however, after my return for the second load, stood on the shore wet from the navel down and black from the mud. Yet he insisted that everything was OK. When I ran into his wife on the portage, I warned her that right at the water's edge was deep mud into which her husband had sunk up to his middle. She just noted leisurely that, "This is typical for him. He did the same thing last year!" It was obvious that they loved nature but they must have belonged to a city elite with neither a great deal of wilderness experience nor much physical fitness. On my third return for the canoe, I saw them paddling in the direction from which I had come. It did not seem that the man had bothered to change. All was probably OK.

The Loon was narrow like a small river. It wound through a land of mixed forest along occasional meadows of waist-high grass and weeds with lonesome old oaks — trees that in Alberta, where I live, one does not see. On the inside of the curves, shallow sand bars formed. More than once, I had to avoid a tree that had fallen into the water. There were signs of beavers here and every once in a while a pair of ducks appeared. At one point, a trio of kingfishers flew in step with my canoe, flicking their bluish wings in bobbing flight from one river bank tree branch to another, further and further down the current. When I at last rounded a 90-degree turn to the right — the north, I finally had the wind in my back. It was an unusual luxury that I had to really appreciate. I paddled in long strokes on a 15-metre-wide river, passing white trunks of birch trees leaning above the water, shoreline rushes and an occasional granite outcropping. As a typical feature of the "rivers" of the boundary water route, one could not discern any current except in a few narrows. I again paddled stripped to my waist like a savage under the blue cupola of the sunny Indian summer day. Just then, the roar of a strong motor in the back announced that soon a motor boat would show up. I squeezed into the sparse reeds by the right bank and paddled on. In a moment, a large boat of outfitters from Minnesota emerged in which about eight men with the serious look of seasoned outdoor professionals sat ranging in age from some 30 to 65. It was evident that they were surprised. They all admired the appearance of a 71-year-old who paddled by mighty strokes with a bare, sun-bronzed back free of a life jacket, only a hat on, in a solo canoe. As they advanced closely along my canoe at a reduced speed to minimize overly large waves for me, one of the younger men lifted a plastic window flap of the boat's transparent canopy and with one raised finger on an outstretched hand, expressed a query by his questioning grimace: "Are you traveling alone?" I understood. When I nodded, all in the boat stretched the corners of their lips down with pushed-out chins in appreciative nodding, some of them with a "V" of raised fingers as a recognition. It was the most effective booster injection to my self-confidence — a shot of courage into the continuation of my lonesome, rough coexistence with the water wilderness.

And of that courage I indeed needed more than a few bunches in the not too distant continuation of my movement to the north. That's because the river widened up after a while, first into a large lake, Little Lake Vermillion, and later into even bigger Sand Point Lake. It was already afternoon and the wind by that time had already gained its maximum strength. It now blew from the southwest. In the narrow sections of the river aiming north, it got expressed as a tail wind, but on the open water of the lakes, it sent strong waves from the rear left. Two motorboats, which I met in the middle of Little Lake Vermillion moving in the opposite direction, were forced to reduce their speed to a minimum because the waves and the wind threatened to throw their bow over the stern. They looked surprised seeing a lone canoeist fighting the waves in the middle of the vast spread of the water like a bull riding rodeo cowboy. They too signaled with the "V" of raised fingers, wishing me victory. Yet however crazy the continuation of paddling on the lake seemed, I could not afford to not take advantage of the natural force that was driving me forward for free. Who knows how long the wind would continue blowing from the back in this part of the route? I was prepared to persist in paddling for as long as possible, perhaps even till dusk. Between 4:00 and 5:00 when I normally started looking for a campsite, the waves were overwhelming. But the near shore, which was the Canadian one, still did not offer any suitable spot. I passed the whole coastline of a large island where I had hoped to camp, searching in vain. The lake now opened into a broad bay to the northeast where I could not see its end. My route called for a diagonal crossing of the lake to the northwest — to a point on the American side, about five kilometres distant across the open water. For a long while I hesitated, pondering the risk, but when the wind weakened momentarily, I suddenly gathered my courage and took off for a hard race across the water. I knew that I had to reduce the time spent in the middle of the lake area, kilometers from the nearest shore, to a minimum. I suspected that the wind and waves would only worsen with the passing of time. I paddled as in a race with my eyes burning a spot in the red-black rock point on the horizon. Yet it seemed to remain at the same distance. When at last it seemed that only half a kilometre remained to reach it, the wind grew mad in an obsessed effort to prevent my possible victory. Every once in a while, an even bigger foaming wave came from the left side that threw the front of the canoe high above the water and at the same time tried to capsize the craft to the right. As I was forced by the wind to paddle on that side, my body weight also happened to rest more on the right. Only with heavy support from the paddle, as I stroked mightily against the water, I managed to resist this tendency. Perhaps even the rock cliff of the point itself was compressing the streaming of the wind along its wall, so that in the moment when I neared the point to within 10 metres and considered the battle almost won, its climax was yet to come. Moreover, the waves, reflected here from the wall, made sure that the boat moved toward the point forward and backward in the infinite snail pace of a sick cha-cha dance struggle.

Oh, what a relief, when finally, I rounded the point and found myself temporarily in its lee from the wind and waves. This, though, was already around 6:00 — high time to immediately look for a campsite. I passed a low, narrow, extended sliver of a granite island, which, in an absolute emergency, could have allowed a sleepover. Yet I wanted to explore better possibilities a little further ahead. I wished, as much as possible, to approach a hidden narrows that would reveal tomorrow's access into the next lake. That was vast Lake Namakan. I hid from the wind by moving through narrow gaps between islands, when to my disbelief, in the small cove of a small island to my left, the corner of my eye discerned a brown sign on a post through the evening half-light that seemed to depict the symbol of a tee-pee. Was this to indicate a campsite? I almost passed the site but now I returned to it. Indeed, there was no doubt that the sign marked a campsite. This one even had a name: "Norway Island," the sign said. On sandy soil here under the crowns of tall pine trees, there were two picnic tables, a metal fire pit, four leveled base platforms for tents, a roofless plastic commode toilette and even sheet metal cabinets for the safe storage of food from bears. A notable curiosity of the island was that everywhere I looked, a bounty of king bolete mushrooms grew — the most prized by European mushroom picking savants. Thanks to their island isolation, they evidently shared the same mutated gene that gave their heads a very light beige color. The whole island was void of people. It was only waiting to soothingly cradle my aching body and help renew its strength and energy for the battles of the near future. I had a pleasant evening here. For the usual swim there was neither time nor mood. The strong wind was too chilling. One important thing distinguished my current water voyage from the previous ones. This time, I carried a small electronic device of pocket watch size that allowed me to send an e-mail message via satellite each evening to a list of recipients that I myself had predetermined. I was able to broadcast information such as if I was OK or if I needed help. The gadget of a "SPOT" brand had — besides buttons for sending out the messages such as "I am OK" and "I need help," — an SOS button protected by a snap cover. The latter had to be flipped open before one could press it. This would activate a full-fledged rescue mission from the appropriate international authorities. One could be responsible for the financial cost of such an operation should he/ she have light-heartedly abused it. He or she thus has to think twice before pressing the SOS, making sure that the request for a rescue is really the last resort for survival. In any case, Milena had a message from me every evening that "I am OK." Besides this text, (which I could compose myself, but only before the trip), the e-mail message also contained an interactive Google map with a pin indicating my exact position, complete with the GPS bearings and the date and time of the broadcast.

The blazing light of planet Venus in the role of the Morning Star in the east and the cold silent constellation of Orion above the southeast horizon welcomed me when, still in the dark, I left the comfort of the tent and started packing. It was necessary to find a very inconspicuous, narrow canal among the wooded shores and islands of a large lake into an even bigger one. Once on Lake Namakan, I was to move for a long distance directly to the west. I had studied the shape of the coastline leading to the narrows in the last light yesterday evening after walking across the island from my camp to its west side. Now I moved through the dawn twilight on the lake's surface very vigilantly so that I wouldn't miss the passage. All was successful, though, and I entered Lake Namakan victorious. It was still relatively early in the morning. The wind had not calmed down completely overnight and it still blew albeit with reduced strength from the southwest. I thus paddled closely along the south — American — side of the lake where the waves were smaller. Only once at the end of the lake, I started to curve the course to the right — north — where I was to enter another narrow passage of a reversed "S" shape. This was supposed to finally lead me to the largest and final lake of the route, Rainy Lake. The wind rose to its full strength on Lake Namakan when I was aiming northwest to the narrows passage. I thus fought again a life and death battle with side waves from the left and a howling wind. Only with utmost exertion and with a sizeable dose of luck, I at last reached the calm water in the passage. Now I paddled for a longer period in a relative wind shelter to a site called Kettle Falls. Its name hinted that it represented waterfalls even if my map no longer showed any further need for a portage on my route. I first heard the name from Dean, the lone water traveler in the opposite direction whom I had met on the portage to Ottertrack Lake. He was curious at the time about how I intended to overcome Kettle Falls. But I followed my time-proven philosophy that I had adopted on my water voyage to not worry about possible problems until I actually faced them. And so I continued paddling along the border until warning signs forbade my further progress because of a dam ahead. I did not see any posted instructions on how to circumvent the dam so I thus started guessing where the most likely portage around it could be. I backtracked from the arm of the dam and entered an adjacent bay on the American side where I had seen motorboats disappearing before. Soon I viewed a group of small buildings with a number of watercraft tied at several harbor piers. I did not see any rails here but I guessed correctly that a smooth dirt road disappearing over a crest represented the portage for powerboats. Those were transported on a trailer behind a truck. Accordingly, I repeatedly transferred my gear on foot under the dam and floated out. After a period of a lost wandering due to brief disorientation, I did find the right channel. At last I floated into the lake of an enormous spread — Rainy Lake. The name comes from the name of the outflow river — the Rainy River, (or Rivier La Plui as the voyageurs called it), because a short distance below the lake was a big waterfall with water spray that precipitated all around as never-ending rain. Today the site is obscured by a hydro dam. But now, I had a long way to that end of the lake and all of this straight to the west.

The sun was low now. The only prospect of a campsite that remained for me was a wild campsite on the Canadian side of the boundary. I thus searched on the right, hugging the right shore with the canoe. After some period of scrutinizing, I found a gorgeous spot that did not bear any evidence of having been previously used. It had all the right attributes: a low, flat granite platform for landing and disembarking; higher up and a short distance away, a granite terrace with a carpet of soft moss and caribou lichen for the tent. There was an abundance of dry wood everywhere around for the fire. I built the fire in a rock cavity so it would be sheltered from wind and conserve its heat by reflecting from the walls. The tent was soon up next to a "whale skeleton" of a fallen old pine with bleached stubs of its bare branches as the ribs. The wind quieted down with the evening and the late sun rays reflected from the smooth water surface into the camp. It was pleasantly warm. The edge of the harbor slab fell off to a considerable depth so there was a natural access for my traditional swim. Yet in spite of the seeming closeness to the finish of my journey, I still seriously worried about what obstacles the giant vastness of the water body that I would traverse to reach Fort Frances would plant ahead of me. Fort Frances was the destination of my voyage and was situated at the outflow end of the lake. In all honesty, at that time I was still not sure if this lake would stop me.

The angry Rainy Lake

The next morning was gloomy. The tent fly was dry, unlike other mornings when it would be wet from the morning condensation of humidity. Black clouds rolling in from the southwest thickened the pre-morning darkness. The air smelled of rain. It was the first time in a long while that I decided to stretch the spray cover onto the canoe. I hurriedly loaded and just as I was frantically unfurling the rolled up cover from the bow to the stern, a downpour started. It managed to form a few small puddles in the bottom of the canoe before I finished covering it securely. But the rain had definitely managed to drench me before I could don my Gore-Tex jacket and my hat. I would have to dry by body heat while paddling. I again hugged the south — the American coastline of the lake — to avoid the big waves that were being whipped up farther on the open water.

I could imagine what kind of a sea surf had to be pounding the distant Canadian shore that was visible only as a thin black hairline in the misty distance. The first rain shower passed after some while, yet the clouds only grew and new showers came one after another for the whole morning. From the map, I had worked out a strategy to take advantage of a narrow passage between the American coastline and the adjacent islands up to a place where it was necessary to turn northwest and aim across the open water toward narrows that separated Rainy Lake into eastern and western parts. The dividing constriction had a name — Brule Narrows. The passage between the coastline and the islands was supposed to protect me from wind and waves. When I reached its beginning, the sun had merrily blazed for some while. As if by some miracle, it found an opening in the rolling clouds. Here was a quiet lee of the coastline and I thus stopped for a quick snack in the boat. For the times where I hadn't had the time to make tea in the evening, I had a filtering straw as a backup. This is a plastic tube with a sucking mouthpiece, inside of which a smaller coaxial ceramic tube acts as a filter. With this device, I could draw water to have a drink directly from the lake without worrying about contracting bacteria like giardia, etc. Before I could finish my refreshment, though, the water surface around me started getting dappled with little rings from rain drops. At first, the sun was still out and it seemed that this was only the passing whim of an errant tatter of a cloud. Yet as the rings grew steadily denser, I packed away my food in a hurry, put on my Gore-Tex jacket and closed the skirt of the spray cover up to my armpits. I pulled down the bottom edge of my jacket over the spray skirt just when it started pouring. Now the sunshine was replaced by gloomy half-darkness. When I looked up to the sky, I saw with horror a menacing black wall of rapidly rolling storm clouds above the black spruce tips on the left bank of the passage. From their violent interfolding, crooked lightning bolts were shooting and above my head thunder claps exploded. Right away, I knew that this would not be something that one could somehow escape. In the blink of an eye, the storm was above my head. The rain turned into a waterfall. Together with the wild wind, it flogged my back and drove my boat down the channel like a broom in violent gusts that chased waves of white, frying boil along the surface of the water. I squeezed to the right shore under the protection of the trees in lieu of lightning rods. I was not going to represent the highest point on the open water, even if I had noticed that the lightning bolts were being exchanged only between the clouds and not between them and the ground. The wind and rain pushed me in my direction without paddling. I held the paddle crosswise in my lap and leaning slightly forward, I tried to protect the waterproof map case in front of me with my body. Yet it immediately rested in a rain puddle on the spray cover anyway. The idea of leaving the canoe and seeking some refuge on shore was totally out of the question. The rainwater accumulated in puddles on the spray cover and poured from my hat down my back at the same rate as if somebody poured one bucket on it after another. I couldn't keep up on lifting the spray cover in front of me and behind the seat to dump the accumulated water in it over the gunwales. It immediately sagged again under the load of litres of new water. When I thought there had been enough and that perhaps the end should be coming, a yet more berserk fit of Nature's insanity arrived. When at long last the worst wrath of the heavens had passed, I again started paddling. With the help of the still driving wind in my back, I soon reached the end of the narrow passage. Here I turned to the north along the shores of the islands that I had earlier predetermined as my navigational guides. The storm had moved over the main area of the lake in a northeasterly direction. The scene of the lake landscape possessed a funereal atmosphere. Under the leaden sky, all the shores looked black and the islands merged with the mainland into one black mass surrounding the open water. No shape of the surrounding coastlines was distinguishable. Yet after the passing of the storm, the surface of the lake miraculously calmed down and sat quietly like the eye of a hurricane. In the southwest, I could see a portent of another wrath of the heavens. I now had to cut across about four kilometres of open water to a narrow channel leading to the next part of the lake. I knew that I only had a short window of time to accomplish it. Should I get caught out there in something similar to what I had survived in the passage, it might sink me. Naturally, under the present circumstances, I discerned no narrows in the black line of shore on the distant horizon ahead of me. I just set a crude azimuth of my desired course to it from the map and from the north on my watch and I commenced the race. I glued my eyes to a lighter spot of rock outcrop on the distant coastline, but as I progressed along the water surface, I more and more tweaked my course to the right in an effort to miss the narrows toward the Canadian side and return along its shore left to it. Just when I at last approached the coastline in front of me to perhaps 300 metres, the gale of another storm roared in from my left. In the ensuing waltz of the devils, furiously paddling, I reached some protection in a gap between the coastline and a near island. Driven by the wind through the gap to the right, I looked for another gap on the left through which I could somehow return to the sought-after narrows. It seemed that several were available here. I was cruising through their network for quite a while. Yet the topography that I could see did not agree with the one on the map. I determined the north from my watch and to my utter disbelief, it was exactly on the opposite side than where I had assumed it to be. I fished out a busola compas from the bottom of the electronics drybag and it confirmed the testimony of my watch. I was yet again disoriented, this time thoroughly. I had a very hard time trying to reprogram my brain to comprehend my present position. When I finally emerged into open water, and assumed that due to some sheer luck, I had passed through the narrows into the next part of the lake, the sun peeked out from under the edge of the cloud cover on one side. That by now had to be in the west where I was supposed to aim. Against my instinct, I thus turned to the right in its direction. Yet on the left where I had planned to follow the American coastline, there was no shore. Everywhere on the left as far as the eye could see, only a vast lake spread. I paddled uncertainly for another half an hour against a strong headwind. After a while, when I knew that something was seriously out of order and I could not continue, a small island appeared in front of me with a cove of a harbor on the shady, lee side. Above a cottage in pines, a Canadian flag flew. I headed directly to the building in the hope that I could ask its owners where, in fact, my position was on the map. But the place was deserted. I was exhausted, chilled to the bone from the cold wind and from the wet clothing that never had a chance to dry on me from the rains and the drenching of the previous and recent storms. I based an emergency camp on the grassy flat at the harbour. Water somehow found its way even into my waterproof map case and the maps in it were a soggy mess. I peeled them carefully apart and spread them to dry. In the meantime, I tried to use all possible means that I had at my disposal to determine my position. I pulled out the GPS unit and determined my bearings. These I transferred into my very non-detailed 1:250,000 topographic map. It was wet but it was the only one that had the degrees and minutes marked along its edges. Yet it did not have the corresponding set of grid lines inside and I therefore only estimated the cross-section of the transferred coordinates by eye. This gave me a nonsensical result, according to which, I should have found myself on the Canadian shore, still somewhere in the part of the lake east before the narrows. I refused to take this revelation seriously. I charged the iPhone and tried to open the app that was supposed to show me my position on a map. The app, however, had always crashed my cellphone in all my repeated attempts. But then, I suddenly noticed that I had one bar of a telephone signal. I attempted to call Milena and … a miracle! … Her voice answered.

Wisely, she suggested that I send her my SPOT signal and she would call me back with a description of where I was. I was a little skeptical about Milena's sense of orientation. From my experience, Milena could normally take "east" and "west" for baking ingredients. Yet as usual, in critical situations Milena outdid herself. She confirmed to me that I was indeed at the Canadian coastline, still in the part of the lake before the narrows — thus to the east of it. She informed me that she clearly saw in the zoomed-in satellite view on the map my island with the cove of the harbor and the cottage. She even had the guts to joke that she could see me there. To my amazement, she even described, how I should move to get to the Brule Narrows. I had her repeat everything several times and, in the end, I believed her. Everything now meshed. It would cost me an extra day, but now I started feeling confidence that with prudent vigilance and self-discipline, I would reach the finish of my voyage successfully. The lion's share of it belonged to Milena's encouraging words.

The next morning, I took off again at the first signs of daylight. Yet I still fought against a merciless southwest wind. A low sun, clearing the eastern horizon, finally illuminated the entry into the narrows. The progress through the passage to the west was once more a Sisyphean struggle. When at last the western part of the lake opened up in front of me, I closely followed its American coastline, seeking protection behind every projecting point and a near-shore island in a prolonged battle with the headwind. I constantly and scrupulously studied and verified my current position on the map so that I would not again lose my orientation. In some places, I advanced metre by metre against half-metre waves. Towards the end of the day, I strayed into a dead-end channel and had to backtrack. Yet in the end, already during dusk, I set up an emergency camp on top of the rocky point of an American island. My tent stood under the huge cross of some religious organization that must have owned the otherwise empty property. I was satisfied that I had accomplished a significant advance toward the final destiny of my journey that day.

Venus and Orion once again welcomed me in the morning as I was folding the tent and carried gear from the top of the point down to the canoe. I paddled through the morning twilight vigilantly because I was to pass through another narrows of the lake leading to its final western spread. I was on a keen lookout for the direction of occasional powerboat traffic through the channels and gaps between the islands. I was following some kind of marine signs that seemed to delineate a shipping channel and appeared roughly about every kilometre in critical locations. The shores were getting more densely populated with cottages and in the background one could hear industrial noise. Dense fog rolled in before 6:00, but by around 7:00, the sun and blue skies triumphed. Suddenly I sailed into wide-spreading, open water. I could not believe that the narrow passage was behind me but this would turn out to be true. Now I just paddled in stretched out, mighty strokes with my eyes focussed on the hazy line of the most distant coastline where tiny light squares of building walls started to be distinguishable. It was Fort Frances. Once again, I raced to reach it before the wind awakened. It did wake up when I neared the coast. The battle intensified when I entered the outflow river, the Rainy, and continued paddling on it up to the municipal marina. Had I started paddling an hour later in the morning, I would not have reached Fort Frances that day.

I grasped the edge of the wooden pier from the canoe as I pulled parallel with it and called Doug, the taxi driver, on my iPhone. The hoarse voice with which he responded betrayed that I probably woke him up. After all, it was only 11:30 in the morning and it was a Saturday. He might have had hectic business the previous night and driven clients till the wee hours of the morning. "Hi Doug, this is

Jan. How are you?" "Hi Jan, where are you?" "I am here in Fort Frances at the marina pier." "You must be kidding! Already in Fort Frances? I am there in a couple of minutes!" Doug did not appear in two minutes, but he arrived in 15 minutes with my Jeep. What a relief that everything ended well! He wanted to help me with disembarking and loading the Jeep, but I thanked him. "Doug, thank you, but that's OK. I am going to work slowly and methodically. I have to savor the feeling that I really have all the hard exertion behind me." I offered to give him a ride home but he lived only a block and a half away. I thanked him again, we shook hands and Doug strode off in his jeans and cowboy boots. Seating myself in the Jeep and setting the course to the west came as the sweetest reward for me. It brought me both mental and physical relief. I had a long road ahead of me. Yet, "So what? The whole way, I will be only sitting and I won't have to paddle at all."

P.S. Only while I browsed in an outdoor store back in Edmonton sometime after my return home, did I discover that what I had always taken for a bear banger (the shorter cartridge), was, in fact, a flare. A bear banger was the longer cartridge. Milena and I verified it by firing both at midnight on New Year's Eve of 2016 at our log house on Lake Kootenay. So those were flares that I used to scare the bear on the Saganaga Lake — not bear bangers!

CHAPTER VI

From Fort Frances towards Lake of the Woods along the Rainy River
(June 24 – 29, 2016)

Does it seem to you that the date span of my expedition for the year 2016 is rather short? You are absolutely right. My plans for returning to the historic water highway of the Canadian fur trade and continuing the canoe voyage of my lonely, adventurous coexistence with wilderness must have been cursed right from the beginning. In Czech and in many other languages, we say that "there had to be a buried dog in there." It started on the long road trip to Ontario eastward across the prairies with the canoe on top of the Jeep. It rained violently the whole way through the provinces of Saskatchewan and Manitoba. My windshield wipers had a hard time keeping the front glass clear even at their highest setting. When I happened to pass a semi, I was blinded completely. It was lucky that the Trans-Canada Highway is divided into two lanes in each direction. It didn't stop pouring until the last moment, when on the second day, I arrived at Fort Frances in Ontario. It was just turning dark. I was stressed out from worrying where I would spend the night, where I would launch the canoe into the waters of the Rainy River and where I would safeguard my Jeep. Before entering the core of the town, I turned into the local graveyard. By then in darkness, I drove to its end on the riverbank. My goal was to survey access to the water from here. It was still raining. When moving through the high undergrowth, I ended up with my boots wet and my jeans soaked up to mid-thigh. Mysteriously, the usual motels and hotels were full. Hence, I ended up for the night in an expensive hotel in the town's center. After I draped my wet clothing over the heating radiator to dry, I tried to contact Doug, the Gold Star Taxi owner. I left him several messages before I finally reached him on the phone the next morning. As I had hoped, Doug was immediately willing to take me to the water in my Jeep. Following the unloading of my canoe and gear, he drove my vehicle to his home for safekeeping. It was to stay there until my reappearance in town. I offered a sum of $200 for these services that Doug accepted without problem.

Once more ambitious to cover a significant chunk of the country across Canada during the starting summer, I set out relatively early. I thus ended up with the canoe on the banks of the Rainy River on June 24. Unlike the last two days, the sky was azure blue and the sun burned mercilessly right from the early hours on the day of my launch. After carefully sorting the cargo and meticulously placing it in the boat, I spread sunscreen on my still delicate skin and wearing a brim hat, I pushed off. The river's surface was smooth as a mirror. Now at the beginning of summer, it was high. The water reached right into the dense, luscious greenery of bushes and trees — mostly deciduous — on both banks. The river, up to its mouth into Lake of the Woods, formed the border between Canada and the United States. On the right bank, I passed Canada, while the left bank was American. This particular part of the historic fur trade route ran off to the south from the Canadian Shield — the vast region of the continent covered with granite of volcanic outflows, dotted with myriads of lakes and lakelets among mostly coniferous woods. Here the surrounding landscape was flat. To me it even seemed boring. It had fertile, loamy soil and deciduous forests. To the voyageurs, this land represented a welcome change from the austere, rocky terrain through which they had laboured on their way here. In variation to my taste, they referred to it as "pays beau" (beautiful land). My personal guess would be that, to them, it seemed to have the potential for, in their time, a standard way of agricultural life. Today this fertile area is indeed strongly utilized for the purposes of agriculture. By the same token, it is relatively populated. Ever since I drove through Fort Frances two years earlier, I've had a detailed map of Lake of the Woods. As a nautical chart, the map even featured a matrix of marked depth measurements all over its water area. I had purchased it in a local roadside souvenir shop while passing by along the lake. That way, I had had a lot of time to repeatedly study it and terrify myself about the huge areas of open water among its multitude of islands. Even locals who knew the lake had warned me against its sudden storms and wind gusts, skeptically shaking their heads. Ergo, I had considerable respect for the lake. Yet from what I had seen about the Rainy River, I regarded it as an easy matter. "It's going to be a piece of cake," I had thought. "It'll only be a matter of several days of peaceful or even boring paddling to gobble the distance between Fort Frances and Lake of the Woods." The American canoeist, Dean, whom I met on one of the portages of the fur trade route in the Boundary Waters a year before, had warned me about its rapids — Manitou Rapids. The river was supposed to feature them somewhere on its course. He confessed to me that these rapids really scared him a lot when, at one time in the past, he had encountered them. "But that's me," he added. "You will not have any problem!" He tickled my ego jokingly as he was judging me from the quick recounting of my accomplishments preceding our encounter. As it would turn out, my expectations for the Rainy River had grossly underestimated it. Why? There was an unfortunate combination of factors that conspired against my progress. In the first place, the river had a continuous series of private properties covering its banks wall-to-wall. That turned the task of finding a wild campsite into an almost impossible challenge. In combination with the high water level of the river where it reached into the shore's growth, one had to resort to stealthy camping in inferior emergency settings. I had to maintain a very low profile and stay inconspicuous out of sight of the land owners. Under the given circumstances, I could not dare to have a fire in my campsites. Moreover, June, as the month with the longest daylight and the sun the highest in the sky, supplied an excess of energy into the atmosphere. It not only turned my peaceful paddling into galley slavery in the searing heat, but also, from the second day on, it brought a daily, abrupt violent electrical storm in the afternoon with downpours and lightning. The looming storm forced me to paddle until the last moment before it started while frantically searching for whatever possible place to put down the tent. I would then hurriedly land and run through the vegetation onto shore, becoming a target of the left and right artillery strikes of lightning while putting up the tent and hurriedly crawling into it. Besides vegetation in the very peak of its growth, the insect population was peaking too. As a result, after the passing of the storm, I was forced to stay inside and spend the rest of the afternoon and evening in a tent that often felt like a sauna.

Manitou Rapids

Manitou Rapids announced themselves some kilometres in advance with distance-muffled thundering. The river had markedly narrowed here and upshots of frothy water beyond its threshold, visible from a distance, signaled a foreboding threat. A small road led to them from the Canadian side off of the main street of a small community that was part of the Indian reservation of Manitou Rapids. Besides a few Indigenous anglers who were likely taking advantage of nature's boost to their fishing luck here, a small audience of white pelicans inflicted a great deal of stage fright on me. They all played the role of witnesses to my indecisive acting aimed at overcoming the rapids. Right up to the last moment as I slowly neared the brink of the whitewater slope while studying it from a standing position in the canoe, I considered it necessary to land and prudently carry around it. Yet in the moment when it would have been high time to head for the shore to land, I noticed that if I moved tightly along the American bank — immediately after entering the throat of the rapids — I could exit their narrow "V" by prying left with the paddle and peeling the canoe into a back eddy under their left side. Having successfully done this, I was able to skirt around the whole turbulence downstream and have it all behind me. I felt pride that I had succeeded in overcoming the rapids without stopping and thus managed to maintain cool dignity in the view of my audience. I had also gained a feeling of peace and safety in continuing the voyage, assuming that ahead of me, there was now only a placidly flowing river without any great surprises. As it would turn out though, the rapids consisted of two parts. The second one introduced itself with a thundering rumble again after about 10.5 kilometres. The geysers of white water beyond their lip once more roused me up from my lethargic dreaming and once again, they put fear into my immediate future. It was already quite late. I had paddled long that day with the goal of covering as much distance as possible while the going was good. And so, when a rare opportunity availed itself to camp at the mouth of a small tributary from the Canadian side about 300 metres before the rapids, I resolved to stop here for the night. The rapids could wait. I considered it wise to sleep on it. Luckily, the daily thunderstorm came late that evening after I had safely crawled into the tent.

Yet when I carefully approached the rapids the next morning, again standing in the boat as I had during yesterday's first part, this one could also be navigated tightly along the American shore. That way, there were no issues. This time, my successful performance could only be appreciated by pelicans who were strategically positioned here to catch fish from the boulders of the entrance into the white water. Once past the second part of the rapids, I was convinced that I should only have a quiet river ahead of me all the way to Lake of the Woods. All the pitfalls were now safely behind.

The scourge of Poison Ivy

The 27th of June, 2016, was especially hot. I paddled stripped, under a hat that had to protect me from suffering sunstroke. During that day, I drank almost the whole supply of my drinking fluids. Yet still, after noon, I was progressing in a dopey lethargy from the heat as I passed the luscious greenery of the banks. Poking out of it, recreational cottages, mansions and farm houses showed in regular intervals. Sometime around 2:30, the Northwest skies turned ominously dark. It was obvious that the storm of that day was arriving early. Yet I was just paddling past a shore where it was impossible to camp. I thus frantically continued on, studying the shore to discover some camp spot — any spot before the storm would trigger its wrath. Nothing was showing up. When circles from rain drops had already started forming on the water around me, I spied ahead of me about a ten-metre-high bank with a hay field on its top. Just below it, I spotted a kind of bench in the waist-high growth of grass and weeds. I aimed a freakish pace towards it. But by then, it was already pouring. I shot with the canoe to slide onto the shore through a jumble of flattened deadwood. I hauled it quickly out of the water and freed out the waterproof backpack with the tent and sleeping outfit. In my shorts and rubber sandals, I raced with it through the shore bushes onto the grassy slope and quickly identified a level spot on its wavy terrain. I foot-flattened the weeds and immediately unpacked the tent to frantically start erecting it in the pelting downpour. By then, the lightning had started to explode. It was hitting the ground all around me like aim-improving mortar fire. I had the tent standing in a blink of an eye. Yet when I crawled into it, everything inside was wet — mainly from my wet body. I completely stripped right away, threw out the wet clothing and drew in a semi-wet towel from the tent's vestibule to dry myself. When the storm had passed and the sun came out, I lay on a wet foam mat waiting for things to dry. It did not take long and the inside of the tent felt like a sauna. Contrary to my hope, instead of drying I was sweating. Yet outside, hordes of biting insects were buzzing and it made no sense to come out. The storms then followed in waves that marched one after another in hourly intervals until darkness. When it cooled off at night, I finally slipped into my sleeping bag. But the whole night my legs were itching from the knees down. I blamed mosquitos and black flies. Overnight, a wind had come from the west. When I left the tent at 6:00 in the morning to start packing for departure, the wind was so strong that it bent trees and drove whitecaps up against the current of the river. It would make zero sense to try paddling against it. I thus continued to sweat in the tent for another whole day. I only came out to drink the rainwater from puddles in the grass with the aid of the filtering straw. My legs were itching more and more. They started to turn red. In the morning, I got up with daybreak. I couldn't wait to push off into the river again. The wind was still blowing but now it had changed its direction. It blew from the side. I descended the slope to the water with the packed tent and sleeping bag in the waterproof backpack. At that moment I froze, gaping awestruck. The water level in the river had risen by half a metre! My canoe that had originally been on shore covering the gear, was floating bottom up in the water. Floating around it were pieces of the load. It was only by luck that the floating items were held captive by the interwoven mess of the deadfall floating around them. I was crushed when I saw the cardboard tube that had contained a full set of special topographical maps. Though it was sheathed in poly tubing, it was now soaked throughout and also floating. I emptied the canoe, loaded it with the wet cargo and pushed off. It seemed useless to stretch on the spray cover. Everything was already wet anyway. I just hoped that it would not rain anymore and that the dark morning sky would clear up during the day. Yet as soon as I rounded the first bend of the river, I could see a wall of rain in the distance that was mercilessly moving straight at me. My spirit hit bottom. On top of everything, my legs were itching insanely and strange sores started showing on my skin. I passed a private lot with two houses on it. It had a paved boat launch ramp down into the water. I returned back to the ramp and skidded the prow of the canoe up the pavement a bit so that the friction held it. I had a cell signal so I called Milena on my cell phone. I needed to discuss my immediate urge to pack things in. She warned me to weigh my decision very carefully so that I would not regret my action later. But when I described to her the mysterious affliction on my legs, it was decided. She said, "You cannot risk a secondary infection from the water and impurities somewhere far away from possible medical help." When the lady home owner noticed me as she was leaving for work in a vehicle, she drove down the ramp to me sitting in the canoe. "Is everything OK?" she asked. "Can I help you in any way?" I asked for permission to unload the canoe onto their property and return for it in my Jeep. She immediately agreed, but as for herself, she had to leave. The road was about half a kilometre from the river here. I called Doug in Fort Frances to bring my Jeep as I started marching along the road to meet him.

According to the latest news from Doug, the succession of storms had had a hard impact on the whole vast area. Allegedly, in Thunder Bay, people were paddling canoes on Main Street.

Shortly after I returned to Edmonton, I had to head for the emergency room. My lower limbs were swollen like elephant legs and were red to black-purple. On the insteps, around the ankles, and on the shins and calves they were covered with bloodshot blisters and they itched insanely. Worried, I pondered if this could possibly be leprosy, or some kind of flesh-eating bacteria. Our family doctor, however, quickly diagnosed the problem as an allergic reaction to poison ivy, or poison oak. As I learned from the web later, this kind of vegetation is found predominantly in this part of the North American Continent and grows abundantly along rivers. I must have run through this plant while looking for emergency campsites. Conceivably, the poisonous oil from their leaves could have even soaked into the trouser legs of my jeans the very first evening in Fort Frances when I walked to the river at the cemetery. Never before had I encountered any problem of this kind and never had I worried about this danger. Consequently, I did not even know what such plants looked like. The affliction did not seem to have any end in sight. I abhorred the possibility of residual scars. But about a month later, the blisters finally disappeared, the skin peeled off several times and not a trace of the malady remained behind. Well, I am now again a bit wiser and more experienced. One must know the dangerous plants in the wilderness and must be able to avoid them. Should one still be hit with this kind of danger, the only wise decision is to abort the expedition and seek medical help. In the least, it is necessary to give the affliction a chance to pass through its cycle of healing in a clean environment. A secondary infection of the disturbed skin somewhere in the middle of nowhere could potentially turn into something much more serious.

CHAPTER VII

Rainy River to and across Lake of the Woods.
(August 26 – September 2, 2017)

Ah, what a feeling to hold the paddle again. The digits of one hand itching to encircle its shaft, the palm of the other — both in fingerless leather gloves — hardly waiting to wrap around the bulbous Tee on its end. The arm muscles are twitching with the anticipation of propelling the canoe to adventures unknown beyond the distant horizons. It has all been long etched in and familiar — no need for refresher practice. It is the same routine as riding a bicycle, swimming, the kick from the wax zone of a cross-country ski, the pressing down of the heels in the stirrups while pumping a horse for a jump over a fence — once you get the hang of it you can never forget it. It is the freedom to move again on one's two legs over the surface of Mother Earth, to live without a ceiling over one's head other than the high sky, to feel the warming sun on one's bare back, to draw in the aroma of coniferous resin, to feel the fresh moisture of the wind-driven rain on one's face while protected by a Gore-Tex windbreaker. It is the refreshing scent of ozone after the passage of a thunder storm; the ever changing daily transformations in nature's beauty scenes; the day's conclusion in the radiant therapy by the embers of an evening campfire. It is the beckoning of that old familiar yearning akin to the salmon's drive to head for his native spawning flats high up the river. It is the return to the liberation of the primeval instincts in me that I inherited from ancestors as distant as those from the Stone Age. Could even the few percent of Neanderthal genes in my genome be responsible? It all heightens the spirit, sharpens the acute alertness and spurs on the flow of adrenaline for overcoming unforeseen obstacles and dangers — the components that make adventure an adventure. And to make it a true adventure, even that ultimate peril must be an integral part of it all — the one that lurks somewhere in the dark background shadows — the one that one must constantly hold in check by wisdom and experience — the danger of death.

Today is excitingly different from all the prior days of my lonely solo canoe water wayfaring from Montreal to here. Though it is a chilly, windy day today with a rain-laden overcast sky, for me its atmosphere is festive. Why? It's because from today on, I will finally paddle again with my proven partner, the only one that I can safely rely upon and with whom I can get along in this crazy undertaking — my wife. How was all this suddenly possible? We had both concurred in a joint decision that the time was ripe for Milena to finally join me in retirement. She had enjoyed a very well paid management position in which she could have stayed for many more years. Yet the ever increasing burden of stress that was weighing on her due to a politics-charged, toxic work environment had threatened to undermine her health. She took a leave of absence to rest and to contemplate the details of this important decision. We both agreed that the best setting for regaining her sanity to accomplish this rationally would be in the caressing arms of nature. In our case, this would be fulfilled by a canoe voyage through the wilderness. Our preparations were quick. The end of August was nearing, not much remaining of the summer. Both the tandem canoe and lightweight tent for two had been ready two years ago when Milena's injury forced her to cancel her plan to join me for the voyage along the Boundary Waters-Quetico canoe route from Lake Superior to Fort Frances.

All that remained now was to sort out the logistics of starting out. Where would we launch the canoe? And where would we safeguard the Jeep until we returned for it? During the whole drive east from Edmonton across the Prairies, I speculated that we would go all the way to Fort Frances. Here we would pay my proven taxi driver, Doug, to take us to the place on the Rainy River where I was forced to abort the voyage last year. Then we would let him take the Jeep to his home in Fort Frances and keep it there for us until our return.

Yet when we woke up into a rainy, windy morning at the motel of the first settlement where we reached the river, a new idea emerged in my mind. Instead of diverging through a large detour upstream to Fort Frances, we would turn downstream and try to find the property with the house on the river bank where I finished last year. We would ask the owners if they would allow us to launch the canoe there — exactly where I had to pull out — and, perhaps, even leave the Jeep with them. The idea worked to a tee. I managed to find the place and the elderly homeowner lady, Maureen. She was taking care of her young grandchildren there while their parents were at work. Maureen recognized me right away, remembering me from the last year. She generously agreed with our request and showed us where to park the Jeep. Following this unexpectedly smooth phase in our logistics, Milena and I changed into our paddling clothing. Then we carefully launched and loaded the canoe. Soon it was ready in the reeds at the edge of the river, waiting to be pushed off. It was a miserable day that demanded Gore-Tex outfits. Milena wore a toque, while I wore my brim hat pushed right down to my ears. Yet we were warmed by the elation from our successful start of the voyage. To my delight, Milena liked the situation and with a final feeling of freedom, she was brimming with humor. Luckily, the chilling wind blew from behind in the direction of the river's current. Hence, the voyage passed quickly. Sometime around 2:00, we floated under the bridge of the highway that crosses from here to the U.S., and with further paddling we rapidly left the last signs of civilization. Two hours later, we were already looking for some campsite. The land along the banks was still divided into private parcels, yet now those were only farms with sparse habitation that were mostly invisible in the surrounding greenery. In light of my last year's unfortunate experience with poison ivy, we were extremely cautious about where we stepped and selected a spot for the camp. We saw poison ivy in practically everything that grew on the shores. Consequently, we rejected several otherwise appealing spots until Milena finally espied a narrow strip of a sand beach beyond a band of reeds that had emerged due to the low water level. This looked promising. Here we enjoyed a relatively comfortable evening. Yet in the morning, still in the tent, we were awakened by the voice of a farmer — the owner. He thrashed his way to our spot with difficulty through reedy shallows in his motorboat to announce that we were on private property. We apologized but since we were leaving the place in a short while anyway, all ended on a friendly note. There was no point in arguing, even though technically, the flood zone of the riverbank up to the high water mark is classified as Crown Land and hence, we were, in fact, not trespassing on private property.

The chilling wind endured till the morning. To top it off, it changed its direction toward us. We thus sought any feeble wind shelter in moving close to the bank. Though the speed of our progress had dropped markedly, we sensed that we were not far from the mouth of the river into Lake of the Woods and this injected us with a strong, optimistic mood. The mouth of the river presented a challenge to us in the form of a labyrinth through a vast spread of reeds. We had followed a kind of canal through it that followed the border. Luckily, we managed to orient ourselves just in time to correctly divert to the north — the Canadian side. Milena's sharp eye then registered something on the kilometre-distant shore that from afar looked like a sand beach. After a while of paddling, there was no longer any doubt about what it was. With gratitude, we sledded the prow of the canoe onto the sand of the shore and went to explore it for camping. The place was very nice. Except for the freakish clamoring of a large crowd of Canada geese conferring in the neighborhood before leaving about two hours later, it was heavenly quiet. The location, surrounded by deciduous woods, was far from any farm buildings that were nowhere to be seen anyway. Our steps still warily avoided leafy shoots growing out of the sand that looked like poison ivy. But gradually, we accepted that we must have been dealing with seedlings of maples — the trees that grew all around. Our exaggerated prudence would gradually subside to a new self-confidence. We went to sleep early.

In the morning, we got up with daybreak. The surface of the lake was as smooth as a mirror, reflecting the rising sun through the low morning mists above it. Above the water, a clear sky spread without any clouds. We quickly struck the tent and loaded the canoe. After pushing off, we turned the boat north, parallel with the shore. We moved away from it only to avoid the vast spreads of the shoreline reeds. The wind had already started to blow from the west, thus from our left. But from my two-year studying of the lake's map, I had wisely chosen a route that was to a great degree protected from the resulting westerly waves. It is because the southern end of Lake of the Woods is relatively shallow. Due to an interaction between the inflowing river that brings sand, and the west-winds-driven lake surf, a huge barrier of a sand bar had formed over the ages that protects the whole mouth of the river. In places, this is up to some eight metres high, 20 metres wide and over six kilometres long across the bay of the mouth. On some of the bar's sections, mature trees are growing. It has several gaps that allow boat traffic to pass through. We moved north through its protected lagoon that had formed between the bar and the shore. At its northern end, it opened up again onto the lake. On the map, this lagoon is named "The Four Mile Bay." We had a nice day and soon the sun burned merrily. A short break to rest and to explore a pretty spot on the bar turned very interesting. Just before our bow touched the sand bar, two juvenile bald eagles, still all brown — prior to the development of the white plumage on their heads and tails — rose from its ridge. They had to be nesting close by judging from the numerous prints of their talons and wing tips in the sand high up on the dune. We concurred that this place would make for very romantic, gorgeous camping. Alas, it was still too early for it today — bad timing! The view from the ridge of the sand dune toward the west opened onto a broad panorama of the enormous spread of the lake. It only reconfirmed the wisdom of our strategy to avoid its mighty waves by moving within the lagoon.

The legacy of La Verendrye and Ochagach

Looking over the vast water expanse of the southern part of the lake reminded me of the tragically rough history of its discovery. I recalled Pierre Gaultier de Varennes, Sieur de La Verendrye — a Quebec-born Frenchman who fought heroically as a soldier for the French king in Europe and suffered several wounds. After he returned to Canada, married and established a farm — at an age when others retire — he planned an exploration aimed at the discovery of the hypothetical "Western Sea." He invested all his possessions into the venture including the involvement of his three very young sons. Only with great difficulty, he finally obtained an assent for the voyage from the king's bureaucracy. Yet he was denied any financial support for the undertaking. He was supposed to make money for his expenses from trading furs. During his prior two-year stint as the commandant of a post at Nipigon on Lake Superior, he met an Assiniboine Native by the name of Ochagach, who described a canoe route to the west from Lake Superior. This man sketched for him a map of it on a scroll of birch bark. It was the line of today's border — the same route that I had followed on the part of my journey west from Grand Portage. La Verendrye set out on the voyage with a fleet of birch bark canoes and a crew of some 50 recruits from Montreal in the spring of 1731. The group included his nephew and three sons. He was envied by numerous enemies of his who had been laying obstacles in his way right out of Montreal. Following some initial glitches when several of his men defected, the expedition arrived at the end of Lake Superior at the end of August of the same year. This was at the place of the later Fort Grand Portage. I found out how the voyage on the Superior was viewed by La Verendrye himself. My own experience could very intimately relate to his every word:

"It was now the end of July, and we still had a long way to go. After a brief rest, I gathered my men together. We embarked once more, and steered our way on that great inland sea, Lake Superior. All that had gone before was child's play to what must now

be encountered. In contrast to the blue and placid waters of Lake Huron, we now found ourselves in the midst of a dark and sombre sea, whose waves, seldom if ever still, could on occasion rival the Atlantic in their fierce tumult. Even in this hottest month of the year the water was icy cold, and the keen wind that blew across the lake forced those who were not paddling to put on extra clothing. They must needs be hardy and experienced voyageurs who could safely navigate these mad waters in frail bark canoes. Slowly we made our way along the north shore, buffeted by storms and in constant peril of our lives, until at last, on August 26, we reached the Grand Portage, near the mouth of the Pigeon river, or about fifteen leagues south-west of Fort Kaministikwia" (where Fort William now stands)."

The troubles for La Verendrye had not ended at the end of Lake Superior. As I already mentioned, his crew mutinied against the hardship of the Grand Portage. La Verendrye was forced to split his outfit. Only the half of his party consisting of the most faithful and most courageous were sent by him to Rainy Lake under the command of his most reliable man, Christoph Dufrost de La Jemeray — his nephew, together with his oldest son, Jean-Baptiste. The rest returned under his command to spend the winter at the mouth of the Kaministiquia River. The first group reached the outflow point of the Rainy River from Rainy Lake during the same fall and managed to build a post, Fort St. Pierre. In the spring of the next year, 1732, they were joined by the rest of the expedition. Together they then reached Lake of the Woods in the early summer. Here they built a new post, Fort St. Charles. By now, La Verendrye was drowning in financial debts. Heretofore, his men had never been paid. Still, he continued his explorations up to Lake Winnipeg and his sons then carried on even further into the region of the prairies. (They were joined by La Verendrye's fourth and youngest son Louise-Joseph in 1735, who would eventually prove as the most active.) During this time, they established a number of new posts. In spite of his enthusiasm, he would be struck with a significant number of tragedies. First, he learned that his faithful beloved nephew, La Jemmeray, had died in an outlying post during the winter of 1735. Perhaps as part of the intrigues, plotted against La Verendrye back east, Fort St. Charles had not received its order of goods before the same winter. Jean-Baptist, who had been made commander of Fort Saint Charles, therefore organized an expedition the next spring consisting of three large canoes and 21 men, including himself and a returning Jesuit priest, Father Aulneau. They were to obtain the supplies themselves from Fort Michilimackinac on Lake Michigan. The party left Fort St. Charles in the western part of the lake and moved in a straight direction across the southern expanse of Lake of the Woods towards the mouth of the Rainy River from where we ourselves entered the lake. After about 20 miles, the fleet stopped to rest and smoke a pipe on a small island. Through an unfortunate coincidence a large war party of the Sioux — the cruelest savage warriors who in those times enjoyed regular terrorizing raids on the relatively peaceful tribes living in the lake country of the Shield — entered the lake. The group numbered some 100 warriors in war canoes. The traditional territories of the Sioux nations Lakota, Dakota and Nakota used to be on the prairies. Hence, they entered from the southwest reach of Lake of the Woods around what is still called Warroad. Fate had it that the routes of both parties were to roughly cross. It so happened then that a sharp eye of some member of the war party penetrated the morning mist above the surface of the lake and discerned the fleet of Jean-Baptiste in the distance as it was about to land at the small island. The plan of the Sioux crystalized instantly. Paddling with a minimum of noise, they landed at the opposite side of the island, sneaked quietly through the forest growth on its top and ambushed the resting Frenchmen with a shower of arrows followed by tomahawks and scalping knives. Those with multiple injuries who tried to swim to the neighboring island were left to drown. Today the island carries the name "Massacre Island." The bodies were not discovered until some two weeks later. It was a scene of utter horror. Jean-Baptiste's body lay headless on its stomach with a deeply cut up back and with the genital area completely missing. A chapel was built on the island where Fort St. Charles was situated and the bodies of Jean-Baptiste and Father Aulneau were buried under its altar.

It ought to be noted that La Verendrye was not necessarily the first European who reached this land. The Hudson's Bay officials who had trading connections with this territory from the north, reported at this time that when La Verendrye was penetrating to the land from the southeast there had been an unusually lively activity of "coureurs des bois" — the independent, gutsy, yet illegal traders of furs who got here most likely by the same way or a very similar way as La Verendrye. There are, however, no official records of these people and La Verendrye does not mention them.

The moving legacy of the Verendrye story would remain in the back of my mind for the whole voyage through the lake. I was constantly trying to visualize if what I was seeing was what they had seen and how our impressions might have differed. It is quite obvious that they found themselves way out on a limb from the security of their starting settlements on the continent, relying only on the knowledge and advice of their befriended local Natives. They had to be constantly on the alert for the unknown dangers of the landscape, the climate, the technical obstacles of the water courses, wild animals and unfriendly native inhabitants. They definitely had not met with the cottages and cabins of fishermen and hunters like us. Yet those had started to appear only once we reached the northern half of the lake and their numbers grew proportionately to the nearness of the city of Kenora on its northern shore. Ergo, here on the southern half of the lake we were, in fact, discovering it just like the party of La Verendrye had in his time. As soon as we reached the end of the Four-Mile Bay sand bar, we emerged onto open water. During the prior study of the nautical chart of the lake, I had felt great apprehension about the danger of being caught in stormy, or at least windy, weather in the middle of open water. I was therefore choosing a line that curved from the close vicinity of one island to another. But in the end, the long crossing of a large span of open water surface came anyway. We had to reach large Bigsby Island. There is nothing on it except for a dense forest. It is protected as a provincial park. We viewed it only as a dark hairline in the misty distance on the horizon from a brief rest stop in the boat at the last little island. After a while, we set a racing pace to it. It was hot and we faced waves from the west where we headed, yet our 17-foot tandem canoe felt much more stable in them than what I had gotten accustomed to in my solo canoe. When we discerned a sand beach on the shore of the island in front of us, we aimed our course straight to its widest middle.

The mysterious experiences

In something over half an hour, we finally pushed the prow of the canoe onto the yellow sand of the beach. Here I will mention one of the strange experiences that Milena and I had in this part of Canada. They were new to those that I alone had already had before on the route between Lake Superior and Fort Frances. The entire area was absolutely devoid of people as far as the eye could see and to where reason could extrapolate. There was no one on the kilometre-long beach. Nowhere could one see any boats. We were sweating from the hot day and from our vigorous paddling. Hence, we stripped naked and immersed ourselves in the clear water of a delightful temperature. Yet before that, thanks to Milena's good ear and a sixth sense perception, she let me know about an incomprehensible noise coming from the inside edge of a deciduous and rather impenetrable forest. She said that the sound could not be described. But I remember that she related it to something like a turbulent water movement, shattering surf, or the rumbling of a waterfall. It sort of reverberated in her chest. Therefore, she automatically perceived that there had to be another shore on the island right beyond the first few rows of trees. While consternated, I assured her that the nearest lake shore in the direction into the trees did not occur until after a 10-kilometre width of the island. She started feeling a little apprehensive. I, in the meantime, walked to the edge of the woods to relieve myself. In spite of my not exactly lynx-like hearing, with great surprise I found myself listening to something that sounded like the muffled mumbling of women's voices. Originally, we had wanted to have a break here for lunch. But when Milena's sound suddenly stopped as if axed-off and a deadly silence ensued, she had had enough. Her sixth sense picked up a strong message for us to leave. She decided that we should pack and paddle somewhere else. Some sort of strange energy in the air dictated to her that it would not be wise to linger in this place. I am no scaredy-cat and am not naive, but for many years, I have researched the subject of the existence of Sasquatch/Bigfoot. I have studied hundreds of reports by witnesses presented on scientifically organized web sites such as bfro.net. I have written about my conclusions and presented a couple of public lectures on this subject. From what I know, this incident and other experiences that I have already described from my solo water voyage and will still describe from the present voyage, fully agree with the typical sensory experience of some witnesses in the presence of Sasquatch. I also know very well that in modern times, no incidence has been reported of Sasquatch ever hurting a human. His aim appears to scare the intruder into leaving his territory. In this regard, though, he can perform an excellent job.

In about another two hours, an opportunity to make camp at last opened up. Our route skirted the east shore of Bigsby Island where we had hoped to find a nice camp. But in this sandy and shallower part of the lake, the shore of the island and its bays were mostly obstructed with dense and extensive spreads of cattail reeds and wild rice. At one point, we got almost lost in it before we finally found the way out. We eventually gave it a wide berth in a large detour toward the middle of the open water. Our campsite now rested on the point of a sand bar that jutted into a narrows between Bigsby Island and another smaller island. Swimming was wonderful here with a soft, sandy bottom. I noticed that the whole bar was imprinted with the small feet of a mink. My assessment was confirmed the next morning. While I packed the gear to load the canoe, my eyes looked in just the right direction to catch the fleeting moment when a mink emerged from the edge of the forest, quickly crossed the beach and submerged under the water surface. A few seconds later, he was followed by another one, likely his mate. From what I had observed during my water voyages, these animals of rapid movements and cute looks feed mostly on water crustaceans. Their crushed shells can often be found densely scattered over some spots of the shore that must be the minks' favorite hangouts. While resting from a strong headwind once in the lee of a small island, a mink suddenly emerged from the water at the rocky shore right in front of my canoe, unaware of my presence. His small muzzle was full of little crayfish.

The next day, we moved through narrow passages among islands, at first still skirting Bigsby Island. Gradually, the granite of the Canadian Shield started appearing again into which we were returning in our advance to the north. Beautiful little granite islets yielded romantic rest stops for us with joyful swimming. Our camping was blessed now with finding splendid scenic places at the end of each day. The next campsite was situated on a smooth granite slab, gently sloping into the water and jutting out as a cape at the end of a long narrows. Already from afar it called our attention to evaluate it. The day was especially hot. The light grey, smooth granite served as a welcome cool down as we walked barefoot on it and when we lay down on it while waiting out the cooking of supper. Walking here was as on a marble floor. In the evening, a series of two thunder storms arrived. They were marching one after the other with a noisy band of thunder and lightning. The drumroll of the bands were downpours of heavy rain from the ruptured sky that threatened to flatten our tent. Yet, the finale of the whole hoopla materialized in spectacular dramatic skies in the east with anvils of cumulonimbus clouds radiating the reflection of the last sun's light. The scene would have made a stunning landscape painting.

A strong wind blew from the north the next day. Luckily, our route was to lead us along the south shore of a huge peninsula to the west. This would provide us with a wind shelter. The peninsula juts into the lake from the east and covers perhaps more than a quarter of its area. It is named after Father Aulneau, the French Jesuit priest who, together with Jean-Baptiste de La Verendrye and another 19 Frenchmen, were massacred by the Sioux. First though, we had to wisely strategize by choosing a course through the passages among islands. We had to work our way to the lee of the peninsula avoiding big waves. Interestingly, the north wind obscured the atmosphere with forest fire smoke that it had carried in from the far north. One could even smell the smoke in the air.

As the essence of adventure goes, we were not always fortunate. We were not spared a share of bad luck. To that, we than had to react with self-help improvisation. So it happened on the previous campsite that through an unfortunate mishap, I broke the plug end of a little cable from the solar charger into the iPhone. I had downloaded a navigation app into the cell phone that showed me our position on the map of the lake. I had downloaded the maps into the phone while still at home in Edmonton. This function then worked even in the absence of a cellular signal, which in this case, was so on most of Lake of the Woods. But now the navigation app worked only while the charge in the phone battery lasted. That reached its end the very next day. From then on, I only navigated by the shape of the shoreline that I compared with the map. Following several navigational errors, which are hard to avoid with this method of traveling, I later recalled that I always carried a busola compass as a backup to my high-tech electronic gear. Heretofore never used on my fur trade route, I successfully fished it out from the bottom of my small drybag with electronics. With it, I was then able to orient the map and set the azimuth for the direction of our course. Another faux pas befell us just as we paddled along the shore of the Aulneau Peninsula. Some 45 minutes ago, as we had steadily worked our paddles, we started hearing a heavy, chugging noise behind us from the east. As we continued, the noise grew slowly louder and closer. Eventually, it escalated to a mighty roar that loomed just behind the stern of our craft, seemingly threatening to roll us under. I finally had to find out what was going on behind us to plan some survival strategy. As I twisted my torso backward as close to 180 degrees as possible with my hand outside the gunwale, the already cracked wristband of my barometric "Pathfinder" watch broke and it immediately sank to what must have been the deepest spot of the lake. I felt the urge to jump after it, yet when I saw how quickly it was disappearing in the dark depths, I capitulated. The source of the all-encompassing noise revealed itself very shortly when we were passed closely by a sizeable barge, the centerpiece of which was a large metallic tank. On its flank, a large sign smiled: "LOTW SEPTIC SERVICES." Slithering at snail relative speed alongside us at first, the pumper barge was slowly winning. From a stand up cabin in the rear a man stepped out of the door smiling, ready to crack some joke. Yet his voice was hopelessly drowned by the thundering motor. Instead, he jokingly gesticulated for us to throw him a rope so he could tow us behind his barge. In another hour or so, we finally lost sight of him until we could not even hear him.

Because of my unfortunate loss of the watch, this encounter was both comical and shocking. After this episode, we could determine time only by the position of the sun. With the lost watch, we also lost the information about changes in atmospheric pressure and hence, the ability to predict the development of the weather. Our water voyage then acquired a much closer taste to what La Verendrye and the voyageurs must have experienced in their time.

At the west end of the Aulneau Peninsula, the late sun of the day found us in a scenically romantic campsite inside a small scallop of a bay with a sand beach. It was situated the closest to Fort Saint Charles out of our entire passage through Lake of the Woods. The post used to be about 25 kilometres distant from here, directly west. Our tent rested on sand surrounded with sparse stems of goldenrod. In back of it was a warm, dry pine forest. With glee, we repeatedly enjoyed swimming over a sandy bottom. While cooking, we savored the views from a sand point, taking in the panorama accented with black silhouettes of small, tree-crowned islands that were strewn over the copper-hued lake surface like theatre props against the setting sun. Just then, like the stereotypical silhouette of Santa Claus's sled with a team of reindeer against the Christmas full moon, a silhouette of the sewer-pumping barge slowly passed across the sunset panorama in the distance, aiming in the direction opposite to that of this morning. Having collected what he was after from the isolated island lodges, cottages and outhouses, the owner of the essential business was returning home with a full load. The distance made the contraption small and muffled its chugging into a nostalgic evening serenade. Even sleep tasted sweeter on the soft sand under the tent.

A camp in the fiord of Kennedy Island

After the push-off in the morning, we fought wind and waves for about an hour. But soon after, we were paddling through narrows where the wind played no role. This is the area of Lake of the Woods that is covered by a great multitude of islands and peninsulas in its center so that it consists more of dry land than of water. Only narrower passages avail themselves here for connecting to the northern spread of the lake. The one that we had chosen is situated in the central area. It connects a relatively long series of really narrow straits that I expected would be especially immune to the effects of wind. It is called "the French Portage Narrows" because during the fur trade era there was a short section of the narrows here where it was necessary to carry. This was because the natural water level of the lake used to be a metre or so lower before the dam in today's Kenora raised its surface. We passed through some sort of a gate here with warning signs for motorboat traffic without any problems. When we again emerged onto the open water, we had our hands full with fighting the wind and waves. I had not been careful enough in determining our course to correctly enter into another protected passage. Thus it happened that after several kilometres of paddling, we missed the passage, overshooting it towards the east. While I was figuring out how to correct my disorientation, a strengthened wind and waves arrived from the east. It was high time to set up a campsite anyway. We decided to escape the wind by entering a pocket-like narrow bay on the nearest island. Originally, we had speculated that the narrow strait would lead us back to the passage that we had missed. Yet eventually, it would show that the strait had a dead end. But before its end, a flat granite point appeared that jutted from the densely wooded shore into the bay. This was immediately inviting for a cozy camp. The spot was nice, but most of all, it was heavenly serene. The inside of the narrow bay was thoroughly protected from the tumult of the wind and waves on its outside. The flat granite point, though excellent for a campsite, was somewhat out of the way and definitely outside the routes of the water traffic. Hence, it had not been discovered very often to be used for camping. As the first task after unloading the canoe, we pitched the tent. It stood here again on the hard flat granite with the corners weighted by rocks over the pegs passed flat through the corner loops of the tent. My next task was to spread the marine chart on the granite and determine where, in fact, we had ended up. This I accomplished by transferring the coordinates obtained with a GPS unit onto the map. I had to stretch a string across the map to substitute for a grid line. It turned out that we were in an out-of-the-way fiord of Kennedy Island. Reassured, we at last enjoyed the safety and peace of a spot that allowed us relaxed recreation in the form of swimming and even chores like cooking and the baking of a "bannock" — Indian bread — by the fire.

As I had promised above, I will now mention further, definitely weird if not outright eerie, experiences and feelings in this location. As the situation would evolve due to the weather, we were forced to spend two nights here. As I've indicated, Milena possesses a sixth sense. An example of it is her ability to read a person's mind. I can never hide anything from her and have already learned not to even try. Another of Milena's gifts in this regard is her capacity to quickly gain the trust of animals and be able to emotionally communicate with them. Be it a dog, cat, horse, squirrel or a raven, they become friends with her in short order. In spite of these — ethereal, lofty abilities — Milena's feet are firmly planted on the ground. She would not be bamboozled with any superstitions or paranormal fairy tales. I have yet to find a woman who, like Milena, would maintain cool composure when facing a bear in a close encounter. In my conviction about the existence of Sasquatch, Milena has always been my most skeptical opponent and a cold shower on my brain to "cure me from my obsession." After our experiences during the voyage on Lake of the Woods together, though, Milena has started to somewhat change her opinion. Not that she would believe in the existence of Sasquatch ("I have not seen one yet," she argues), but she has accepted that there was something wildly strange here that could not be explained with normal phenomena. It's because her good hearing and sixth sense were telling her that in this campsite we were being constantly and secretly watched by somebody or something. During the bread-baking for example, she heard a branch crack no farther than 10 to 15 metres away in the thicket — but no little branch — she estimated that from the sound, the limb had to be over 10 centimetres thick! And there was no wind at the time. Not a leaf stirred. My attention was distracted by something so I did not hear the crack, but that is no wonder anyway. My hearing is not the best and indeed, following the hearing tests that our family doctor had prescribed, it was recommended that I get a hearing aid. During my prior solo voyaging, I might have thus outright frustrated the Sasquatches more than one time, when in my ignorance, I did not respond to their acoustic provocations. So as it is now, I contribute experience and strength into our travels through the wilderness while Milena fills in the function of eyes and ears. Hence, we perfectly complement each other and are armed for anything. Well then, before the first night, at Milena's suggestion, I mounted a wildlife camera that was motion-activated on a tree trunk that could take pictures and videos even in total darkness thanks to an invisible infrared flash. Milena slept lightly, alert to strange noises. I, on the other hand, fell asleep right away like a log. Yet however soundly I slept, even I was abruptly awakened and startled when in the middle of the night, something slapped the wall of our tent hard. "What was that?" whispered Milena, horrified. "Well, it had to be some bird," I tried to calm her down. Yet to myself, I was not able to find the explanation. Those birds that fly at night can see in the darkness. Bats navigate by echolocation and are able to perfectly avoid much more complicated arrays of obstacles than the wall of a tent. I kept listening for quite a while before I was able to fall asleep again. In the morning, it turned out that due to my beginner's inexperience, the wildlife camera was still waiting for the start button to be pressed. Hence, it had not taken any pictures.

On the following day, circumnavigating the east shore of Kennedy Island, which was exposed to a huge open expanse of the lake from the east, would be risky. We thus got up before daybreak and immediately started packing and loading the boat. It was quiet in our campsite, yet when we looked up at the tips of the trees, it immediately became obvious that on the outside of the bay, wind ruled with fury. As it was dawning and the sun started pushing its fiery edge from beyond the water horizon, looking from our fiord through binoculars we could see very rough whitecaps in the distance. In spite of that, we finished loading and set off toward the exit from the bay. We knew that the effort would be risky but we hoped that we would somehow survive the skirting of the island and then find shelter in the more protected passages among the islands. At the moment, though, when we emerged beyond the sheltering edge of the bay, we were caught in mighty waves racing from the right — the east. We fought with them for 300 metres, precariously maintaining our balance. But when water started splashing to terrified Milena's bow over the gunwale with no possibility of landing at the steep rocky shores, it was time to implement emergency measures. We carefully turned the front of the canoe right against the waves and continued to turn the direction of the boat 180 degrees back. It was clear that the only way out from the acute crisis rested in returning into the safety of the fiord. We thus kept on precariously holding our balance, racing back in the side waves that were coming from the left now and praying that we would not tip over or swamp the canoe before reaching the lee of the bay. Once there, we were at peace again. It was obvious that we would have to renew our camp on the granite point where we would then be forced to wait until the weather wised up. Milena apologized to the Sasquatches as soon as we landed and stepped on shore again. In a little while, the tent stood in the same spot as before.

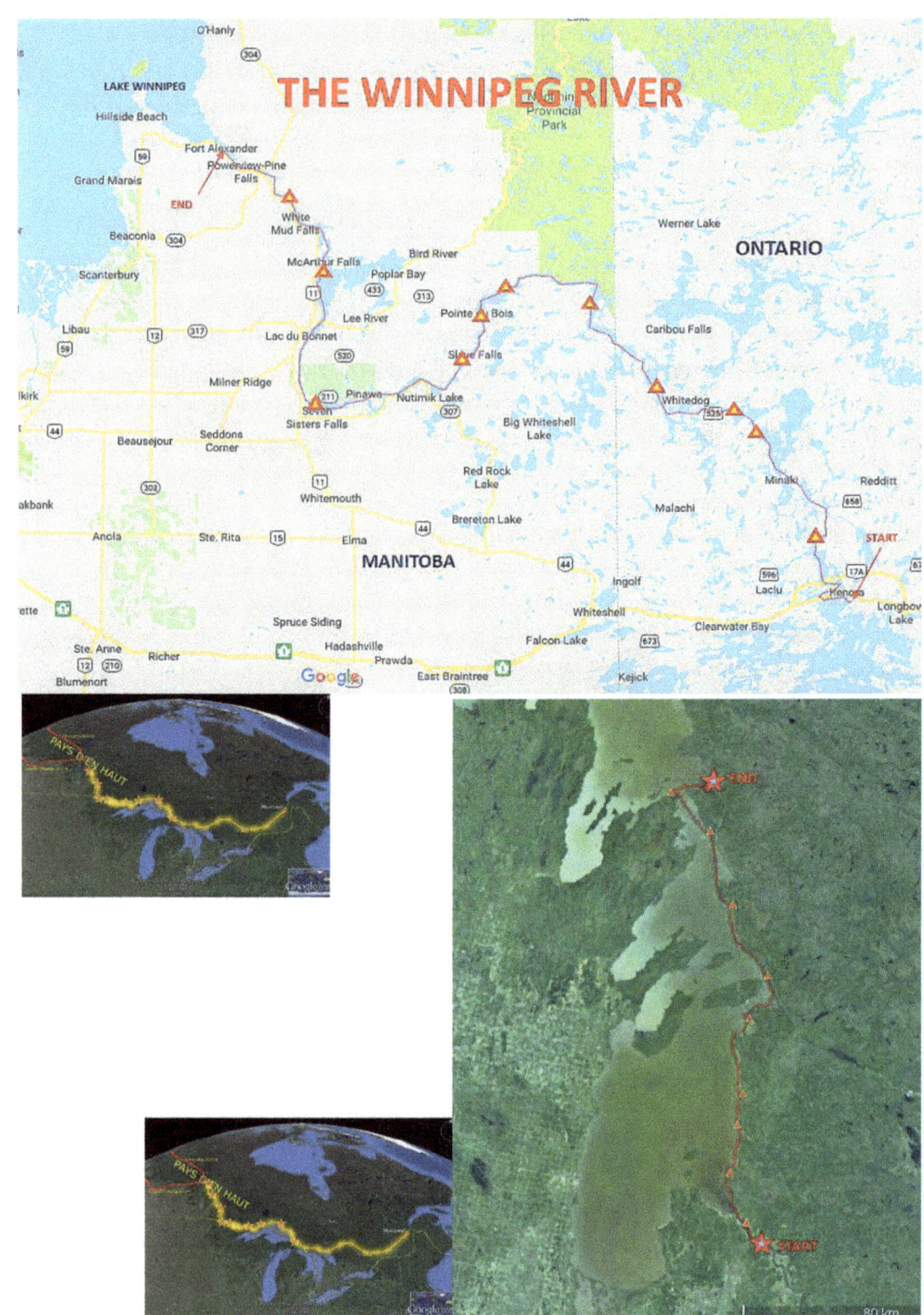

Lake Winnipeg.

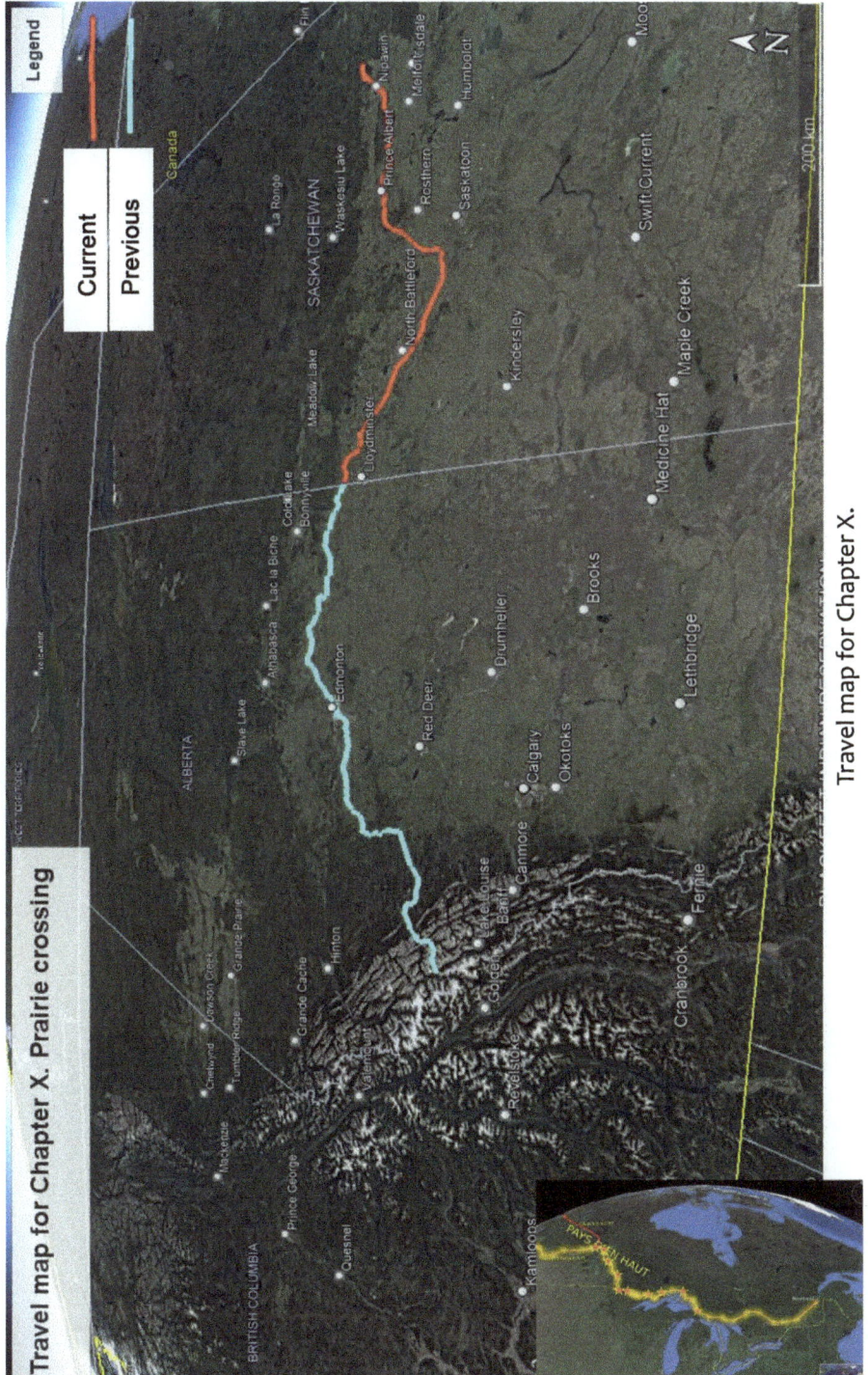

Travel map for Chapter X.

CHAPTER VIII.

A majestic bald eagle watching over us passing by on the Winnipeg River below near Kenora.

Entering the rat-hole underpass below the railway causeway from Keewatin Bay to find the portage into the Winnipeg River.

The portage from Lake of the Woods behind us, we are ready to push-off into the Winnipeg River.

Pelicans "own" Canada's Shield country outside the winter season.

By the sunset of the first day on the Winnipeg River, we enjoyed a scenic campsite with lovely swimming on the boundary of Les Dalles First Nations Reserve.

Our home-made spray cover protected the canoe from a rainy morning on Rough Rock Lake.

But after a thunderstorm, we enjoyed a nice late afternoon and evening in a camp above White Dog dam.

Ready for a portage around White Dog dam.

After the dam and Wabaseemoong community, we were blessed with a nice island camp featuring a horse shoe arc of a sandy beach.

While I study maps for the next day's journey in the evenings, beavers usually start their "witching hour" frolicking around.

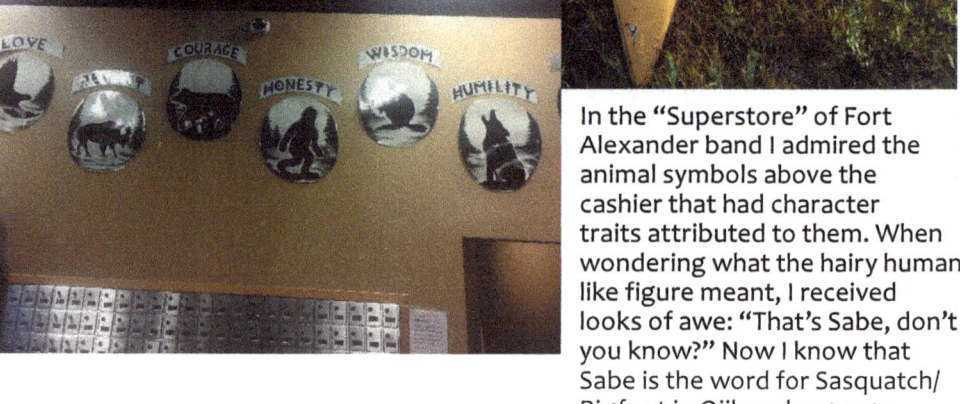

After we had missed our chance to camp before the town of Pinawa, we got trapped into endless paddling slavery against searing sun to cross the length of Lake Natalie in an evening scorcher to reach the Seven Sisters Dam. Utterly exhausted, we then resigned to camping right on the concrete of the dam.

In the "Superstore" of Fort Alexander band I admired the animal symbols above the cashier that had character traits attributed to them. When wondering what the hairy human-like figure meant, I received looks of awe: "That's Sabe, don't you know?" Now I know that Sabe is the word for Sasquatch/Bigfoot in Ojibwa language.

CHAPTER IX.

In my struggle against a powerful headwind in the mouth of the Winnipeg River on the first day, I sought shelter of all shore protrusions, overhanging trees and reeds.

Pelican is a frequent sight on Lake Winnipeg. They are efficient fishers and very graceful fliers.

My windy first camp atop a windy, grassy butte in the mouth of the Winnipeg River.

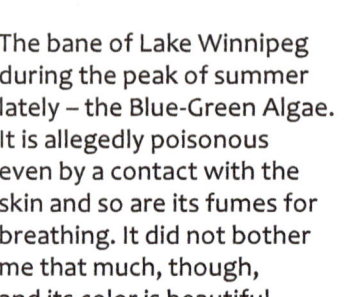

The bane of Lake Winnipeg during the peak of summer lately – the Blue-Green Algae. It is allegedly poisonous even by a contact with the skin and so are its fumes for breathing. It did not bother me that much, though, and its color is beautiful.

I often woke up to find fresh bear prints right up close to my tent. Yet I never met with any kind of a mischief from them. The ones that I had seen seemed smaller and they displayed rather cowardly behaviour. This is my camp at the mouth of the Black River.

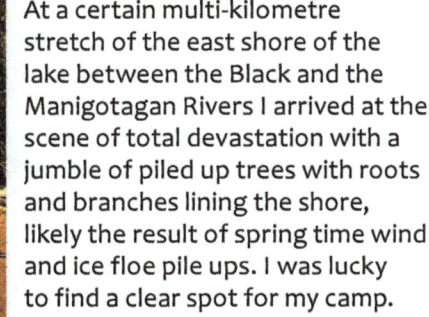

At a certain multi-kilometre stretch of the east shore of the lake between the Black and the Manigotagan Rivers I arrived at the scene of total devastation with a jumble of piled up trees with roots and branches lining the shore, likely the result of spring time wind and ice floe pile ups. I was lucky to find a clear spot for my camp.

While paddling along, I witnessed an acted-out scene that involved a large dead fish, turkey vultures that discovered it and were getting ready to start a feast and a black bear who smelled it from afar and invited himself to the table rushing and jumping out of the bush.

At the sight of the bear the vultures flapped off with their wings and the bear in turn, at the sight of me in a passing canoe, bent his trajectory back into the bush.

Top: Finding a safe harbour for a beach camp after a day of hair-raising paddling in wind and waves. Bottom: After I had to abort I set out early to re-cross the lake back to the east and Bloodvein River.

A territorial otter

My ride from Bloodvein to Powerview and my Jeep. Gloria waiting for her husband Richard.

CHAPTER X.

I gladly accepted my Kootenay friend Tony's offer to join me for the prairies. We made a good team.

Clockwise from left: My canoe travel on the North Saskatchewan River started from above its crossing of Jasper-Banff Highway in The Rockies some years ago.

Passing through Edmonton in 2014.

Above: Some twenty five years ago I traveled up the frozen North Saskatchewan River from Edmonton to Drayton Valley on skis, followed by three Alaskan Malamutes that were pulling a sled with food and camping gear. We used to breed these magnificent dogs (ALAYUK Kennel).

My voyage on the North Saskatchewan River from above Edmonton to the Saskatchewan border in 2014.

As the river's deep channel of the main current is constantly changing sides, we would often run into shallows and had to lead the empty canoe back to depth. On lunch breaks, we had ample opportunity to study wildlife prints in mud. The wolf print fit my hand in size.

Open sandy islands provided our favourite campsites to avoid mosquitoes. Past Prince Albert the shores became rocky, making it difficult to find good campsites.

A short distance past Prince Albert the river swapped its placid character for a steeper slope and speed. For a day and a half we tackled almost continuous class 2 rapids with big-volume waves.

The few people that we had met along the river were all nice and helpful. Our notoriety of two white-haired old men preceded us and gained us admiration from both young and old.

The rest of the day in the reestablished camp was spent mostly in cooking around the fire because the weather was windy and not exactly warm. In the evening, a series of three violent thunderstorms arrived with lightning, thunder and downpours. But I have to mention a rather intimate experience that I would otherwise not write about, yet it is important again in regards to the possible signs of Sasquatch. At one point, I felt nature's urge to fulfill my daily duty. I wanted to go as far as possible from the camp, yet since the bushes and trees behind it were very dense, I tried to gain distance along the edge of the water. The growth reached up to the water so I was moving in acrobatic lurches, catching the branches. With `surprise, I noticed several game trails to the water that I was cutting across in my trek. As often happens, my call of nature waned and in repeated lurches I returned back to the campsite without having performed my ritual. Therefore, I was stumped when Milena, holding her nose, chastised me with the words: "I hope that you thoroughly buried it!" Yet at that moment it hit my nose too. An unexplainable and indescribable stench was exuding from the thicket which was a mixture of rot, carrion and waste dump. After some five to ten minutes of perplexed looks at each other and in the direction of the source of the odor, it stopped as suddenly as it started. I have read about these cases and was only surprised, if not maybe even a bit honored, that this kind of episode would have happened also to me. For the uninformed Milena, though, the event had exactly the result that affects the majority of witnesses, i.e., it brought up an urge in her to leave the place as quickly as possible. But this was already close to the evening and our attention got distracted by a more tangible threat in the form of a rapidly approaching storm with thunder and lightning. The drumroll of a downpour bombarding the forest foliage from the southwest chased us into the sanctuary of the tent. The deluge came in multiple waves. The water accumulated on the impervious granite and flowed under the polyethylene ground sheet of our tent. Yet besides my quick momentary exit from the tent to add weight to its corner rocks and Milena's quick assembling of a small rock dam for deflecting the rain water from flowing under the tent, the night passed in peace.

The important thing was that the storm had changed the direction of the wind. It blew from the southwest in the morning. With the sun just bobbing up from the water horizon, we pushed off from the scene of our possible coexistence with Sasquatch and had it at our backs. The sky had cleared after the stormy night and it reflected blue in the waves under our paddles. We watchfully sailed out of our bay. This time, we were able to continue through the mist of the early morning around the east point of Kennedy Island and northward to remerge our movement with the preplanned route. From now on, I carefully oriented the map, and with the use of the busola I determined the azimuth of our direction across the spreads of open water very meticulously.

Originally, I had planned a much safer route straight west from the north tip of the island that came next after Kennedy Island and then moving along the west coast of the lake. This route would have been especially justified in case of the prevailing westerly wind. Yet this detour would be much longer. It might add perhaps a whole day to the overall voyage. Presently though, the wind did not blow from the west and hence we decided for a bolder and riskier yet much straighter route that followed a chain of small islands across a spread of open water. At its end, we would have an opportunity again to move through protected narrow passages among larger islands. Along the way, I pondered, how ideal the environment of the isolated, food-rich islands of Lake of the Woods would be for the theoretical Sasquatch. They would enjoy relative peace from human disturbances. Yet how would they get to the islands? Are they such good swimmers? But then it struck me: Isn't the lake frozen over during winter? They could simply march to the islands on the snow and ice, babies and all. Indeed, I later learned from a local man in Kenora that during the winter, there is a regular multilane winter highway on the lake that allows supplies to reach the cottages and fishing/hunting lodges on the islands. It also explained to me how the cottages are built. All these constructions are performed, or at least supplied with building material mainly during winter.

The Devil's Gap

When we successfully conquered about half of the route connecting the series of islands across the span of open water, Milena raised a (naive for me, at first) question: "Is there any chance that we could paddle all the way to Kenora today?" I understood where the question was coming from. Our layover yesterday due to being wind-bound worried her. This was clearly about the waves and wind that made her wonder if we would ever be able to finish the voyage. Now that it had become apparent that under today's conditions we could proceed with caution, she would rather have it all with certainty behind her. I explained that if she didn't know that, we still had about 35% of the total length of the lake remaining between us and Kenora. To my surprise, Milena declared that so far, she was not at all tired and that she could paddle for a long time today. To shore up my manly role of a tough leader, I responded that I was accustomed to long paddling myself and could endure if she could. We both agreed to try. During the first half of the day, we sailed predominantly to the north. The wind had shifted to the northwest and made waves yet not such that would cause any serious problems for us. In the later phase, we would be moving towards the northeast. I now meticulously focused on accurately determining the azimuths of the direction of our progress so that we would enter the passages between the islands correctly and follow the correct line of the narrow straits. The day was warm to hot. Hence, I paddled stripped to shorts yet under a hat while Milena toiled in a sleeveless shirt. While constantly moving, the wind was relatively welcome in that it cooled us. As we neared the north of the lake and the city of Kenora, the density of cottages grew. On some islands, whole villages sprawled. It happened to be the Saturday of a Labor Day long weekend. As a consequence, everywhere around the lake was astir with fun and pleasurable recreational activities of families, teenagers — people of all ages. In the straits a humming rush hour was just peaking with motorboat traffic of all sizes and powers of motors. As we approached to within some 20 kilometres of Kenora, we suddenly realized that perhaps we would not even find a spot for camping. All the useful places seemed to have a cottage or a log cabin on them. We thus continued further and further. In the end, I finally succeeded in correctly guiding the canoe to the distant lighthouse that marked the entrance into a long final narrows before Kenora. Its designation on the nautical chart sported a no less disquieting name than "Devil's Gap." As it turned out, it would live up to its name. In some places, this was merely about 10 metres wide and it stretched for some three kilometres. It quickly revealed itself as a favourite race track of the local hormone-packed, younger show-off population. The motorboats zoomed through it in both directions trying to outdo each other in showing off the power of their motors and how quickly and riskily they could maneuver the turns through narrow curves. Many could not see around the corner yet they sped with the finesse of out-of-bounds skiers. Threading its humble way in all this mayhem was our fragile craft. Some boat captains were courteous in slowing down to lessen waves as they passed us. On the contrary, though, there were also those who wanted to show us that we had no business being in the channel — consequently, shooting right by us at full speed. Terrified, Milena turned around at the end of the gauntlet, when right behind us, totally quiet and tall like a three-story house, the towering sightseeing boat MS Kenora slowly shuffled its way through.

I had known about a beautiful public campsite at the south outskirts of Kenora. The park carried the name of "Anishinabe," by the indigenous confederation who owned the campsite and managed it. I knew that it had a lakefront with a boat pier. Yet I had visited the campsite only briefly from the road with my Jeep when I was traveling to Fort Frances two years before. Now from the water, I could not recognize where in the complicated shoreline of many small bays it might be located. In this way we had suddenly emerged in the middle of Kenora with the hotels, shopping center, hospital, etc. on the shores around. It was clear that we had overshot the campsite. Fortunately, a local man at the city docks knew the campsite and was able to describe to us how to find it. We had to retrace our paddle strokes for about a kilometre. But in the end, we succeeded in docking at the right place and securing a scenic tent spot with a nice lofty view of the bay and the boat traffic emerging from Devil's Gap. The campsite served mostly visitors with vehicles and RVs. Since it was the long weekend, it was almost full. Yet because the tent spots were located on terraces of a steep, grassy slope toward the water and thus less conveniently accessible to the RVers, they remained unoccupied.

In the evening and at night, though, a storm arrived that changed the weather. The hot Saturday turned into a cold, rainy and windy Sunday. As a result, most of the campers packed up and left. Had we not overdone ourselves reaching Kenora on Saturday, we would have been hopelessly stranded. We would have been wind-bound now, squatting somewhere in an emergency camping spot within the overcrowded zone of the lake.

Only once we reached Kenora, did we receive news from home for the first time. Due to a combination of circumstances regarding the sale of our house in Edmonton (we had received an offer), as well as the finalization of the official details for Milena's retirement, we decided that for now, we would terminate the voyage. We determined that we would return here the next summer and continue down the Winnipeg River to Lake Winnipeg and further as we wished. We would not be limited by time then. First, though, we had to find a means of getting back to our Jeep. There was no public transportation between Kenora and Fort Frances. Milena then came up with an ingenious idea. I could not have used it in my previous lonely mode of travel and thus I had never thought about this option. She suggested that we try to rent a car. There were two of us. We would drive the rental together right up to the Jeep. On the way back, Milena would drive the rental while I would drive our Jeep. Fantastic idea! Yet it was the long weekend with a holiday on Monday and the single car rental company located in Kenora was closed till Tuesday. When the two beautiful young Indigenous women who ran the Anishinabe park's office extended our camping in it until Tuesday morning, we gained time to get to know Kenora. We walked a lot of kilometres on Sunday and Monday and visited the historic town's many interesting sites. We enjoyed an excellent breakfast in a Natives-owned cafe every morning and the Indigenous personnel began to like us so much that they even tried to find us a ride to the Jeep. Alas, even after many phone calls, nobody was found who might happen to give us a ride to the boonies-like neck of the woods where we had left our Jeep. We thus booked the rental vehicle over the internet from the cafe. At 8:00 in the morning on Tuesday, the manager of the rental agency brought the vehicle right up to the gate of Anishinabe Park just as Milena and I walked to it from our tent site. After driving the manager back to his office, we set out right away. Everything worked out splendidly. The car was brand new. Its rental fee was less than $50 for the whole day and it performed very economically. After we had accomplished our goal and were ready to return the vehicle, there was almost nothing needed to refill into its tank. When canoe-voyaging in two, we will now always practice this idea for retrieving our vehicle. With the Jeep back in our possession, we now explored Kenora on a farther ranging scale. Hence, we surveyed the site of the portage from Lake of the Woods into the Winnipeg River that we would tackle next year. It used to play a very important role in the fur trade era. The voyageurs called it the "Rat Portage." "Rat" in this case meant a muskrat whose pelt also used to be an important commodity of the fur trade. The initial settlement of Rat Portage, which had formed around this spot, would eventually grow into today's city of Kenora. In the end, we extended our camping in the park by another night. In the evening, we loaded the Jeep with everything — including the canoe on the roof — except for the tent and the sleep set. The weather now worsened to the degree where a frost occurred overnight. With a frosty windshield in the gloomy morning dawn, we said goodbye to Anishinabe Park and left the city behind in a freezing fog.

CHAPTER VIII

From Kenora on Lake of the Woods down the Winnipeg River to Lake Winnipeg (July 29 – August 9, 2018)

Well, how else than back into the embrace with the Canadian wilderness? With the return of spring in Edmonton, ice floes start to churn down the North Saskatchewan River ("Swift Running Water" in Cree) and the "V" shapes of migrating birds in the blue sky aim their points to the North. Every spring, in tandem with them, my wandering instinct begins to gain ever mightier strength to rip free from the ties of settled urban life. It whispers in my ear to head out with the easy lope of a tireless wolf once more and aim for the forests, meadows, mountains, lakes and rivers. The return to my physical declaring of love to Canadian Nature by steady paddle strokes in a silently slipping canoe is an old routine now. Still, as with my first launching out of Montreal, I anticipate it with joyful trepidation. Ahead is the vision of a thrilling adventure.

Once again, my wife Milena joined me as a faithful partner. The distance of the yearly return eastward from Edmonton to the renewed continuation of our canoe voyage along the Water Highway of the Canadian fur trade was getting shorter with each new stage. For the last time we returned into the largest Canadian province of Ontario to its westernmost city, Kenora. From it, we would leave behind Lake of the Woods, and along the Winnipeg River we would head northwest towards Hudson's Bay. We at last would cross the boundary of Ontario into the first prairie province, Manitoba.

Our road return to Kenora with the canoe on the roof of the Jeep had its start from as far as British Columbia. That is because this time, we set out from our log house in the mountains above Lake

Kootenay where we had moved our household following the sale of our house in Edmonton last October. In Edmonton, we now only keep a cozy condominium.

We traveled through Edmonton where we delivered my niece and her daughter to fly back home to Prague after visiting us. Having dropped off a trailer that we had needed for the extra cargo, we headed eastward. Gone are the days, when it would take a five-day trans-Canada trip to return to the start of each new leg of the voyage. With the shortened trip back to the water route, we arrived in Kenora the second day.

Our starting point was again the public campsite of Anishinabe where we had ended our voyage last year. During the two days that we spent there, we arranged the safekeeping of our Jeep at the house of a friendly park custodian. We were thus able to push off with peace of mind on the second morning, Sunday, July 29, before most of the camping population woke up.

The Rat Portage

The day hatched out splendidly right from the cock's crow. The smooth surface of the lake, sliced only by the prow of our 17-foot Kevlar canoe and dabbed with paddle stroke eddies, reflected the blue sky with scattered, little white clouds. It was Sunday morning; hence, the north shore of Lake of the Woods, which is rimmed by the city of Kenora, was still free of busy motor boat traffic. We needed to cut across it in roughly an hour of paddling to reach the lake's outflow arm, Portage Bay. This was near the suburb of Keewatin. A portage used to be situated there called "Rat Portage." Originally, even the city of Kenora that sprouted in this locality used to bear this name. The topography of the historic portage, though, is obstructed today by a causeway embankment of the Canadian Pacific Railway. A short tunnel cuts through the causeway under the railway to allow paddling through to its other side. Shortly beyond, the canal ends in a boat launch ramp that serves motorboats. About 200 metres from it is a similar ramp, this time sloping into the Winnipeg River. The latter has its water surface some five metres lower than Lake of the Woods. For canoeists, though, there are metal steps here that lead directly from the first ramp to the river, shortening the carrying of the canoe to some 20 - 25 metres. The price of the shortcut is a breakneck-steep descent on the steps and the launching from a bank of sharp rocks.

It was only around 10:00 in the morning when the transfer of the load, including the canoe from Lake of the Woods into the river, was finished and the loaded canoe was ready to be pushed off into its waters.

Soon, the hot morning made us take off our tops and spread sunscreen on our exposed complexions. The character of the Canadian Shield reflected itself in the landscape of the river. Though the water had a barely discernible slope here, it spread into a multitude of crooked arms, filling cracks of irregular widths in the Earth's crust of granite outcrops. In this way, it formed numerous lakes and islands, spiked up with resin-scented coniferous growth. Based on the images from my life's experience, it was difficult for me to attach the term "river" to what I was seeing in front of me. From a bird's eye view, this land would remind one of a granite sponge, saturated with innumerable lakes, lakelets and water arms interconnected by inconspicuous junctions in the forms of narrows or short flows. The surplus contents of water from periods of rain and from spring snow melt, as well as the inflow of similar excesses from the higher elevations of the watershed starting as far east as the divide that I crossed shortly after leaving Lake Superior behind, drained here in an northwesterly direction towards Hudson's Bay. What was meant by the river here, was an imaginary crooked curve that connected a series of outflow narrows. Only in them was any current discernible. It was not until the river neared the boundary of Manitoba and started to leave the granite Shield that it gained more slope and a clearer definition of its river course. The name of the river derives from the indigenous name of Lake Winnipeg, which in the Cree language sounded like *Win-nipi* (Murky water). Many partners of the Northwest

Company spoke of this river, as the most beautiful part of the fur trade water highway. In that time, there used to be a number of dangerous waterfalls here that had to be portaged. Today, they have been tamed by a series of hydroelectric dams that, to a great extent, flooded them. Yet the step-like topography under the surface of waterfall narrows remained. And this still poses a challenge to canoeists today in the form of large waves and unpredictable, chaotic eddies. A map and vigilant navigation were absolutely indispensable here. Without these instruments one could not avoid getting hopelessly lost.

Although for quite a while, we still moved through the thinning density of human dwellings and communication structures, the wilderness was already asserting its territorial claim here in a combination of picturesque crag formations, wild tree growth and in bare rock outcroppings strategically occupied by birds. High upon the tips of the majestic white pines along the banks here and there, sharp-eyed bald eagles watched over us; on the bare rock islets in the water, lilly-white pelicans were congregating. The white of their plumage contrasted with the orange of their long, pointed beaks, the underside of which was fitted with a landing net-like sac with a capacity good for fish of trophy size. The presence of pelicans is thus an indicator that fish of this size are indeed living in the local waters. It is joy to observe pelicans in flight. It seems unbelievable how these large birds can shorten their cumbersome neck by folding it into a compressed "S" and point the long spear of their beaks straight forward. The result is an aerodynamic transformation worthy of envy from the modern aviation industry. At the same time, the appearance of a flying pelican can bring up the image of a pterodactyl from the age of the dinosaurs, which, in fact, pelicans really are like all birds. At one moment, a wing-squadron of six pelicans silently flew by us, moving like fighter planes in great speed without flapping their wings, perhaps only 30 centimetres above the water. Despite their prehistoric appearance, pelicans seem to be uncommonly intelligent and socially well organized. They can estimate exactly when the degree of danger from an approaching watercraft with a human reaches the point when it is necessary to spread their mighty wings and take off in an aerial evacuation. Hence, it would not be very easy to try hunting them. The experience of native hunters, though, tells that it would be foolish anyway, due to the unusual toughness of pelican flesh. Seeing pelicans always reminds me of a joke that I heard at one time from an Indigenous person of the Canadian North:

The recipe for how to prepare a pelican:
Take a large pot. Cut up the pelican into it. Fill all with water. Make a big fire and set the pot with the water and pelican on it. Cover the pot and boil it for three days and three nights. Meanwhile, cut up a two-by-four into short pieces. After three days of boiling, open the pot and add into it the pieces of the two-by-four. Continue boiling for another three days and three nights. Then take the pot off the fire and let it stand to cool off a bit. You then eat the two-by-fours.

Before we camped the first evening, the last remains of people-built structures had long petered out and the sun slipped past its zenith. As with every time on the first day of the water voyage, fatigue arrived early. We thus aimed our attention into finding a suitable campsite. With the rocky, wooded banks of about 100 metres wide, mutually criss-crossing water channels did not offer such a spot immediately. Only after another few kilometres, we at last espied a friendly-looking tip of an island that was formed by low, flat granite with sparse tough vegetation. It was high time because we ended up on the boundary of an Indian reservation that was beginning just ahead of us. This one was called The Dalles Ojibway Indian Reserve by the narrow, several kilometres long water channel that the voyageurs used to call Les Dalles. It means tiles, or paving in French, perhaps relating to rock slabs that might be lining the bottom of the channel. It is one of the locations on the Winnipeg river where a somewhat strong current is felt. Since the canoe route was traveled in both directions, the quality of the bottom might have played a role here during the movement upstream. It was waiting for us to pass through it the next day.

The evening in the first campsite yielded pleasant contentment and tranquil rest when we swam in the lukewarm water that surrounded the flat platform of the narrow, granite projection of the island. The sun, lowering itself to the sunset in a clear sky, warmed us for a long time while we walked barefoot on the glacier-smoothed rock floor. Then it finally burned its way beyond the flat horizon.

In the camp during the evening, we had the opportunity to observe several dwellings in the nearby reservation with binoculars. The next morning when we continued our voyage, we admired the apparent wealth of the residents. Our route wound through the reservation past their houses. Besides the luxury, fast motorboats that were moored at the piers, we even saw an occasional float plane. The houses, set on small islands, abounded with artsy log architecture, some possessing complex, curved water slides for children. Following about a kilometre of paddling through the reservation, we sensed a current and entered into the long narrow channel of Les Dalles. It felt comfortable here that the current carried us, yet other than the need for an occasional paddle stroke to correct the aiming of the canoe among eddies, we never met with any technical challenge. We could thus admire the greenery-embellished crags on the flow-confining high cliffs, and the game, including deer, beaver and waterfowl.

Emerging from Les Dalles, the river widened. The day was hot again and Milena protected her back when paddling with a Superwoman-like cape made of a silk scarf. After a few hours of paddling, a bridge of the Canadian National Railway appeared in the distance ahead of us. It marked the Native community of Minaki. As I found out later, the name means "Blueberry Grounds" in Cree. Quite probably, the Indigenous people used to pick the berries here when in season, mixing them with dried and pulverized bison meat. With melted tallow poured over this into long moose hide or deer hide tubes, this turned into a practically non-perishable concoction. This was then called pemmican (from pimihcan — Cree for grease). It used to be the basic staple for the nomads of the time, whether they traveled on foot, on horse, by dogsled, or by water as the canoe brigades of the fur trade did. Pemmican thus enjoyed the role of a good trade commodity at the time. Today, the surroundings are populated, not just by Indigenous people but also by weekend cottages of the non-Indigenous population thanks not only to the railway but also to a road that passes through here. It is notable that another, equally important item of nutrition that Native peoples traded with the canoe brigades of the Europeans was wild rice. This plant appears in great abundance throughout the lake country of western Ontario where, like reeds, it covers many quiet shallow bays. The locals bent the stems of the rice over the gunwales of a floating canoe and thrashed the seeds with sticks straight into the bottom of the vessel. In camps on shore, they then winnowed the seed and the separated grain was bagged for trade. The camps for this purpose had existed in this area until the 50s of the last century.

After passing through the narrows spanned by the railway bridge, the water sprawls into vast elongated Sand Lake that contains numerous islands. It was here that we experienced the first of a series of disappointments related to the disappearing nostalgia of canoe travel through the deserted wilderness on a Canadian heritage river. The impressions described below would later surprise us and bring a bitter taste to our lips more frequently as we neared and crossed the Manitoba border. As we followed the west shore of the lake, the time arrived to start looking for a campsite. Yet the shore was steep and rugged. It did not offer a suitable spot. If a low, usable platform appeared, it was occupied by a private cottage. The islands were low and had a shore of broken, rough angular rocks. When we finally discovered a place on an acceptably flat granite tip of a roughly half-a-kilometre-long island, we unloaded our gear on it. Just as we unrolled our tent and were about to start erecting it, a man appeared in a plastic kayak with a question of, "What are you thinking of doing there?" He sternly informed us that the island was private. We responded that we had already searched fruitlessly for a long time and that we just needed to sleep over somewhere. To his objection that we could not have a fire, we countered that we did not need one, we could eat dry food. The next objection was: "And what about your waste?" The ensuing exchange started to acquire a bit of a disgusting taste. Yet thanks to Milena's diplomacy, the man eventually, albeit reluctantly, agreed to let us stay on the spot. From his constant hesitant turning back, however, as he was leaving, it was more than obvious that he rued his decision. After the man disappeared, Milena and I mulled our situation over for a while. In the end, we decided that his unwilling help was not worth it. We packed everything back into the canoe and set out to look farther. It cost us another two hours of paddling before we finally, exhausted and late in the evening, discovered a roundish head of an igneous granite tongue on the pate of which we were able to erect the tent. We were now situated far from the access road in Minaki. Thanks to that, the whole vast surroundings appeared wild and deserted. In the advancing darkness, the place even seemed somewhat spooky to Milena, but our fatigue finally made sure that we would quickly fall asleep and awaken from this bad experience into a bright new morning.

Yet the third morning on our water voyage was not quite bright. The sky was almost completely overcast and the threat of rain was imminent with a high degree of probability. Hence, after loading the canoe, we for the first time, stretched on its brand new, homemade spray cover that we had carried with us last year but had not needed to use then. It now sat splendidly on the boat and its deep red color could not have better harmonized with the bright yellow color of our slender, 17-foot canoe. With great pride from our successful job, we immortalized the covered canoe for posterity in more than one picture before setting out. The spray cover not only protected the canoe's load from rain and the accumulation of a rain puddle on its bottom, but it also protected the contents of the canoe from getting blown away. It also protected the bottom halves of our bodies on windy, chilly days on the water. Indeed, a couple of rain showers caught us as we were crossing the water spread of Roughrock Lake. At the same time, a wind from the southwest rose, i.e., from the port side. The paddling exertion in the waves then demanded a short, scenic break with a rest and snack in the boat. The right spot for it was provided by the lee of a small island that hid an entry into new, long narrows. The latter ushered us in the direction of an old Indigenous village that bore the name after a one-time waterfall, "Wabassimong," which in the Cree language means "White Dog," White Dog is today the name of both the indigenous village and a dam on the river, the only one on the Ontario side at the location of the former waterfall. After about a kilometre of paddling in the westerly direction through the narrows, a dark sky appeared in front of us, predicting a storm. After the exhausting, long journey of yesterday, we had planned to camp early anyway. Hence, when a scenic point of flat granite appeared jutting out from the left bank, it was a short decision-making to terminate the cruise here for the day. A short rain spell was spent here under the protection of a just erected tent. We than whiled away the rest of the late afternoon and evening in a pleasant rest while cooking supper on the base of the smooth granite. Again, we found ourselves totally forlorn within the entire range of visibility.

In the morning following the loading of the canoe, we set out, conscious that we could not be too far from the White Dog dam. When at last we spotted the distant dam structures in front of us, we proceeded warily. We closely skirted the right bank where our old map indicated a portage. We found its start on a flat granite slab just as the map described it, but now it was surrounded by trailers of a construction company that worked for the Hydro dam. We thus carried the gear on our backs, including the canoe, through the industrial camp first and then along a nice dirt and gravel road through woods from there. The portage route was well marked and about 800 metres long. It ended on a beach of coarse sand below the end of the turbulent water outflow from the dam. Following a few zigzags, the narrow passage after the dam widened and in the distance on a high right bank, the silhouette of the White Dog settlement emerged, dominated by its water tower.

According to the records of the Northwest Company partners, the early name of this locality was "Wabartim," where various posts existed, including one possibly operated by coureurs de bois prior to 1730. (Note that this was before Pierre Gaultier de la Verendrye appeared on the scene here.) "A very old French fort" was noted by David Thompson in 1797.

1789 Toussaint Lessieur & Simon Fraser maintained "Fort du Portage de l'Ile" for the N.W.Co.

1793 James Southerland and John Mac Kay of the H.B. Co., arriving via the English River from Albany, set up nearby. Alexander Henry remarked that it took 5 days for the N.W. Co. brigade to reach Lake Winnipeg from this point.

When the course of the river changed to the north-northwest again, having left the settlement of the White Dog in the distance behind, it broadened up here into an elongated Lake Tetu. Before the lake's narrowest point, at about one-third of its length, an island of medium size appeared, in front of whose left side, a tall, craggy, small island was situated that appeared very close to it. As we came closer, I discerned a sandy beach on the bigger island that stretched all the way to where it became hidden behind the small island. As we neared even closer, it became evident that the two islands were actually connected by a sandy isthmus with a tree and bush growth on its ridge. The whole configuration thus created a cove of serene water with a splendid beach of fine sand curving into the shape of a horseshoe. It was a gorgeous campsite, moreover, completely deserted. About an hour later, when our camp had already been erected and we were cooking supper on a granite platform, a fleet of six red canoes emerged from behind an island about a kilometre back from where we arrived. We had seen them earlier as a group of young people with guides who were leaving a log cabin camp on an island that extended the trend of a peninsula jutting from the White Dog village. We guessed that it was a camp of some Christian organization, like the YMCA, or simply just some "Bible Camp." It is likely that the fleet had originally aimed for the campsite with the beach where we were now situated. We were ready to share the paradise with them. Yet as soon as they saw that somebody was already camping on the spot, the canoes stopped and it became apparent that the group was deliberating. Then the crews began to survey the island where they were. For about a half an hour, we observed with binoculars how they circled the island and stepped on shore in different places. In the end, they pitched their tents on a rough and also sloping terrain. The distance made it impossible for us to invite them over. This was the only appearance of canoes or any kind of muscle-powered, non-motorized craft we saw while traveling the entire length of the Winnipeg River.

The tragic reputation of the river's many falls

We paddled most of the length of Lake Tetu along its left shore the next morning. At its end, we again entered a narrow course where we felt the current. On a high crag we spotted strange looking, big birds. They were dark brown with featherless red heads and partly red necks. We quickly realized that they had to be turkey vultures as they were hopping and bobbing, most likely about a carcass of some large animal resting on a rock ledge where we could not see it. Having passed through another narrows, we finally arrived at a place that we had anticipated with some trepidation. Our old map placed a waterfall there that had a portage, "Portage de l'Ile," over a scree of blasted rock on the tip of an island on the left. The location happened to be very close to today's boundary between Ontario and Manitoba; hence, now it is called "Boundary Falls."

In 1760, Alexander Henry the Younger gives a tragic account of one of his canoes that tried to shoot the rapids: ".....But alas! He sank under a heavy swell, and when the bale arose the man appeared no more..."

We were aware that some hydrological elements on the river Winnipeg have changed since the times when the voyageurs passed through here but some of them have not. Of the present state of

Boundary Falls, we knew nothing. We thus advanced very slowly and warily toward the tip of the island on the left where the portage was. Fortunately, a motorboat moved ahead of us, very cautiously progressing toward the waterfalls. Naturally, we glued our eyes onto it. After it crossed the line where we estimated the lip of the waterfall was located, the boat momentarily disappeared from our sights as it dropped over the horizon. In an instant, though, it reappeared again and continued on. When we came to within 30 metres of the drop, I stood up in the canoe and studied the water. I could see the whole passage without any kind of obstacle besides smooth, fast water dropping over the shiny ramp of a low drop wave. With a pounding heart we then passed through the narrows without a problem. About five kilometres through a long narrow course, we finally crossed the boundary into Manitoba.

Now we found ourselves on about 20-kilometers long Eaglenest Lake that curved to the north. Since a northwesterly wind was blowing, we kept to its left (western) shore. It was already time to find a spot for camping so we closely studied both the islands and the left shore. Roughly at two-thirds of the length of the lake, a small bay of quiet water emerged where, at last, a nice setting appeared on the flat area of a granite beach. We passed the late afternoon and evening in the peaceful tranquility of the camp while we cooked supper and made the obligatory four litres of tea for the next day.

By the next morning, though, the tranquility vanished. The sky was overcast with a gloomy half-light and a strong wind blew from the southeast diagonally across the width of the lake and partly from the rear. Occasionally, a rain drop fell to maintain a damp wind chill. As we set out, we planned to cross the small bay where we had camped, yet otherwise keep closely along the left shore of the lake. In a violent battle with the side waves that occasionally splashed over the gunwale of the canoe, we fixed our eyes to the nearest point of shore on the other end of the bay and struggled to reach its proximity as fast as possible. However, we did not notice that the western shore of the lake was separated by a well camouflaged, very narrow gap from a large island. Having missed the gap, instead of moving north along the shore of the lake, we followed the shore of the island toward the northeast in the continuing melee. Waves came at us from across the whole length of the lake, practically broadside. When we reached the end of the island, we continued along the extension in the same direction, assuming that we were moving in the extended direction of the main shore toward the north. After a merciless battle with the waves across a vast spread of open water, we finally arrived at a shore whose geographical features did not agree with our presumed position on the map. As always, when disoriented, I again invited the advice of whatever electronic navigational tools we had at our disposal. The Gaia App in our cell phone indicated that we had actually cut across the whole width of the lake diagonally to its northeast corner. From here, we had to follow the north shore back to the west to an outflow narrows that issued from its northwest end to the west. Now the wind blew from aft and only a tad from the left so we were able to finally relax and rest. In the narrow channel with its entry protected by a group of islands, the wind at last played no role. Moreover, the sky had now cleared and the warming sun graciously made its appearance on the set.

The long, scenic channel with numerous islands and wild deserted banks now led us to the west through a flat arc. After the center of the arc's bend reached the northernmost point of the river Winnipeg that still finds itself within the Shield country, the river began to curve toward the southwest. And here, according to our old map, we were to expect the next, potentially dangerous challenge. Our map announced it as:

"Chute à Jacqueau" — 1760 — "Lamprey Falls" — dangerous waters — portage across point on right side — 100 paces (campsite & shelter).
"We passed the "Chute de Jacques," so called from a man thus named, who, being dared by one of his companions to run his canoe

over a fall of 15 or 20 feet, an exploit never attempted before or since, unhesitatingly essayed the bold feat and pushing off his frail bark, jumped into it, and on rounding a small island darted down the main sheet, his companions meanwhile anxiously watching for his safety from shore. As might have been expected, he was dashed to pieces and no more seen." — Paul Kane, June 9, 1846.

The same as the last time, we knew nothing about the contemporary state of this waterfall. We approached it very prudently close to the right side, prepared to land for the portage. When close enough to the line across the narrows where one would expect the edge of the waterfall and being able to study it from a standing position in the canoe, I could see that the waterfall was flooded by a dam that was located farther downstream. It was therefore navigable, but the fast current of the water that was backstopped by the constriction of the waterfall narrows still had a significant drop over its drowned edge. As a result, there were chaotic waves and eddies here that stretched for more than 200 metres downstream.

After some 400 metres below the waterfalls, the water opened broadly to the right into a vast lake held up by the first hydro dam in the territory of Manitoba, "Point au Bois," that displaced another two drops of the river, some 15 kilometres farther downstream. It was high time to find a campsite. Prodding us to it was both our fatigue and a strong wind from left front that was forming whitecaps on the suddenly open vast surface of the lake formed by the dam. We had hoped to find something in the narrow bays on the right yet the shore there proved unsuitable for camping. We were already at the brink of desperation when I finally put my last bet on a small, tree-covered rocky island that was appearing about a kilometre away toward the center of the lake. Following the experience that we had had earlier involving the private island, Milena was highly skeptical. We almost blew up into an argument when she predicted that the island would be private and settled. I was arguing that without making sure by inspecting it, any objections were pointless. Reaching the island in the waves straight against the wind was no simple matter. We had to literally battle our way to it. Until the last moment, Milena insisted that she saw a motorboat tied at the shore. Yet it turned out that it was just a driftwood tree stranded on shore. Similarly, what Milena identified as the wall of a cottage showing through the trees, morphed, after circumnavigating the whole island, into the bare bark of a different, higher clump of coniferous trees. Indeed, the island was undeveloped and unpopulated. It was simply devoid of a human soul. We touched on the lee side of the island. Yet even so, it was not easy to disembark and haul the canoe upon the steep, slippery granite. I then shimmied hand-over-hand, grabbing tree branches to a higher granite point where I expected the possibility of an emergency spot for the tent in a more or less horizontal little saddle. As soon as I reached the spot, though, I immediately discovered that just beyond it, somebody had already cleared a flat, protected spot for a tent on bare mossy soil in a group of thick, young spruce trees. Given our present conditions, the place turned out to be an ideal campsite. We dragged away a few dead trees that had fallen since the last time somebody camped here and then we erected the tent. It was thoroughly protected from the wind that was now bordering on a tempest on the open water. Before I retired to the tent to sleep, I revisited the canoe and in the starting rain, made sure that it was secured even more reliably to the trees with ropes and straps. I made it rest still higher from the reach of the ever-increasing surf. The main storm struck around midnight. The lightning and thunder seemed to be exploding directly above our heads, all accompanied by the howling of the wind and a machine gun barrage of pelting downpour. We were protected by the surrounding thicket of spruce but I feared that some of the tall trees closer to the high center of the island might be struck by lightning with a resulting forest fire. The entire Canadian west was suffering from them this summer and the land was shrouded in persistent smoke that stretched eastward across the continent from the Pacific almost up to here. In the giant waves and the darkness, there would be no escape from the island for us. Only after we had finished the expedition, we learned that not too far from our storm survival island, a tornado touched down on the same night and tragically claimed a human life.

In the morning, the surface of the lake was quiet. We got up early and without much dilly-dallying accomplished the acrobatic process of prudently lowering the canoe into the water from the steep, slippery granite, loading it with the gear, and then our own embarking. We successfully dodged the high probability that somebody would end up in the water up to their neck. The fly sheet of the tent was still wet after the night storm; hence, it was draped over the load in the boat as the last item to quickly dry in the wind and sun. Now in the morning, only a gentle breeze blew from the west — so far, merely a hint of where it would rise around 10:00. We thus aimed our course in a straight line to the west shoreline in the lee of which we intended to move southwest towards the dam. We still had some 15 kilometres of paddling to it. While paddling, we could not resist congratulating ourselves again and again in being blessed with the good fortune of finding our island refuge of safety yesterday and happily surviving the night of the dance of devils. According to our map, the portage around the Pointe au Bois dam was to be on the right. The original name of the portage prior to the building of the dam sounded in Cree as "Ka-mash-aw-aw-sing" (where one carries twice). The map described it as 700 paces across the parking lot of the hydro plant. Before we arrived at its start, the sky grew overcast and the threat of an inescapable storm loomed. We quickly disembarked and divided the load into three burdens for our backs plus the canoe, as well as a few smaller hand carried items. I set out first with the heaviest and most misshapen load strapped on a pack frame, which contained two crosswise drybags with food, together with one paddle and the bags in our hands. Milena followed carrying the waterproof framepack and a second paddle. I surveyed the route and hurried to have the agony of a mule's work over with as fast as possible. It turned out that the description of the portage on our map was obsolete because the parking lot that we were to cross had grown, was fenced in and had become a vast machine park of the hydro plant. It now had to be trekked around. On top of this, the place where the boats used to be relaunched below the dam was also fenced in; hence, one had to continue carrying for another three-quarters of a kilometre downstream. Thus, the overall length of the portage suddenly grew from 700 paces to some two-and- a-half kilometres. In my tortuous Calvary, I quickly lost Milena far behind, leaving her desperate and in tears when she lost her way. After shedding my burden at the end of the portage, I immediately turned around and trotted back to meet her. Before we reached the end, it started raining. Hence, we quickly selected a spot for the tent and hurriedly unpacked it. We almost started putting it up, when we realized that we did not have the fly sheet for it. This time, it had ended up in the yellow drybag with the hardware that was still at the beginning of the portage. The tent was therefore quickly stashed back into the waterproof pack again and I set out at a trot back to the start of the portage for the missing load. Exhausted and demoralized, Milena stayed at the end of the portage to protect the already delivered load. I almost trotted out my second carry with the heavy yellow pack because I knew that Milena was waiting at its end in a downpour. Fortunately, at the end of the portage was a billboard that had a small roof over it. Milena thus covered whatever needed protection from the rain with her Gore-Tex windbreaker and sought refuge standing under the narrow roof of the billboard. Finally, we erected the tent as quickly as we could to avoid getting its inner walls too exposed to the rain. While Milena organized its interior, I set out for the last load that was comprised of the canoe and packs attached at my waist. It was pouring in both directions and lightning was blasting. The thunderstorm reached its climax. With my hands holding the gunwales of the overturned canoe on my shoulders, the sleeves of my Gore-Tex windbreaker collected the water draining from its surface like the downpipes of eavestroughs. Every once in a while, I had to turn my arms downward one by one to empty the sleeves. The adversity-packed story ended happily after all. Following our thorough drying with towels, the cozy comfort of the inside of the tent protected from the downpour, tasted even sweeter contrasted with the adversity test outside that we had just passed. We then whiled away the rest of the storm and rain in a well-deserved nap.

In the late afternoon, the storm was displaced by a warming sun. It would soon turn out that the location of our semi-emergency campsite at the end of the portage, where our tent stood on a granite platform next to a small sandy beach, happened to be the favourite swimming spot of a local family. The father of the family foggily remembered that during his youth he canoed with a group down the river. He recalled that they had to carry around another dam that was waiting for us tomorrow. He was able to weakly confirm my suspicion that a much shorter and better portage existed there than what was described on our old map. The map recommended a portage around the dam on the right side while the satellite view revealed the possibility of keeping to the left side above the dam and then landing on a smaller island in the middle of the river that divided the dam wall into two. The left part of the dam was a great deal smaller and removed some 300 metres downstream by the length of the island. There was evidence that it should be possible to portage across the island to the right below the main dam.

The man added a sobering and cautious reminder that a tragic incident had happened almost exactly a year ago. According to him, a solo kayaker left the spot where we now camped at around 5:00 in the morning. He had to carry around our dam of tomorrow, (which, by the way, was called "Slave Falls" after the falls that it replaced), and continued on. After some while, he arrived at another one-time waterfall, now flooded yet still dangerous due to waves, rock reefs and chaotic eddies — "Sturgeon Falls." The tragedy must have occurred at this location because the items of the kayaker's gear were later found scattered over the surface of the lake below the waterfalls. The drowned body of the kayaker wearing his life jacket was not found until quite a while later.

The next morning after three hours of paddling, we carefully approached the Slave Falls Dam. We were not sure yet whether our speculated portage on the left over the island would be possible.

We dreaded the chance that we might have to backtrack a long distance upstream if the opposite side portage proved to be the only choice. Yet surprisingly, besides the orange signs warning against approaching the zone of the dam wall, I could spy from a great distance a sign on a tiny island at left with blue text. When at last my eyes could discern what the sign said, my expectation that it would give instructions for the portage on the left was happily confirmed. The instructions recommended closely following the left bank where signs with the symbol of a walking figure toting an overturned canoe on its shoulders would appear at reasonable intervals. When we got close to the dividing island, the same but much larger sign indicated the landing spot for the start of the portage over it. Oh what a luxury and a welcome confirmation that we had invested our physical energy correctly! The landing at the portage was at a low bank with mowed grass. A roughly 400-metre long portage trail led through a cutline along the island first, which also had a mowed path, and then slipped down from it through woods to a river beach on the right. The setting at the end of the portage below the dam was inviting for establishing a camp. It possessed a peaceful atmosphere with a flat base for the tent, this time on sand. A plentiful supply of dry driftwood for fire was not lacking here either. The view across the river indicated that the portage along the right bank could prove to be not only long but also somewhat arduous thanks to steep, rocky terrain. The dam itself was only partially visible from here. I have found a source that explains the origin of the name of the one-time waterfalls and of today's hydro dam:

"Chute aux Esclaves," or *"Slave Falls." "Tradition tells that a slave of a ferocious master, maddened by long continued cruelty, calmly stepped into a canoe above these falls in the presence of the tribe, and suddenly pushing off from shore, wrapped her deer-skin robe round her face and glided over the crest of the cataract, to find rest in the surging waters below."– Y. H. Hind – 1857.*

When one hears this touching story, one ought to regard the name of this place completely differently. Unaware of its origin, one might take it like any generic name — simply a geographical designation. Yet now I know that in its background, a very soul-stirring, sad history lurks that attests to the cruel character of certain types of humans, who, intoxicated with possessed power, take ill pleasure in exercising control over another human's life, turning it into such pain and suffering that the victim seeks liberation in ending it. Apparently, similar situations could have existed and still exist anywhere on our planet. Could it be some character aberration in the DNA of Homo Sapiens that threads back to archaic times? As far as the present locality, the typical props on the scene were: birch bark canoes, waterfalls, deerskin dress and a stop for a portage. Yet a similar evil drama can play in different settings in different eras, including modern times. Musing about this story, I value even more the freedom that destiny generously dealt to me. I savor it in full gulps.

A new importance in our attention to the challenges of the river Winnipeg was conquered by yet another waterfall, Sturgeon Falls. As La Verendrye reports in the 1730, lethargic sturgeon that were harvested in these waters by the ton, used to be the staple fish of the local natives. Until the time when we heard the tragic news about them from the father of the family that bathed at our campsite below the Pointe au Bois dam — this time from modern times (last year) — we again knew nothing about these waterfalls. Our old map warned: *"dangerous waters — portage to the left or canoe close to the left shore, keeping away from the center."* Towards the evening, two jolly fellows beached their motorboat at our campsite at the end of the portage below the Slave Falls dam and went to look for something on the portage trail. On their return, we gleaned advice from them for running the Sturgeon Falls. They had to pass on the left but allegedly there were big waves and eddies. They recommended passing at the right shore where there is quieter water. It was shallow there, but "With the canoe you should be OK," they said. After some 15 kilometres, we finally approached the location the next morning. From a distance, the rock outcrops were visible in the middle of the falls' narrows that we were to keep away from. Heeding the advice of our visitors yesterday, we aimed for the right side. For as far as it could be viewed among the boulders, there was indeed timid water. Yet as it turned out very early, there was not enough of it. When the bottom of the canoe touched the flat bottom of the passage, we had to back up and turn the canoe back upstream. We then ferried in a big arc to an approach on the left side. When I stood up in the canoe 30 metres above the narrows, I could see that there were big waves there. Yet with a simple maneuver, it was possible to almost avoid them provided that one could aggressively swerve to the right immediately past the waves and return to the main direction of the current before the waves could thrust the boat against a long crosswise "whale back" of smooth granite barely sticking out of the water that extended from the left shore to almost the center of the left passage. After that, I just allowed the canoe to follow the main train of the current waves, steering hard to prevent eddies from playing a game with the boat's orientation. The waves continued for some 300 metres, gradually dissolving into Lake Nutimik below the falls. After that, we could only feel the current under the canoe for another half a kilometre.

Looking back, I have been trying to understand the tragic incident at the Sturgeon Falls the year before our own passage through there. I found the reported news of the accident on the web. The victim was a very capable and qualified individual who loved and enjoyed the outdoors and outdoor adventure. It turned out that he was a former chief of the Kenora police who retired in his 50s to enjoy his adventure hobbies. These notably included even base jumping from a hot air balloon in California. He set out alone down the river from his town in mid-May, 2017, with the aim of crossing Lake Winnipeg and continuing on to The Pas, Manitoba. I imagined that in May there had to be a significantly higher level of water in the river. Perhaps it just submerged the "whale back." If he struck it, could he have hit his head on it and drowned while unconscious, floating face down in his life jacket?

Lake Nutimik led through a narrow channel into the next lake, Lake Dorothy. This lake happened to have access from behind by a road. As a result, its shore was lined with one cottage after another. As we emerged into it from the channel, we could see youths in motorboats who, buffeted by their turbulent hormones, carved mad curves with their motorboats, jumping on the roiled up waves that they created themselves. All was accompanied with drunken yelling that sounded like Apaches preparing for a war path. It did not bode well for the paddling of the miles ahead. Every cottage along the shore had its own harbor, its technical equipment competing with that of its neighbor. Moored to each was a motorboat, if not two, with as powerful a motor as possible. That is, of course, if they did not just slice the surface of Lake Dorothy barreling like an ICBM missile, or creating the undecipherable Brownian motion zigzags of a "mad house fly in a milk canister." A handful of marinas clearly ruled supreme as they harbored a float plane. With mere muscles and paddles propelling our craft, we represented an absolute zero — nada. In the humiliating role of total misfits, we had to exercise our paddling motions for the next 10 kilometres before we could sequester ourselves again in narrow, unpopulated channels. The river divided itself here into two channels. The northern one, the Pinawa, which used to be run at times of sufficiently high water — today closed, and the Rivière Blanche, which is turbulent — leading to the west. In it, one has to be wary of rocky reefs and waves. Surprisingly, we found ourselves surrounded here by a small group of sea kayakers — all retired teachers who resided nearby — on a day's outing. We were prepared to camp at the first opportunity when a town emerged on the right bank. I must admit that I had not studied the map far enough for that day to expect that. It was the town of Pinawa, which, as a nuclear physicist and nuclear engineer, I soon, with respect, recognized. Besides the summer homes of recreational users, it also included a famous research laboratory of nuclear reactor technology. Never during my professional career had I had the opportunity to visit this place. Counting the research institute in Chalk River, this was the second most famous place of Canadian nuclear research alongside of which I paddled on my water voyage from Montreal.

Entering the prairies

The river bank along Pinawa was again lined with an uninterrupted chain of summer cottages. It was clear that our chance for camping could only emerge past it. Yet, alas! As soon as we passed Pinawa and the last cottages, the landscape radically changed. We had left the Canadian Shield. All of a sudden, the granite crags disappeared, the land opened up into a vast plain with a flat horizon of a forest of reeds that surrounded a rapidly sprawling dam lake. One could see only individual trees here and those beyond the reeds at a great distance somewhere. The prospect of camping appeared suddenly impossible. What could we do? The end of the day was nearing yet no choice remained but to paddle. A seemingly infinite Lake Natalie opened ahead of us, filled by the "Seven Sisters" hydro dam. This is how the voyageurs named a onetime series of seven portages that followed each other so closely that, as sir Alexander Mackenzie writes: *"Here are seven portages, in so short a space that the whole of them are discernible at the same moment."*

Today, this series lies at the bottom of the lake of the hydro dam that assumed its name.

The horizon, flat as a pancake, was proving that our water voyage had at last reached the Canadian Prairies.

The sun had now descended to the west and, reflecting on the surface of the lake, blinded our eyes from two angles. The brim of my hat screened only one. On top of it all, however late, the sun still blazed hot. It was clear that up to the dam there would be no possibility to camp. Yet we still had at least some nine kilometres to it. In a slavery stupor, we continued sweating in monotonous paddling with our eyes hanging onto the finish point — our salvation, that was represented by the growing silhouette of the hydro power house atop the dam wall. When we finally stepped up onto the berm of rough rocks immediately to the right of the end of the concrete wall, there were no signs with instructions or any hints about how to go around it. Everywhere were signs forbidding entry with "no trespassing." It was past 6:00 in the evening. Moreover, it was a long weekend. Ergo, there was not a living soul in the whole huge building of the power plant to ask for help. Whatever the outcome, we had not an iota of energy left in us to start any kind of a portage. "We will deal with it in the morning," we decided. I left a few voice messages on the phone that hung on the wall outside one of the entrances to the plant building. Then we erected the tent directly on the concrete of the dam wall and retired to rest. In the morning, I was out before 6:00. I had to catch someone among the employees as they arrived for their shift. They might be able to help me. I engaged a young secretary who parked her car and kept shrinking away from me as if I were a homeless hobo to kindly find the employee who should bear the responsibility for that kind of public relations and send him to see me outside. In the meantime, I went to search for a possible portage alone without a load. When I ignored a warning sign and continued along a gravel road on the right side of the river below the dam, the portage route suddenly became obvious. Yet I was shocked by its length. It had to be, perhaps, two kilometres to the put-in. When I returned to the tent, Milena was already engaged in a conversation with two friendly, energetic men who apologized for the difficulties that we ran into in regard to carrying around the dam. As I had secretly hoped, they suggested that we pack everything while they returned with a company pickup. They loaded us and our gear and took us to the end of the portage. We thanked them warmly and they wished us a bon voyage.

The river under the Seven Sisters dam was relatively narrow and hence the current could be felt here. Its banks were perhaps up to 30 metres high. Thus, one could not see the surrounding land. Later, though, the river gradually widened before the town of Lac du Bonnet into another large hydro dam lake. Also, the banks became lower. First, one could see grain fields upon them; later, both banks were lined with recreation cottages. For the water traveler whose design was to re-enact the way of traveling along the historic river when it was the only artery connecting the east and the west of the country, this situation was crushing. No campsites existed here. Wherever a suitable spot would avail itself, a cottage occupied it. Only second-rate spots remained among the reeds in low bogs, etc. One was unable to plan the day. Frequently, one was forced to paddle long into the evening till such a place would appear. When wind and waves arrived it was risky because there was nowhere to come to shore. Also, the landscape had changed here since the time of the voyageurs. The hydro dams flooded the fast water and spilled it into vast lake spreads with flat drab horizons. The remainder of the river Winnipeg up to its mouth into the lake of the same name is etched in our memory as making us feel like slaves on the waves and the portages under a searing sun.

We bade farewell to the Winnipeg River on its south bank — opposite to the bank with a promontory where a modest fort, Fort Maurepas, once stood. It was erected in 1734 by the advanced party of the exploration recruits of Pierre Gaultierre de La Verendrye, surrounded by a palisade wall of pointed poles. Involved in the construction were mainly his most trusted second-in-command, his nephew Christophe Dufrost de la Jemmeraie, and La Verendrye's oldest son, Jean-Baptiste. Christophe succumbed to an illness here during the following winter and Jean-Baptiste, together with a brigade of 20 others, was massacred a year later by the Sioux near Fort St. Charles on Lake of the Woods. The explorers named the fort after the French minister of the Navy, the count of Maurepas — an official who oversaw the colonies — in hopes that they would glean his support. As far as the financial backing is concerned, this never happened. According to his surviving sons who carried on further explorations far into the prairies, La Verendrye never received due recognition after his death, thanks to the jealous envy of his peers.

With regard to Fort Maurepas, somebody recorded in 1793: *"not a vestige remaining except the clearing."*

I feel it important to mention an interesting finding here. When we finished the canoe voyage, we rented a U-Haul truck because it was the only local option for retrieving our Jeep in Kenora. When we returned with it to Pine Falls to collect our canoe, we looked for a store to buy some food. The locals recommended visiting the Superstore on Fort Alexander Indian Reserve, a mere 10 minutes away. When we arrived, we did not find the stereotypical "Real Canadian Superstore" building but a large barn that proudly sported the same name. It combined a gas station outside with aisles of store goods on the inside as well as a post office and even a Tim Horton's coffee outlet. The complex is owned and run by the Indigenous community. As I waited in a cashier lineup, I noticed that at the top of a wall of P.O. Boxes up ahead, there was a display of wild animal silhouettes with character traits that they symbolized. So there was a bear to symbolize bravery, an eagle to stand for love, a buffalo for respect, a wolf for humility, a beaver for wisdom. But there was also a hairy bipedal figure among the wild animals that represented honesty. Being curious, I asked the pretty, young Indigenous cashier lady about what that particular figure on the wall was. She was surprised that I did not know. Even the burly Native man who stood behind me in the line volunteered to help. "It is Sabe, everybody knows that." As I found out later, Sabe is the name for Sasquatch in the Ojibwa language. Interestingly, in the Indigenous cultures, the existence of these creatures is not in question. It is taken for a fact. There are close to a hundred different Indigenous languages in North America. All of them have a name for this being.

"Kitchi-Sabe" in Ojibwa means "to walk tall", or "to have integrity."

CHAPTER IX

From Powerview-Pine Falls near the mouth of the Winnipeg River up Lake Winnipeg (August 8 - 18, 2019)

Well, hello! Another year has passed since we chatted the last time. I must admit that things are getting harder and harder with age. The kids prepared a wonderful surprise party for my 75th Birthday with an expensive cake ordered online. It featured a tent, a campfire, a canoe, a lake, a couple of spruce trees — all made of marzipan. It even featured — hold yourself — a Sasquatch — all hairy with individual hairs made of marzipan! Because my family was scattered across Canada from Montreal to the Sunshine Coast on the Pacific, the party was online with most of them participating via Face Time. It was nice to see the children and grandchildren, some of them in person, others on the screen — all healthy and radiant with success and happiness. Yet the plans for continued voyaging along the historic fur trade canoe route seemed to be facing more challenges than just the logistics and supplies. I was extremely happy during July in our log house on Lake Kootenay in British Columbia when I managed, by myself, to conquer a peak that sticks out above the surrounding mountainous landscape like a giant shark tooth. I needed to prove to myself that at 75, I could still stand on the summit of Mt. Loki (2771 metres) that is visible from pretty much everywhere around Lake Kootenay. It had challenged me to it from the first sight.

But Lake Winnipeg, to which I had planned to return in the month of August, was a different story. For one thing, I would not dare ask Milena to join me again. I could see how even the vast spreads of the open water above each of the power dams on the Winnipeg River lower down in Manitoba had intimidated her, not to mention the final arrival into the endless spread of the inland sea that Lake Winnipeg presented at the end of our journey the year before. So it was going to be a solo voyage again. All my gear was at the log house, which is where I had prepared myself and reconditioned my solo canoe. All packed, we then went to Edmonton where we put together the food for a month of my voyaging. In the next phase, Milena remained in our city condo and I set out east to Manitoba. As usual, I had butterflies in my stomach related to how I would manage all the necessary arrangements for the safekeeping of the Jeep at the start of the journey and about how I would get the canoe and gear to the water. Nevertheless, I kept driving on to gain as much distance towards the goal as possible and then worry about the arrangements when I got there. After sleeping in a motel in Yorkton, Saskatchewan, I arrived at the expansive mouth of the Winnipeg River on the second afternoon. I first asked about the possible Jeep storage at the "Superstore" on the Fort Alexander Indian Reserve where we had shopped the year before. I got a tip there to seek Henry's Towing business in Powerview higher up on the river. Alas, Henry had his yard full. After unsuccessfully visiting two more businesses, I finally entered the office of "Papineau Motors" near their closing time. I had to wait for the owner who had been delivering a repaired car to a client. Because of my previous experiences I was not very optimistic. Yet when Ed Papineau arrived, it felt as if sunshine just broke through the clouds. He proved to be very sympathetic to my cause and though he was leaving for an extended weekend at their summer cottage right after closing, he instructed one of his mechanics to take me with my Jeep to a boat launch in Pine Falls the next morning. After that, he was to drive the vehicle for safekeeping to the Papineaus' house. Ed seemed to have lukewarmly brushed away my offer of a $50 payment for the service and deferred it till my return after the trip.

Windy start

Getting up very early in a local hotel the next morning, I was waiting at the front door of Papineau Motors before it opened. When the mechanic, Armand, arrived, we drove to the boat launch. After helping me unload my gear, he departed with my Jeep. I had harboured serious worries ever since I first looked out from my hotel room window because I could see all the flags in front of its entrance whip-crackling fully extended toward the east by a very strong westerly wind. It did not bode well for the start of the voyage west against it. Yet I could not postpone it. Things were all irretrievably arranged. With apprehension, I watched the big waves streaming in a race pace up the river's current. It took me another hour to distribute and secure the load into the partially launched canoe. A couple fishing from the launch could not believe that I would be setting out in my frail craft into the wind-whipped madness. Yet I proceeded with the determination of a preprogrammed robot. In the end, I pushed off and paddled like a canoe racer with mighty, extended strokes across the raceway of the waves. My logistical aim was to cross the half-a-kilometre-wide river to its opposite, north bank and move tightly along it. I hoped to find some shelter behind its trees, shoreline reeds and protrusions. The main purpose was to find a spot for pitching a tent for waiting out the wind. The far shore, due to being part of an Indian reserve, had a relatively small density of human habitation as opposed to the south bank that was part of the stretched out and practically connected communities of Power view, Pine Falls and Fort Alexander. It did not matter how far I progressed on the first day but I had to be able to sleep in a tent somewhere and hoped that the wind would die down overnight.

Once I had reached the north shoreline, I was forced to fight a heroic battle to win a metre-after-metre progress against the westerly gale for many hours. The shoreline was either reedy and rocky, occupied by houses, muddy, teeming with a growth of poison ivy, or otherwise unsuitable for stopping and setting up camp. Finally, at the brink of utter exhaustion, I chose the clayish butte of a point with grassy, flat top for erecting a tent. I first had to spread and flatten two healthy plants of poison ivy right at the water's edge for which I had changed into boots and long Gore-Tex pants. Then, making sure that the canoe was secured from being blown off, I scrambled with the waterproof backpack up a near-vertical clay wall of the butte. Stomping flat the waist-high grass on the top, I finally erected the tent, spread the bedroll in it and fell asleep. The sun was still shining and the wind's rattling of my abode's nylon walls sang me a roughneck's lullaby.

The wind had not died down by the next morning. I methodically packed everything up and stuffed most of the camp equipment into the waterproof backpack. With it, I then descended the clayish cliff down to the canoe. I expected to find in it my Jacaru hat. Yet it was nowhere! After I finished loading the canoe, I went back up the cliff looking for it. Unsuccessful, I boarded the canoe and slowly paddled downwind close to the shore checking if the hat had not been blown off the canoe into the reeds. No success! I must have repeated the climb up the butte and the search of the downwind shoreline at least three times before, sadly, I accepted that my favourite protector against the merciless extremes of weather from searing sun to drenching rains was lost. I then resorted to wearing my khaki green army visor cap and rammed it down up to my sunglasses. With somber resolve, I finally resumed my battle with the headwind. I was not quite out of the Traverse Bay yet that was formed by the river's mouth. I hoped that soon I would start tracing its flared-out shoreline and turn my course more to the north along the eastern shore of the lake. The wind should then be coming a bit from the left — not head on. While paddling, I still mused about the fate of my hat. In hindsight, I speculated that most likely, it might have ended up hidden and flattened under the long grass that I stomped down to stretch the poly ground sheet and place my tent on. Oh well, it was too late now to risk another delay by returning for another search with uncertain results.

The wind was strong but the day was hot. As the army cap had no brim except for the visor, I prudently stopped and applied dollops of sunscreen on the sides of my face. The sweat of paddling forced me to strip off my t-shirt and apply the sunscreen also onto the unadapted skin of my denuded back, shoulders, arms and thighs. As the shoreline curved to the north, becoming the coast of the main lake, it gradually became less overgrown with vegetation that had thrived in the richer soil along the river's course. More and more of its scallop-like shallow coves displayed sand and beaches. I was taking shortcuts from one successive point to another, conquering these as the milestones of my progress. Two observations struck me as rather interesting. The first was the lack of motorboats. Except for one motorboat that moved up and down the mouth of the river fishing as I was struggling against the wind yesterday, there were no boats on the main lake. As I would learn later, Lake Winnipeg is very shallow and features a lot of rocks and rock outcroppings visible above the surface or hidden just underneath it, making things treacherous for this kind of craft. The second observation was the frequent occurrence of pelicans. Even more than on the rivers and lakes of western Ontario, these birds that are both magnificent and awkward at the same time seem to rule on Lake Winnipeg. They are the birds of the largest wingspan (2.7 metres) among Canadian migratory birds and I consider them the most graceful fliers. It was fun watching them pick one large fish after another, each time throwing their head and long beaks upwards to let their quarry slide down their gullets.

Blue-Green Algae

One serious worry that I acquired just a few days before I arrived in Manitoba, was the media news about the infamous toxic "blue-green algae" that has plagued Lake Winnipeg during the last couple of decades. It was to have reached its highest ever level of spread. Nourished by the leaching of nitrogen-rich fertilizers from the vast agricultural fields of Manitoba into the lake during the almost annual floods of the prairie rivers, the algae flourishes during the peak of summer. The affected water is poisonous not only when ingested, but also by contact with the skin. To be prepared, I carried about a 30-litre reserve of drinking water. I kept its weight close to the bow of the canoe to keep the boat's front profile low in fighting headwinds. The algae plant also produces gas that can be harmful when breathed in. I was therefore surprised during the first part of the day that I was moving through a refreshing water of pleasant temperature that was clear, only having a muddy hue that gave the lake its name wīnipēk (ᐄᓂᐯᐟ), meaning "muddy waters" in the Cree language. I later went through one such green underwater cloud streak that announced itself by a different smell. To my relief, I passed through it and re-entered clear water. But by the time I looked for a campsite, I merged into it again. The new location featured beautiful coves of granite rock with nice little beaches between them. The spot could not be passed by without camping in spite of the fact that the water all around was thick with blue-green algae. This, when dry, lined the sand along the water's edge with a foot or two-wide strip of beautiful turquoise color as if it had been painted on. I set up my tent on the sand a few metres from the water where the smell of the algae gas was reasonably weak. I then cooked my supper and brewed four litres of weak, green tea from my bulk supply of water as drinking fluid for the next couple of days.

The third day on the water was beset with two main challenges. The first one was that following the strenuous paddling against the winds of the two previous days, my body had become achy. This I had expected. The second was that the wind had gradually shifted from the western sidewind of the main part of yesterday to a north-northwest one. That meant another headwind. Furthermore, nature decided to test my resolve by throwing in some rain. I quickly landed on the nearest beach and laced the spray cover onto the canoe. I protected myself with a Gore-Tex windbreaker on which I deployed a seldom used hood from its collar. I had always hated wearing the hood as its front edge kept sliding over my eyes. With the Jacaru hat, I never needed it. Yet now, in combination with my army hat, it seemed to work OK because the hat's visor kept the hood edge in check. From my emergency stop site, I had to pass through a shattered rock point where the wind-whipped waves exploded in a very intimidating dance. I spent some two hours waiting here in the rain, hoping that the wind might abate a bit. In the end, I pushed the canoe off the shoreline breakers, embarked in it and gave the wave gauntlet through the point an honest fight. As the shoreline after the point curved more to the northeast, I had the wind now a bit more from the left front, not head on. Exhausted, I reached the mouth of the Black River, crossed it and established a campsite on the north end of a relatively long stretch of nice beach. Besides animal tracks in the sand, I could also see the tracks of some quad wheels. Indeed, after I had already retired into my tent, two couples emerged on two quads onto the beach from a nearby Indian reserve. Yet when they saw my tent, they respectfully settled for holding their small but somewhat noisy party at the other end of the sandy stretch. Around midnight, their versatile machines finally revved off into the darkness of the bush.

In the morning, I could see fresh bear prints in the sand, some of them quite close to my tent. Their size was relatively small, though, and the important thing was that nothing got disturbed. My food bag, the kitchen/hardware bag and all the other gear remained stashed under the overturned canoe on the sand some 20 strides away from the tent — totally unmolested. The day's beginning was largely sunny. The most welcome change for me was my observation that the wind had shifted to the southwest overnight — thus ready to propel me with a partial tailwind. Encouraged, I pushed the loaded canoe past the shoreline chop, boarded it and arced my course to parallel the shoreline about a half to a kilometre away from it to avoid surf-reflected wave effects. As no threat of rain seemed to be evident, I left the vessel uncovered, free of the spray deck. My progress was relatively fast thanks to the friendly wind and I quickly got used to the sideways rocking of the canoe on regular swells that were coming from my left rear. Even the achiness in my tired body seemed to be subsiding. In my distance from the shoreline, I was also giving a wide berth to a plethora of shattered rock outcroppings, reefs and islets of granite that lined the shore and mainly its points. After about the second or third day on Lake Winnipeg, the fur trade route gets reunited with the granite Shield country. I had passed through several areas of the algae bloom in the water that I recognized now by its characteristic smell. On the water, the smell seemed reasonably subtle mainly thanks to the strong breeze. In confined coves though, where the air circulation was limited, it could be quite pronounced. Contrary to what I would have expected before I had actually experienced it, it did not have a foul, rotting odour, but rather a chemical-type gas smell — something like latex paint.

Mindful of the fact that muscle fatigue reaches its peak after some three days of journeying before the body has a chance to adjust to the daily routine, I resolved to make the day's trip shorter. Otherwise, when pushing it, one can suffer negative effects that can frequently result in injury. Towards the later part of my paddling, I arrived into an area where vast stretches of the shoreline were devastated with a jammed up jumble of whole, massive trees apparently uprooted by some gigantic storms and deposited by violent surf as a desolate shore liner. Perhaps this effect might have had help from westerly wind-driven ice floes of the spring break up against the eastern shore. When I saw in the distance that the unruly tangle left some width of a sand beach between it and the water, I immediately set my aim for the espied spot. I beached the canoe, moved it loaded, end-by-end, onto the sand out of the reach of surf waves and walked along the sand to survey the beach for a tent spot. I successfully nestled it on a nice, flat, slightly elevated platform of firm sand among the bleached tree limbs and roots that were reaching wildly in all directions. In the absence of any surrounding rocks, I secured the tent pegs with chunks of heavy, water-soaked wood. The setting sun gilded my beach camp with a mighty, orange glow as I tended to my evening chores. Both the sun and I retired to sleep at the same time.

My fifth day on the water hatched into gloominess. The day was windy, the northwest wind driving herds of rain-threatening streaks of clouds overhead across my northerly course. I somberly paddled a spray-covered canoe braving the swells from the left front. Now and then, I felt some sprinkles on my face, but no deluge. I moved at least a kilometre from the shoreline, skirting the closest rocky treed points. The passage of each new point revealed a new section of the immediate coastline with its distant, bulgy protrusion constantly visible as a dark forested line on a far away, misty horizon. With the progressing day, I started discerning some large island horizons off the nearing western coastline. When I finally reached and skirted the big bulge of the coastline on my side, my attention got drawn to a conspicuous rock among many, strewn along the edge of the water. It looked like a big bird of prey sitting on the ground with its back to me. The rock was a solid brown color and perfectly still. I just took it as such, when to my surprise, as I got close, it spread its wings and lifted off. It really was a bird. I would have taken it for a juvenile bald eagle, yet I was puzzled by how solid the brown color of the plumage was. Only when my bird joined two more of the same kind circling up ahead of me, did I realize that I was looking at turkey vultures. They obviously sensed some prey along my course. Indeed, I suddenly watched them land on a flat rock by the shore, and just as I was passing by the closest, I could see that they were attracted by a huge, dead fish that somehow ended up on the flat rock. They were just about to start their feast when another diner invited himself to it. Jumping over a felled tree, a black bear emerged from the shore bush huffing and puffing from haste. He was aiming straight for the fish that he must have smelled from some distance. His appearance scared the vultures into spreading their wings and flapping off. My appearance on the scene, in turn, scared the bear, resulting in him bending his trajectory right back into the bush without even losing stride. The whole play must have resumed after I was deemed to be at a safe distance.

Following my exciting bit of a show, the shoreline started bending to the right — east. When I recognized that it led into a deep bay whose distant opposite shore I could now also see, I decided on a risky undertaking, paddling straight across its five kilometres of open water. I discerned a group of small, rock islets in its middle and charted my course closely by them in case I needed an emergency landing. They turned up to be just gathering outcrops for birds like pelicans, cormorants and ducks of all kinds that congregated here in great numbers and coated the rock surface with streaks of white guano. Its richness totally killed all vegetation on the islets and only a few dead, bare, tree skeletons remained, serving as roosts for more birds. With the islets behind me, I could now watch the grim forested mass on the other shore of the bay. After a while, I suspected that I was seeing the roof of some house. I also could see that the shoreline had a strip of beach along its lowest edge. I aimed my mighty paddle strokes toward it. It was a while before I could discern more details. Suddenly, I could see that my beach was totally surrounded by large cottages in the trees — thus, hopeless for camping. I bent my course more to the left — towards the exit from the bay. I was now following the shoreline strewn with many treacherous rocks in the water, beyond which was the beach. Yet in the trees above it, there was a continuous chain of recreational cottages. I consulted the Gaia App in my IPhone and confirmed my surprised suspicion that I had reached the mouth of the Manigotagan River — a popular recreation area of the province's local population. Also, my benefactor, Ed Papineau, who generously agreed to guard my Jeep in Powerview until my return, was to spend his extended weekend at the family cottage here and maybe was still here somewhere. I tried to follow the shoreline until the series of cottages ended, yet, when it did, it was only because the shore transformed into a swamp. I had to backtrack a bit and aim for the widest section of the beach. My only option was to camp on it in front of the cottages hidden in the trees. The beach belonged to the flood zone of the lake that qualified it as crownland — thus, not private property. Getting to the shore through the maze of rocks in the water was quite a challenge. Then I selected an elevated spot of sand among a sparse growth of waist-high weeds and pitched the tent. Next to it, I placed my baggage and stretched out the spray cover to dry. There was no cooking that night as I did not want to make fire. A dinner of protein bars and jerky washed down with cold tea had to do. As it turned out, the cottages might have been unoccupied anyway because no people appeared on the beach during my stay.

Friendly encounter

The next day was beautiful right from its start. After I loaded the canoe, I prudently walked it through the band of rocks that lined the shore, embarking it on their outer edge. I paddled past the swamp part of the shoreline and rounded a picturesque, rocky point peninsula with trees that was almost an island except for a small isthmus connecting it to the mainland. More cottages appeared on the main shore past it, stretching thinly along the coast up to the boundary of Hollow Water Ojibwa First Nation Indian Reserve. A village of its Indigenous inhabitants appeared after an unpopulated stretch of shore on a hillside rising high from the water. I did not see any people when I was paddling some half a kilometre from the shore, yet they might have observed me as I learned later. The shoreline here had curved east to another deep bay of the mouth of the Wanipigow River (Wanipigow actually meaning "Hollow Water", or "Hole in the Water" in Cree). When abreast of the village, I bent my course straight to the north, aiming to cut across the big bay to its north shore. This represented some five- and-a-half kilometres of open water crossing — a calculated risk for me. The sun was hot and I paddled shirtless in shorts with mighty, elegant strokes. My vessel rocked on heaving side swells from my left, driven by a westerly breeze. The prow of the canoe sliced eagerly through the water as I tried to move fast as I always do when I find myself far out on a limb from the safety of a shore. As I was nearing closer to the shore, I felt more secure. I was also able to resolve more details on the shore. It was free of any signs of human activity and quite scenic. It was truly wild and forested. Close to the water were rocky peninsulas jutting into the lake crowned with clumps of contorted trees that made them worthy of an artist's painting. Between them, beautiful beaches nestled in coves. It was still early for setting up a campsite, so I continued. I started curving my course from a two-kilometre distance to slowly converge with the coastline towards the northwest. Where the forested bulk of a huge island approached from the left, narrowing the lake, I spotted a motorboat speeding straight toward me. It was the second one that I had ever seen on the whole lake. The boat was occupied by five Natives who were curious about how I was traveling. The man who operated the craft was an older wise character with an air of authority who reminded me of Chief Dan George — the famous movie character. They had watched me earlier as I passed their village and must have been admiring my skill in paddling a solo canoe — the classical Ojibwa culture symbol from the history of their own travel — especially as I was disappearing across the vast stretch of the open water. I greeted them with: "Hello my friends!" and complimented them on the beauty of their land. In turn, they responded in a very friendly way to me. I felt the warmth of their admiration once they asked about and heard my story of how I had got to them all the way from Montreal. The elder showed me where he had a fish camp across the water on the huge, looming bulk of an island and offered that I could stay the night there. I thanked him kindly but explained that the logistics of my travel required a different option. We then parted warmly, they aiming for Hollow Water village, me searching for a suitable cove with a possible beach. The shoreline here had lost its earlier character and the coves with beaches became rare. When I finally found one, I grabbed it. It was small but snug and relatively deeply incised — pocket-like. I pulled the canoe onto the coarse beach and jumped back into the water for a refreshing swim. I then pitched the tent and selected a spot for the kitchen right next to a granite wall that bracketed my cove. I managed to get another swim and washed my hair before I tended to the kitchen. Not even an hour had passed since my landing when a huge wind started from the northwest that sent a train of racing, wild whitecaps past the entrance of my harbour. In no way would I be able to move even an inch against it. I was glad that I had been already protected in the shelter of my mini-fiord deep within the shore.

As soon as I emerged with the canoe from my shore pocket haven, I was pleasantly surprised. This was because the wind had changed direction overnight and the strong morning breeze was now coming from the southeast — a friendly wind for my direction of travel. I took advantage of the lee that the shoreline posed to the wind as it was coming over it from the rear right. The waves were minimal here and streamed offshore. At the same time, a component of it was pushing me on my way. Still, before noon the wind strengthened and shifted more to the south. The coastline here was very shattered with many rugged islets and randomly strewn rocks and reefs extending into a bulging array far from the mainland. I thus had to move far from shore where I was driven practically straight in the direction of my travel on sizeable waves. When the time came to start looking for a suitable camp spot, the shore did not offer any. In a distance of some six kilometres, I could see a tiny strip of shore edge that appeared bright in the now oblique sunshine. I put my bet on it being a beach. Aiming straight for the spot far from shore as I shortcutted a long, shallow bay, I literally surfed on driving whitecaps. My movement was fast yet very intimidating. I felt very much on edge, thus putting on a mighty pace both to better control the aiming of the canoe and to get the crossing over with as quickly as possible. It took at least 45 minutes, though, before my eyes could confirm that my wager was worth it. I discerned a horseshoe of a small beach flanked by two granite outcrops, its open entry guarded by an array of helter-skelter, scattered rocks like a mine field. The northern outcropping was, in fact, a small peninsula connected to the mainland by a narrow sandbar. I prudently slowed down and warily approached the surf-battered rocks, searching for a safe passage through to the sand. As I landed, the combination of the sudden safety with the awesome beauty of the scenic setting made me feel as if I had just reached the haven of a tropical island in the middle of nowhere. I moved the loaded canoe onto the surf-stepped-up sand and returned into the splashing waves barefoot to cool off and wash off sweat. Then I took a walk, still barefoot to explore my new territory. The sand was smooth and firm where it was wet and sloped close to the water. It was dry and loose with sparse weed growth in it farther inshore. Beyond that, came an edge of sun-warmed, dry coniferous woods. I could see the tracks of big wolf pads emerging from it that continued on the wet band to the rock peninsula and then north along the shore. When I looked closely, I also recognized some bear prints — not clearly defined in the loose, dry sand. I picked a nice, level spot in the elevated, dry band with the weeds and erected my tent there. For the kitchen and cooking, I chose a spot some 20 metres away to the south next to the bounding rock outcrop. There was plenty of dry driftwood for fire to be picked up anywhere along the beach. In my loneliness, the sunset expressed itself in a very nostalgic way here.

The wind was back in from the west by the next morning. It was relatively subtle at first, yet within an hour and a half, it became quite forceful. I proceeded north-northwest following the coastline, frequently seeking shelter from the left-coming waves in the lee of many rocky islets. Especially when I had to stop paddling to hold my breakfast, or a break for a snack in the boat, I had to make sure that I found a wind-sheltered cove on the lee side of some outcropping. Among the islets, the waves were particularly shattering due to many reflections that made my vessel often sway wildly, traversing the slopes of the waves — mainly from left to right, making it impossible for me to reach for a camera and photograph the action. I carried a GoPro camera that was waterproof and could be worn attached to a headband on my forehead. This would not interfere with the paddling. Alas, this would have required making the preparations under quiet conditions beforehand. That I had not done, as I had not anticipated action worthy of documenting. Once in the dance with the waves, I had my hands full, wielding the paddle in a brutal battle for survival. Only afterwards was I rueing the missed opportunity to enrich my photo narrative with proof of what I had to overcome to escape the designs of nature for quashing my daring resolve to persevere. Hypothermia was not an issue in connection with capsizing or crashing the canoe on a reef this time. The water of Lake Winnipeg was warm enough to survive in it maybe for hours. Reaching the shore by swimming, though, could not be declared as survival by any stretch of imagination. Rather, it might be just the beginning in a dead-serious game. Even with salvaging a limited amount of supplies from the crash, one would have to struggle for many days if not weeks on foot along a very rugged, desolate coastline that alternates sharp crags with swamps, deep multiple inlets and thick bush, to reach, if at all, some help. The land on the east side of the lake is totally empty save for isolated Indian reserve villages that are spaced some 90 kilometres apart. As I mentioned before, the lake has zero boat traffic.

The Fist of Nature

By mid-afternoon, I was shortcutting another large notch in the coastline. The wind had abated a bit by then. Once I reconnected with the distant shore, I searched for a suitable campsite. Luck had it that in the end I found a protected cove in this otherwise camping-unfriendly area that sported a nice beach in its depth. I placed my tent on a flat slab of granite this time, weighting its corners with heavy rocks over the peg ties. I was able to use lake water to cook with. It was green with algae at one end of the beach, but the other end had clear water. The late afternoon and evening were very serene in the cove and I took several scenic pictures. After it got dark around 10:00, though, and I was falling asleep, all hell broke loose. A violent thunder storm with pelting rain and a berserk wind came ambushing me like a puma stalking its prey. I had to exit the tent to put more rocks on its corners, returning into it soaking wet to hold the pole structure from the inside against the gusts that tried to rip it apart. I held the top corners with my arms for over two hours, constantly praying and pleading with it to end. No other name for the storm came to my lips than "Fist of Nature."

The morning of the ninth day on the lake pretended innocence. Its bright sunshine and glassy water surface reflecting the blue sky tried to distract the mind from remembering last night's war dance of the devils as if nothing had ever happened. As I exited the tent, I noticed that it was limp on one side of its top. When I took it down, I discerned that the socket of the central cross joint on the roof poles got cracked in the storm. Fortunately, the tent came with a repair kit that contained an emergency sleeve to slip over the cracked tube and thus, theoretically, strengthen it. By the time I had the canoe loaded and was curving my paddling course from the cove onto the open water to follow the coastline, the surface was no longer glassy. The water rippled with an ever livelier chop, yet luckily, from the southeast. Mother Nature must have felt guilty for the last night. With her friendly push now, I gained enough confidence to shortcut another large notch in the coastline.

I regarded today as a very important one because I anticipated, with some butterflies fluttering in my stomach, that I would reach the key narrows in the shape of Lake Winnipeg where the historic fur trade route traditionally crossed from following the east coast of the lake to its west coast. Looking at the lake in Google Earth while still at home before my expedition, I could see that to play it safe and follow the western shoreline fairly closely, one would have to inscribe several really deep zigzags in it. It also showed the rectangular pattern of farm fields carpeting the surrounding land. Furthermore, with direct road access from Winnipeg, I strongly suspected that the best parts of the shore suited to camping would be densely occupied with recreational cottage subdivisions from what we had seen on the Winnipeg River. At the same time, it seemed clear to me that following the east coast and rounding the north end of the lake to the mouth of the Saskatchewan River in Grand Rapids would be fairly smooth. In the absence of any zigzags there, the distance to the destination might not be much longer than when switching to the west side. Another argument against the west coast was that it consisted of uneven limestone cliffs that did not leave much of any beaches for camping. To the opposite, the east coast was represented by the scenic Shield landscape with granite and conifer woods. Musing about the geological origins of this environment, I pictured that the area used to be the sea bottom plain with eons-accumulated layers of limestone from dying sea animals. The weight of the volcanic lava that later blanketed the whole Canadian Shield area broke and collapsed the limestone plate. The relatively shallow depression formed between the jagged edge of the limestone break and the granite edge of the Shield topping then filled with water — forming Lake Winnipeg. The limestone break became its west shore.

In any case, my initial speculation was to follow the east coast all the way and arrive at Grand Rapids by rounding the north end of the lake. My plan eventually received strong encouragement when I revealed it uncertainly to Ed Papineau — the local. He fully agreed, mentioning that higher up the shore was really beautiful and even lined with scenic islands that should provide shelter from the prevailing winds.

Was there any catch to it? You bet! Nothing comes for free! The catch was that, except for a few widely scattered Native villages where some have only fly-in access during the summer, there was absolutely nothing but endless wilderness in that part of the world. This, for a solo traveler, sounded a bit intimidating in regards to getting help in case of misfortune.

As I approached the narrows, carefully judging my rate of progress, the remaining food supplies and the actual experience related to population density regarding hopes for help, I changed my plan. I decided to switch to the traditional route after all. I hoped that I would have good enough weather to shortcut the zigzags of the west coastline by daring open water crossings. Under such circumstances, albeit less romantic, the west coast alternative would have to be shorter and, with the higher population of dwellers along it, also safer.

With continuing favorable wind and sunny weather, I crossed over toward the west shore of the lake from quite a distance before the constriction in its shape that represented the shortest and safest location for switching sides. It represented a daring shortcut already there. Stripped to my shorts, I sliced through the smooth water of large, undulating swells with the prow of my canoe while rhythmically stretching the paddle strokes. I eventually identified the initial, thin, black line on the horizon as a densely forested shoreline. Approaching it as I aimed for the distant point of the left side of the narrows, I saw a white, moving motorboat. Apparently, the west coast must have been safer due to a lack of hidden rocks and reefs. When I was close to the point, I saw a beautiful, sloping sand beach on its eastern face. My aim, though, was to round it and get reasonably close to the island community of Matheson Island that was connected to the outside world by a ferry and a road. I was hoping that I would be able to buy some supplies at the ferry. Having the famous narrows-crossing behind me brought me great relief. It represented success in my sought-after accomplishment for the day. I was determined to find a suitable spot and camp out early to rest in anticipation of the daring open water shortcuts in the next few days. If I had been a little skeptical about the rumours of the difficulty in finding spots for camping on the west coast of the lake, my eyes confirmed it now. As I followed the shoreline closely, having passed the point of the narrows, I was able to see its details. It was indeed a continuous, crumbling cliff of layered limestone where the surf had mercilessly undermined it, causing rock scree and whole slabs to fall off and litter the shoreline into a helter-skelter junkyard. It seemed hopeless to find a spot for putting my tent down. Finally, I noticed that one of the layered slabs was perched horizontally following its fall and fairly high from the surf waves. I passed by it and had to return to inspect it from a standing position in the canoe. I then landed and walked to it to have a look. It was large enough and horizontal enough for the tent. I immediately set up my campsite here. Facing north, it was shady here which was welcome during the hot peak of the afternoon. I watched Matheson Island from here. What appeared from this distance as cliffs or a beach got identified after dark by its lights as cottages of the village that lined the shoreline.

Same as the night before, when it was dark and I fell asleep around 10:00, the Fist of Nature struck again, totally unexpected after a nice, quiet evening. The tent was buffeted like the sails of a poor sloop in the middle of a raging ocean hurricane. I immediately exited to put more rocks on the corners and, the same as the last night, returned soaking wet inside to prop the top of my tent with achy raised arms. I had to endure it for another two hours. The mad yanking with the tent managed to loosen the reinforcing sleeve on the top joint of the tent's pole frame and a chunk of the cracked, tough aluminum alloy flaked off the end of the tube making any kind of a makeshift repair hopeless. During a brief lull in the tempest, I again exited into lightning-strobes-illuminated darkness. I had to locate the spare kayak paddle by the canoe that rested inverted on shore. The paddle could be separated into two halves. With one of them I returned into the tent and used it as an internal tent pole. Luckily, its length turned out to be almost perfect. I was then able to get a restless sleep by curling my body around the erected paddle.

By the next morning, the Fist of Nature was gone. Yet, the rain and gusty wind remained to frustrate my plans. I was wind- bound, spending most of the time flat on my back in the tent while holding the blade of the tent-propping kayak paddle between my knees. Suddenly, I had plenty of time to ponder my situation. With the failed tent compounding all the existing challenges of the voyage, continuing on the way appeared unreasonable, if not irresponsible. I knew that I had to abort the trip. The burning dilemma was how. I was not far from the road crossing by a ferry to Matheson Island. Yet following its connection to the outside world on the map, it appeared to be a very circuitous route that required going all the way south to Winnipeg and then switching to the east around the bottom of the lake to go to Powerview for my Jeep. Then I would have to retrace the route all the way back for my canoe and the gear that I would have to have hidden somewhere near Matheson Island or gotten somebody to guard it for me there. I also eyed a different option, albeit dangerous. I could see on the map that back across the lake to the east there was a very large bay at the mouth of the Bloodvein River around which a village of the Bloodvein Indian Reserve was situated. This village had a gravel road connection directly to Powerview east of the Lake. The distance was only around 300 kilometres. I decided to risk it.

A perilous self-evacuation

I got up early the next morning and pushed off with daybreak. The lake surface was temporarily quiet and I did not want to lose the window of opportunity to cross the lake's narrows again, this time back to the east. The swells started coming from the west-northwest by the time when I was abreast of the west point of the narrows and started to discern the thin black line of land on the east shore. By the time I was in the middle of the narrows, the wind and the waves were coming in earnest again. I was paddling like mad with long, race-pace paddle strokes. Every once in a while, a big wave arrived and in a weird manner made the waves pile up under the canoe, lifting it almost like a surfboard. Luckily, the wind blew roughly in my direction. With no surprise, this scary roller-coaster made me cross the narrows in a significantly shorter time than it took in the opposite direction two days ago. When I came across the narrows, I reached a small archipelago of shattered granite islands. This provided a temporary shelter from the wind to stop for a breakfast of a dry, yogurt-coated oatmeal bar and cold tea in the canoe. When I finally found the quiet lee of a small island where my unpaddled canoe would not grind against rock, I discovered that I was violating the sovereign territory of an otter. After first noticing some fleeting, suspicious displays of a shiny, snaking body out of and into the water, the show got explicit. Finding that I was too brazen to be intimidated by the snaking, the otter stuck his whole head and neck out of the water challenging me with direct, angry looks accompanied with rattly snorting. After reaching for my camera, the otter emerged completely out of the water onto his favourite rock perch and arced his water-polished, furry body like a cat in an attempt to intimidate me into leaving. This I eventually did when I finished my breakfast. I was happy to let the otter think that he made me do it.

After reaching the archipelago, the battle was far from over. I had just reached the southern point of the huge bay with more than 10 kilometres left to reach the mouth of the Bloodvein River. The going here was particularly treacherous. The water was shallow everywhere and there were many hidden rocks in it. I had to leave the islands, passing through what seemed like a minefield and bypassing the arrays of rocks far from the shoreline where the wind blew with full force. Yet even here, there were constellations of rocks that, in combination with the wind, were making my eyes pop out of their sockets. Luckily, the rocks whose tops were just above the level of the water surface or just below it, were made visible by the wind-driven waves similar to the foaming bubble veils and characteristic waves trailing rock disturbances in river rapids. Yet some were still dark and invisible. One had to estimate where they could occur from studying the trends of the reefs shattered into rock series. The wind drove the waves straight east. To reach the inlet of the Bloodvein River, I had to aim northeast. I therefore tried to steer my course in that direction, as otherwise, after reaching the inside shore of the bay, I would have to go straight north with the wind becoming a dangerous side wind. The wind was now at full force. I was surfing on the waves at an angle. It was terrifying. When I barely escaped two close shaves with capsizing, I had to turn my canoe directly down the waves. I was more than a kilometre from the shore and I was praying to capsize only at a manageable distance from it. To top the sick fun, as I got closer, I had to steer the canoe through a labyrinth of rocks and reefs.

I thanked God when I finally touched a granite shore slab and pulled the canoe from the reach of the surf. I was thankful to be alive and did not want to do anything but lie down in a sheltered, sunbaked spot, watching the clouds fly on the blue sky to the east. I was hoping that the wind might abate but after idly waiting for some two hours, during which I studied the approach north to the presumed mouth of the river, there was no sign of it. It was now about 1 pm. I sensed where the entrance to the river had to be, but I still could not see any signs of the river or the village. To get there on foot appeared impossible thanks to a vast water-filled swamp that extended far inland. The rest of the terrain was rugged crags or dense bushes. I studied the possible canoe route. If I stayed relatively close to the shore, I could actually hope to find some shelter from the waves by them being shattered on the broad band of rock formations strewn throughout the shallow water. This, though, would make it into a high stakes poker game to get through them. I kept looking at the water, the waves and the rocks, feeling momentous impulses to launch the canoe. Finally, I mentally charted my way and, with shaking knees, I went for it. I moved slowly in a huge arc looking for passages among the rocks, sometimes having to detour far out. I rubbed a rock a few times, yet I was carefully winning. Finally, I could see the entrance into the river inlet. It had strange boat signs, apparently requiring them to be lined up by a motorboat when entering, or leaving the inlet along the only safe line. With the canoe, I could still dare to shortcut through a side channel that finally brought me to a relatively sheltered water spread of the river's mouth. It looked almost like a smaller, extended lake with mildly choppy water.

I could now see a stretch of houses lining its north shore. Earlier, I had expected a triumphant arrival with the whole village watching and cheering from the harbour. Yet I saw no harbour and, moreover, I did not see a living soul anywhere. The setting was dead quiet except for the wind's sighing and moaning in the granite gaps and its wistful whispering in the reeds as if the village had died of some fatal epidemic. I aimed towards the first houses on the left where I finally discerned a broken wooden pier sticking out into the water. The houses around were mostly engineered mobile homes in a rather neglected state. I could see that broken windows or damaged walls were simply patched up with a piece of weathered particle board. The pier was surrounded with all kinds of junk, mostly children's banana seat bikes, plastic riding toys, broken barbecues, etc., all submerged in the water. I figured that the pier might have served as a favourite resting and gathering bench during winter activities on the frozen river ice. Having been propped up against the pier and then forgotten, the riding toys and bicycles likely ended up in the water during the spring thaw. I hoped to find somebody whom I could ask to arrange for a ride to Powerview. I could see a building not too far away that looked like a community hall with a radio tower next to it. When I had seen it from a distance, I took it for a possible microwave tower, yet trying my iPhone proved otherwise. Now I hoped that the village had their own local radio station that could help my cause. Finally, I spotted a youth, maybe a senior high school student, who was walking along the waterfront with his cap's visor turned typically backward. I called him to get his attention, yet he kept walking on, unaware of my presence. I started shouting and almost performed jumping jacks standing in the canoe before he looked in my direction and, pulling out his earbuds, came a few steps closer to me so we could talk. I learned from him that the "community hall" had sat empty for several years now and the radio tower was never used. No hope to get any help there. But he suggested something that in hindsight turned up to be life-saving advice: It was to go and ask for help at the RCMP detachment. He pointed to another, smaller radio tower, which served the police, and marked the location of their building not too far away.

The intrepid RCMP officer at Bloodvein

I tied both ends of my canoe to the pier, took my cameras in hand and walked to the RCMP building. It turned out to be closed. I realized that it was a Sunday. In desperation, I turned back to a house that I had walked by seeing a truck with RCMP insignia parked in front of it. I rang the doorbell and waited for a long time before a head with a dark, square, brush cut — an unmistakeable identifier of the members of the Royal Canadian Mounted Police force (normally with a moustache which this young man did not have) — opened the inner door. In an instant, a fierce pitbull dog thrusted himself at the screen door baring his white fangs at me, salivating with berserk barking. The man waved him away and, with sleepy eyes betraying that I must have woken him up from a Sunday afternoon nap, skeptically turned his ear to what I had to say. It seemed that he was a bit suspicious about my story. After all, I realized that I must have looked like a weird, homeless vagrant with a scruffy beard, shorts worn over pulled-up silk long johns and bloodshot eyes from staring into the sun reflected on waves. He pulled up a little notepad and took my name and address. Then he disappeared back into the house. I waited and waited, perhaps for 20 minutes, confused, before the officer emerged from the door, this time in full uniform with a bulletproof west and sidearms. "Where is your canoe?" he asked. "We have to fetch it right away before it gets stolen!" We jumped into his truck and drove the block and a half to the ramshackle pier. Strangely, a van with several youths was already parked next to it, all of them eying the contents of my canoe. We could not have come a minute later. The van disappeared and having loaded all my stuff, including the canoe, into the bed of the RCMP truck, we took it to the detachment building.

On the way to the pier, I tried to reveal my plan to the constable: "I had thought that I would pitch my tent on that sandbar over there to sleep and arrange the ride tomorrow." This, because I thought that there was no way to accomplish it any sooner. The officer just gave me a silent "you must be nuts" smirk and categorically ruled it out. "You would be dead by the morning! I would have another homicide on my plate. I am already in the middle of processing two homicides here right now." He took me inside his office and sat facing his computer. He pointed to a folding chair for me to pull up and turned on a large-screen TV near the ceiling so I would be entertained while waiting. Otherwise, he was a man of action — hardly uttering an unnecessary word or smile. "We have to get you out of here before tonight! I have to find some reliable persons to take you to Powerview. Otherwise, you would be in jeopardy even on the way there." I could not believe it. When I pulled up my chair, I placed it next to him, facing the computer as I am used to from my work. He immediately stopped me. "There you sit!" pointing to the other side of the computer where I could not see the screen. He was on the computer for a long time without a word while I watched some noisy sci-fi concoction involving "Transformers" on the TV. It occurred to me only much later that he had to be checking for my crime record and credit profile to make sure he was not dealing with some kind of a scam artist. He must have been satisfied with my squeaky clean record. Finally, he asked how much cash I carried. When I replied "About 300," he announced that he had arranged for a couple who were willing to take me and my gear, including — hold yourself — the canoe, to Powerview this afternoon. Soon, a road-dust-covered van arrived and the older, quiet, small Native woman driver introduced herself as Gloria. "He wants 200," she peeped, half whispering, uncertain. "Agreed!" I happily replied and we started loading my stuff. The officer himself took the initiative to tie the canoe onto the roof of the Dodge Caravan. In the absence of my foam blocks for the canoe gunwales, he produced some Styrofoam packing and, using my machete, he chopped it into suitable substitute chunks. Then he also produced some nylon ratchet straps and we cranked the boat to the roof rails of the vehicle. "Those rails may come off, but the canoe won't!" was the only joke I ever heard him utter. In the meantime, Gloria's elderly husband, Richard, arrived from his afternoon nap and, after I thanked the wonderful officer from the bottom of my heart for his extremely efficient help (he did not want his name or picture used here), we were ready to set out onto the dusty gravel road. But first we went to their house in the village so that I could use their phone to call Milena. Until now, she had only received my Spot device message, "I am OK," with the GPS coordinates of a confusingly strange location. I also paid Gloria right at the door.

A very funny event happened when I exited the van and made a few steps toward the house. A lab-like, very friendly black dog came forth, excitedly wagging his tail and jumping with his front paws on my chest, trying to lick my face. That was relatively normal.

What was shocking, though, was that a few seconds later, around the corner between the house and a garage, a smaller-size lanky, black bear ran out and was seemingly just as friendly and excited to be included in welcoming the stranger as the dog. Richard shooed him away and walked toward the bushes behind the house where he berated another black bear. This one was a mother with two small cubs. She seemed to be stubbornly talking back, reluctant to miss on the excitement at the house while her two babies swayed at the tops of two young six-foot poplars, each with barely a two-inch diameter trunk. Richard was white and had lived with Gloria in Bloodvein for a few decades. Gloria had been born there. During several hours of riding together, I learned a lot from them about life in the area. I was curious about how the lifestyle in the village had changed since the times of Gloria's now deceased mother. It had to be much healthier and prouder then. I mentioned my surprise about seeing practically no motorboats on Lake Winnipeg and heard horrifying stories of accidents that resulted from collisions with rocks in the water. One boat allegedly struck an underwater reef and summersaulted stern over bow in the air, crushing the pilot to death. An RCMP powerboat that I had seen parked on a trailer next to the detachment building had a huge dent in its bow — obviously the result of a rock collision. Although the landscape along the road might have seemed impenetrable and monotonously boring to me, I could sense that both Richard and Gloria loved it, pointing to its features with pride. At one time they pointed to a spot where, right after a curve, the gravel road bed was somewhat elevated over a crosswise granite rock ridge like a broad speed bump. "This is where our priest got killed one winter when his vehicle got thrown and rolled over many times". Neither one of them drank any alcohol but Richard tended unhealthy habit of chain smoking. Out of respect for me, he kept his window open and blew the smoke outside. I learned that the intrepid RCMP officer was notorious in the surrounding land for being very brave. Allegedly, he had been involved, in the diving recovery of some drowned snowmobilers who had broken through ice crossing the Winnipeg River at Powerview. Being skeptical, I checked with Gloria and Richard to see if they thought that the situation in the village was really as bad as the RCMP officer had implied. To my surprise, they confirmed it. According to them, the culprits were boredom and a steady supply of drugs and alcohol among the youths. They gather in the evenings to get high, and with impaired judgment, they have committed suicides and several murders. With my wilderness-travelling experience of always being able to establish a friendly, helpful relationship with the First Nation People that I meet, my mind was unable to accept this alleged truth. While paddling through the beautiful sceneries along the boundary route and Lake of the Woods, I often sympathised with Pierre Gaultier de La Vérendrye, trying to visualize his tragic conflicts with the war-mongering cruel Sioux that cost him the life of his eldest son together with a priest and 19 men. I appreciated the safety of modern times by which the savagery of local Indigenous tribes had long mellowed down. Is it possible that the modern time hobby explorer could still run into "bad Indians?"

I was happy with the transportation deal. The $200 was nothing for the unexpectedly smooth extraction of me and my gear from the very scary situation in which I had found myself within the previous two days. Moreover, my Jeep was spared from having to drive some 600 kilometres on a dusty gravel road. And importantly, Richard and Gloria were also very happy as my job for them provided spending money and an opportunity to go shopping in the Fort Alexander Superstore along with a night on the town.

We reached Powerview by about 6:00. Papineau Motors was already closed but we spotted my Jeep right from the Main Street at a house that had to be the Papineaus'. Funny thing is that, as it turned out, it sat at the house the whole time unlocked with the keys in the ignition as Armand had left it during the Papineaus' absence. It surely attests to a safe atmosphere of life in this town. When I handed $50 cash to Ed for the service he wouldn't accept it. On the contrary, his wife invited me in for dinner. But I thankfully declined because it was late and I wished to put in some distance before I checked into a motel somewhere.

With the loaded Jeep, I set out towards home. From the news on the car's radio, I learned that the Fist of Nature storm that hit me just two nights ago wreaked quite a havoc in a First Nation pow-wow not too far to the west from my camp by Matheson Island. After children had been laid to sleep in a large military base style tent and the adults had gathered to continue socializing long into the night, the sudden arrival of the storm blew the children's tent off. When several adults scrambled to catch it, lightning struck the ground in their midst. The surge of induced current through their bodies knocked them out and for several days in a hospital afterwards, they suffered from severe burning in their lower limbs.

For an unclear reason, all the accommodations along the way were fully booked. Milena constantly tried to find something on the web while on the phone with me as I moved. I decided to continue driving into the night until I got tired and then snooze in the Jeep parked somewhere out of the way. Not until Portage La Prairie was I lucky enough to find a room in a hotel just as the owner was closing the office. The next day, I made it all the way to Edmonton. The fact that I was safely home the next day after the ultimate battle for survival seemed utterly miraculous.

CHAPTER X

Closing the remaining gap in my paddling between Montreal and the Rocky Mountains by traversing the Canadian prairies down the Saskatchewan River from Alberta/Saskatchewan border toward Lake Winnipeg (August 9th – 23rd, 2022)

Oh, the prairies! — What a difference from the Shield country of Quebec and Ontario! Canada is so vast and varied in its natural beauty! While your eye scans the endless flat expanse of agricultural fields when you are driving along a prairie highway, you might get convinced that traveling through it by canoe ought to be boring. I am always trying to imagine the landscape as it might have looked when it was enrobed in the prairie wool grass, strewn with scattered groves of trembling aspen and adorned with wild rose and wolf willow bushes along gullies and ridges. Even past the era of the endless herds of the prairie buffalo, the mental scene is awe-inspiring, with the distant sight of pronghorn antelopes — the image shimmering distorted in the sun-heated air. An intoxicating scent of sage is permeating the red sunset evenings. The star-studded nights are pulsing with the chirping of crickets and cicadas, the sounds punctuated with barks of a Swift fox and yammering of a coyote. I visualize the landscape traversed here and there by horses trailing travois, or oxen pulling Red River carts. It all is irreversibly gone — its graveyard the museums and archives. Yet the courses of the prairie rivers are invariably incised into the plain. Thanks to their topographical irregularity the river valleys have mostly escaped any practical attempts by people to tame their wildness by cultivation. From the canoe, at the level of the river water they look the same as they did a thousand years ago when they served as birch bark canoe conveyances to the far-ranging nomadic roams of the Indigenous Peoples of the plains. By the same token, these enclaves remain the last refuge of the original plains fauna. Moving across the Canadian prairies by paddling a canoe down the Saskatchewan River is quiet, dreamy, stimulating the sense of nostalgia. It possesses its own poetry. A big role in this feeling is played by its beautiful wide-open sky. You are aware of the wheat, canola and other, mostly cereal crop fields beyond the horizon of the river valley, but you do not see them and neither you see any humans around. Other than the cities of Edmonton, North Battleford and Prince Albert, all settlements lie unseen outside the valley, on top of its valley banks. What you typically see in the heart of the prairies — in Saskatchewan — is the wide river, broadly wallowing throughout its spacious valley and splitting around its numerous old and newly forming islands made of the rich prairie soil. The valley bottom and the islands are mostly covered with trees of cottonwood and white poplar — the silvery, shimmering and rustling foliage of which might have reminded the French-Canadian voyageurs of "liard" — the monetary small change. There are also trees of ash, bushes of alder, willows and wild rose, berry bushes of saskatoons, choke cherries and high bush cranberries. Higher up the valley sides you see sage and prairie wool grass. You may glimpse a black bear loitering at the shore and scooting back into bushes the moment he detects your approach. You can see a deer curiously watching you as an unusual moving apparition on the river; you will spot beaver, otter, coyote, moose, geese, ducks, cranes, great blue herons, pelicans, bald eagles, hawks and turkey vultures. The coniferous trees like spruce, fir and pine only appear higher upstream, towards the Rocky Mountain foothills of Alberta and in the frontier character of the river downstream, starting at and beyond Prince Albert. The natural setting could not have changed since the times when David Thompson led through here the North West Co. canoe brigades up the river to his base in Rocky Mountain House and then on to cross the Rocky Mountains and explore the Kootenays and the Columbia Basin.

Filling the gap.

OK then, this part of Canada was the last stretch of land that I had not had the privilege to know yet in my paddling between Montreal and the Rocky Mountains. In spite of being seventy-eight now I buckled under to the gnawing inner temptation to break all my earlier promises by launching the canoe again, this time into the North Saskatchewan River to cross the prairies. My age only provided me with the excuse to accomplish this traverse downstream on the river, from west to east, instead of struggling against the current and prevailing westerly winds. Now ... over the years, I have already covered the part of the river from the Rocky Mountains to the Alberta/Saskatchewan border. This stretch had been spliced from shorter, overlapping expeditions. There I moved solo from Saskatchewan River Crossing (launching above the Jasper-Banff Highway bridge near the start of the Howse Pass — the favourite Continental Divide crossing by David Thompson) to the Abraham Lake dam. With my wife, we paddled from Nordegg to Rocky Mountain House. On one Thanksgiving weekend I paddled solo from Rocky Mountain House to Drayton Valley. I not only paddled multiple times from Drayton Valley to Edmonton in a canoe, but I also covered this stretch in the opposite direction on cross-country skis upon the frozen river. My three Malamute dogs were pulling a sled behind me with camping gear and food. In 2014 when I could not find a partner for tackling the Boundary Waters between Waterfowl Lake and Fort Frances, I launched the solo canoe in Edmonton and paddled to the Alberta/Saskatchewan border.

So, what remained now was to launch the canoe at the above-mentioned border and paddle to Lake Winnipeg. I started preparing for the solo expedition at our log house on Lake Kootenay where we spend summer seasons now and where our canoes are stored. Yet when one of our numerous, nice Czech friends in this area heard of my plan, he immediately offered to go with me. Tony is a very creative, fit and tough outdoorsman who cycled solo across most of Canada during the COVID shenanigans and can survive in all situations. It is different from going solo, but at both of our ages (150 combined) it felt safer. I liked the idea. I could not wish for a better partner. So, Milena and I loaded the 17ft Nova Craft Prospector onto our Nissan Rogue and took it to Edmonton, where Tony arrived on the 7th of August from Proctor on Kootenay Lake. Milena drove us to the Saskatchewan border where we launched on the 9th. Just as I remembered it from July 2014, when I arrived here on the river from Edmonton, the shore was extremely muddy here for loading and launching the canoe. We used some sparse rocks to step on and Tony applied his creative inventiveness early when he used my machete and harvested some young green willow branches to fashion stepping mats over the gooey clay mud. Unlike in my solo travels, having combined our outfit from two different sources, we ended up with a substantial load in the boat that contained duplications. It was too late, though, to start re-sorting the already water-tightly sealed equipment. Besides, we were comforted by the knowledge that there would be no need to portage it for a long time on the river before the food load would be already fairly depleted.

On the way.

After I helped Milena bring the Rogue back up from the river to the highway and kissed her goodbye, I joined Tony, seating myself in the stern of the canoe. We carefully pushed off, washing the mud off our feet in the river water over the gunwales before we brought them in and started to paddle in earnest down the main current. It was a gorgeous early afternoon. The vast blue sky was strewn with scattered cotton balls of small white clouds. In spite of the day being hot we kept on T-shirts and hats to protect the unaccustomed skin. In the haste of loading and pushing off I only neglected to protect my lower legs that stuck out of my shorts with sunscreen. It cost me a fairly severe sunburn on them on this very first day that then hounded me for the rest of the trip — be careful! As it usually is on the first day of the expedition, we did not feel any pain from straining the muscles yet. We thus pushed with determined paddle strokes past the lonely banks following the gentle curves of the river valley. It was only after a ninety degree right turn of the river at Frenchman Butte that we started feeling any sense of fatigue and commenced thinking about a campsite. With my previous experience we were planning to camp on an open island with natural air circulation that would keep mosquitoes away. We hoped that we would find one as close as possible to a river-crossing bridge that the map showed up ahead and to which we had assigned the milestone for the day. We were indeed able to pick a sliver of a sandy island with patches of low willows that was about a metre higher than the fast-flowing water. The latter eroded its edges into a half-meter drop-off. As we would find out, the muddy character of the river edges from our launch day would escort us on its whole stretch through the prairies. The river carried the fertile prairie soil down its current and it formed islands and bars from this material all along. On the top of smaller islands, it was dry, behaving like very fine, wind-packed sand. But along the edges where it was wet it behaved like deep, gooey, clay mud that we sank into half-shin deep. It sucked on our rubber sandals refusing to let them go, hence we got used to living with bare feet for the whole time that we were moving on the river. Yet moving about barefoot turned up actually very pleasant because there were no rocks on land, nor on the river bottom and we felt that it was healthy for our feet. We just conscientiously washed the mud from them before swinging them into the canoe.

Though our first camp was located only a couple of kilometres upstream of the Deer Creek Bridge, by the time it came into our view we were fighting the first of our many nasty headwinds that we would experience on the Saskatchewan River. It was a shock to me who had fought the prevailing westerly winds in my solo canoe movement from east to west — Montreal to Lake Winnipeg. Here I expected wind in my back based on the travel from west to east. But no cigar! It would turn out that today's easterly wind was no aberration. It seemed that whenever we had wind on the river it was a headwind, whether we moved east, southeast, or northeast. I do not actually remember ever having a tailwind.

But this first one was by far the worst. While we were passing under the bridge, we were engaged in a water rodeo, bucking over half-metre waves. Only thanks to two of us paddling a tandem canoe we were making any, if very hard-earned progress. With my solo canoe I would have been wind-bound. That day we advanced significantly less than during the previous one, in spite of paddling longer. We again chose a sand island with low willow patches, this time quite a bit larger, about a kilometre upstream of Milleton Bridge that we could see from our camp.

While my daily routine in my solo paddling used to be such that I would spend the whole paddling day in the canoe having the breakfasts of cold tea and granola bars, the lunches and snacks all in a drifting vessel without stopping at a shore, this time, on Tony's suggestion, we would always stop on some airy island for about an hour of a lunch break. Because the weather was hot and the water was pleasantly warm, we would always have a swim in the swift current. We would rest a bit, sometimes even snooze in the shade on a bed of young, green willow branches that Tony had mowed with my machete. There would always be wonderful opportunities to study what animals had left their tracks in the soft mud. It would be mostly deer, moose, coyote and waterfowl like geese and ducks. In fact, we would be swimming three times a day on most days: mornings after brushing teeth, during the lunch breaks and evenings after setting up the camp. In the absence of any humans within our range of sight on the river, there was never any need, or sense in making a swimsuit wet. Interesting was my comparison of the Saskatchewan River with the lakes and rivers that I had traveled by paddling in a canoe from Montreal to Lake Winnipeg regarding hardships due to a current. Apart from short, discrete steps like waterfalls and drops ("saults" in the voyageur lingo) that had to be portaged, the rivers of the latter are all relatively friendly to the travel in both directions — i.e., not possessing a drastically fast, or turbulent flow that would pose problems whether moving downstream, or upstream.

The Saskatchewan River is in comparison significantly faster. In fact, its name comes from the Cree "Kisiskâciwan-sîpî", or swift flowing river. Especially past Prince Albert, the river picks up slope and speed in a series of many high-volume rapids. The fur trade canoe teams and the oarsmen of Hudson Bay's York boats, when they could not use the sail, experienced thus quite a workout in moving west — upstream. Poling and dragging on ropes from shore had to often supplement paddles and oars. Especially the few steamboats that were later deployed around Fort Carlton had quite a challenge moving not only upstream through the lower river rocky rapids, but namely in navigating through them downstream.

On the third day, Tony in the bow first reported seeing a black bear sow with a cub at the shore up ahead. I was busy studying the map and by the time I looked in the pointed direction the bears were gone. But we both observed a deer buck that seemed very excited by our, to him confusing, appearance. He was prancing skittishly up and down the beach, constantly looking in our direction. In the end he displayed a splendid, highly energetic gait of bouncing off all four feet at once and bounding forward in arcs higher than himself.

When the day turned the hottest after our lunch stop, we started detecting flashes of the sun reflected on wet paddles in a great distance up ahead. In our strong, determined pace of paddling we soon caught up to a mixed bunch of some giddy, happy people randomly drifting in five daringly overloaded canoes. Each was carrying some five younger men and women which, together with their gear, was giving the vessels barely a ten-centimetre freeboard. Our appearance of two white-haired athletic seniors pushing a canoe at a fast pace visibly arose their admiration. This so especially after they asked and heard that we were headed all the way to Lake Winnipeg and Tony mentioned that I had already canoed half-way across Canada from Montreal to this lake. They had launched at the Milleton bridge and were more or less drifting to North Battleford. We had an exchange of friendly jokes that ended with them offering us cold beer. Being modest, I politely thanked them declining and pushed the canoe on our way. Yet Tony boldly responded that, sure, he would take one. So, we made a U-turn and Tony picked up his prize. "Why did you not take one too?" Tony asked me after we passed them. "You would have made them happy by accepting their friendly offer!" "Well, that's just me. I am too sheepish." I responded. Perhaps it was my intrinsic pride that would not allow me to reveal any unpreparedness, or lack of self-sufficiency. "But that's OK, we'll share the one that you've got". I added. It did not seem that Tony liked the outcome, but being a courteous gentleman, he passed me the can to drink the first half. In the given situation, the beer tasted absolutely heavenly. I was truly sorry now that I did not take one too. I guess that any ole cold beer would have fit the bill in these circumstances, but I made sure that I would remember the brand: Pabst Blue Ribbon.

Another episode — funny to one person, not so funny to the other — happened later in the afternoon. The sky had darkened due to the spread of a large cumulonimbus cloud that threatened with a thunderstorm. When the first drops of rain hit, we quickly brought the canoe to the right shore and feverishly unfurled the spray cover onto it. Tony took care of lacing-on the spray cover on the starboard side while I, with longer legs, offered to lace the port side where I stood on uneven bottom in deeper water. Just before that I managed to protect the dryness of my upper body by donning the Gore-Tex windbreaker and my hat. But now, pushing and tugging on the canoe between Tony and myself, I lost balance and fell into the water backward. I got thoroughly wet from head to toe. We then paddled the canoe protected by the spray cover. Tony paddled protected by his raincoat and a hat. I had absolutely no dryness left to protect. I could have just as well paddled naked. But soon the shower stopped and we looked for another sandy island campsite.

Most of our camps on sandy islands of the North Saskatchewan River were chosen near some big, flood-deposited tree, or a pile of driftwood that provided both the firewood for cooking and shelves and hangers for dishes and cooking utensils. Invariably it also offered raised seating to rehabilitate the overworked backs from the fatigue of some eight-hour paddling. By this time, entirely voluntarily, Tony had gravitated to what turned out to be his natural niche — the role of a camp cook. He then spoiled me with wonderful meals that his wife, Irena, professionally freeze-dried using mostly the products of her vast garden. And, compared to my usual type of expedition food that used to make the heaviest item in my load, hers was featherlight to boot. Tony forced me to abandon my "unhealthy" habit of not eating any breakfast by making me consume substantial meals, like chili, scrambled eggs, risotto with turkey breast meat, delicious vanilla custard, etc. before we would set out each morning. "You have to eat to have energy!" he would say. Besides his wonderful cooking, Tony amazed me with his inventive creations of kitchen structures like table tops, or wind screens for the cooking fire made mostly from the young green willow branches.

The next day we expected to reach the vicinity of the Battlefords. Those are two cities situated on the opposite sides of the North Saskatchewan River. I have never visited the Battleford on the south side — not visible from the river, nor from the highway — but I regularly traveled through North Battleford that spreads on the north side of the valley. It was when the Yellowhead Highway, which I followed on my way east to reconnect with my previously conquered progress in the canoe-crossing of the country, switched from following the south to the north side of the river. One crosses on a bridge here followed by a climb through this city. The history of the area is related to fur trade with several trading posts that used to be scattered around the confluence of the North Saskatchewan and the Battle Rivers. The place briefly served as the capital of the then Northwest Territories and it had also figured in the North-West Rebellion — all this in the nineteenth century. Throughout the day I could gradually discern the signs of the highway, asymptotically approaching the river on its south side. I could recognize the silhouettes of occasional power poles, or notice a flash of a sun reflection on the windshield of a vehicle moving in the distance along the gaps in the treed valley-edge horizon. Eventually, the highway lowered itself down the side of the valley and its large, river-crossing bridge with lively traffic came into view in a great distance. Soon we were moving under it, passing a few people, for a change, who were fishing in the river. It was time to look for a campsite. But around here it did not avail itself. We just continued down the current until the city disappeared from view. Some five kilometres downstream we finally chose a narrow channel that separated a suitable sandy-dune island with the young green willows. Here we set up a scenic camp with very pleasant swimming in the narrow channel.

Because the river split into numerous channels around a number of islands along its right side, we somehow totally missed its confluence with the Battle River next morning. Our movement was now streaming toward the river's major bend that was bringing it the farthest south in the province of Saskatchewan. It was altering its average course from aiming southeast to northeast. Yet before that, close to the time to camp for the night, we were again hit with a progressively strengthening headwind. With it came the threat of a large thunderstorm, evident not only from a growing anvil of a cumulonimbus overhead, but also by a plethora of many more thunderstorm cells spawning all over the vast prairie sky. We thus quickly selected a sandy island with low willows and started pitching the tents. By now the wind from the east had become a real gale. The dust was blowing along the ground, my tent refused to stand to it. While Tony chopped out a rough tent spot in the midst of the willow bushes, I had to move my tent some fifty metres into a relative lee of a large, willow-covered sand dune. I had to tie on and deploy all the body guy strings of the tent to anchor it securely. In the meantime, the overturned canoe blew off and the wind chased it tumbling some thirty metres over the ground before I managed to catch it just as it was about to hit the water. By the time the magnificent fireworks of the overnight thunderstorms started exploding in the heavens, it was dark. Being too tired, we could not get distracted by it from indulging in a well-deserved sleep.

Passing an incised ravine of the in-flowing Eagle Creek, we finally reached the end of the south easterly trend of the North

Saskatchewan River. From here we flattened the curve straight east during which time we had the opportunity to watch a pair of Great Blue herons fishing. Then we finally aimed northeast. Our complete passing of the bend got confirmed definitively by an appearance of a bridge on the Yellowhead Highway again — here aiming east for Saskatoon. Just past the bridge I noticed a group of RVs on a high bank above us. Is it a campsite? We touched the canoe to a steep, rough boat launch and while I held onto some willow branches to keep the canoe anchored, Tony climbed up with our water canister to explore if he could refill it there. Soon he reappeared beaming with success. In turn, I collected a number of empty two-liter soda pop bottles and went up to refill them at the campsite's water tap too. It turned out to be truly delicious-tasting, cold water. We were again full to capacity. I should mention that, following my experience from canoeing solo down the North Saskatchewan River in Alberta with its oil industry, cattle and spraying of canola fields along the shores, I decided against ingesting the river water even after boiling it. We thus carried a 23-liter canister, plus half a dozen two-liter pop bottles of drinking water that we were able to replenish with luck.

A couple of kilometres downstream from a second bridge, this time a railroad type, we chose an island for a camp. Besides the usual low, sandy area, the core of the island was elevated by another metre-and-a-half or so with a dense growth of cottonwood trees and bushy undergrowth. This higher area had been spared of a high-water overflow that shaped its upstream side into a round point reminding one of the prow of a ship. Behind my tent which was placed on the flood-smoothed low sandy flat I discovered a curious, turned grisly scene. The sand bar was dug up in one spot about a meter deep revealing a skeleton with more bones pulled outside the hole. My detective intuition deduced the following scenario: A young deer got swept by the river in flood and drowned. His body got embedded in a newly formed sand bar. When the water level subsided and exposed the bar, a bear smelled the carcass in the ground, dug it up and devoured the pickled delicacy, leaving just cleanly picked bones.

The next day we again paddled, refreshed by a morning swim, in bright sunshine under vast azure blue sky. Before I saw them, I detected the presence of sandhill cranes that were flying overhead by their characteristic calling sounds of crackling "g'roo-g'roo" from the great heights. By the time Tony looked up, alerted by me, he had to look backwards and could not see them straight against the searing sun. But, yet again, we caught up to reflection flashes from wet paddles up ahead. The group we met consisted of a canoe carrying a mature fifty-some-year man with one young man and a second young man paddling a kayak. They were all Hutterites from the neighbouring Riverbend Hutterite Colony. The older gentleman, Chris, was very cheerful and full of humour. The young men were politely quiet, perhaps following the Hutterite courtesy etiquette. They were on a day trip down the river passing alongside their 20,000-acre common property. We had a very friendly chat in which we learned a lot about the communal life of this industrious religious group that counted some 120 people. They enjoy a great deal of independence from the government regulations and are self-sustaining thanks to producing food and most daily needs in collective cooperation. They would share with us anything that could help us, offering a cottage by the river stocked with non-perishable food, etc. Yet it turned out not fitting into our logistics. One thing that Tony and I craved on this hot day was beer that, unfortunately, they could not help us with. They do not drink alcohol.

My old topo map with 1:500,000 scale showed a number of ferries across the river. Some of them had already been replaced with newly built bridges by the time we arrived at the spots, yet a few of them remained, small and picturesque, bringing the nostalgia of the old times. As the main current of the river constantly wandered from one side to the other, it would create challenges into the navigation of the canoe. Frequently, we would run into shallow bars where the underside of the canoe touched the bottom. We were then forced to step out and lead the canoe "on a leash" into deeper water. The walk was not unwelcome. It served as a refreshing stretch for the legs and the back. The barefoot walking in the water was on a soft firm sand.

I was safe at the stern, but Tony, walking in the front, was more than once surprised by a sudden drop in depth when he reached the current channel. This is when, in turn, he got soaked to the bone.

In one spot on the river, we were witness to a curious gathering of an unusually large number of turkey vultures. There were cows grazing on a steep slope of the river valley when more than a dozen of these buzzard-like ugly birds congregated in one spot hopping and circling. Was there a dead cow, perhaps? We stopped and ventured onto shore in two places. The first was a spot recommended to us by the Hutterites called Shekinah Resort where there is an interesting observation tower that offers nice views of the river from above the treetops. The second one was the place where historic Fort Carlton once stood. It used to play an important role in the trade with the west. Red River Carts brought here pemmican, steamboats precariously plied the river — highly dependent on the river's water level — with trade goods and fur. Today there are only information panels with archival photographs. But both the above places overwhelmed us with clouds of biting mosquitoes as we were moving in thick high willows. We were only happy to hurry back to the safety of our moving canoe. As we were finally approaching the city of Prince Albert we were again chased by the threat of a looming thunderstorm. A huge storm cloud darkened the sky and when thunder rattled from the flashes of the first lightning, we feverishly sought and found a spot for a camp, again on an island, about five kilometres short of the city. After beaching the canoe, we sprinted with our packs containing tents to pitch them in a record time before the deluge would be triggered. Yet, somehow, the wrath of the tempest just skirted around us, shedding only a few raindrops from its weak side wing. We were then treated to a nice, serene evening, tinted with the red-orange sunset. Our gleeful feeling of unrestrained freedom resonated in my heart with a lonely yammer of a coyote. This, though, contrasted sharply, time and again, with the distant blast of a siren that was enforcing a strict daily regime in a prison that we discerned by its corner watchtowers far in the direction of the sound's source.

It did not take long the next morning before our paddle strokes brought us to within the sight of the first buildings of Prince Albert. Just before the bridge that extended as the Main Street, we touched the right shore with the canoe. It was in a spot where it would be hidden from view by thick overhanging willows. The disembarking here was the worst ever. The mud was the deepest here and widespread. Moreover, sinking with bare feet into it was dangerous as it contained unseen discarded garbage. My foot sank right next to an old rusty car bumper with peeling chrome plating. Using branches as ropes to climb a steep slippery mud bank to a paved sidewalk, we proceeded towards the waterfront streets. I carried my sandals which I donned after washing mud from my feet in a puddle. Tony continued in bare feet. We carried a couple of water containers with hope to fill them somewhere. A couple on bicycles warned us that leaving the canoe unattended was highly risky. According to them, the city waterfront near the bridge was a hangout of desperate homeless people, who would sleep out their hangovers from the previous night there. Sadly, many of them were Indigenous. In spite of moving among modern building structures we felt that we were visiting an area that belonged to First Nations dwellers, in this case to the onetime proud Cree. All the working personnel that we met were Indigenous. They were very helpful, whether it was in the local museum where they graciously allowed us to fill our water containers in their private washroom, or in A&W where we bought breakfast. Many of the street people were just transients who visited Prince Albert temporarily from their home up north and applied their skills of living and sleeping under the open sky to which they were accustomed in their frontier world. Although in this particular setting their presence may have expressed a clash between their lifestyle and the modern conventions, I have never stopped admiring their traditional abilities to live in harmony with nature and survive under adverse conditions in the northern wilderness. Never leaving our canoe out of our line of sight for too long, we managed to return to it unmolested. I brought the fresh water while Tony managed to procure a six pack of beer. Funny thing is that the East-Indian liquor store owner insisted on carrying the purchase transaction out on the sidewalk since nobody was allowed to enter in bare feet.

My rather outdated 1:500,000 topo map that I had Xeroxed from the University of Alberta map collection showed three bars across the river with "R" letters indicating rapids in one location already relatively close to the confluence of the two Saskatchewan branches — the North and the South Saskatchewan Rivers. In reality, we encountered the first rapids soon after passing a small ferry called Cecil Ferry, not far past Prince Albert. That is where the river starts dropping steeper and meanders, constrained by an incised river valley. We then ended up with two whole days of tackling rapids, one after another. Technically they were only class II, but, with the volume, they made huge waves in places. I put my GoPro camera on my forehead only after the biggest ones. They remained only in our memory, undocumented. The 17-foot overloaded canoe proved rather hard to maneuver quickly and, only with luck, we barely squeezed by some big rocks several times. To me, it provided a more realistic picture of what it was like to navigate through here the fully loaded fur trade canoes. The next campsite availed itself right after we passed a strange-looking concrete structure that jutted out of the right bank. It looked like a telescoping dam that might be extended from a half to across the whole width of the river. Yet it appeared old and disused. It had erosion holes and was covered with graffiti scrawls. Only at the time of this writing did I find that the location has a name: "Lacolle Falls". Our campsite had a large beach and mowed weedy grass on the elevated shore. A steel cooking fire-stand proved that this must have been a weekend campsite, now deserted, of local First Nations whose land we were passing through. For once, we were not camping on an island.

Next morning it seemed to be taking forever for us to reach the anticipated confluence of the two Saskatchewan Rivers. Finally, I identified the right topographical features and joyfully announced: "We have reached the confluence!" Tony did not see it: "Where?" For one, there was a ridge of land across the course of the river that made it turn 90 degrees to the left. Secondly, what looked first as a deep bay on the right-hand side proved to be the inflowing South Saskatchewan. "Hooray!"

We were now tackling the rapids with a spray cover on the canoe. At the end of battling them for the whole day we could not find a campsite. Everywhere there was either deep, wide-spreading mud with reeds, or, this time, rough rocks. We finally settled for emergency squatting on a really rocky, mini-delta of a small incoming stream. It was very uneven and sloping, with rocks everywhere. While Tony made a base of chopped grass and reeds for his tent, I lay myself on the ground among the rocks to check where it was feasible and determine where to put my tent over the spot. Barefoot walking was no longer possible here. Our consolation reward was a flood of wild stunted sunflowers that covered the base of a sedimentary cliff and a creek gulley behind us, swaying cheerfully in the orange light of the setting sun.

Very shortly after leaving our rocky bivouac next morning we were paddling on a smooth river again. A bridge appeared, followed by a notch in the shoreline immediately past its right end. The spot featured a few cottages and a park-like setting including picnic tables. We asked a couple who were fishing from a dock, if one could get drinking water from a structure that looked like typical park washrooms. Their answer was negative, but across the notch, from a mini-marina, a man who was washing his boat with a garden hose disputed their answer that he also heard and said that: "Actually yes, you could get water there, but I have the same water here in my hose and I can fill up for you." He was a nice engineer of Ukrainian descent who was spending a vacation with his wife in their cottage here. We had a very nice conversation. While we were filling our containers from the hose, the gentleman's wife emerged on a trail from the bushes followed by a few hens and joined in in the introduction niceties. Their retiree friends appeared next. The latter couple volunteered to take a group picture of us with the engineer and his wife using my camera. We all chatted for over an hour, us acquiring a status of heroes of their age category. Before we parted, the engineer whispered something to his wife. She briefly disappeared to their cottage and then quickly returned with friendly gifts: a six-pack of cold beer, a dozen of fresh eggs and a package of freshly filleted walleye meat. It was a proof that nice people have not yet gone extinct!

We had learned from our generous friends that their area was a recreational resort called Wapiti Valley. One of its important features was a winter ski facility. Interestingly, this area was to be indeed abundant in Wapiti elk. They also informed us that from here on we were moving on a lake of a dam that filled the narrow, deep river valley. In fact, in my rather superficial research for this expedition I had not been aware of this, the Nipawin Hydroelectric Dam. I knew about the farther one, called Tobin Lake, but this one was built later, in 1986 — after the printing of my old topo map. It still looked like a somewhat wider river, only perhaps sitting higher in the river valley. It was brim full, the water reaching into wooded banks and leaving no shore beaches to land. Our only hope was to find a campsite resort which, we were told, was some eight kilometres down the lake. We were greatly relieved when we found it at long last. We pulled the canoe out on its, likely artificial beach and went barefoot looking for a store further inland that somebody had mentioned. When we found it, about a kilometre in, we had a friendly encounter with its owners. All that was available from the store was water that was free from a hose and ice cream that we paid for. As a friendly gesture, we also bought it for the owner couple. The Smits were slightly younger than us, but we resonated in a lengthy exchange of stories, sitting on benches while licking the ice cream. We got a free camping permission right for the riverfront spot where we had landed. We learned that the hydro company had the responsibility to transport our canoe and gear around their dam. The owner lady, Shirley, arranged for us in a text exchange to be met with the power company truck at the dam the next morning at 10:30. To make sure that we would not be late for our rendezvous with the truck, we pushed off already at 7:10 the next morning. Everything still slept, but Shirley arrived to their marina, jumped into her kayak and chased us up to say goodbye. We snapped pictures of each other for a memory while paddling together for a while. She showed us a couple of Wapiti elk grazing high up on the bank and turned her kayak to paddle back.

When we eventually rounded a point and spotted the dam about four kilometres up ahead, we realized that we would arrive almost an hour early. I tried to call the number that Shirley had given me and probably woke up the employee who had the duty to transport us around the dam. I forgot that it was a Sunday. Yet, he promised that he would do his best to come earlier. Once we finally succeeded in finding a way to the shore through a mess of drift logs and unloaded the cargo, including the canoe, onto the grassy shore, we had been snoozing for almost an hour before the truck showed up. It even had a trailer to accommodate our 17-foot canoe. It was a short ride to a small beach below the dam.

Our next stop was Nipawin. We learned from the truck driver that its name comes from what Cree used to call a flat river dale nearby, now flooded, where Cree women, children and the elderly were spending time camping while waiting for men who gathered here at certain times of the year and went hunting. ("Nipawin" meaning bed, or resting place, also "nipawewin" meaning waiting place, or place where one stands in Cree.) It was only about five kilometres to its marina and park, but we were once again fighting enormous headwind to it. Here, in Ray's store, we could finally buy some refreshments and junk food. In our discussion with some seniors, mostly fishermen gathered here for a Sunday morning coffee with Ray on the deck, we were told that "in this wind and waves against you, you won't get anywhere, especially when you enter the 75 kilometres of the open water in its direction on Tobin Lake." We nevertheless pushed off after a while and continued fighting the elements. The camping outlook was the same as on the previous lake. The water reached into the woods and left no beaches. Luckily, just after we reached the open stretch of Tobin Lake and the next progress became next to impossible, some kind of a sanctuary, announced by a sign board with somebody's name, opened up on the right bank. It was a thinly treed meadow with waist-high weeds. Here we established our base for the evening. Tony chopped out a spot for his tent, I just stomp-rolled the vegetation for mine. The wind had not calmed down overnight. In the morning it blew at full force and, to top the adversity, it started to sprinkle. We loaded the canoe handing pieces down a high slippery bank and navigated out through channels in reeds onto open water. We moved under gloomy, dark, overcast sky, paddling like robots in hats and rain gear against the wrath of wind, rain and waves. Hardly making any headway, there was no prospect that we would reach a spot to camp today, or even to stop somewhere to rest in the canoe. I at first clenched my teeth and paddled with mechanical determination, but after a while it seemed insane. Tony was silent, yet the moment my sense of responsibility hinted that this did not make any sense, he instantly agreed. We were at the end of our strength. Dejected, we decided that we would turn the canoe around and paddle down the wind and waves the 15 kilometres back to Nipawin.

Once we reached the mobility signal, I contacted Milena to inform her about the change of our plans. She immediately found on-line that there was a U-Haul dealer in Nipawin. Ergo, once we docked at Ray's Marina, I changed, put on my hiking boots and headed for the dealer in town, some five kilometres away from the river. While walking, I tried to phone ahead to quicken the transaction. Yet, I only learned that there were no trucks available to us for booking. As it turned out through my phone calls after I returned to the marina, no U-Haul trucks were available anywhere else from all dealers within a 300-kilometre radius of Nipawin. Ray and a few locals who had offered to drive us up to Prince Albert and to other outlying dealerships could not help. I did not ask for it, but seeing us stranded, Milena took it bravely upon herself to rescue us. In spite of her worries about her sense of orientation, she set out the same afternoon from Edmonton and, after a few hours of sleep in a motel in Lloydminster, she materialized with the Rogue at the spot where I was waiting for her on the highway near Nipawin at around noon. Thank Nissan for the GPS navigator in their vehicles! After we loaded up, I took the wheel and we were home the same evening.

Tony and I ended up some 300 kilometres short of our goal, but we have gleaned the experience. In the end we were happy and proud with our achievement. At 78, this was my final stab at retracing the fur trade canoe route between Montreal and the Rocky Mountains.

EPILOGUE

Feeling my adopted country — not inherited by birth, but associated with by a conscientious choice — with the soles of my feet and by paddle strokes through its waters, I have got to know her intimately. She gave me a chance and freedom to thrive when I arrived here 54 years ago as a strapping young 24-year-old. She allowed me to add a PhD in Nuclear Physics to my curriculum vitae. I have repaid her gratefully and full-heartedly, dedicating my whole productive life to helping establish her respected name on the frontier science field of Particle Physics. My professional life involved work in world famous Particle Physics research facilities in Canada, the United States and Europe, including the Large Hadron Collider at CERN, Geneva, Switzerland. Especially the view of the Canada`s bountiful natural beauty from the perspective of foreign countries during my modern science work there made me appreciate the true value of its unspoiled wilderness.

Besides my accomplishments in the professional life, I have been able to build a house and participated in raising four healthy, intelligent children who have become Canada's patriotic, productive citizens. In my spare time I served as a Ski Patroller, coached swimming, cross-country skiing and English riding in the Canadian Pony Club. I have served as a president of AMPA (Alberta Modern Pentathlon Association).

But my most loved hobby has always been what made me choose Canada in the first place, the return to nature and spending time in the Canadian wilderness. Once my children grew up and flew the nest, I found time to enjoy it fully, especially after I retired. The investment of always devoting time to exercise and healthy physical activity throughout my life provided me with the dividend of excellent, fit quality of life into my retirement. During my solo escapes, the Canadian wilderness taught me self-discipline, patience, use of wisdom and experience to arrive at the right judgment. It helped me build self-confidence and skills to observe. It instilled in me respect for all life. Through my love of nature, I have arrived quite naturally into relying only on myself, as opposed to surrendering my fate into the hands of some divine authority. I try to man the helm of my fate with the use of wisdom and intelligence of Homo sapiens. My religion is the harmonious, eons-established, refined-to-perfection order of nature with its objective physical laws. I regard my returns to nature as my "mental hygiene". I am a great admirer of the adventurous wanderlust of Vikings and of the Viking philosophy. Over the years, I have completed 30 Canadian Birkebeiner Cross-Country Ski Marathons. I like to think and hope (tongue-in-cheek) that when my time will come, my life's exploits would qualify me for the acceptance into Valhalla. I am aware that to be admitted inside its gates I have to hold a sword, or some kind of a dagger when dying. I will make sure that, in emergency, I will clutch at least a plastic cutlery knife.

P.S. Nature has returned my love for her with a generous gift at last: I was blessed in November two years ago with chancing upon what I can only explain as Sasquatch tracks in the first snow of the season barely one kilometre up the steep forested mountain side from our log house above Kootenay Lake in British Columbia. See the blog on my website for the details:
https://janskp0.wixsite.com/wildpaths/single-post/a-sasquatch-at-last

Printed in the USA
CPSIA information can be obtained
at www.ICGtesting.com
JSHW070252301223
54538JS00016B/58